FOI 10 years on: freedom fighting or lazy journalism?

EDITED BY
TOM FELLE and JOHN MAIR

Published 2015 by Abramis academic publishing

www.abramis.co.uk

ISBN 978 1 84549 646 3

Printed and bound in the United Kingdom

Typeset in Garamond 11pt

Abramis is an imprint of arima publishing.

arima publishing
ASK House, Northgate Avenue
Bury St Edmunds, Suffolk IP32 6BB
t: (+44) 01284 700321

www.arimapublishing.com

Contents

Section 1. Critical reflections on freedom of information
Tom Felle

1. The 'nincompoop' Blair's greatest mistake? 10 years of FOI in the UK
Maurice Frankel assesses 10 years of FOI in the UK, which has seen much released the governments of the day might have wanted kept secret. But despite its transformational impact on the rights of citizens to be informed, the pressure to clampdown on hard-won freedoms is

2. A 'very British revolution': the MPs' expenses scandal
From a bill to clean a moat to dodgy mortgage receipts, the MPs' expenses scandal had it all. But attempts by MPs to block their outlandish expenses regime from investigation under FOI made the story all the more shocking when it was finally revealed. Nicholas Jones explores the

3. Freedom fighting: why FOI is important for democracy
The cost of biscuits at council meetings is hardly front-page news, but the work of journalists in holding those in power to account using the Freedom of Information Act serves an important

4. The development of FOI in Britain
FOI in the UK was part of a raft of reforms aimed at making British administrative systems, and government, more open, transparent and accountable. But it would never have been introduced were it not for constant pressure from the civil society, opposition MPs and the

5. Information in the secret state
10 years after the introduction of the Freedom of Information Act, the UK is still obsessed with secrecy. Information is not a 'right' if access to it is in the gift of the Government, writes

iv

Table of figures

Acknowledgements

This book, like the many others in the series, has been possible only because of the collective efforts of our many contributors, and to each of them we are truly grateful.

Gracious thanks are due to Danielle Eriksson for her careful, considered and meticulous comments on drafts, and her support at various stages during the editing process.

Jacqui Taylor and her team at FlyingBinary who designed the cover illustration for this volume is due our gratitude for their innovation, creativity and tremendous patience.

Thanks, as ever, go to the publishers Abramis, in particular Richard and Pete Franklin and their staff.

Finally, we would like to thank our families who have born the brunt of our long nights locked in conclave while this labour of love sidled its way from an idea born at a conference in Sheffield to the volume you now hold in your hands.

Tom Felle, London
John Mair, Oxford
January 2015

About the editors

Tom Felle is acting director of interactive and newspaper journalism at City University London, and was formerly head of journalism at the University of Limerick. Prior to that he was a career newspaper journalist and worked for a decade as a reporter and correspondent at the *Independent* (Dublin); as Bureau Chief of the Leb News Agency (Beirut); and as Deputy Editor of the *Irish Echo* (Sydney). He has contributed to a number of books on issues including media policy, press regulation, investigative reporting, media and democracy, local journalism, and is co-editor of two books on FOI. In 2013 he was appointed by the Irish government to a national expert committee examining the implementation of that country's freedom of information legislation. Email tom.felle.1@city.ac.uk, Twitter @tomfelle.

John Mair is a senior journalism academic currently teaching at Brunel and Westminster universities in London. He is a former BBC producer working in current affairs and investigations. He helped to invent 'Question Time' in 1979. He is the editor of 12 previous 'hackademic' texts for Abramis on subjects ranging from the Arab Spring to journalism after the Leveson report, mostly with Professor Richard Keeble. They invented the sub genre, which is much admired in and out of the academe. All the books have had much effect. Lord Justice Leveson read *the Phone Hacking Scandal* whilst preparing his report. The most recent *Is the BBC In Crisis?* (published 1 March, 2014) made *The Sun*, and *The British Journalism Review* inter much alia.

Foreword

Peter Preston

Freedom of information? It sounds such a simple, sweeping, irresistible idea. Try Article 19 of the UN's Universal Declaration of Human Rights: 'Everyone has the right to freedom of opinion and expression; this right includes freedom to hold opinions without interference and to seek, receive and impart information and ideas through any media and regardless of frontiers.' Or, slightly closer to home, try the first couple of sentences of Article 10 from the European Convention on Human Rights: 'Everyone has a right to freedom of expression. This right shall include freedom to hold opinions and to receive and impart information and ideas without public authority and regardless of frontiers.' But then the legal weevils get to work. Article 10 doesn't end on a high note, even before the balancing acts with Article 8 and privacy get underway. It rattles on about state licensing of broadcasters, duties, responsibilities, national security, disorder, crime, public safety, health, morals, old Uncle Tom Cobleigh et al. Here's where freedom struggles to survive amongst the fine print. Here's the inevitable detritus of negotiation and political pondering. And here, inevitably too, is the real freedom of information you discover from this collection of essays: a freedom to examine, refine, target, persevere and jump through innumerable hoops in search of facts that may or may not still be hidden behind some official shroud. In short, a true challenge of a freedom.

Freedom of information didn't arrive in Britain overnight. To the contrary, it took many years of campaigning - by, above all, the wonderful Maurice Frankel - to put it on the statute book. Some of its political initiators during the Blair era now openly regret their enthusiasm: too much time, effort and expense, too much damned trouble. Members of Parliament who helped put reform in place also fought tooth and nail to keep their expense claims - real and confected -

1

from public view. Local councils and trusts, obliged to co-operate, frowned and played for time. Local journalists, lacking the investigative resources of their national press colleagues, carried on much as usual, lazily declining to jump through FOI hoops in search of a scoop.

All of these stories, and many more, are told here in a way that echoes the progress of Freedom of information itself: tales of the heartening, depressing, crusading and inert. Tales, in sum, of a modern life where principle, sloth and cynical calculation perpetually jostle for supremacy.

But I also increasingly feel that there's a much bigger, more symbolic story lurking amongst these pages: one that addresses the most perplexing problems of journalism in our globalised, digitalised age. For freedom of information is not some small, special cause that stops at Calais - or never escapes from Silicon Valley. It is a tide of history. And there are more waves sweeping, with it, onto beaches far and wide.

Examine two of the great media dislocations (and controversies) of the 21st Century thus far. One, bitterly contested, are the issues of personal privacy as outlined by Lord Justice Leveson in his monumental report. The other is summed up by one name and one man: Edward Snowden. And both, as the mists of debate clear, mirror the experiences of FOI; both show us what lies in wait for us all, just around the corner.

Take Snowden first because he's a warrior for freedom, a foe of walls, secrecy, official dissembling – and intelligence practices that no-one who is at last allowed to see them, whole and in detail, can easily defend. Read Barry Turner's description in 'Information in the secret state' and the pieces slip swiftly into place. Snowden, an American, reveals America's illicit surveillance record to the editor of *the Guardian* America website in New York. That editor and other diligent reporters travel back and forth to Washington bearing de-coded texts. They know they must be published. There's a shattering story here. But they also know that publication could put individual operations and lives at risk. So, at the National Security Agency, the Pentagon, the White House, officials talk about and help edit the stories before publication. They don't like the central revelations, but the First Amendment to the constitution means that they'll be published, like it or not. So the name of an essential game is setting basic information, the kernel at the heart of so much encrypted detail, free – which means free, amongst other things, to put the President of the United States on track to reform the surveillance state.

Now this whole episode, of course, has very little to do with freedom of information legislation per se. But it has everything to do with those tides of history. Remember how this 'freedom' began in muted, often neutered legislative American form in 1966. Remember how the debacle of Nixon blew so many of its restrictions out of Watergate in 1974. Now think of the new, digital world and how it must, logically, almost automatically, operate. There is no simple formula called 'information denied' any longer. There is no fortress of silence. Edward Snowden exists, just like Julian Assange; and when Snowden reveals the excesses of government agencies, in America, in Britain, news travels in a digital instant. You can't keep secrets in one country. Nor can you threaten meaningful reprisals against publishers in one country, especially if the country where the news began is, as in this case, the USA, with a First Amendment that makes injunctions against *The Washington Post*, *The New York Times* or *the Guardian* America impossible.

'Congress shall make no law… abridging the freedom of speech, or of the press…' Of course the Founding Fathers weren't thinking of Snowden in 1791. Of course Planet Google is an utterly changed place. But the principle still holds: and the need to see it span and encircle the globe becomes ever more imperative.

Toil through long hours of discussion with representatives of MI5, MI6 or GCHQ. Watch, as *the Guardian* did, as computers in the paper's basement were destroyed in the name of 'national security'. Then ask the absolutely fundamental, absolutely unanswered question of the 21st Century: Is there anything real called national security left? Shouldn't we be talking insistently about international security?

Perhaps, surfing over to that other tidal wave, such arguments become much less high-flown once the topic is privacy – the right of film stars, models, sports wizards and ordinary people (caught up in extraordinary events) to shield their lives and loves from public gaze. The information freedoms involved here have nothing to do with the recesses of government. They are personal, and thus no part of the FOI Act. Yet still, watch the ocean churn.

America's privacy laws - indeed, its whole assessment of public figures and public life - is totally different from Anglo-Saxon (or wider European) attitudes. Thus Tiger Woods, once exposed as a serial fornicator in Florida, has no means of shutting down the ensuing furore by good, old-fashioned British legal practice i.e. an injunction. He's just the most obvious case of something that you now see every day (on the *Mail* Online website, but fuelled by hundreds of other website sources). Simply: the celebrity gossip industry begins, but does not end, in Hollywood. It pours out across America and thus, in the nature of the technology, across the world. Gallant British lawyers may offer to staunch its impact in the Strand (for a suitable fee). Gallant politicians may threaten new laws and new approaches. But basically this is more information without borders: a flow not just of celebrity news, some of it confected, some of it hugely damaging, but of something that cannot be staunched or controlled.

And so the logic of universal declarations rides again. Freedom of information is an idea and a global crusade: a democratic gift to the world. It does not advance consistently. Sometimes (see Charles N Davis' essay on its 'sorry state' in the US) it stutters and slides back. Always (see Dean Jobb in Canada) the gaps between promise and reality have to be lugubriously closed. Only slowly (see Sankaran Ramanathan on Malaysia and Singapore) do you find information, the right to know, chipping away at the walls of one-party government. Yet - from Zimbabwe to China, from India to Australia - there is an idea of such freedom, a wave that never retreats.

3

No-one - this year, this decade, perhaps this century - can see a world where one concept of freedom of information, perhaps as enshrined in one consistent global treaty, will rule OK. But it's coming; and with it will gradually come one doctrine of international security and one binding definition of personal privacy, the logical essentials of online expansion. Freedom doesn't come in penny parcels. Freedom (as FOI brilliantly demonstrates) is the common currency of human existence.

So, for me, this fine collection of reports and examinations from at home and abroad, is much more than a 10-year report on Freedom GB. It shows us where history itself is taking us. It shows, a million miles from Sir Brian Leveson's courtroom or the Houses of Parliament, how that journey will seem, with all its disappointments and frailties along the way. But it is also, amongst many other things, a template for the day after tomorrow. Hear, distantly, the march of feet along freedom's long road.

- Peter Preston is the former editor of *the Guardian*

Preface

Tom Felle

F.O.I. Three little letters but one powerful word. FOI laws have brought down governments; sent corrupt politicians to jail; given closure to those abused in state institutions; and allowed victims of forced adoptions to be reunited with their families.

When modern FOI legislation was first introduced in the US in the 1960s, the trickle down effect of that openness spread. To Australia, Canada and New Zealand in the early 1980s, then to other European states, and eventually to the UK in 2000. Around the world today, nearly 100 countries have freedom of information laws on their statute books. FOI overturned the long-held presumption of a government's right to keep secrets from its people. It was the people's *right* to know, and the media's *right* to inquire. And for a few years, despite the embarrassments and the political damage caused by FOI disclosures, the legislation proved effective.

Chapters by Peter Timmins (Australia), Brant Houston (USA), Michael Foley (Ireland), Dean Jobb (Canada) and Martin Rosenbaum (UK) all list the honours the law has achieved. Himalayan incompetence was unearthed; ministers asleep at the wheel were outed; political feather-bedding, pork-barrelling and corruption was uncovered; unethical and unlawful practices were revealed; unsafe and dangerous threats to public health and safety were discovered; institutional abuses were exposed, and gross wrongs were righted. Investigations by journalists disclosed massive public spending overruns in Ireland and India; civil rights abuses by public authorities in the USA; corruption in Australia and Canada; citizen stripping in the UK; and many other international scandals.

But, as Dean Jobb writes, despite these successes – or perhaps because of them – FOI laws in Western democracies, and the work that investigative journalists do, is under threat. 'Politicians and bureaucrats, the public officials that freedom of information laws are designed to hold accountable, have mounted a determined and highly successful counterattack to evade requests and frustrate applicants,' he argues. States are almost in unison moving (as if there was a secret FOI-avoidance manual for mandarins) to exempt large parts of their decision-making apparatus from disclosure under FOI. Letters received by ministers; papers prepared for cabinet; and documents that form the basis of important public policy decisions are increasingly not being released under FOI.

Bureaucrats have become expert at finding ways to frustrate inquiries by journalists, with excuses such as commercial sensitivity; privacy and data protection; and increasingly the catch-all 'national security' used to thwart legitimate investigations. In the UK, the Home Office even went as far as to ban investigative journalist Alice Ross (see her chapter on citizen stripping) from submitting FOI requests, labelling her a 'vexatious requester', before that decision was overturned on appeal.

It is often overlooked, but there are two 'freedoms' of information operating simultaneously in most countries. One is the access freedom of information laws grant to ordinary citizens. Their *right* to know – to inspect a planning document; obtain personal medical files; to see safety reports of public utilities; to examine inspection reports of crèches, schools and care homes; to view restaurant hygiene ratings – is commonplace around the world. Almost without thinking these freedoms have become the norm in the last decade, and might now be considered part of the package of fundamental liberties that any citizen can expect, and should demand. They promise an element of openness from bodies that interact with the general public, and they assure trust and transparency for civil society.

These sorts of rights hardly need a freedom of information law at all, as this information is routinely proactively published, or available on request. Any government who tried to row back on those rights would soon find a public in revolt. Chapters by contributors from India, Malaysia, Singapore, South Africa, China, and Zimbabwe demonstrate that even in weak democracies and non-democratic regimes, these sorts of basic freedoms are expected, even demanded, by citizens. As Peter Preston writes so eloquently in his foreword to this volume, 'freedom of information is not some small, special cause that stops at Calais - or never escapes from Silicon Valley. It is a tide of history. And there are more waves sweeping, with it, onto beaches far and wide.'

However there is another freedom of information, that practised by journalists, activists, and similar groups – and that is the *right* to know which secrets governments are keeping hidden. That *right* goes to the heart of the role of journalists in a democracy – to hold those in power to account, to ask the uncomfortable questions, and to speak truth to power. This is a far more fragile freedom, and one we must seek to protect.

Much has been written about the worldwide move away from open government and back toward state secrecy post 9/11. Many contributors report with alarming similarity the lengths Western governments are now going to, to avoid disclosing information under FOI. This 'gaming' of FOI includes the overuse of exemptions and the unjustified classification of material; the use of excessive fees and charges to deter journalists; delaying tactics; and in some cases even political interference in FOI requests, especially if the requests relate to material that is likely to be politically embarrassing or damaging.

Offices of Information Commissioners worldwide are being run down to the point where Commissioners can no longer function. Offices are poorly staffed and drowning under the weight of appeals. Often such appeals are as a direct result of refusals of information on political grounds – certain to be overturned by an Information Commissioner – but long forgotten news stories by the time they are. There is evidence that public bodies are wilfully failing to keep records and in some cases refusing to assist in investigations by journalists.

Society has gone through radical change in the last 30 to 50 years, but FOI laws have hardly changed at all and the legislation is hopelessly out of date in many states. Worse still, with increased moves worldwide toward privatisation, many legitimate areas of public inquiry are now beyond the scope of information laws entirely. Whistleblowers laws are inadequate and do not support or protect those who shout stop.

The distinguished US FOI campaigner Professor Charles N Davis, in his chapter 'The sorry state of FOI', calls for a new generation of FOI warriors to carry the flag. He's right; it is time for a new campaign to let in the light. It's time for laws that punish political interference, and that place FOI requests on a par with demands for discovery in court cases. It's time for laws that protect Information Commissioners, with extra powers to investigate public bodies and punish them for poor (or deliberate) decision making, not just in adjudicating long after the fact. It's time for Information Commissioners to be given the power to compel the release within 20 days of documents relating to issues of major national public importance so that the public can be informed when it matters, not months or years after the fact.

FOI laws, narrowly interpreted, work to provide citizens with access to their personal records, and guarantee a personal *right* to know. The more widely interpreted *right* is that of civil society - through the media - to ask uncomfortable questions of those in power. Emerging democracies, and countries with little or no democratic credentials, have some distance to travel before such principles emerge. Unfortunately what might be considered advanced democratic states have regressed and long-fought for and hard-won freedoms are being ceded in the name of national security, and for political obediency.

In a post-Snowden era, there has never been a more critical time for citizens to set demands of what they expect of their governments in terms of openness.

The long-fought for and hard-won freedoms are worth fighting for once more. Journalists – the freedom fighters we are – must lead that charge.

The tide of history beckons.

Section 1:
Critical reflections on freedom of information

Tom Felle

'My greatest mistake.' It was an odd thing to say for a man who had ordered the British invasion of Iraq. Yet the former British Prime Minister Tony Blair singled out the legislation for that special mention in his 2010 memoir. In the first chapter of this section - in which many contributors examine freedom of information in a more conceptual way - Maurice Frankel, an early pioneer and director of the Campaign for FOI in the UK, looks back on 10 years of freedom of information legislation in Britain. The initial White Paper, as Ben Worthy observes, was watered down, but the Act was still far stronger than the Bill, which had included a raft of exemptions and no legislative standing for a public interest test. Some 10 years later the Act has stood the test of time, and the public interest test has been interpreted far more widely than many public bodies, ministries, and officials might have preferred. He notes:

> 'Unfortunately, the public interest test does not apply to all exemptions. And an obstructive authority has a powerful card to play: delay. Each stage of the process can be spun out over many months. Requesters with lives to live may find other uses for their time but plenty have been prepared to go the distance.'

The media have played a critical role in using the Act to report on stories in the public interest, but resentment about the high volume of requests from the media – and the impact on the work-load of public officials – threatens the Act. There has been pressure to increase exemptions; to remove government policy papers from the FOI process; to introduce fees for requests; and to allow more requests to be refused on cost grounds. 'There is no iron law that says FOI is never rolled back - and pressure for that seems certain to continue,' he rightly warns.

The scandal of MPs expenses in the United Kingdom is without equal as one of the biggest domestic stories of the last decade. FOI had been around for nearly four years before the *Daily Telegraph* obtained its scoop, exposing the hypocrisy and illegality at the heart of Westminster with MPs fiddling their expenses. The former BBC correspondent Nicholas Jones re-tells the story of how the *Daily Telegraph* broke the MP expenses story, including the lengths to which MPs went to keep their expenses secret. While not released under FOI, the legislation was the catalyst as the introduction of the act brought the scandal to public attention. As Jones writes:

> *The parliamentarians of Westminster must rue the day their predecessors vowed to do all they could to keep the financial affairs of MPs beyond the reach of the 2000 Freedom of Information Act. If the House of Commons authorities had co-operated with journalists from the outset, rather than obstructed a new era of openness, the collateral damage could have been better controlled, if not minimised, and MPs might have gained a degree of respect for having taken the initiative in cleaning up their expenses system.*

Tom Felle (City University London) takes a step back from many of the other chapters in this volume by asking pertinent questions of the roles that investigative journalism, and freedom of information, play in democratic society. While acknowledging that the media sometimes engage in 'churnalism' he argues that accountability journalism is important so that citizens can have faith in the democratic process. Many powerful public interest investigations have been conducted by journalists using FOI; corrupt officials have been ousted; poor practices have been exposed; and wrongs have been righted. The occasional request concerning amounts spent on biscuits at council meetings aside, FOI has played an important role in reporting on the democratic process, and in holding those in power to account. Felle writes:

> *'The real power of freedom of information, if well used by journalists, is as an investigative tool.... Serious and the important news is often outweighed by entertainment and scandal – that is the society we live in. Stories about the cost of biscuits at council meetings and toilet rolls at Number 10 are the price we pay for democratic accountability. Given the choice between FOI and none, it's a price well worth paying.'*

Ben Worthy (Birkbeck College, University of London) traces the development of the culture of official secrecy in the British administrative system crystallised by the Official Secrets Act, 1911. He examines why the UK was so slow to introduce freedom of information legislation, despite its introduction in the US in the 1960s and in Canada, New Zealand and Australia in the early 1980s. The first moves toward incremental openness in the UK's administrative system started in the 1960s, but it would be nearly 40 years before FOI would be introduced. Despite Tony Blair's later aversion to FOI, Worthy describes Blair and his ministers as being enthusiastic supporters when they came into government, though the 2000 legislation was a much watered down version of their original 1997 White Paper, *Your Right to Know*. In fact, the act may have been shelved completely were it not for a sustained media and civil society campaign:

> *The media were central to this process. As occurred in the US, they were crucial in mobilising support and applying continuous pressure for change. The succession of information related "scandals", from leaks to court cases, generated a self-reinforcing momentum – each failed Official Secrets Act trial generated headlines and made the stronger case for reform.'*

Barry Turner, of Lincoln University and Nottingham Trent University, argues that despite the 'right' to know, little has changed in how the British Government releases information, which is still in its gift. Britain has a centuries old penchant for secrets, and that culture has been slow to change. Turner charts how the British establishment operated throughout the centuries, including cooperating with newspapers to (amazingly) keep stories out of the press via the D Notice Committee. A system of 'grace and favour' has always been favoured over any legislative right. He writes:

> *The culture of secrecy is alive and well 15 years after the passing of the Freedom of Information Act 2000 and we are a very long way away from the transparent open government we were promised by those who introduced it. More than ever we rely not only on those 'lazy journalists' who employ the Act to get stories, but on those who obtain information the old fashioned way by stealth and guile. Let us hope that the next generation of journalists will be well trained in the latter skills.'*

Investigative journalists Guy Basnett and Paul McNamara of OpenWorld News discuss their use of the legislation in a series of national news stories during the last 10 years, including how miscarried and aborted foetuses were being incinerated as clinical waste, sometimes in waste-to-energy power plants; how trigger-happy police officers used 50,000-volt Taser stun guns on children, including a mentally ill 12-year-old girl; how police officers avoided sexual abuse investigations by resigning; how hospitals secretly stored the remains of dead children for years; and how vulnerable children - even babies - have routinely vanished from council care. They offer sage advice on using the FOI Act:

> *'Constantly think up ideas; get the requests in; and be prepared to argue. If you do, then you'll produce great stories and investigations, and the Freedom of Information Act can carry on doing exactly what it's designed for: uncovering the public interest stories that would otherwise remain hidden and untold.'*

Journalism professor Paul Bradshaw, of City University London and Birmingham City University, looks at the practicalities of operating FOI mass requests and offers key tips on how to make it work. A single FOI request to a single agency may give results, but more often than not journalists working on national newspapers may want national figures, not available unless the media organisation decides to collate the figures themselves. FOI requests to reveal the comparative statistics for all hospital trusts, or all councils, for example, require significant effort, a lot of patience, and a well oiled system to deal with replies. His advice: it's all about planning and preparation:

> *'The Freedom of Information Act has opened up a raft of possibilities for watchdog journalism, allowing journalists to hold power to account in ways that would have been prohibitively costly or time-consuming previously…. Combining your legal rights with effective planning and information management makes it possible for a single journalist to do in days or hours what would have required a team of researchers decades ago.'*

Finally, researchers Savita Bailur and Tom Longley examine the use by journalists of FOI request sites in a number of countries worldwide, and find that while the sites are regularly used by the general public, and are popular as repositories, their use by journalists is limited because of the competitive nature of journalism; the 'leak' culture; and the danger of being out-scooped for a story. They argue:

> *'The critical role journalists play is in advocating for an opening up the FOI process, irrespective of whether they use the sites or not – they can raise FOI awareness and create a "culture of asking"…. The more awareness there is of ways to hold government accountable, the better, and online sites facilitate the process.'*

The 'nincompoop' Blair's greatest mistake? 10 years of FOI in the UK

Maurice Frankel assesses 10 years of FOI in the UK, which has seen much released the governments of the day might have wanted kept secret. But despite its transformational impact on the rights of citizens to be informed, the pressure to clampdown on hard-won freedoms is mounting

Introduction

In 1991, BBC Radio 4's 'Face the Facts' programme reported on the closure, at two weeks notice, of a hostel for the homeless. The presenter asked to see the report that led to the decision. The then social security minister Anne Widdecombe replied:

> 'You cannot obviously have detailed reports made available to every outside organisation and everybody who wants to come along and look at them. There's no organisation in the country which could function on that sort of basis... there is no way that I am interested in having umpteen organisations looking into every last detail of all our papers... No, I will not show you the report. I see no reason to show the BBC the report. You know the contents of the report. If you don't believe me, that is tough luck' (BBC, 1991).

The following year, the Chief Constable of Merseyside Police replied to a requester who had asked for an explanation of one of his decisions. 'I have not the slightest intention of giving you any information why I reached the decision I did,' he observed. 'To sum up, I would please ask in future you direct your inquiries to me personally but I can assure you, you will certainly not receive any answers' (*The Independent*, 1992). Remarkably, that rebuff was not directed towards an ordinary member of the public, but to the chairman of a statutory body, the Police Complaints Authority.

A radical reform

Such outraged outbursts are rarely heard today. Ministers and officials may secretly feel that requesters are invading their privacy – but neither the public nor the law now accept that. The Freedom of Information Act provides, in the words of the High Court, 'a radical change to our law and the rights of the citizen to be informed' (Burnton, 2008). The results can be seen every day in the press: FOI stories revealing lapses in public services; policies falling short; regulators that can't keep up; lobbying by special interests; undeclared conflicts of interest; reckless spending and authorities acknowledging in private what they have publicly denied.

Tony Blair famously described FOI as his greatest mistake and himself as a 'nincompoop' for introducing it. But even if he was, as Lord Falconer - who took the FOI Bill through the Lords - wryly observed, being 'typically modest about his achievements', some of what Blair says is spot on. FOI was, as he wrote in his memoirs, 'a quite extraordinary offer by a government to open itself...to scrutiny. Its consequences would be revolutionary' (Blair, 2010).

No revolution was intended, of course. After an initial, bold White Paper (Cabinet Office, 1997) the Government published a draft FOI bill so weak as to have snuffed out any right to know (Home Office, 1999). Some 10 pages of exemptions were coupled with a purely voluntary public interest test, which the Information Commissioner would have had no power to enforce. In a parody of a public interest test, authorities would have been entitled to ask requesters why they wanted the information, what they intended to do with it and - if satisfied with the reason - reveal it on condition they did not make it public. That this would have constituted disclosure 'in the public interest' was a neatly Orwellian touch. Faced with a gale of criticism, these elements of the Bill were eventually dropped. The public interest test became legally binding but ministers insisted on the power to veto decisions made under it by the Commissioner and Tribunal. Jack Straw who, as Home Secretary, introduced the FOI bill has since acknowledged that he and the prime minister considered killing the measure off altogether. Only Labour's manifesto commitment to FOI and Blair's personal promise to deliver it restrained them (Straw, 2012).

In the public interest
The public interest test has proved to be the heart of the Act. It has turned exemptions from the fierce barriers to access originally intended to a nuanced balancing of the pros and cons of disclosure. The section 35 exemption for government policy formulation was intended to protect internal discussion from disclosure other than in exceptional cases. But the High Court has ruled that there is no presumption against disclosure under the public interest test (Burnton, 2008). If you ask for policy discussions before any decision has been taken, the answer will normally be no. But if the request is made *after* the decision, a genuine weighing up of competing factors should follow. Will disclosure of information of that sensitivity (or lack of it) after that length of time inhibit the future recording of similar views? Does the public interest in protecting the official stream of consciousness outweigh the benefits of scrutiny, public understanding and accountability?

The section 36 exemption for the frankness of advice or deliberation and the 'effective conduct of public affairs' was devised as an easily invoked catch-all. All that's needed is a 'reasonable opinion' from a minister or senior officer that disclosure would be harmful. But the Tribunal's approach, which the Government cannot have expected, is that while this elevated person's opinion triggers the exemption it carries no weight under the public interest test (Information Tribunal, 2007). If the evidence of harm is poor or the case for disclosure good, the information must be revealed.

The ministerial veto, which in theory could overturn such public interest decisions, has been invoked on only a handful of occasions in the Act's 10 years. A commitment that the cabinet must endorse its use on every occasion has erected a procedural obstacle to its casual exercise. So while disclosure of the cabinet minutes on the war with Iraq has been vetoed, the government has complied with Tribunal rulings to disclose ministerial working party papers discussing the benefit rights of Eastern European workers (Information Tribunal, 2009) and information about British officials' role in soliciting bribes for Saudis involved in the Al Yamamah arms deal (Information Tribunal, 2008).

Unfortunately, the public interest test does not apply to all exemptions. And an obstructive authority has a powerful card to play: delay. Each stage of the process can be spun out over many months. Requesters with lives to live may find other uses for their time but plenty have been prepared to go the distance.

Media requests

The media have played an absolutely critical role. They have not only opened up streams of important news stories but demonstrated to the wider public that FOI works and is worth using. Requests cost nothing and are simple to make – particularly via the informative WhatDoTheyKnow.com web site, which allows requesters to first study how related requests have fared in the past.

But there has been a backlash. According to one survey some authorities believe that many requests are made solely 'for what was seen as illegitimate use i.e. a "good" media story or to irritate organisations' (Ministry of Justice, 2011). An appeal for information about 'problems' caused by the Act, circulated on behalf of the Local Government Association in 2014 sought statistics on requests by the media and others while complaining about 'the use of the FOI process by researchers and campaigners for their benefit at our expense' (Lawyers in Local Government, 2014). The depressing implication is that they believe the Act is there to help householders discover why their rubbish collection was late but anyone using it to document or influence policy is hijacking FOI for an improper purpose.

The press's use of FOI undoubtedly irritates some authorities. Is this just resentment at the scrutiny, exposés and criticism? Complaints about the high volume of journalists' requests are common. FOI is sometimes used as a survey tool with the same request going to multiple authorities. Some of the results have been spectacular, as with *the Guardian*'s survey of the mortality rate of individual cardiac surgeons. The paper published figures adjusted to take account of the severity of the patients' conditions, so as not to unfairly penalise surgeons prepared to tackle risky cases (Boseley, 2005). The exercise gave extra impetus to the publication of such data by the Society for Cardiothoracic Surgery, which has now occurred. Critics had argued that it would make surgeons less willing to operate on high-risk patients, to avoid jeopardising their statistics. But this has not occurred, at least from the publication of hospital-wide mortality data (Bridgewater, 2007).

Another complaint is that journalists use FOI for 'fishing expeditions' – requests fired off with no express target in the hope of a lucky strike on a newsworthy item. FOI officers may resent having to find and process large volumes of material most of which will be judged too mundane to report. The Commissioner who enforces Scotland's FOI law has ruled that a request for all 'if asked' answers to potential press questions, prepared by the Scottish Government during a four month period, would have required such a wide and expensive trawl of files as to make it 'manifestly unreasonable' and thus vexatious (Scottish Information Commissioner, 2013). A ruling from the UK Upper Tribunal has established that requests that do not exceed the FOI cost limit may be vexatious if answering would cause a disproportionate burden not justified by the value of the information (Upper Tribunal, 2013). The UK Information Commissioner's guidance expressly cites 'fishing expeditions' from journalists as a potentially vexatious category if they are part of a disproportionately burdensome pattern of 'pot luck' requests covering large amounts of information of limited value. However, he cautions against its use by authorities where the requester is following a genuine line of enquiry (Information Commissioner's Office, 2013). At the time of writing, only one such journalism case had been decided, and that in the journalist's favour (Information Commissioner's Office, 2014). This development will undoubtedly require some requesters to moderate the volume of requests they make. Under a regime where access is completely free of charge, such self-restraint may be wise if only to avoid further restrictions.

Pressure for restrictions
Within 18 months of the Act coming into force in 2005 the Blair government attempted to make it easier for authorities to refuse requests on cost grounds. The measure was blocked by the then Chancellor, Gordon Brown, and dropped when he became prime minister in May 2007. Simultaneously, a private member's bill to exclude Parliament and thus MPs' expenses from FOI was approved by the Commons but stalled in the Lords (Campaign for Freedom of Information, 2007).

In 2010 the government came close to excluding all cabinet and cabinet committee papers from the Act (Ministry of Justice, 2010). There has been high-level support for moves to bar access to government policy discussions altogether and the Prime Minister, David Cameron, has complained that FOI 'furs up the whole of government' (House of Commons, 2012). Information about communications with the Monarch and the next two in line to the throne has already been removed from FOI.

There has been pressure for application fees to be introduced with some authorities calling for them to apply to commercial bodies, which they suggest should include the media. The Local Government Association has twice released lists of the most bizarre FOI requests received by local authorities, highlighting the total cost of FOI to councils and warning about the need to ensure value for money. In fact, requests about preparations for possible zombie attacks (the kind of example that features) cost nothing, because FOI officers do not spend time on them. But the publicity promotes the idea that FOI has gone too far.

At the time of writing the coalition government is still considering options to allow more requests to be refused on cost grounds - and the introduction of charges for appeals to the Tribunal. It says its concern is to focus on those who impose 'disproportionate burdens' by making 'industrial' use of the Act. But the key proposals would make it easier to refuse *all* requests including those from occasional applicants raising issues of real public interest (Campaign for Freedom of Information, 2014).

So far attempts to restrict the Act have largely been unsuccessful. But there's no guarantee of that in future. The introduction of charges under Ireland's FOI Act in 2003 (which has just been partly reversed) led to an immediate 75 per cent fall in the volume of official information requests. The Office of the Australian Information Commissioner is being abolished which will require challenges to the merits of decisions to go to the Administrative Appeals Tribunal at a cost of AUS$800 (£435).

There is no iron law that says FOI is never rolled back - and pressure for that seems certain to continue.

References

BBC (1991) 'Face the Facts,' BBC Radio 4, September 1991

Blair, Tony (2010) *A Journey*. London: Vintage.

Boseley, Sarah, Carvel, John, and Evans, Rob (2005) 'Hospitals deny patients facts on death rates,' in *the Guardian*, 16 March

Bridgewater, Ben et al (2007) 'Has the publication of cardiac surgery outcome data been associated with changes in practice in northwest England: an analysis of 25,730 patients undergoing CABG surgery under 30 surgeons over eight years,' *Heart*, 93, 744-748

Burnton, Mr Justice Stanley (2008) *Office of Government Commerce & Information Commissioner & Her Majesty's Attorney General*, [2008] EWHC 737 (Admin)

Cabinet Office (1997) *Your Right to Know, The Government's Proposals for a Freedom of Information Act*, CM 3818

Campaign for Freedom of Information (2000) 'Things you would not have believed possible under a Freedom of Information Act', available at http://www.cfoi.org.uk/2000/03/16-things-you-would-not-have-believed-possible-under-a-freedom-of-information-act, accessed 20 October, 2014

Campaign for Freedom of Information (2007) 'Attempt to remove Parliament from FOI Act', available at http://www.cfoi.org.uk/campaigns/attempt-to-remove-parliament-from-the-foi-act/, accessed 22 October, 2014

Campaign for Freedom of Information (2007) 'Blair Government's proposals to restrict FOI requests', available at http://www.cfoi.org.uk/campaigns/blair-governments-proposals-to-restrict-foi requests, accessed 22 October, 2014

Campaign for Freedom of Information (2014) 'Stop FOI restrictions', available at http://www.cfoi.org.uk/campaigns/stop-foi-restrictions, accessed 22 October, 2014

Home Office (1999) *Freedom of Information: Consultation on Draft Legislation*, Cm 4355.

House of Commons (2012), 'Evidence from the Prime Minister to the Liaison Committee,' Question 438, 6 March

Information Commissioner's Office (2013), *Dealing with Vexatious Requests (Section 14)*, 20130514, 522278 Version: 1

Information Commissioner's Office (2014), Decision Notice FS50522278, Welsh Assembly Government

Information Tribunal (2007), EA/2006/0064, *Mr R Evans & Information Commissioner & Ministry of Defence* (decision of 26 October 2007)

Information Tribunal (2008), EA/2007/0071, EA/2007/0078, EA/2007/0079, *Nicholas James Gilby & Information Commissioner & Foreign and Commonwealth Office*

Information Tribunal (2009), EA/2008/0073, Cabinet Office & Information Commissioner

Lawyers in Local Government (2014) Bulletin No 14, April 25

Ministry of Justice (2010), *Government Response to the 30-Year Rule Review*, Cm 7822

Ministry of Justice (2011), *Memorandum to the Justice Select Committee, Post-Legislative Assessment of the Freedom of Information Act 2000*, Cm 8236

Scottish Information Commissioner (2013), Decision 211/2013 *Mr Martyn McLaughlin and the Scottish Ministers*

Straw, Jack (2012) *Last Man Standing: Memoirs of a Political Survivor*. London: Macmillan

The Independent (1992) 10 June

Upper Tribunal (2013), *Craven v Information Commissioner & DECC* [2012] UKUT 442 (AAC)

Note on the contributor

Maurice Frankel has worked for the Campaign for Freedom of Information since it was established in 1984 and has been its director since 1987. He was actively involved in persuading the government to introduce the FOI Act and in improving what started out as an extremely weak bill. His work for the Campaign includes providing training for requesters and public authorities, assisting requesters, monitoring the Act's operation and seeking to defend and improve it. He can be reached at admin@cfoi.demon.co.uk

A 'very British revolution': the MPs' expenses scandal

From a bill to clean a moat to dodgy mortgage receipts, the MPs' expenses scandal had it all. But attempts by MPs to block their outlandish expenses regime from investigation under FOI made the story all the more shocking when it was finally revealed. *Nicholas Jones* explores the errors of judgements that led to self-inflicted humiliation

Introduction

The parliamentarians of Westminster must rue the day their predecessors vowed to do all they could to keep the financial affairs of MPs beyond the reach of the 2000 Freedom of Information Act. If the House of Commons authorities had co-operated with journalists from the outset, rather than obstructed a new era of openness, the collateral damage could have been better controlled, if not minimised, and MPs might have gained a degree of respect for having taken the initiative in cleaning up their expenses system. In the event the purchase by the *Daily Telegraph* of a purloined computer disk containing one and a half million receipts in 2009 gave a national newspaper the opportunity to dictate the news agenda for weeks on end as each day's revelations about their extravagant and outrageous expenditure exposed the extraordinary lengths to which the country's elected representatives had gone in order to profit at the taxpayers' expense from their second-home allowances. MPs were at the mercy of the news media, as were ministers and party leaders. Rarely had there been an occasion when reporters and editors had been so united in their collective determination to help exploit and manipulate data stolen from the parliamentary fees office, in what the news media was convinced was investigative journalism of the highest order and most definitely in the public interest.

If ever a testament was needed to the folly of not accepting the full consequences of the greater transparency demanded by freedom of information, there could hardly be a more pertinent reminder than the prison sentences imposed on five Labour MPs for false accounting. But whereas the illegality of claiming for a non-existent mortgage was inevitably a matter for the courts, it was the court of public opinion that shamed numerous Conservative Party grandees, the Tory knights of the shires, who for years had milked their allowances in order to subsidise their highly desirable country houses and lavish private amenities. Such was the public outrage at the deception and duplicity of the House of Commons Commission in overseeing the lack of accountability, and then in trying to perpetuate a cover-up, that the Speaker Michael Martin had no option but to resign in disgrace, the first time in more than 300 years that a Speaker had been forced out of office.

Shattering public trust in MPs

In the immediate aftermath of the expenses scandal, newspaper opinion polls indicated that trust in MPs had fallen to an all-time low. By the end of the first week a YouGov survey indicated that 60 per cent of those questioned believed MPs had been 'ripping us off' (*The Sun*, 15 May, 2009). Public revulsion intensified as the extent of the abuse was exposed. Five months into the scandal 73 per cent of those surveyed believed MPs were 'still dishonest' (*The Sunday Times*, 18 October, 2009). Another poll showed that only 13 per cent of people trusted politicians to tell the truth, MPs' worst score in the 26-year history of the survey and lower even than the rating for journalists (*The Observer*, 27 September, 2009). Although many of the unusually high number of 148 MPs who stood down before the 2010 general election had been tarnished by their expenses claims, the newly-elected House fared no better. Early in 2013, when MPs were debating a pay increase, there was no sign of any recovery in their public standing: one poll suggested that only 14 per cent trusted MPs (*Sunday Express*, 10 February, 2013); another found only 18 per cent 'generally trust politicians to tell the truth' and they remained the least trusted profession after journalists on 21 per cent (*Evening Standard*, 15 February, 2013).

Given the widespread public support for the news media's role in holding politicians to account there is no likelihood of a quick fix for the House of Commons. Deeply embedded in the mind-set of journalists is a narrative that MPs were exposed as having been not only unbelievably greedy but that they were also only too willing to put themselves above the law. As a result, readers are reminded regularly, especially in the tabloid press, of the extravagant claims that were made in the past; any proposal to increase MPs' pay to compensate for a stricter and less generous expenses regime is greeted with critical banner headlines and damning editorials; and there remains a lingering suspicion that given half a chance MPs would once again try to impose a blanket of secrecy over the finer points of their remuneration and expenses.

Scoop of the decade

Political correspondents could not remember an occasion when a single newspaper had succeeded in keeping the Westminster establishment on the defensive for so long. Initially, after the *Daily Telegraph*'s opening salvo, 'The truth about the Cabinet's expenses' (8 May, 2009), there was stunned disbelief in Whitehall and Westminster. The then Prime Minister Gordon Brown, his ministers, party leaders and the House of Commons authorities had been given no advance warning that a group of journalists had gained exclusive access to four years worth of MPs' receipts and their private correspondence with the parliamentary fees office. For a relatively modest outlay of £110,000 a newspaper had acquired four million separate pieces of information, a treasure trove of illicit material, but also potentially incriminating evidence. For several weeks the country became transfixed by the grasping ingenuity that had been deployed by MPs as they went to inordinate lengths to take full advantage of an additional costs allowance worth just over £23,000 a year. A claim for purchasing a floating duck house and another for cleaning a moat seemed out of this world to the average citizen, as did the realisation that an MP had dared to claim for a phantom mortgage. Amid the ensuing hue and cry the House of Commons' original culpability in having defied the Freedom of Information Act seemed to have been rendered a mere footnote when set against the more immediate demands that excessive and fraudulent claims should be repaid and that heads should roll. But the public's trust in the probity of their elected representatives had been well and truly shattered and a generation of MPs have found it impossible to shake off their responsibility, however limited, for having impeded FOI requests and for then having acquiesced for so long in an attempted cover-up.

Heather Brooke, an American journalist who had already established herself as a doughty investigator of politicians' expenses claims, was one of the first to prepare for the day when MPs' financial affairs would be within the scope of freedom of information. In February 2004, 10 months before Act would finally come into force, she asked if the House of Commons intended publishing details of each MP's expenses. She was assured information would be released in October 2004 but in the event publication amounted to no more than a summary of the total paid out to each MP for office costs, travel and the additional costs allowance for maintaining a second home. Although there was no detailed breakdown, the figures did even more to fuel the news media's interest. A number of political correspondents had spent years trying to penetrate the secrecy surrounding MPs' expenses and their appetite had been whetted yet again by the vast range in the individual amounts being claimed and then reimbursed. Once the Act took effect in January 2005, Ms Brooke put in an FOI request for the expenses claims of all 646 MPs. She was not alone in taking the initiative: two other reporters had filed similar requests. Jon Ungoed-Thomas of *The Sunday Times* submitted a request for the expenses claims of the then Prime Minister Tony Blair and the Secretary of State for the Environment Margaret Beckett; Ben Leapman of the London *Evening Standard* (who later joined the *Sunday Telegraph*) asked to see the claims of six MPs, including Blair. An FOI request had also been submitted by the Liberal Democrat MP Norman Baker, who had been investigating abuses in the expenses system.

These initial requests were all rejected by the House of Commons Commission. Ms Brooke had tried several different approaches, narrowing down her requests. She was told that it would be too expensive to collate such a huge volume of information. 'They pretty much laughed in my face' she said, speaking of the event later (Winnett and Rayner, 2009: 20). Baker said his 'modest request' for a breakdown of MPs travel costs by mode of transport was 'fought tooth and nail' by the parliamentary authorities (Baker, 2008). After refusing to take no for an answer the journalists appealed to the Information Commissioner Richard Thomas who agreed in April 2005 to conduct an investigation. Two years elapsed before Thomas ruled in June 2007 that the claims of 14 MPs named by the reporters should be made public. Each MP's annual claim would be broken down into categories such as rent and household goods, but without receipts or further detail.

Leaked emails subsequently obtained by the *Sunday Telegraph* indicated that in a draft decision in 2006 Thomas had proposed ordering publication of the full details of MPs' expenses but he had 'watered down' his final judgement after pressure from the House of Commons (Leapman, 2009a). Jack Straw, then Leader of the House, held a meeting with the Commissioner between his preliminary and final rulings. Straw denied that the meeting had played a 'fundamental' role in the about-turn. Nonetheless, instead of accepting the amended ruling, the House of Commons Commission appealed to the Information Tribunal. When the Tribunal decided in February 2008 that the expenses claims should be published in full, including receipts, the parliamentary authorities went to the High Court to try to get the ruling overturned. The case was rejected and three judges ruled in May 2008 that information relating to the 14 MPs should be released on the grounds that the 'expenditure of public money through the payment of MPs' salaries and allowances is a matter of direct and reasonable interest to taxpayers' (Winnett and Rayner, 2009: 27).

Rearguard action continued to impede FOI requests

As a result of the judgement the House of Commons agreed to make preparations to publish the claims for all MPs for the period 2004 to 2008. FOI campaigners were in no mood to celebrate: the original publication date of October 2008 slipped to December and that too passed without any details being released. Speaker Martin and the senior MPs who made up the Commission had shown by their dogged obstruction, and by their appeal to the High Court, that they would not give up without a fight. Ben Leapman for one sensed further obstruction was imminent. The claims of the six MPs that he had obtained were for the period 2001 to 2004 but despite it being a test case, he subsequently discovered that once the Commission realised the vulnerability of MPs, it had 'destroyed all other MPs' receipts from the 2001 to 2004 period' (Leapman, 2009b). His revelation about the steps that were still being taken to protect the secrecy surrounding MPs' allowances was another indication of the unprecedented action that FOI campaigners believed the House of Commons would continue to sanction in order to impede the reach of the legislation.

Perhaps the most audacious rear-guard move had been the attempt by the Conservative MP David Maclean to introduce a private member's bill to exempt Parliament from FOI. His Freedom of Information (Amendment) Bill was passed by 96 votes to 25 on Friday 18 May 2007, the day of the week reserved for backbenchers' legislation. Norman Baker was one of the MPs to vote against the Bill, which ultimately failed to proceed beyond the House of Commons because a sponsor could not be found in the House of Lords. The Bill was still being considered at Commons committee stage when the Information Commissioner ruled in June 2007 that the claims of 14 MPs should be released to the three journalists – the ruling that was then challenged by the House of Commons Commission, of which Maclean was a member.

Despite losing its appeal to the High Court in May 2008, and finally agreeing that it would publish MPs' expenses for 2004 to 2008, the Commission had evidently not given up the possibility of obtaining a last-minute change in the law to maintain the confidentiality of MPs' expenses. Behind-the-scenes pressure on the Labour government paid off in January 2009 when, after the two promised publication dates had passed, the Leader of the House Harriet Harman tabled a motion to exempt MPs' claims and allowances from FOI requests. Labour MPs were told there would be a three-line whip on the motion and that they had to give it their support. But after Conservative and Liberal Democrat MPs indicated their opposition, the government backed down, withdrew the motion and announced a new publication date of 1 July, 2009.

MPs' addresses key in exposing worst abuses
Although the Government and the Commission had been forced to accept defeat, and the parliamentary fees office was engaged in the mammoth task of preparing for the July release of MPs' expenses, there had been one little-noticed success for the opponents of FOI. A motion had been approved the previous year, in July 2008, to exempt MPs' addresses from any FOI requests, despite this having been rejected in the ruling of the Information Tribunal and the High Court judgement. Both had accepted the argument of the three journalists that unless MPs' addresses were disclosed there would be no way of checking whether a second-home allowance was being abused. Ben Leapman's intention was to see whether bogus claims were being made, perhaps for properties that were not genuinely being lived in.

The willingness of MPs to put party differences aside and close ranks in their doomed attempt to frustrate FOI investigations by withholding their addresses was perhaps only to be expected after the way some of their colleagues had been picked off, one by one, and had their claims trawled over by the news media. In the two years immediately preceding the *Daily Telegraph*'s publication of what became a daily rogues' gallery of errant MPs, there had been widespread coverage of several highly embarrassing abuses of the system. One MP was pilloried for having paid a salary to his student son when there was no record of any work having been done; another was found to be paying a nanny from her parliamentary expenses; and two parliamentary pairs of husbands and wives were accused of having gained financially by jointly pooling their second-home allowances.

The next MP to find her expenses had become headline news was the then Home Secretary, Jacqui Smith. In her case it was not only her second home that had attracted attention but also the additional claims she had made. 'Jacqui Smith put adult films on expenses' was the front-page headline of the *Sunday Express*, one of the first newspapers to make use of the vast accumulation of data purloined from the parliamentary fees office that included claim forms, receipts and correspondence (Groves and Giannangeli, 29 March, 2009). Her expenses had included a bill for two pay-per-view adult films that her husband later admitted to having watched and an additional 88p for the cost of a sink plug.

At least six newspapers had been offered access to a computer disk stolen from the Stationery Office, which had been given the task of scanning a mountain of paperwork in preparation for publication. Initially newspapers were offered access to an individual MP's file at £5,000 a shot and there had been two earlier exclusives in the *Mail on Sunday*, about the second homes of Jacqui Smith and the employment minister Tony McNulty (although the source of both leaks was not identified). Only the *Daily Telegraph* promised to publish information relating to all 646 MPs, irrespective of party affiliations. Once a deal was agreed, it paid £100,000 for the disk and £10,000 to two businessmen who had acted on behalf of the whistleblowers, thought to be several disgruntled soldiers on leave from Iraq who had been employed to guard staff scanning the documents and who had been scandalised by what they had seen. The disk was an 'unregistered', unedited copy of the original hard drive and was unlike later versions from which MPs addresses had been redacted along with other identifying details in accordance with the terms of the 2008 House of Commons motion for dealing with FOI requests.

To flip or not to flip: a 'no brainer' for many MPs

Having an uncensored disk enabled the *Daily Telegraph* to coin a new word in the House of Commons vocabulary: 'flipping', the practice of an MP changing the designation of a 'second home' back and forth to enable improvements to be carried out at each address at the taxpayers' expense. Flipping between properties in order to claim the maximum allowance was an abuse that had not been exposed until the *Daily Telegraph*'s team of journalists started checking individual claims against addresses. Their step-by-step guide to working the system explained how an MP could nominate a London property as a 'second' home for refurbishment and then flip the designation to a constituency home, so that it too could be improved. MPs' calculated exploitation of their allowances in order to extend and improve their property holdings had become common practice among MPs from across the House and any doubts within the news media about the justification for the theft of private information were swept away once the *Daily Telegraph* revealed that even some of Gordon Brown's cabinet ministers had joined those who had been busily massaging their expenses in order to benefit from rising house prices.

Heather Brooke told *Channel 4 News* on the evening the story broke that the public had every right to know how MPs were using public money (*Channel 4 News*, 8 May, 2009). If they were so arrogant as to claim for a bath plug on expenses or flip their allowances between two different properties, they had to realise they were not beyond scrutiny. 'MPs came up with the excuse of personal privacy but this is all about very personal embarrassment.... This will make MPs think before they put in their claims in the future' she said, interviewed by the BBC the same evening (BBC News, 8 May, 2009). The extent of some of their property portfolios was no surprise to the former Conservative MP Michael Brown, who had become a columnist for *The Independent*. He described his first trip to the fees office on the day he entered parliament in 1979. He was asked for his national insurance number and was told his salary would be £7,000 a year. 'As my constituency was 200 miles from London I was given a book of claim forms for the additional costs allowance of £3,000 a year. The fees office suggested I claim £250 a month. I could stay in London if I chose, no one was going to ask, and no receipts were required. Staff in the fees office were the servants of the House and the House took MPs on trust' (BBC Radio 4 *Today*, 9 May, 2009). Brown said that over the years the allowance steadily became more generous. The turning point was during Margaret Thatcher's premiership: 'In 1983 the additional costs allowance was increased and MPs were allowed to use it to pay for a mortgage on a second home; that was the beginning of MPs joining the property business' (ibid).

Amid the furore generated by its exclusive stories the *Daily Telegraph* always took care not to reveal MPs' addresses in print, although the publication of photographs of their properties meant their location was hardly a secret. Nonetheless the paper was praised for having taken this precaution by the Conservative MP Dr Julian Lewis, who had supported moves to keep addresses secret because he feared the identification of MPs' homes was a security risk. In March 2009, two months before the expenses scandal broke, Dr Lewis had successfully moved an amendment to the Political Parties and Elections Bill to allow all candidates in parliamentary elections to keep their home addresses secret. MPs argued that the move was justified on security grounds to protect them from attack by terrorists or harassment from angry constituents. Harriet Harman was challenged by the *Channel 4 News* presenter Jon Snow when the *Daily Telegraph* first revealed that addresses had been vital in exposing flipping between properties. He accused MPs of having engaged in 'a step-by-step cover-up' to block FOI requests but Ms Harman insisted that it had been the House of Commons that had decided to keep addresses out of the public domain (*Channel 4 News*, 8 May, 2009).

Only themselves to blame

Initially the Speaker and the Commons Commission seemed intent on vengeance, demanding a police investigation. Their fury had been stoked by the earlier stories which they were convinced were based on information leaked from the fees office. Speculation in March 2009 about illicit files being offered to newspapers had been heightened by an investigation on *Newsnight*. After the programme's reporter Michael Crick described how copies of receipts for every MP were up for sale, Sir Stuart Bell, a leading member of the Commission, claimed the asking price was £300,000; a figure also quoted by *The Times*. He said the House had a 'pretty good idea' about the source. An investigation was underway into the theft of data and what appeared to have been a breach of the Official Secrets Act (BBC *Newsnight*, 30 March, 2009). Once the *Daily Telegraph* broke the story, Sir Stuart was the first to confirm the accuracy of the leak. He acknowledged that four years' worth of receipts appeared to have been stolen (*Channel 4 News*, 8 May, 2009).

On the fourth day of disclosures the Conservative Party leader David Cameron, then being advised by the former *News of the World* editor Andy Coulson, tried to seize the agenda in a series of television interviews in which he said it had been another 'bad day for parliament' and 'we are sorry about that' (BBC *Ten O'Clock News*, 9 May, 2009). Next morning Gordon Brown followed suit saying he wanted 'to apologise on behalf of politicians, on behalf of all parties'. Yet in his first response, rather than build on the Prime Minister's apology, Speaker Martin went on the offensive, setting out the reasons for calling in the police. Because the unauthorised disclosure included details of 'bank accounts, style of signature and verbal passwords' he thought a 'criminal offence' might have been committed and the person who sold the data could not be left 'in situ' able to offer the material to the 'highest bidder'. Martin compounded his failure to join the chorus of apologies by unexpectedly rounding on MPs who dared to suggest parliament should be reforming itself rather than calling in the police. Norman Baker was admonished for being 'keen to say to the press whatever the press wants to hear' after he suggested expenses claims should be always be published as soon as possible.

Campaigners for greater openness believed the Speaker had sealed his own fate: Martin had consistently encouraged the Commission to thwart FOI and was considered the principal roadblock to reform. An early day motion tabled that evening by the Conservative MP Douglas Carswell called on Martin to stand down. His misjudgement of the mood of the House became all the more embarrassing as details emerged about the subsidies being paid to Tory grandees for the upkeep on their country estates. That weekend the press identified Martin as the likeliest scapegoat. Several editorials accused him of bringing parliament into disrepute. In his second statement, on the eleventh day of the scandal, Martin bowed to the clamour for an apology but remained as combative as the week before. He said they must 'all accept blame'; he was 'profoundly sorry'; and he called for an urgent meeting with party leaders to discuss reform of the expenses system. MPs were aghast at Martin's attempt to brazen it out and by his refusal to accept Carswell's motion for a vote of confidence. Lobby correspondents had been briefed that the Prime Minister would 'accept the will of the House' and a discreet meeting with Brown that evening in the Speaker's house was the prelude to what the *Daily Telegraph* would claim was 'A very British Revolution' (20 May, 2009). Next day, at the start of business, Martin made a brief 33-second statement announcing that he would relinquish the office of Speaker the following month.

The public interest

From the outset the *Daily Telegraph*'s editor William Lewis had been convinced there was a clear public interest in their investigation if the details about MPs' expenses were genuine. Neither the Commons Commission nor the Stationery Office had taken the precaution of giving the scanned documents a security classification and his journalists believed there was no danger of falling foul of the Official Secrets Act (Winnett and Rayner, 2009: 37). Lewis was also advised that the disk did not constitute stolen property; it was simply a copy (ibid: 75). Although still fearful as to how the police might respond, there was widespread relief on the second evening of the investigation when the paper's deputy political editor Robert Winnett received a text from 'one of the country's most senior police officers, congratulating him on the scoop' (ibid: 157). Within days of Speaker Martin telling parliament the police had been called in, Lewis received information from 'a highly placed source that the Metropolitan Police Commissioner, Sir Paul Stephenson, had decided not to launch an investigation into the leak' (ibid: 239). In his statement confirming the decision, Sir Paul said the Crown Prosecution Service had concluded that a public interest defence would be a 'significant hurdle' to any successful outcome.

References

Baker, Norman (2009) 'Never in my 20 years in politics have I seen the public as angry as today,' *Mail on Sunday*, 10 May

BBC (2009) David Cameron interview, *Ten O'Clock News*, 9 May

BBC (2009) Heather Brooke interview, *BBC News*, 8 May

BBC (2009) Michael Brown interview, *BBC Radio 4 News*, 9 May

BBC (2009) Sir Stuart Bell interview, *Newsnight*, 30 March

Channel 4 (2009) Harriet Harman interview, *Channel 4 News*, 8 May

Channel 4 (2009) Heather Brooke interview, *Channel 4 News*, 8 May

Channel 4 (2009) Sir Stuart Bell interview, *Channel 4 News*, 8 May

Daily Telegraph (2009) 'Only the start of a very British revolution,' Editorial comment, 20 May

Evening Standard (2013) 'Ipsos Mori poll', 15 February

Groves, Jason and Giannangeli, Marco (2009) 'Jacqui Smith put adult films on expenses,' *Sunday Express*, 29 March

Leapman, Ben (2009a) 'T'sar's plan to publish "watered down",' *Sunday Telegraph*, 31 May

Leapman, Ben (2009b) 'My four-year battle for the truth,' *Sunday Telegraph*, 10 May

Sunday Express (2013) 'Editorial: Vision Critical', 10 February

The Observer (2009) 'Ipsos MORI', 27 September, 2009

The Sun (2009) 'YouGov poll', 15 May

The Sunday Times (2009) 'YouGov poll', 18 October

Winnett, Robert (2009) *Daily Telegraph*, 'The Truth about the Cabinet's expenses', 8 May

Winnett, Robert and Rayner, Gordon (2009) *No Expense Spared. Daily Telegraph* Books

Note on the contributor

Nicholas Jones was a BBC industrial and political correspondent for 30 years. He has written extensively on the relationship between politicians and the media. In his book *Campaign 2010: The Making of the Prime Minister*, he investigated MPs' obstruction of the 2000 Freedom of Information Act, the leaks leading up to the MPs' expenses scandal of 2009 and the way it was exploited in the lead-up to the 2010 general election. His other books include *Trading Information: Leaks, Lies and Tip-offs* (2006). News archive: www.nicholasjones.org.uk

Freedom fighting: Why FOI is important for democracy

The cost of biscuits at council meetings is hardly front-page news, but the work of journalists in holding those in power to account using the Freedom of Information Act serves an important democratic function, writes *Tom Felle*

Introduction

Journalists have long argued their central role as the 'fourth estate' in democracy. The media's role in asking the tough questions, in holding power to account, in exposing wrong doing, maladministration and corruption in public life is centrally important for any democratic society. It is probably why authoritarian regimes desperately seek to control the press, and why the rich and powerful often try to stymie journalists through court injunctions and other legal means. The role of the press in accountability journalism – reporting on public bodies' decision making and spending – is just as important in a democratic society even where there is no wrongdoing, as it forms part of the debate and discussion process in civic society: different ideas can be considered and other voices can be heard. Of course, there are many other reasons people watch TV and buy newspapers, but the provision of news, current affairs and authoritative opinion are central elements.

Freedom of information is fundamental in all of this because it grants the *'right to know'* to all citizens – not just to the media. That right is independent of government, so the news media are - in theory at least - able to access information those in power may not want released, if it is in the public interest. Of course, as many other contributors to this book argue in later chapters, the reality is not always so simple, and there are many problems with governments, even the democratic ones, trying to block FOI requests. There are also many problems with journalists' use of FOI laws, not least their obsession with minor spending by politicians that offer cheap headlines.

Democracy and the 'right' to know

Freedom of information is important because it makes government open, transparent and accountable. The philosophy behind such legislation is that citizens have a right to know how and why decisions are made by government in their name. It is directly connected with notions of democracy – in particular transparency and open government. Democracy is an enigmatic term, an essentially contested concept (Gallie, 1956). More recently, Phillips (2004: 57) described the aims of democracy as 'not very high' but offering protection against tyranny and arbitrary rule. Democracy does not weed out careerism or opportunism, neither does it ensure far-sighted policies nor enlightened legislation, but it does require 'political leaders to subject themselves to regular bouts of accountability through the election process' (ibid: 57). In essence, therefore, there is the concept that democracy empowers people to elect leaders, and to deselect them, and that government is accountable to the people.

Openness and transparency in government are then closely related to democratic rule. Citizens have a legitimate expectation that they will be informed how and why decisions of government are made in their name. Indeed, they have regular opportunities to voice their own views via referenda, local and national elections, and public meetings on issues such as planning. Wright (1977: 2) argues that the principal definition of an open government is one in which it is assumed the public have a right to know unless there are specific reasons such as national security why information should not be divulged. This view is at odds with the traditional Westminster view of government, more inclined toward secrecy. As McCrann argues, all governments have a 'penchant for secrecy' (2007: 1), which is at odds with the concept of open democracy.

Freedom of information is designed to shed a light on the process of government, making it more accountable and transparent (Banisar, 2002: 5-7; Hazell, 1989: 189-190). The principal philosophy is that open government is good government. Legislation exists in most western democracies where the right of citizens to know how and why governments make decisions on their behalf is a well-established precedent, and one that is recognised internationally, for example in the Swedish Constitution, the First Amendment to the US Constitution as interpreted by the US Supreme Court, and in international conventions such as the European Convention on Human Rights and in the UN Convention on Civil and Political Rights. The legislation has its foundations in Sweden, where it has existed since 1766, and today is enacted in most Western democracies – though known as 'Right to Information' (RTI) in a number of Asian states, and by other acronyms elsewhere (see section three for chapters on the workings of FOI in several states worldwide).

Making government open

FOI laws are based on the premise that people have the 'right' of access to public documents, save for certain exemptions (Doyle, 1997: 68). The aims of the legislation, according to Hazell (1989: 189), are to increase public awareness of policy-making; increase public participation in decision-making; and to improve the quality of the legislative process. It can be viewed as part of a raft of legislation such as public service reform; ombudsman legislation; strengthening powers of public auditors; police oversight; and ethics laws that have been introduced in democratic countries during the last 30 or so years with the aim of making government more open, transparent and accountable (Banisar, 2002: 5-7; Hazell, 1989, 189-190) with the right of access to documents leading to a more open political process (Doyle, 1997: 77). Such laws have the potential, at least then, to lead to more open and accountable government, less corruption and better democratic outcomes for states.

While the details of legislation differ, the principle of the legislation is similar in most Western democracies in that there is a general rule that all public documents should be available for public scrutiny, save for specific exceptions. These exceptions are also broadly similar, namely documents dealing with security and defence, international relations of the state, on-going deliberations, commercial interest and individual privacy (McDonagh, 1998: 10). Legislation usually also includes public interest overrides and harm tests, so documents may be released if this is in the public or national interest in some circumstances, though specific countries apply specific rules depending on individual circumstances (ibid: 12). A central theme can also be identified, namely the presumption of a right to know. Appeal to independent bodies such as an Information Commissioner is also a common feature (Bugdahn, 2007: 129-130). Information disclosure is important to allow opposition parties, the media and the public to judge the quality of decision making, but at a citizen level it ensures fair treatment at the hands of bureaucracy, including, for example, the reasons for decisions concerning access to public services such as social welfare entitlements (Doyle, 1997: 65).

States that have the longest records of open access to government have the best records of democratic engagement and lowest levels of corruption in public life. Western countries with long traditions of open access to government, that have transparency and accountability structures in place to provide scrutiny of public services, fare best when measured against others who do not have such procedures in place (see, for example, Group of States Against Corruption evaluation on Norway, 2006: 1-5). International indicators on issues such as trust, corruption and democratic engagement in government and public office also demonstrate this. Transparency International's global *Corruption Index* reports show that countries such as Sweden, Norway, Denmark, New Zealand and Canada, which have long-established practices of open government, fare best in the anti-corruption league (see, for example, Transparency International, 2013). It is not clear whether open democracies are less likely to have corruption because of the fact that they are open, or whether other causal factors have contributed to high levels of honesty among public officials, both elected and in bureaucracy.

In a contemporary context the United States government introduced FOI in 1966 amid calls for greater accountability in government following the McCarthy era 'witch hunt' Senate hearings of the 1950s. FOI has been in operation in Canada, New Zealand and Australia since 1982, and in Ireland and the UK since 1998 and 2005 respectively. Most EU countries have also adopted FOI legislation (Banisar, 2002: 7, 16-18), as have almost 100 states worldwide. Governments do not particularly like the legislation, but once introduced, the expectation of access is created and it cannot be reversed. It is, as one scholar has noted, a 'small but significant shift in the balance of power between the citizen and the state' (Hazell, 1989: 202).

Freedom of expression and FOI

Freedom of expression is considered a fundamental right both in the European Convention on Human Rights and in the UN Convention on Civil and Political Rights. The European Convention defines this right expressly as the right to 'hold opinions and to receive and impart information and ideas without interference by public authority and regardless of frontiers' (Article 10). However, the UN Convention goes further, guaranteeing the 'freedom to *seek*, receive and impart information and ideas of all kinds, regardless of frontiers, either orally, in writing or in print, ... or any other media of his choice' (Article 19; emphasis added). That freedom to seek information is an important right in the context of citizens' rights to be informed of the actions of governments in a democracy. Similarly, the constitutional protection of freedom of speech enshrined in the first amendment to the American constitution has been interpreted by the US Supreme Court much more widely to include the freedom of inquiry, also allowing citizens this freedom to seek information, and has led to more open government in American democracy (McCrann, 2007: 1-3). In the British context, although there is no explicit constitutional provision giving citizens a right to know how and why government makes decisions, the Kennedy judgment in 2014 – for the first time recognising a common law right to information – was a small but significant step in granting that 'right' to know (*the Guardian*, 27 March 2014).

The concept of freedom of information, then, is closely linked to the concept of democracy. The right to seek information is crucial in understanding why freedom of information laws are important in any democratic state. The media, acting on behalf of the citizen, very often carry out that function in what has become labelled their 'professional citizen' role (Felle and Adshead, 2009).

Journalism and the public interest

There is an explicit public interest function for journalists working in the news media, regardless of platform. While most news organisations (save for the BBC, a handful of state-owned public service broadcasters; and a minority of trust-owned newspapers internationally) are commercial enterprises, journalists working for these companies rarely see the pursuit of profit for their owners as their primary motivation. Many scholars agree that news journalism has an important role to play in democracy (Galtung and Ruge, 1965: 64-90; Harcup and O'Neill, 2001: 261-280). In contemporary society, the role of the journalist and the news media might be said to be to entertain and to titillate as much as it is to inform, to engage, to analyse, to uncover, to report and to hold power to account. Entertainment scoops, sports, gossip and comment receive as much (and in many cases more) space in newspapers than news receives. Despite this, the public interest role of news organisations in advanced democratic societies is unquestionable, with virtually all news organisations performing that role in some shape or form.

The question of what is the role of journalism – and of the journalist – in a democracy has perhaps received contemporary relevance given *the Guardian*'s publication of classified material in 2013, leaked to it by the former US National Security Agency (NSA) contractor Edward Snowden. The series of stories, which detailed the extent of electronic surveillance undertaken by state security agencies in the US and the UK against its own citizens and foreign governments, was an undoubted scoop of international significance. However, the reaction by the security forces in the UK, who used counter terrorism legislation to detain the partner of Glenn Greenwald (the journalist who broke the story) at Heathrow Airport, demonstrated on the one hand how important a role journalists play in bringing such stories into the public domain, but on the other hand how difficult that role can be, even in an advanced democracy (Borger, 2013; Rusbridger, 2013). Put plainly, it is arguable that governments, no matter how democratic, have a penchant for secrecy. There are some secrets – such as areas of national security, counter-terrorism and defence – that are rightly kept undisclosed, but by-and-large most democratic governments keep information secret for far less than national security concerns. In some cases it is simply to protect their own political interests. And even when national security exemptions are applied, it is arguable that they are applied far too eagerly by over-zealous securocrats (see Tim Crook's chapter for a discussion on national security).

The fourth estate

In advanced democratic societies the differing branches of government – an executive that is separate from the legislature and the judiciary – are set up to ensure checks and balances. The news media, in carrying out an investigating and reporting function, in essentially keeping an eye on government and elected office holders, have often been labelled the 'fourth estate'. The concept was first espoused by Edmund Burke (1729-1797) (Schultz, 1998: 49). The term was originally applied just to newspapers or 'the press' by virtue of the fact that radio, and later television, had yet to be invented; however, it is contemporarily understood to encompass all news media. It is arguable, therefore, that the news media have a crucial role as public interest defenders or as 'professional citizens' in a democracy (Felle and Adhsead, 2009).

The role of journalism in democracy is so important that a number of states, including the US, offer some limited privilege and protection to those working in the media. The First Amendment to the US Constitution states: 'Congress shall make no law … abridging freedom of the press' (Federal Government of the United States of America, 1787). No such explicit protection is offered in the UK, though almost all advanced democracies recognise the right of journalists to investigate and criticise government, and transparency legislation such as FOI is commonplace (Felle and Sheridan, 2015, forthcoming).

Many will argue that this places the news media on a pedestal, where it does not belong. There have been numerous examples where these high standards were not lived up to. Most news organisations in the US and the UK collectively failed to question the validity of both governments' claims' that Iraq had weapons of mass destruction in 2003 (Kumar, 2006: 48-69) – though, as Amanda Geary Pate notes in her contribution to this book, the UK's FOI laws were not yet in force at this time, and requests on this topic were among the first to be lodged in January 2005 when the legislation became operational. The UK media itself became the story after a series of allegations of criminality against the *News of the World* (Davies, 2009) – was there a role for journalists in using the Freedom of Information Act to examine potential police corruption? In a number of Eurozone countries including Spain, Greece and Ireland, most news organisations failed to seriously question their governments' economic policies in the mid-2000s (Schechter, 2009). The economies of those countries later collapsed with severe social and financial consequences for citizens. With FOI-type laws in force in all of these states, the media collectively failed to hold their politicians to account.

However, despite falling short on occasion, the news media in advanced democracies have developed sophisticated roles as public interest watchdogs. It is to that role of holding power to account that, albeit perhaps an arrogant notion, most news journalists espouse. Not all journalism brings down governments, but human interest investigations that expose the impact of heath cuts, or that uncover favoured treatment or sharp practice in the awarding of public contracts – very often conducted using FOI requests – are every bit as valuable to citizens as investigations which lead to political resignations or sackings.

The obsession with chocolate biscuit costs

Many contributors to this book (see, for example, chapters by the BBC's Martin Rosenbaum; Paul McNamara and Guy Basnett; and Alice Ross) cite their own examples of the use of FOI in important journalistic investigations that have had profound and lasting consequences for the public. And they are to be congratulated. Why then have the media become obsessed with the cost of biscuits and chocolates? For every public interest investigation of how hospitals incinerated dead babies as waste, there is another of the 'scandal' of a council's spending on cappuccinos and biscuits. Requests under the Freedom of

Information Act in the UK have included: How many toilet rolls were used in No 10 during Tony Blair's administration? How many accidents have there been in the BBC Television Centre toilets? What is John Prescott's weight? And what type of tea is drunk in the Ministry of Defence? (*the Guardian*, 4 January, 2010).

Does it really matter what a Manchester council spent on tea and biscuits for a council meeting? Or that the Foreign Office has a rather impressive wine cellar? That an Australian MP flew business class on an official state trip to Europe? Or that the former Irish prime minister Bertie Ahern spent more than £150,000 of the taxpayers' money in 10 years on makeup? (He really did!). Actually, yes it does. Some of this is capricious, yes, but journalists have always had a watchdog role and investigating and reporting on public spending is a legitimate area of inquiry. Not all journalism brings down governments; much of the job is ordinary reporting, and as previously discussed, accountability. How civil servants and politicians spend public money is important for citizens. At a time of cutbacks in health or education, for example, isn't it right that journalists seek to expose hypocrisy in spending decisions? Why can't councillors all chip in to a kitty for their tea, as happens in many offices? Why can't a Member of Parliament fly flexible economy? And if the former Irish prime minister really felt he needed to spend £150,000 on makeup, surely he could have paid for it himself?

That said, the media has always been fond of low hanging fruit, and headlines that 'prove' councillors are gorging on fancy biscuits are easy pickings. A somewhat more important criticism – and in this I have personal experience from my time as a working journalist – is the over-reliance on FOI for stories, and the careful presentation of FOI 'investigations', often distorting facts and selectively reporting the truth to make for a better headline. In some cases, the failure by journalists to give important context can significantly distort the real story, and cause a lot of harm – creating an impression among the public that may in fact not be true. This sort of reporting often gives ammunition to critics and opponents of open government, who argue that the media cannot be trusted to report fairly and impartially, and in the public interest.

Equally the development of FOI 'churnalism' (see chapters by Lynn Wyeth, Alan Geere and Paul Francis on local journalism) adds little to civil society's understanding of decision-making by public bodies, one of the key roles of freedom of information laws. In an era of cutbacks and over-stretched resources in newsrooms, many reporters have little time to actually 'report' on anything anymore. FOI requests, which if carefully targeted and worded can all but guarantee a story, have become a crutch in some newsrooms. The practice of emailing a public body and regurgitating their response 20 days later without any further reporting is commonplace. News writing has always been about talking to sources, gathering and checking facts, and most importantly finding the human-interest angle. In that sense FOI should only form part of the investigation. Old-fashioned reporting is still important and unfortunately there is ample evidence - in the UK and elsewhere - that in some cases FOI has created a generation of lazy journalists.

Such behaviour by journalists is ammunition to critics of FOI, especially among officials who claim their work is severely hampered by being swamped with FOI requests (which are costly to administer) and adds nothing to the public's understanding of decision-making processes. The former British Prime Minister Tony Blair described the Act as his worst mistake in 10 years of government, lamenting:

> *'Where was Sir Humphreys when I needed him… [the] Freedom of Information Act. Three harmless words. I look at those words as I write them, and feel like shaking my head 'til it drops off. You idiot. You naive, foolish, irresponsible nincompoop. There is really no description of stupidity, no matter how vivid, that is adequate. I quake at the imbecility of it.'* (Blair, 2010).

It is somewhat understandable that the media in the UK (with almost identical experiences in Ireland, Australia and elsewhere) were perhaps over-zealous in their initial use of the Act, firstly overwhelming the system with requests and secondly failing to understand the nature of the material that was being released. Documents that revealed the normal internal due diligence processes of various public bodies suddenly became exclusive front-page stories about dire warnings to government from senior civil servants. Routine disagreements between departments, properly minuted by officials, were turned into political theatre in Ireland, in Australia, in the UK and elsewhere.

One of the lasting legacies of freedom of information laws in countries where it has been introduced has not been the work of journalists at all, who remain, by comparison, a small percentage of overall users – 10 per cent in the British case (Information Commissioner's Office, 2006-2014) – but rather its use by ordinary citizens. FOI has transformed the relationship between citizen and the state, which traditionally was a distant one. In Westminster-influenced democracies, the legacy of the Official Secrets Act loomed for generations. Citizens voted for political parties, but could not make independent judgments on their performance and decision making because information was officially 'secret'. Even citizens' own personal interactions with public bodies were 'secrets' – in Ireland up until the introduction of FOI a citizen had no right to see their own medical files; or to access documents concerning them held by public bodies. FOI has changed that relationship fundamentally (Felle and Sheridan, 2015 forthcoming).

Conclusion

Freedom of information is important in society because it gives citizens a 'right' to know how and why decisions are made in their name. Journalists, acting as the fourth estate or 'professional citizen' most often use such laws to hold those in power to account; to investigate how public money is spent; how decisions are made by public bodies; and hold those elected to public office to account.

News and current affairs journalists, by their nature, do things that annoy those in power, but that is the price those elected to office are expected to pay to ensure democratic accountability. The news media's presence, then, assures transparency. Through their reporting journalists act as public interest champions as much as investigators of corruption, very often using tools such as freedom of information laws. As European Ombudsman Emily O'Reilly and others have argued, FOI has the capacity at least to 'keep government honest' (2008).

While FOI is designed to keep government open and accountable, that is not to suggest that all governments are corrupt. Rather FOI has the potential to discourage corruption and maladministration by assuring accountability and transparency. Sometimes journalists uncover bureaucratic incompetence, and occasionally political corruption. More often no significant wrong may have occurred, but newspapers report on stories that may be embarrassing for those in positions of power; may highlight hypocrisy, feather-bedding or pork-barrelling; and sometimes may even generate public debate on the merits and demerits of policy decisions. FOI requests by journalists in several countries (and discussed in later chapters in this book) have shown politicians asleep at the wheel in their departments; attempts by the political class to proffer favoured treatment; in some cases attempts at political interference by politicians; and occasionally it has brought down politicians, and governments.

The development of 'FOI churnalism'; the use of FOI to sensationalise and to report in a partisan way; and the obsession with political spending – which is very often quite small when compared with overall budgets – is regrettable. The real power of freedom of information, if well used by journalists, is as an investigative tool. There are countless examples of outstanding FOI reporting – in some cases leading to awards for public service journalism – that have had profound impacts on the lives of citizens, and changed society for the better. But equally the media have used FOI to report on frivolous issues. Serious and important news is often outweighed by entertainment and scandal – that is the society we live in. Stories about the cost of biscuits at council meetings and toilet rolls at Number 10 are the price we pay for democratic accountability. Given the choice between FOI and none, it's a price well worth paying.

References

Banisar, David (2002) *Freedom of Information Around the World*. London: Privacy International

Blair, Tony (2010) *A Journey*. London: Vintage

Borger, Julian (2013) 'Why *the Guardian* destroyed hard drives of leaked files' in *the Guardian*, August 20, 2013

Bugdahn, Sonja (2007) 'Does the EU stifle voluntary policy transfer? A study of the introduction of the Freedom of Information Act in Portugal and Ireland' in *Public Administration*. 85(1), pp123–142

Council of Europe (1950) Convention for the Protection of Human Rights and Fundamental Freedoms (European Convention on Human Rights). Strasbourg: Council of Europe

Davies, Nick (2009) 'Murdoch papers paid £1m to gag phone hacking victims' in *the Guardian*, July 8

Dowell, Ben (2010) 'Freedom of Information: caught in the act' in *the Guardian*, 4 January

Doyle, John (1997) 'Freedom of Information: Lessons from the international experience' in *Administration*. 44(4), pp64-82

Felle, Tom and Adshead, Maura (2009) *Democracy and the Right to Know: 10 years of the Freedom of Information Act in Ireland*. University of Limerick: Limerick Papers in Politics and Public Administration

Felle, Tom and Sheridan, Gavin (2015) 'Freedom of Information and the Citizen' in Adshead, Maura and Felle, Tom (eds) *FOI@15: Ireland and the Freedom of Information Act*. Manchester: Manchester University Press

Galtung, Johan, and Ruge, Mari Holmboe (1965) 'The Structure of Foreign News The Presentation of the Congo, Cuba and Cyprus Crises in Four Norwegian Newspapers' in *Journal of Peace Research*, 2(1), 64-90

Greensalde, Roy (2014) 'Supreme Court ruling opens door to revelations of Freedom of Information' in *the Guardian* online, 27 March, available at http://www.theguardian.com/media/greenslade/2014/mar/27/medialaw-thetimes, accessed 15 September

Group of States Against Corruption (GRECO) (2006) *Second Evaluation Round Compliance Report on Norway* RC-II, 11E. Strasbourg: Council of Europe

Harcup, Tony, and O'Neill, Deirdre (2001) 'What is news? Galtung and Ruge revisited' in *Journalism Studies*, 2(2), 261-280

Hazell, Robert (1989) 'Freedom of Information in Australia, Canada and New Zealand' in *Public Administration*. 67(2), pp189-210

Information Commissioner's Office (2006-2014) *Information Commissioner's Annual Report and Financial Statements* (for various years). London: Stationary Office

Kumar, Deepa (2006) 'Media, war and propaganda: Strategies of information management during the 2003 Iraq war' in *Communication and Critical/Cultural Studies*, 3(1), 48-69

McCrann, Grace-Ellen (2007) 'An examination of the passage of the 1966 US Freedom of Information Act' in *Open Government*. 3(1), pp1-17

McDonagh, Maeve (1998) *Freedom of Information Law in Ireland*. Dublin: Roundhall

O'Reilly, Emily (2008) 'Freedom of Information: The first decade' *10th Anniversary Conference of Freedom of Information in Ireland conference proceedings*. Dublin: Office of the Information Commissioner

Phillips, Anne (2004) 'Democracy, recognition and power' in Engelstad, Fredrik and Osterud, Oyvind (eds) *Power and Democracy: Critical Interventions*. Burlington: Ashgate

Rusbridger, Alan (2013) 'I would rather destroy the copied files than hand them back to the NSA and GCHQ' in *the Guardian* online, available at http://www.theguardian.com/world/video/2013/aug/20/alan-rusbridger-miranda-snowden-nsa-gchq-video accessed September 9, 2013

Schechter, David (2009) 'Credit crisis, how did we miss it' in *British Journalism Review*, 20(1), pp19-26

Schultz, Julianne (1998) *Reviving the Fourth Estate*. Cambridge, England: Cambridge University Press

Transparency International (2007) *Global Corruption Index 2007*. Berlin: Transparency International

United Nations (1966) *International Covenant on Civil and Political Rights*. Geneva: United Nations Publications

United States Government (1787) *Constitution of the United States of America*. Washington DC: US Government Printing Office

Wright, Ronald (1977) *Open Government: A British Interpretation*. London: Royal Institute of Public Administration

Note on the contributor

Tom Felle is co-editor. See 'about the editors' section for full biography.

The development of FOI in Britain

FOI in the UK was part of a raft of reforms aimed at making British administrative systems, and government, more open, transparent and accountable. But it would never have been introduced were it not for constant pressure from the civil society, opposition MPs and the media, writes *Ben Worthy*

Introduction

Before the Freedom of Information (FOI) Act of 2000, successive UK governments initiated a series of incremental openness reforms from the 1960s onwards. This process took place on two levels. At central government level, the debate began through growing pressure to reform the Official Secrets Act of 1911, which then transformed into a discussion around access to information. At local government level, there was a more consistent and coherent opening up of access to meetings and decisions, with significant statutory access legislation passed each decade between 1960 and 2000.

Access to information legislation, despite its powerful symbolism, is rarely a reform that attracts votes. It is frequently a 'vote-less' policy, exciting little electoral interest and reliant on media pressure, lobbying and a series of focusing events, helped intermittently by politicians pressured into action. As seen in other FOI regimes, in the UK the media helped provide the vital momentum. In the 1960s and 1970s, through highlighting (and inadvertently triggering) scandals, exposing secrecy in local and central government level and allying with a strengthening lobby group, the media continually kept openness on the political agenda. By the 1980s it formed part of a growing network of NGOs and MPs pressuring for FOI. It remains a key defender, innovator and user of FOI (Hazell et al, 2010).

Figure 1: A Timeline of the development of openness in the UK

Year	Event
1960	Local Government (Access to Meetings) Act
1969-70	White Paper Information and the Public Interest Labour and Conservatives commit to reform of Official Secrets Aitken Trial
1974	Labour enters power with manifesto pledge to pass FOI
1977-78	Croham Directive introduced and controversial ABC trial takes place
1979	Government White Paper Clement Freud's FOI Private Members' Bill
1984	Data Protection Act
1985	Local Government (Access to Information) Act
1994	John Major's Code of Access
1996	Tony Blair commits to an FOI Act
1997	Your Right to Know White Paper
2000	Freedom of Information Act receives Royal Assent-comes into force 1 Jan 2005

FOI and central government 1960-1997

At central government level, initial pressure for reform focused on the 'secrecy' created by the draconian Official Secrets Act (OSA) of 1911, rather than access to information. The Act, passed in 1911, followed a failed attempt in 1908, blocked by intense media resistance (Hennessy, 2003). The OSA, and specifically the 'catch-all' section 2, was subsequently seen as the cornerstone of government secrecy, one part of a wider culture of secrecy that some argued was deeply rooted in the 'English' psyche (Vincent 1999: Hennessy 1990).

1960s

Little was done to 'open up' government until the 1960s, with the first attempt coming as a by-product of the 1968 the Fulton Report into reform of the civil service (Hennessy, 2003). One of the report's recommendations was to reform section 2 of the OSA. This led to a follow-up 1969 White Paper Information and the Public Interest, which marked the first official examination and acknowledgement of secrecy as a political issue (Theakston, 1992; Hennessy, 2003; Civil Service Department, 1969). It was described as 'truly feeble', as it indicated, for example, that the Official Secrets Act did not stop the release of information (Hennessy, 2003). In parallel, then Prime Minister Harold Wilson also reformed the Public Records Act to create a 30 rather than 50-year non-disclosure period for archived records.

Even these minor changes were carried out 'in the face of opposition within the Cabinet and in Whitehall' (Theakston, 1992: 179). A proposed review of the Official Secrets Act never took place following strong resistance (Theakston, 2006: 163). By the end of the 1960s, openness remained a 'minority interest' even with the Parliamentary Labour Party and one that clearly faced entrenched opposition (Dorey, 2008: 186). Nevertheless, Wilson's actions marked a first step.

1970s

The next push came when Edward Heath, then Leader of the Opposition, committed to reform the Official Secrets Act at a Press awards ceremony and Wilson, at a celebration of the press a week later, followed suit (Hennessy, 2003). Heath's electoral win in 1970 led to the Franks Inquiry of 1972 that carried out a far-reaching examination of secrecy and called for increased openness. Meanwhile, within the opposition Labour party, ex-minister Tony Benn and a small group of Labour MPs urged a commitment to FOI on a future Labour administration (Dorey, 2008). As the decade progressed, controversy relating to the press helped to provide the momentum lacking from within government. Outside of the main parties a controversial trial of journalists in 1970-71 led to an embarrassing climb-down for the government when OSA charges failed to stick and the judge advised that section 2 be 'pensioned off' (Wraith, 1979: 206). The following year another case involving leaks to the *Railway Gazette* again 'petered out' (ibid: 207). Both cases attracted attention and criticism over unnecessary government secrecy.

The Labour administration of 1974 entered power with a manifesto pledge to reform OSA and introduce some form of FOI. However, despite the support of Home Secretary Roy Jenkins, the proposals were greeted with disinterest from other ministers (Dorey, 2008). Cabinet Minister Tony Benn claimed there was 'deep hostility' (Benn, 1982: 54). The new Prime Minister James Callaghan was 'decidedly unenthusiastic' about openness, and his arrival led to the temporary abandonment of any plans following two years of vacillation (Dorey, 2008: 191). Despite this, pressure continued to build and the year 1977 'was the year open government legislation ideas reached adolescence...in Britain' (Michael, 1982: 201). Two Private Members' Bills and a draft Bill were drawn up on the subject and a new lobbying coalition, the Outer Circle Policy Unit, began drafting legislation (Michael, 1982: 201-203). Labour's National Executive Committee then published a draft FOI Bill (Benn, 1982; Wraith, 1979). At the same time yet another controversial Official Secrets Act trial involving two *Guardian* journalists again led to the very public failure of the section 2 charges (Wilson, 1984: 127).

To head off the growing calls, the Government responded with the so-called 'Croham Directive', a non-statutory commitment that ordered the separation of policy advice from the factual background, with a view to publication of the latter (Wraith, 1979). Vincent describes the directive as a 'complete failure' (1998: 261). Between May and October 1978 some 28 different departments released a total of 200 documents but this flow soon 'slowed to a trickle' and by 1979 the initiative was 'dead' (Vincent, 1998: 261). The media were heavily critical and a lead article in *The Times* stated: 'The Government demonstrated blatantly yesterday it cannot be relied upon for the voluntary disclosure of official information' (Leigh, 1980: 270). In March 1979, a new government Green Paper proved somewhat equivocal, claiming the government 'took no position' on openness. In parallel, a Private Members' Bill for FOI pushed by Liberal MP Clement Freud led to 'absolute panic' as Freud MP used the opportunity to mobilise widespread support across Parliament and the press (Benn 1982, 53: Wilson 1984). The government fell before the bill could progress.

1980s

The 1980s is traditionally seen as the decade of secrecy under Margaret Thatcher. In 1977, when asked whether Britain would benefit from an American style Freedom of Information Act, she replied 'not at all' and advocated reform of the Official Secrets Act 'but only to make some of its provisions against the disclosure of information stronger not weaker' (Cockerell et al, 1985: 14-15). In 1984, Thatcher described proposals for an FOI Act as 'inappropriate and unnecessary' (in Wilson 1984, 34). The Thatcher governments were 'resolute in their defence of secrecy in high politics' (Evans 2003, 201). A succession of high profile secrecy scandals proved Thatcher's unbending support; from the Government's attempted prosecution of civil servant Clive Ponting over Falkland's War leaks to controversy over a former intelligence officer's memoir. In 1989 the Official Secrets Act was also reformed, though, as Thatcher promised, to enhance its effectiveness. As before, each 'secrecy' controversy proved counter-productive, highlighting secrecy and heavy handedness.

Yet underneath this the pressure for openness continued. In 1984, a concerted push for FOI, led by the Campaign for Freedom of Information, garnered widespread attention. It attracted support from the leader of the Labour party and the new Social Democratic Party (Wilson, 1984). It also led to editorial support from national newspapers, from *the Guardian* to *The Times*, as well as regional and local papers up and down the country (Wilson, 1984). The pressure was no longer just external: in March 1984 former permanent secretary to the Treasury Douglas Wass came out in favour of FOI (Vincent, 1999). There was also gradual legislative reform. The 1984 Data Protection Act, originating from the EEC, gave subject access rights to personal information and the 1985 Local Government Act extended public access to council meetings and documents. Small pieces of legislation gave access rights to particular pieces of information such as medical files (Robertson, 1999). Alongside this there were a series of attempts to pass FOI legislation via Private Members' Bills. These changes, although often 'forced upon a reluctant and unwilling government' nevertheless moved the UK towards access (Robertson, 1999: 141). By the end of the 1980s there was a clear campaign for FOI, led by the Campaign for Freedom of Information (CFOI) but with supporters in Parliament and the media, at national and local level.

1990s

In the early 1990s, John Major's government was the last to try reform short of an FOI Act, following a commitment in the 1992 manifesto to open up government (House of Commons Library, 1997). In a 1993 White Paper, the Major government explicitly rejected an FOI Act, calling it 'costly and cumbersome' and instead created a voluntary 'Code of Access'. The Code offered 'practical steps' that would 'meet the principal objectives of those who have sought a full statutory Freedom of Information regime...without the legal complexities' (Cabinet Office, 1993: 2). The 1994 Code extended across government unless statutory authority or established convention argued 'to the contrary' (Cabinet Office, 1997: 1). It provided access to information, within 20 days, to 'copies, compressed short hand notes' or summaries of documents (ibid: 42). The Ombudsman could be used in the event of problem or controversy (ibid: 3). Parallel to the Code, a number of documents were declassified early, covering controversial topics from Rudolf Hess to Churchill's wartime correspondence with Roosevelt (HMSO, 1993: 7). By 1995, the 'Waldegrave initiative' released over 100,000 'highly sensitive' documents (Hennessy, 2003: 35). Further symbols of the new 'open' political climate occurred in 1995 with the publication of a guide to the intelligence services and the naming of the head of both MI5 and MI6 (Willman, 1994: 71).

Major claimed that the Code was a central part of his 'desire... for nothing less than an information revolution' (Major, 2003: 73). Like previous reforms, senior ministers were not enthusiastic. While Major provided the policy drive, only two colleagues supported it while most of Major's Cabinet were against 'on the grounds of *realpolitik*' (Seldon, 1997: 399). Aside from the Prime Minister, the policy had 'no clear champions' (PCA, 2005: 36). It also created 'division and conflict' within the Civil Service (Vincent, 1998: 303). The 'voteless' nature of openness led sceptics to consistently 'dismiss the cry for open government' as an issue 'confined to the chattering classes of north London' (Seldon, 1997: 400).

In terms of its operation, the Code did 'not constitute a right of access to documents or records' (Cabinet Office, 1993: 3). It thus had no 'legal basis' and 'could not override the 250 or so separate statutory restrictions' to information release (CFOI, 1995: 2). The information available had 15 exemptions including 'tax, Monarchy and internal discussion' (CFOI, 1995: 2). Major admitted that 'institutions were rarely enthusiastic...there was a widespread reluctance to publish information' (Major, 2003: 73). Some departments refused to even give exemptions and 'simply said no' (PCA, 2005: 31-32; 35).

Viewed from the other side, the Government did little to elicit support from the growing group of advocates in the media. The Code had an 'inconspicuous start', launched on a bank holiday during a Parliamentary recess and journalists were given little opportunity to scrutinise or publicise it (CFOI, 1994: 5). The policy was 'launched very quietly without much encouragement for anyone to use it' (PCA, 2005: 36). In any access regime, the media serve as a key driver for use, innovating and passing on disclosures to the wider public (Hazell et al, 2010). Some 10 years after the Code, the Ombudsman concluded that the Code was 'barely known outside the small group of users with a professional interest', who were identified as a mixture of MPs and investigative journalists (PCA, 2005: 29-30). There were 6,000 requests under the Code between 1994 and 1996 (Wilkinson, 1998: 17). While individuals made up 49 per cent and NGOs 9 per cent of these requests, journalists appeared to make up only 3 per cent of the total (Wilkinson, 1998: 17).

Local government 1960-2000

While central government displayed a decidedly sluggish response to pressure for openness legislation for itself, it had a noted enthusiasm for 'other people's openness' (Wilkinson, 1998: 13). Local government in the UK has long been subject to rigorous political and financial control from central government (John, 2014). As part of this, it has frequently been 'pushed' in the direction of openness by central government (Worthy, 2013). Many of the local openness reforms concerned press, rather than public, access rights and were driven by political controversy. Local authorities had granted informal access to the media to council meetings since 1900. However, in 1908, a court ruling in *Tenby Corporation v Mason* affirmed the common law right for councils to meet in secret (Chandler, 2010). The Liberal government, the same year it sought and failed to pass a strengthened Official Secrets Act for itself, gave the press a legal right to be admitted to local government meetings (Chandler, 2010).

Press access to meetings drove the second major access reform in 1959 when a number of Labour councils refused access to local journalists involved in a strike (Chandler, 2010: 106; Moore, 2013). This controversy led newly elected MP Margaret Thatcher to push a Private Members' Bill granting press and public access to council and committee meetings (Thatcher, 1995: 111). What she viewed as a 'socialist connivance with trade union power' became an issue of 'civil liberties' and access to information (ibid: 111-112). Thatcher was supported by the Newspapers Editors Guild and other parts of the press. The Bill met substantial opposition from what she claimed were officials 'echoing the fierce opposition in local authorities' (ibid: 112). However, her own front bench was also concerned about stirring up 'unnecessary conflict' and, wishing any legislation to do as little as possible, inclined to a code rather than statute (Moore, 2013). The result was a compromise that gave statutory access to full meetings for both the press and public but not to local authority sub-committees. It was greeted by both the Left and the Right as a victory (Moore, 2013).

Between 1960 and 1970 a series of reviews of local government, including the famous Maud Review of 1967, pressed for greater openness as part of a 'groundswell' of support (Chandler, 2010: 107). In 1972 the Heath government passed the Local Government Act that gave further access to sub-committees within authorities (Chandler, 2010: 107). A succession of local government corruption scandals kept the issue of 'town hall' secrecy in the headlines (Wilson, 1984; Chandler, 2010). By the middle of the 1980s, local and central government was locked into a 'bitter conflict' over finance with new left councils in Sheffield, London and Liverpool engaged in open revolt against the Thatcher government (Chandler, 2010: 108). As part of a wider campaign to control these authorities, further legislation, again beginning as a Private Members' Bill, meant local authorities' 'documents, agendas and minutes' were open unless there was good reason not to be (ibid: 108). The succession of small pieces of legislation on data protection and access to files also effected local authorities (Robertson, 1999). The final piece of local government reform came with New Labour. In the same year FOI received royal assent, the Local Government Act 2000 authorised local authorities to pro-actively publish a range of information on its decisions as part of a wider structural reform (Chandler, 2010).

New Labour and freedom of information

In 1997 the 'New Labour' government came into power with a 179-seat majority and a commitment to radical constitutional reform (Evans, 2003). In 1996 Blair had personally committed himself to an FOI Act in a speech to the Campaign For Freedom of Information (CFOI, 1996). Pushed by the Lord Chancellor Lord Irvine and Cabinet Minister David Clark, in 1997 the FOI White Paper *Your Right to Know* received wide acclaim. It offered wide information rights, with a high level harm test and no exclusion, even for Cabinet documents (Cabinet Office, 1997). It was greeted with 'widespread applause...indeed the scale of the proposed legislation came as a surprise to many' (Vincent, 1998: 321). Clark proudly commented that 'I don't think there are many White Papers that can actually claim praise from newspapers as far apart as *the Guardian* and the *Daily Mail* but we did that' (CFOI, 1998: 35). Others were concerned that it did not have the full understanding or support of government itself - that it was, as one put it, 'too good to be true' (Hazell, 1998).

In the following months, as resistance and second thoughts accumulated, the FOI policy was transferred to a strongly sceptical Home Secretary Jack Straw, who claimed the White Paper was unworkable (Straw 2012). The re-worked draft Bill presented in 1999 was far weaker than the White Paper, with a new power of veto and more exclusions – though, as an after-thought the new Bill included Parliamentary administration under the ambit of the law. This was less the result of Straw or the Home Office than the severe anxiety from Ministers and a change of mind from Tony Blair (Flinders, 2000). Anxiety over a 'too liberal' Act was motivated by fear of the media. Alastair Campbell recorded in his diary his concern that the press would 'abuse' any FOI legislation (Campbell, 2011).

Following internal battles, the revised policy was only agreed upon following the insertion of a five-year implementation 'pause'. The Government's increasingly lukewarm commitment was driven by New Labour's acute concern at 'failing' a policy, their fear of press criticism and backbench pressure (Worthy, forthcoming). The *Guardian* and the *Times* applied consistent pressure for a stronger FOI Act, with the former leading a nationwide campaign supporting a stronger Bill as it passed through Parliament (Dorey, 2008). Together this pressure improved the legislation, leading to lessening of the veto power and a series of compromises that helped build a more successful and dynamic Act (Worthy, 2010).

Conclusion

The pre-FOI history of openness in the UK is of a series of compromise reforms forced upon uninterested, if not hostile, politicians seeking to do as a little as possible to 'head off' Parliamentary and media criticism. A Select Committee looking into Major's Code concluded that UK openness reforms over the previous decades had been 'ignored, avoided, quietly forgotten or otherwise rendered ineffective' (in Robertson, 1999: 150). However, each half-hearted reform moved government a step closer to statutory access to information. The process and the failures also helped create a growing network of supporters across Parliament and the media, making future legislation more likely.

The media were central to this process. As occurred in the US, they were crucial in mobilising support and applying continuous pressure for change. The succession of information related 'scandals', from leaks to court cases, generated a self-reinforcing momentum -each failed Official Secrets Act trial generated headlines and made the case for reform stronger. Ironically, it was the fear of the media that also shaped the dual reactions of the Labour government that finally passed an FOI Act -the concern that the Act would be used by the media but the anxiety that dropping the bill would generate criticism.

References

Benn, Tony (1974) *Speeches*. Spokesman Books: Nottingham.

Benn, Tony (1990) *Conflicts of Interests: Diaries 1977-1980*. Hutchinson: London.

Cabinet Office (1969) *Information and the Public Interest* [Cmnd 4089]. HMSO: London.

Cabinet Office [Green Paper] (1979) *Open Government* [Cmnd 7520].HMSO: London.

Cabinet Office [White paper] (1993) *Open Government*. [Cmnd: 2290]. HMSO: London.

Cabinet Office (1997) *Code of Practice on Access to Government Information* [2nd Edition].

Campbell, Alistair (2011) *Diaries Volume Two: Power and the People*. Random House: London

Campaign for FOI (1995) *The Campaign's View on the Operation of the open government Code*, available at http://www.cfoi.org.uk/1995/03/the-campaigns-views-on-the-operation-of-the-open-government-code-of-practice/, accessed 12 July, 2014

Campaign for FOI (1996) *Speech by the Rt Hon Tony Blair MP, Leader of the Labour Party* [transcript of a tape] available at http://www.cfoi.org.uk/1996/05/speech-by-the-rt-hon-tony-blair-mp-leader-of-the-labour-party-at-the-campaign-for-freedom-of-informations-annual-awards-ceremony-25-march-1996/, accessed 8 August, 2014

Campaign for FOI (1998) *Conference on the Freedom of Information White Paper*, available at http://www.cfoi.org.uk/1998/02/conference-on-the-foi-white-paper/, accessed 8 August, 2014

Chandler, Jim (2010) 'Freedom of Information and Participation: comparing central and local government' in Chapman, RA, and Hunt, M [eds] *Freedom of information: Local government and accountability*. London Ashgate, pp103-12

Cockerell, Michael, Hennessy, Peter and Walker, David (1984) *Sources Close to the Prime Minister*. Macmillan: London and Basingstoke

Dorey, P (2008) *The Labour Party and constitutional reform: a history of constitutional conservatism*. London: Palgrave Macmillan

Evans, Mark (2003) *Constitution-making and the Labour Party*. London: Palgrave Macmillan

Flinders, M (2000) 'The politics of accountability: a case study of freedom of information legislation in the United Kingdom' in *The Political Quarterly*, 71(4), pp422-435

Hazell, R, Worthy, B, and Glover, M (2010) *The Impact of the Freedom of Information Act on Central Government in the UK*. London: Palgrave

Hazell, R (1998) *Commentary on the Freedom of Information White Paper*. Constitution Unit: London

Hennessy, Peter (1990) *Whitehall*. Glasgow: Fontana Press

Hennessy, Peter (2003) 'The long march? Whitehall and open government since 1945' in Platten, Steven [ed] *Open Government: what do we need to know?* Norwich: Canterbury Press, pp20-37

John, P (2014) 'The Great Survivor: The Persistence and Resilience of English Local Government' in *Local Government Studies*, (forthcoming), 1-18.

Leigh, David (1980) *The Frontiers of Secrecy: closed government in Britain*. London: Junction Books

Major, John (2003) 'Afterword' in Platten, Steven [ed] *Open Government: what do we need to know?* Norwich: Canterbury Press, pp72-79.

Michael, James (1982) *The Politics of Secrecy: Closed Government in Britain*. Bury St Edmunds: Penguin

Moore, C (2013) *Margaret Thatcher: The Authorized Biography, Volume One: Not For Turning*. Bury St Edmunds: Penguin

PCA (2005) *Access to Official Information: monitoring the non-statutory Code of Practice* 1994-2005, available at www.official –documents.co.uk/document /hc0506/ hc00 /0059/0059.pdf, accessed 20/08/2014

Rees, Merlyn (1987) 'The parameters of politics' in Chapman, Richard and Hunt, Michael [eds] *Open Government*. Kent: Croom Helm, pp147-168

Robertson, KG (1999) *Secrecy and Open Government: why governments want you to know.* London: Macmillan

Seldon, Anthony (1997) *Major: A political life.* London: Phoenix

Straw, Jack (2012) *Last Man Standing.* London: Macmillan

Thatcher, Margaret (1995) *Margaret Thatcher: The Path to Power.* London: Macmillan

Theakston, Kevin (1992) *The Labour Party and Whitehall.* London: Routledge

Theakston, Kevin (2006) 'Whitehall and reform' in Dorey, Peter [ed] *The Labour Governments.* London: Routledge, pp147-168

Vincent, David (1998) *The Culture of Secrecy 1832-1997.* Oxford: Oxford University Press

Willman, John (1994) 'The Civil Service' in Kavanagh, Denis and Seldon, Anthony [eds] *The Major Effect.* London: Macmillan, pp64-83

Wilkinson, D (1998) 'Open Government: The Development of Policy in the UK in the 1990s' in McDonald, AJ, and Terrill, G [eds] *Open Government: Freedom of Information and Privacy.* London: Macmillan, pp 13-25

Wilson, D (1984) *The Secrets File: the case for freedom of information in Britain today.* London: Heinemann Educational

Worthy, Ben (forthcoming 2015) *The Politics of Freedom of Information: How and Why Governments Pass Laws That Threaten Their Power.* Manchester: MUP

Worthy, Ben (2013) 'Some are More Open than Others: Comparing the Impact of the Freedom of Information Act 2000 on Local and Central Government in the UK' in *Journal of Comparative Policy Analysis: Research and Practice*, 15(5), pp395-414.

Worthy, Ben (2010) 'More open but not more trusted? The effect of the Freedom of Information Act 2000 on the United Kingdom central government' in *Governance*, 23(4), pp561-582.

Wraith, R E (1979) 'United Kingdom' in Rowat, Donald, C [ed] *Administrative Secrecy in Developed Countries* pp23-28. Macmillan Press: London and Basingstoke

Note on the contributor

Ben Worthy is a Lecturer in Politics at Birkbeck College, University of London. His PhD examined the development of FOI in Britain. Between 2007 and 2012 he was Research Associate in Freedom of Information at the Constitution Unit at University College London. He has written widely on FOI and open data and is co-author of the Book *Does FOI Work?* He is currently writing a book examining why and how FOI laws are passed (forthcoming 2015) entitled *The Politics of Freedom of Information: How and Why Governments Pass Laws That Threaten Their Power.*

Information in the secret state

10 years after the introduction of the Freedom of Information Act, the UK is still obsessed with secrecy. Information is not a 'right' if access to it is in the gift of the Government, writes *Barry Turner*

'No other western democracy is so obsessed with keeping from the public information about its public servants or so relentless in plumbing new legal depths to staunch leaks from its bureaucracy'

- Geoffrey Robertson QC

Introduction

The United Kingdom prides itself on being the Mother of Parliaments and the inspiration to all democracies. The democratic traditions of the UK are, somewhat exaggeratedly, extended back through history to the signing of the Magna Carta by King John in 1215 and throughout the 800 years since this event the idea of Britain being a free country has been trumpeted by politicians of all ideologies. There can be little doubt that some of these self congratulatory claims are true and that the residents of the UK enjoy, and have enjoyed for a lot longer, freedoms denied to many populations of other countries. What remains a paradox, however, is that the country has another tradition that is less often spoken of, let alone boasted about. Britain has been called the 'Secret State' (Hennessy 2010) and with good reason. It is against the background of that less endearing aspect of the British state that this essay on Freedom of Information is set.

In spite of its reputation, or at the very least claim as an inspiration to the rest of the democratic world, the institutions of UK government have jealously guarded the information generated and collected by state agencies. Even more ironically this has most often been done in the name of the preservation of freedom, rights or even the lives of its citizens. 'What you don't know can't hurt you' has been for most of the history of modern Britain the motto on which those ruling it have relied. As well as being the 'mother of democracy' the United Kingdom can rightly claim to be the birthplace of spying, especially spying on its own citizens. Our traditions of espionage undoubtedly go back before the establishment of United Kingdom or even England existed in any political sense but the origin of the modern secret state should perhaps be credited to Sir Francis Walsingham, the super efficient spymaster to the court of Queen Elizabeth the first in the 16th Century. Walsingham has been described as 'one of the great unsung heroes of English history' (Hutchinson 2006) yet his story is described as a 'dramatic tale of subversion, cruelty, greed, disloyalty and deception', a world the author describes as being 'still very much with us in the realms of international politics, diplomacy and espionage'. Walsingham's world might appear on the face of it to have little to do with a discourse on 21st Century legislation on the rights of the citizen to information about the state but our traditions of secrecy can clearly be traced back to his times, and traditions born in adversity are often the ones that are least easy to abandon. Since the 16th Century England and the United Kingdom have excelled in maintaining state secrecy.

Towards the end of the 19th Century Britain had evolved from the fragile divided country of the 16th Century into the largest and richest empire in history. The very real threats that 'Catholic' Europe presented to Queen Elizabeth's England had long gone, but the fear of them remained. That fear was not so much of armies of foreign soldiers rampaging through sleepy English villages but of the 'enemy within'. Indeed the most disturbing aspect of the work of Elizabeth's spymaster was not his relentless pursuit of foreigners, but of English traitors loyal to foreign masters. It is that dark tradition that has perhaps most influenced our secret state to this day.

In 1889 the UK parliament enacted the first of the Official Secrets Acts. The Act curiously was not so much based on the fear of foreign spies but of British traitors and it began a long tradition of keeping secret all activities of government. The Act was strengthened in 1911 to become a potent weapon and was used on a number of occasions against journalists and others whose motives were far from a threat to the state. Britain has the distinction of being the first country in the world to have formed an espionage and intelligence service wholly operated by the state and with a curious mission statement. There were of course throughout history spies and espionage but they were, like Walsingham, operatives of monarchs rather than the state. The *Oprichnina* created by Czar Ivan IV (The Terrible) was wholly devoted to him and operated against state interests to protect him. In 1909 however the UK created the Security Service (MI5) and the Secret Intelligence Service (MI6) curiously operating out of the premises of a private detective (Andrew 2009).

The intelligence agencies had been born out of a growing fear of the expansion of Imperial Germany, especially its naval power and an almost paranoid belief that the country was riddled with German spies (Knightley 2003). In 1908 it had been the government's intention to introduce a new Official

Secrets Act specifically to prevent the press from revealing any details about Britain's naval forces but this had been defeated by a concerted effort from the press. The formation of a state-run intelligence service and the later introduced Official Secrets Act 1911 was the culmination of a policy designed to keep government of the UK secret.

Long established traditions

It is not the purpose of this essay to give a blow by blow account of the activities of the intelligence services between 1909 and the introduction of a less draconian Official Secrets Act in 1989 but an observation of the intelligence agencies in combination with an ever more secretive system of government gives a good insight into why Britain, of all the democracies, was so late in introducing legislation enabling freer access to state information. It simply went against long established traditions.

Other remarkably British traditions mitigated against the introduction of a Freedom of Information Act and one of these was the D-Notice Committee. What is most interesting about this secretive organisation is that it was fully supported by the owners of the establishment press who, far from being dictated to by it, actually took part in its decisions. This body, founded in 1912, was a committee founded on 'honourable relations and trust' between government and journalists - a committee often referred to as 'Chaps together' (Lustgarten and Leigh, 1994). Within this structure editors and politicians knew each other and frequently met informally. Their same background and outlook produced a consensual, implicit understanding and permitted substantial voluntary agreement. The D-Notice Committee - now known as the Defence, Press and Broadcasting Advisory Committee - was so efficient at its job of keeping information from the public that the committee itself remained a secret for 40 years. The 'chaps together' in their informal gatherings were quite capable of preventing information getting into the press and this traditionally British approach backed up by the fearsome provisions of the Official Secrets Act kept the UK a secret state for most of the 20th Century.

A latecomer to FOI

In light of the Britain tradition of secrecy, and of an opaque and exclusive establishment, it is not surprising that the UK is a latecomer to the idea that its citizens should have a right to know what is carried on in their name and paid for by their taxes. It is notable that in virtually all states that now have legislation granting access, often limited access to the workings of the legislature and executive, these rights were hard won against fierce opposition. It is also notable that even with rights to access of government information there is still often a strenuous effort to prevent or restrict as much access as possible. We may have laws giving us access to state 'secrets' but we are a long way from having a tradition of open government or an establishment at ease under scrutiny.

While Britain was first to introduce a set of state run agencies dedicated to maintaining its own secrets (while stealing those of others) it was, with its long standing traditions of secrecy, one of the last to introduce a freedom of information law allowing its citizens access to the workings of those who rule them. This is hardly surprising when set against the background of an almost paranoid attitude to any government information being available to the population at large. The Official Secrets Act 1889 at section 1 made it an offence to disclose state secrets. In its original drafting it also included provisions for criminalising criticism of the government but sufficient pressure from the press forced the legislature to introduce a public interest defence facilitating criticism of politicians and policy but still maintained provision for punishing disclosures that 'could be shown to be contrary to the public interest' (Maer L, Gay O, 2008).

The 1911 Official Secrets Act was aimed at the traitorous civil servant with the notorious section 2 directly referring to persons entrusted with information and in the employment of His Majesty. This piece of legislation has infamously been used many times against writers and journalists who 'took the liberty' of disclosing information that the government wanted kept secret. Perhaps the most absurd use was against the author Sir Compton Mackenzie who had published in his memoirs information about the activities of the secret services during World War One. He revealed not only the existence of MI6, then known as section MI.i.c. War Office 7 but that its head was referred to as 'C' and that it operated in passport offices (Mackenzie, 2011). Hardly information that represented a threat to the realm but even 80 years after it was written the original book is still banned.

Freedom of information legislation seems to have always been born out of scandal. The scandal of the government cover up, still very much with us today, is the basis of most FOI legislation in the countries it is found. It could be argued quite convincingly that our culture of secrecy has always been more about protecting the interests of the establishment than protecting the security of the state.

The birth of FOI

The first Freedom of Information Act in what would have been then called the free world was enacted by the United States Congress in 1967. The US had traditionally had a more ambivalent attitude towards its government since its founding and while the US had similar traditions, the deference towards authority as evidenced in the UK was less prominent. The United States government and governing agencies, in common with all of those who exercise authority, nevertheless maintained a position that government officials should operate their business under an 'executive privilege' principle. This principle arising out of the 'Housekeeping Statute' or the Act of July 27, 1789, ch. 4, 1 Stat. 29 (Department of Foreign Affairs) and the Act of Aug. 7, 1789, ch. 7, 1 Stat. 50 (Department of War). All of this legislation maintained the position that

> '[T]he Secretary for the department.., shall... be entitled to have the custody and charge of all records, books and papers in the office of the Secretary...'

This left the decision on what official information would become public up to even minor officials of government - a state of affairs that was hardly conducive to a nation whose constitution spoke in such bold terms about freedom of expression.

In 1953 Dr Harold L Cross published a comprehensive study of restrictions on the people's right to know about the workings of government. James S Pope who was chairman of the American Society of Newspaper Editors wrote in the forward of *The People's Right To Know.*

> *'We had only the foggiest idea of whence sprang the blossoming legend that agency and department heads enjoyed a sort of personal ownership of news about their departments'* (Cross 1953).

In 1958 Congressman John E Moss and Senator Thomas E Hennings introduced a bill to the House to provide what was described as a correction to the 180-year-old statute that apparently gave executive authority to minor officials of government over the release of official information. In 1962 President Kennedy affirmed that executive authority on this matter could be invoked by him alone and this was affirmed yet again by President Johnson in a letter to Congressman Moss on the 2 April 1965. In 1966 the Freedom of Information Act for which Congressman Moss had worked so hard was passed and came into force in 1967.[1] Over the next several decades however it became apparent that a simple law allowing citizens access to the workings of government did not prevent many more cover-ups. President Johnson himself presided over a major cover up, exposed in *The Pentagon Papers* (1971) in the run up to the presidential election in 1964 had deliberately misled the American people stating 'we seek no wider war'. The United States administration had escalated the war in South East Asia bombing Cambodia and Laos and authorising raids on North Vietnamese territory. The media and US population were kept in the dark, and the secrecy was entirely political and had little to do with the actual prosecution of the war.

Other states followed the example of the United States in introducing freedom of information legislation but in the majority of cases it was a hard fought battle to break down centuries old traditions of secret government. In the UK, the very idea of freedom of information was staunchly resisted by all mainstream political parties for decades[2] and behind the scenes government officials equivalent to those with 'executive privilege' in the US resisted, and resist to this day. Politicians of all shades and all levels were also sceptical and guarded about giving the population access to information. This was probably most starkly observed in the activities of local government officials and elected representatives who conducted a great deal of their business behind closed doors on the grounds of commercial sensitivity. Commercial sensitivity being very like its national security cousin, extremely difficult to define and with very vague boundaries.

FOI, secrecy and security

FOI legislation in most countries with such laws are remarkably similar and contain obvious exceptions to access. It is hardly surprising that the work of the security services in any country would be such an exception. Since the changes to the Official Secrets Act in 1989 people in the United Kingdom are now allowed to receive information about the security services, albeit in large part what the security services themselves want us to know.

The tradition of the secret state can still make obtaining information about public bodies exceptionally difficult. One of the most secret state bodies after the security services and the military is the NHS and all matter concerned with healthcare will cause problems for journalists investigating what is going on. The structure and philosophy of the NHS contributes greatly to the veil of secrecy that covers it. The service is the most monolithic of all public bodies and its structure is labyrinthine and contains a myriad of vested interests that pre-date the provision of free medical service by many decades. First and foremost of these is the obvious medical secrecy surrounding patients. This is one of the most fundamental laws of medical ethics and it is neither surprising, nor in any way contentious that medical confidentiality needs to be protected. Patients, in order to have confidence in the NHS, need to be constantly reassured that their medical records are totally private. Leaks about the state of health of royalty, politicians or their families have caused great controversy in recent years and it is clear that this information is sought out by journalists for stories. Few people would consider that a story based on confidential medical information had any journalistic merit or that the public had any right to know of the medical conditions of individuals even if they were 'public figures'.

The use of secrecy in matters concerning the NHS does not stop there however. While the NHS is a public body it is serviced by a significant section of the private sector who fall outside the scope of the Freedom of Information Act. The largest of these sectors are the pharmaceutical industry and medical device industry, which after health professional salaries form the largest expenditure in the health service. Of all the industries the pharmaceutical industry is the most secretive of all. In the last two decades there has been scandal after scandal involving the drug companies. This has ranged from price fixing to the deliberate hiding of adverse effects of their products. The seriousness of this practice cannot be overstated and many deaths have been caused by adverse reactions that patients and even many medical professionals were unaware of. The press has had some success in reporting the matter but the odd relationship between the press and the medical professions, ambivalent and not unlike the one it has with the police, has often directed press attention away from a detailed analysis of this behaviour.

The press quite rightly will argue that information held by the NHS is in the public interest. While it is unlikely that the majority of citizens of the UK will ever have dealings with the security services, our relationship with the NHS begins at birth and continues throughout the lifespan. Even the healthiest of us will need to see a medical professional and even those who use private medicine will almost certainly at some point encounter the NHS. On top of all that of course all taxpayers finance it. It would be incredibly difficult for either politicians or NHS executives to claim we had no right to know. In spite of this in fact they do. The NHS has proved to be as tenacious as the security services when it comes to transparency. When the NHS was established under the then Health Minister Aneurin Bevan, he famously stated that that if a bedpan dropped on a ward the noise would reverberate around Westminster. It is very clear today that many NHS officials and politicians believe those reverberations were never meant to be heard outside it. FOI has done little to provide the press and public with an insight into what really goes on in this gigantic organisation.

The *Daily Mail* has sometimes a questionable record when it comes to health related stories. Like most tabloids it prefers the two basic plots of scare stories intermingled with 'great breakthroughs' and false hopes. It does however have a better reputation in examining the lack of transparency in the NHS. On 21 and 22 February, 2014, it drew attention to the huge amount of money being paid in settlements and 'gagging clauses' to staff to prevent them from speaking to the press. In true tabloid style it pointed out that the £14.5m spent would have financed the employment of 500 nurses. It did however point out that the culture of secrecy was supported by ministers and officials alike, and that it took two years of effort by Steven Barclay MP to obtain this information under the Freedom of Information Act (*Daily Mail*, 2013). In spite of a much-vaunted Public Interest Disclosure Act[3] supposedly complementing the Freedom of Information Act it was still possible to silence criticism and keep the public in the dark by using taxpayers money to gag those with inconvenient views.

FOI is not for lazy journalists
The Freedom of Information Act 2000 is relatively easy for an official or politician to circumvent or even neutralise. There are many commentaries on this and politicians in particular have often repeated the somewhat absurd assertion that the Freedom of Information Act was not provided for lazy journalists or for journalists and the media to get hold of information for commercial purposes (House of Commons Justice Committee 2012). While the purpose of journalism is indeed commercial, in that the stories are ostensibly a 'commodity for sale' the information contained within them is the essence of what the legislation is about. In a famous case involving reporting from the courts rather than directly to do with official information Brooke J stated: 'The news media are the trustees of the general public whose eyes and ears they are.'[4]

It can be reasonably argued that journalists availing themselves of the legislation are doing it for the public good as much as for the good of their employers commercial wellbeing.

In any case it is not true that obtaining information via the Act is easy and therefore lazy as was adequately demonstrated in the efforts made by Steven Barclay. The exceptions are very broad and the administration cumbersome and expensive. The expense alone can be sufficient to prevent access under the Act and this goes some substantial way to supporting the view that journalists obtaining information this way are acting precisely in the spirit of the legislation. The individual member of the public entitled to the data may not have the financial resources of a mainstream media outlet.

The exceptions in health care matters are easy to manipulate and occasionally have not been helped by the attitude and behaviour of the press themselves. Medical confidentiality is one area where the greater need of the patient and those treating them outweighs transparency and suggested public interest. Scandalous attempts to publish the state of health of politicians and their families and the use of material obtained in breach of confidence have sullied the media's otherwise justifiable insistence on transparency. In a famous case involving two HIV positive doctors,[5] a tabloid newspaper was prevented by injunction from publishing the story. The court decided that the risk they posed to patients was far outweighed by the effect that a breach of confidentiality would have. There would never have been any public interest served by the release of this information and the application of secrecy here is understandable. However in significant numbers of other cases the secrecy is not being guarded in the public interest but in the interest of protecting reputations or policy. For example, on 8 May 2012 the Health Secretary, Andrew Lansley, with cabinet approval vetoed publication of a confidential risk assessment of the government's health reforms. This information had already been cleared for release by an Information Tribunal. The document sought would have given vital information to the public on whether or not a proper risk assessment of the proposed reforms had been carried out. Mr Lansley declared that the information needed to remain secret in order that the government could 'retain a safe space where officials are able to give ministers full and frank advice in developing policies and programmes,' (*The Independent*, 2012).

The cabinet agreed and the publication was prevented. It graphically demonstrated the most obvious weakness of the Freedom of Information Act 2000, access to official information was clearly not a right but a gift of government. What exactly this safe space was and whom it was keeping safe were never defined but it might be justifiably argued that it was contentious government policy and nothing that really need a veil of secrecy thrown over it. Mr Lansley did however assure us that while taking this step he did still believe in 'greater transparency'.

Learning the lessons of the secret state
During the 1990s the Conservative government had always preferred a grace and favour system of granting access to information over a legal right (Vincent 1999). A system of unenforceable charters allowing limited access underpinned by the age-old view that communication of government business was a privilege granted by the state. Some 15 years after the Freedom of Information Act was given Royal Assent it is clear that many politicians believe that still to be the case.

At the time of writing another huge scandal is developing in the press and once again it demonstrates the British tradition, indeed obsession with secrecy in the state. Once again a local authority is at the centre of the secret state. At the time of writing Rotherham Social Services and South Yorkshire Police are under the spotlight for what looks like a major cover up of a series of very serious child sex abuse cases that took place over several years under their noses.

The culture of secrecy is alive and well 15 years after the passing of the Freedom of Information Act 2000 and we are a very long way away for the transparent open government we were promised by those who introduced it. More than ever we rely not only on those 'lazy journalists' who employ the Act to get stories, but on those who obtain information the old fashioned way by stealth and guile. Let us hope that the next generation of journalists will be well trained in the latter skills.

Notes

[1] Freedom of Information Act (FOIA), 5 U.S.C. § 552 (1966)

[2] Freedom of Information Act 2000

[3] Public Interest Disclosure Act 1998

[4] *Attorney General v. Guardian Newspaper (N°3)* [1992] 1 WLR 874

[5] *V. X v. Y* [1988] 2 All ER 649

References

Andrew C (2009) *The Defence of the Realm: The Authorised History of MI5.* London: Allen Lane/Penguin

Cross HL (1953) *The People's Right to Know.* New York: Columbia University Press

Daily Mail (2013) 'Culture of secrecy is killing trust in NHS', Editorial comment, 22 February

Hennessy P (2010) *The Secret State: Preparing for the Worst 1945-2010.* London: Penguin

Houses of Parliament (2012) *Report on post-legislative scrutiny of the Freedom of Information Act, 2000.* Westminster: House of Commons Select Justice Committee, 2 July 2012

Hutchinson R (2006) *Elizabeth's Spymaster: Francis Walsingham and the Secret War that saved England.* London: Phoenix

Independent (2012) 'NHS reform risk report to remain secret' 8 May, 2012

Knightley P (2003) *The Second Oldest Profession: Spies and Spying in the 20th Century.* London: Pimlico

Lustgarten L. Leigh I (1994) *In From the Cold: National Security and Parliamentary Democracy.* Oxford: Oxford University Press

Mackenzie C (2011) *Greek Memories.* London: Biteback Publishing

Maer L. Gay O (2008) *Official Secrecy.* (Standard Note) SN/PC/02033. House of Commons Library

Robertson G QC (1999) *Freedom, The Individual and the Law.* 7th Edn. London: Penguin

United States – Vietnam Relations, 1945–1967: A Study Prepared by the Department of Defense (Hébert Edition 1971)

United States Congress (1989) (5 USC 22) Act of July 27, 1789, ch. 4, 1 Stat. 29 (Department of Foreign Affairs)

United States Congress (1989) Act of Aug. 7, 1789, ch. 7, 1 Stat. 50 (Department of War).

Vincent D (1999) *The Culture of Secrecy in Britain* 1832-1998. Oxford: Oxford University Press

Note on the contributor
Barry Turner is a senior lecturer in media law, public administration and science and environmental journalism at the Lincoln School of Journalism, University of Lincoln and at the Centre for Broadcasting and Journalism at Nottingham Trent University. He is also a judicial observer at the European Commission for the Efficiency of Justice working group on the quality of Justice.

Uncovering the state's secrets: how to use FOI effectively (by two experts in the trade)

Investigative journalists *Guy Basnett* and *Paul McNamara* routinely use FOI to uncover the secrets of our public bodies. Their work has revealed how foetuses are incinerated as clinical waste, police shoot children as young as 12 with Tasers, and children vanish from council care. Here they tell you how to get the most from FOI - by generating ideas, using FOI smartly, and fighting for the information you have a right to know

Introduction

Imagine somewhere in the vaults of Government buildings, the offices of an NHS hospital, or the custody suite of a police station lies information that you'd like to see. Well, you can - this is the Freedom of Information (FOI) Act. You don't need to justify why you want it, or explain what you want it for, or even how you're going to use it. If a public authority holds the information, and doesn't already publish it, all you need to do is put your request down in writing, and give your name and details of where to send the response. We promise you it's that simple. Send a request off to a public body, and within 20 working days they must send you their reply. This is the power of FOI: you have a *right* to that information. The law is in your favour, firmly on the side of disclosure. Unless there's a good reason, the public authority must give it to you.

We regularly break big stories through FOI. Stories the authorities would rather you not know. Stories with impact, and stories that affect real change. Through FOI requests we revealed how hospitals in the UK were incinerating miscarried and aborted foetuses as clinical waste, sometimes in waste-to-energy power plants (*The Sunday Times*, 23 March, 2014). We discovered trigger-happy police officers are using 50,000-volt Taser stun guns on children, including a mentally ill 12-year-old girl (*Sunday Mirror*, 2 June, 2013). We've shown how councils waste millions in public money (*The Sunday Times*, 16 June, 2013); how police officers avoid sexual abuse investigations by resigning (*The Sunday Times*, 24 April, 2014); hospitals secretly stored the remains of dead children for years

(*Daily Telegraph*, 18 March, 2014); and how vulnerable children - even babies - have routinely vanished from council care (*The Sunday Times*, 8 June, 2014). These stories have been turned into documentaries, led news agendas, and been reported on front pages. They've been debated across all forms of the media, and at the highest levels of government. And it's very likely all of them would have remained hidden and unknown if it wasn't for FOI.

Despite this, some journalists don't use FOI at all. Many fear it's too complex, and gathering stories using legislation is beyond them. This is wrong. FOI is actually quite simple. You don't need to be an expert to make it work for you. And after almost a decade of using it, we think some of the greatest success in using FOI comes from three simple actions:

1. Having great ideas (constantly think what can I ask?);

2. Getting the requests in (don't get bogged down – just send them); and

3. Fight (always push for information you have a *right* to know).

There are other points to consider as you use FOI more and more, such as ensuring your requests are razor-sharp and targeted, and staying organised, but just by following these three basic points, FOI can help you break agenda-setting public interest stories.

Great FOIs start with great ideas
Countless times we've seen the results of a good FOI and kicked ourselves screaming: 'Why didn't we think of that?!'. People seem to think the ability to generate ideas is somehow innate: either you have it or you don't. We disagree, and there are some things you can do to increase your chances of latching on to a good idea even in a fast-flowing news environment.

Think about the big issues
The topics driving the news agendas, or constantly bubbling away and exciting news editors – such as police brutality, child sexual exploitation, NHS failings, slave labour, radicalisation, obesity, and so on. What information on these exists but isn't routinely published, and who holds it? As more officers were armed with Tasers we started to think of the details they would hold that would give us a clearer picture of how they were used. We asked all forces for details on the number of times they'd used Tasers on children, with a breakdown of each child's gender, age, and the reason Taser was deployed. The revelation that the youngest to be shot was a 12-year-old girl threatening to harm herself led to a national debate about Taser use (*Sunday Mirror*, 2 June, 2013).

Be reactive
Many stories focus on one event, but beg questions such as what led up to it, what was happening behind the scenes, or how many times have similar events happened. When we heard of a young child admitted to hospital due to obesity, we asked how many babies and toddlers across the country had been admitted

(*The Sunday Times*, 13 October, 2013). And when we learned one police officer escaped prosecution for alleged sex crimes by resigning, we asked how many others had done the same (*The Sunday Times*, 24 April, 2014).

Read everything

Our team reads every national paper each morning, along with any other media we can get our hands on. You'll always find the germ of an investigation or the nugget of a great future story buried somewhere. One of our strongest FOI investigations came from a back-of-the-book real-life feature in Sunday tabloid *Sunday People*, about a couple who discovered their baby who died minutes after birth was buried in a mass grave (*Sunday People*, 21 July, 2013). We finished the story thinking: 'Is this common? And what happens across the country to aborted, miscarried and stillborn babies?' A few calls on the subject told us in some hospitals foetal remains were being incinerated as clinical waste, but confirming it was harder. FOI requests enabled us to ask all NHS trusts how many remains from abortions and miscarriages they disposed of, and how this was done. We revealed thousands were being incinerated, hundreds as clinical waste, and some in waste-to-energy power plants. When our Channel 4 *Dispatches* documentary on the investigation was broadcast, the Government announced an immediate ban on incineration of all foetal remains (*The Sunday Times*, 23 March, 2014).

Look for open doors

You'll often hear journalists accuse public bodies of wanting to hide information, but sometimes the authority is desperate to get information out there. For political reasons they can't and FOI can unlock this. It might be two warring Government departments, where one would happily stitch up the other. Or a regulator itching to show that they've taken on a delinquent industry, but needs their hands 'forced' through FOI. Or FOI can simply bring cooperation. When we heard organ donors were in such short supply that doctors resorted to using donations from former drug addicts, alcoholics and smokers, we FOI-ed NHS Blood and Transplant. Within days we'd discussed and refined our request with help from their Associate Medical Director, who also appeared for interview when the investigation was broadcast on *Channel 4 News* (Macdonald, 2014).

Get them in

Once you have the idea, the most important thing is getting the request in. We're constantly amazed by journalists we speak to, who write thousands of words a day, yet feel flummoxed if they try to pen a FOI request. It's often through over-thinking what is actually a pretty simple process. You can get great results from straightforward requests. A request can be as simple as:

Dear FOI Officer,

How much did your organisation spend on external freelance consultants last year (2013/14)?

Guy Basnett and Paul McNamara

Please reply to: foi@openworldnews.com

Just 20 working days later you should have your information - and hopefully a story.

But what if in our example we didn't say 'last year'? What if we asked for every penny spent on consultants throughout the entire history of this authority's being? For a very old public body it is easy to imagine them saying that gathering the information is impossible as - even if they could locate such records - it would take an unfeasibly long time to collate it. That's just common sense. At this point it might help to understand the most common scenarios for FOI requests being refused in order to avoid situations like this.

Firstly, there is a cost limit as to what you can ask for, measured in how much time it takes to search for, find, and retrieve your information. The limit works out as basically 24 hours work for central Government, Parliament and the Armed Forces, and 18 hours work for all other public authorities.

And secondly, while FOI means public bodies are obliged to hand over information, they don't have to if it comes under one or more of 23 exemptions in the Act. These range from clear-cut situations such as information relating to national security, to more woolly reasons, such as disclosure being 'prejudice to the effective conduct of public affairs'. Some of these are 'qualified' exemptions, which means they should be weighed up to see if it is in the public interest that the information still be disclosed. While others are 'absolute', so basically public interest won't help. These are all detailed in the Act. But the point is you don't need to master - or even read - all of it. You're a journalist, not a lawyer or Information Officer. You should aim to understand enough of the Act so you don't waste your time and authorities' time requesting clearly exempt information, or far too much material. But that's all.

Later we will explain how to argue against refusals. In the meantime, however, just remember not to let fear of refusal stop you from submitting a request in the first place.

Be smart
Once the basics have been conquered, it's a relatively small step from putting in a simple FOI request to using FOI to produce in-depth investigations capable of affecting change. Here are some tips and tricks to taking that step.

Talk to sources
Like any story, FOI investigations need human sources. Specific knowledge will make your requests much more powerful. The more targeted you can be, especially considering the cost limits, the more likely your request is to succeed. When we looked into the growing number of child sexual exploitation cases across the UK, we spent time talking to social workers dealing with the aftermath. They told us teenage girls were routinely going missing from council care, and falling prey to predators. They explained how logs are often kept of

each missing episode, along with details of the children going missing. We were able to ask all councils how many children had gone missing from their care over the past three years, the number of times a specific child had gone missing, and their age and sex. Aside from revealing the thousands of teenage girls that go missing, we also discovered that toddlers and even babies go missing, sometimes for up to a year. The story ran as an investigation for *Channel 4 News* (Long, 2014) and *The Sunday Times* (8 June, 2014).

Do your research

It pays to understand the architecture of how the information you want is gathered and stored. Try to find out exactly what information is held, how, and under what phrasing, categorisation or even code. This information could be buried in reports, descriptions of data files, or the minutes of an authority's meetings. Knowing this can bring a laser-like focus to your request and give you the results you want. For example, we used the NHS coding system to ask for details of the growing numbers of babies and children admitted to hospital due to obesity (*The Sunday Times*, 13 October, 2013).

Think ahead

Imagine the first four paragraphs of your investigation, or sections of your documentary, and think what extra details you might need. Request figures from previous years, so you can get a picture of trends, or request contextual figures that allow you to calculate rates that will tell the real story when comparing performance levels between organisations. Ask for the summaries of individual incidents so your story will have more than just numbers. These are all tactics that can make the difference between obtaining a fairly bland set of numbers, and rich information that will tell a compelling story.

Phrase it clearly

Now you understand what information is available and exactly what you need to tell your story, ask for it in a clear and methodical way. We outline the gist of our request before stating what we are 'specifically' seeking using numbered questions. These should be unambiguous. We set out the date ranges of any information we're interested in, and are clear whether it's calendar or financial years we are looking at. If we ask for information to be broken down, we'll include examples of the type of details we require. We may specify the digital format we want to receive the information in. And we may even provide model tables for them to follow. With this clarity and focus FOI becomes a very powerful tool.

Be organised

Now your request is in, it's time for the unglamorous bit - managing your data. Journalists aren't known for being organised, but if you want to FOI on a national level and achieve a comprehensive response rate from all police forces, or NHS trusts, or county, unitary, and district councils, then you need to find a way to stay on top of things.

Everyone has his or her own method. We use Google Sheets, which allows a whole team to work on the same spreadsheet simultaneously, keeping tabs on which requests have been acknowledged, need to be appealed, or have come back successfully. We religiously update our lists of FOI contact details, so we're not caught out when authorities change them. And we have a number of folders to keep every email in the correct place. It sounds boring, but it's vital in large investigations. When we examined council spending for Channel 4's *Dispatches* we submitted multiple separate FOI requests to all councils in England, Wales, Scotland and Northern Ireland. Each request could generate more than 400 acknowledgements, and 400 responses, not to mention clarifications and appeals. We couldn't have achieved 90 per cent response rates and 100 per cent accuracy in reporting the responses without being obsessively organised in tracking everything.

Fight and fight again

With all that said, even with the best practice, your requests will frequently be refused. It's very important that you put up a fight. This is another area that separates consistently successful requesters from those who don't seem to get results. FOI is partly a numbers game between over-stretched FOI officers and time-poor journalists. And sometimes it seems some public authorities refuse requests as a matter of course. It's a successful tactic, because many journalists immediately give up. Don't be one of them. Faced with a list of exemptions, or a lengthy public interest test that comes down decisively for the other side, most feel there's no point arguing, or don't know where to start.

Firstly, go back to the Act and read up on the exemptions and sections they've mentioned. Compare what the authority has said with what you see written in the Act. Does their reasoning fit? Do you agree? Go to the Information Commissioner's Office (ICO) website and look at their guidance (Information Commissioner's Office, 2014). Has the public authority used appropriate arguments, or do you think they should have given you the information? You can even search for ICO decision notices for previous appeals on similar refusals. Do any of them come down in your favour? As a first step we'd advise you to go back to the authority and either amend your request, for example narrowing or refining it, or stick to your guns and ask for an internal review. If after that they still refuse, follow the ICO complaints procedure.

FOI is a running battle between freeing up information, and keeping it hidden. If you believe you have a right to that information, you have a duty to fight for it otherwise public authorities will think they have a right to keep it secret. You'll be surprised by the results. We've had FOI responses adamant that information is not easily retrievable within the costs limit. But when we've questioned this and asked for more information, they've instantly relented. We've had refusals citing long lists of exemptions, putting up barrier after barrier. In one case an NHS Trust refused information because they believed answering our request would reveal personal data, or confidential information, or put health and safety at risk. We replied with a five-line email amounting to, 'No it won't', to which they instantly conceded.

Sometimes we'll put together thousands of words of argument. Other times, in the heat of day-to-day journalism, we'll only manage a quick paragraph or two. What's important is that we're asking for the refusal to be reviewed, and signalling that we're not going to be fobbed off with a refusal, and will fight to get the information we're entitled to. All these steps are key in making FOI work for you as a journalist. Constantly think up ideas; get the requests in; and be prepared to argue. If you do, then you'll produce great stories and investigations, and the Freedom of Information Act can carry on doing exactly what it's designed for: uncovering the public interest stories that would otherwise remain hidden and untold.

References

Basnett, Guy and McNamara, Paul (2014) 'Alarm raised as 19 babies vanish from council care,' *The Sunday Times*, 8 June. Available online at http://www.thesundaytimes.co.uk/sto/news/uk_news/National/article1420225.ece, accessed on 31 August 2014

Basnett, Guy and McNamara, Paul (2014) 'Thousands of foetuses burnt as ward waste,' *The Sunday Times*, 23 March. Available online at http://www.thesundaytimes.co.uk/sto/news/uk_news/National/article1391109.ece, accessed on 31 August 2014

Boyle, Sheron (2013) 'Hospital dumped my baby in unmarked mass grave without us knowing,' *Sunday People*, 21 July. Available online at http://www.mirror.co.uk/news/uk-news/hospital-dumps-premature-babys-body-2071119, accessed on 31 August 2014

Donnelly, Laura (2014) 'Hospital blunders mean foetuses stored for years,' *Daily Telegraph*, 18 March. Available online at http://www.telegraph.co.uk/journalists/laura-donnelly/10705487/Hospital-blunders-mean-foetuses-stored-for-years.html, accessed on 31 August 2014

Herbert, Dominic and Drummond, James (2013) 'Cops use 50,000 volt Taser on girl aged 12,' *Sunday Mirror*, 2 June. Available online at http://www.mirror.co.uk/news/uk-news/tasered-aged-12-teen-hit-1926398, accessed on 31 August 2014

Information Commissioner's Office (2014) *FOI Guidance Index*. Available online at http://ico.org.uk/, accessed on 31 August 2014

Long, Jackie (2014) 'Thousands of children in care disappear each year,' *Channel 4 News*, 23 May. Available online at http://www.channel4.com/news/missing-children-care-homes-foi-babies, accessed on 31 August 2014

Macdonald, Victoria (2014) 'Patients' dilemma over rise in high-risk organ donations,' *Channel 4 News*, 21 January. Available online at http://blogs.channel4.com/victoria-macdonald-on-health-and-social-care/patients-threatened-rise-highrisk-organ-donations/1787, accessed on 31 August 2014

Summers, Hannah and Mansey, Kate (2013) 'Pedicures on £440m council credit card bill,' *The Sunday Times*, 16 June. Available online at http://www.thesundaytimes.co.uk/sto/news/uk_news/National/article1274701.ece, accessed on 31 August 2014

Weekes, Rob (2013) 'Babies caught up in obesity epidemic,' *The Sunday Times*, 13 October. Available online at http://www.thesundaytimes.co.uk/sto/news/uk_news/Health/article1326826.ece, accessed on 31 August 2014

Weekes, Rob (2014) 'Police quit to dodge sex abuse investigations,' *The Sunday Times*, 24 April. Available online at http://www.thesundaytimes.co.uk/sto/news/uk_news/National/article1401829.ece, accessed on 31 August 2014

Note on the contributors

Guy Basnett and Paul McNamara are investigative journalists and the founders of OpenWorld News, an agency and production company providing content to Fleet Street and broadcasters. Their work has appeared in flagship documentary series including Channel 4's *Dispatches* and BBC's *Panorama*, along with *Channel 4 News* and newspapers such as *The Sunday Times*. Their freedom of information investigations have led to a ban on the incineration of foetal remains; a review on the MoD's care of dogs; and a national debate on the use of Tasers. Contact Guy at guy.basnett@openworldnews.com and via Twitter at @guybasnett. Contact Paul at paul.mcnamara@openworldnews.com and @PGMcNamara on Twitter.

Multiple FOI requests: saving time and effort

Journalist and journalism professor *Paul Bradshaw* navigates through the seemingly complex world of multiple FOI requests, and offers advice for reporters on how to make it work for you

Introduction

Many of the strongest FOI stories involve a reporter submitting the same request to multiple authorities. You may hear that local nurses are being hit by parking charges - but establishing that they - or nurses elsewhere - are being hit *harder* than others in the country or region is another, better, story altogether. Likewise, if you want a national story you need to get figures covering the nation - often only obtained through querying all authorities in that country or region. If you want to identify the 'worst' offender or 'biggest' spends - 'outliers' in statistical jargon - you can only establish this by getting all the facts.

In 2014 the *Mirror*, for example, led one FOI story with the headline: 'Nurses charged almost £200 a month just to park their cars at work' (Hayward, 2014). £200 was the highest charge they found in dozens of responses to FOI requests from NHS trusts across the country. Multiple requests allowed the tabloid to add all sorts of detail to their reporting, including the biggest earner from parking charge income ('NHS trusts are raking in up to £3.9m a year in parking fees from their own staff, outpatients and visitors')' the number of trusts making significant amounts from the practice ('at least 10 Trusts make more than £2m a year from parking. Another 36 trusts earn £1m.'), and the 'worst offender' when it came to penalising staff: at one hospital 'more than HALF the penalty notices handed out were slapped on the cars of its own workers' (ibid).

Multiple FOI requests can also be used to paint a regional picture on a topical issue: when zero hour contracts were in the news, for example, BBC Bristol reporter Ian Parker submitted FOI requests to 18 councils in the South West to find out how many staff were on the contracts. He then obtained a critical response to the figures and led on that:

"Councils in the West have been criticised for employing hundreds of staff on zero-hours contracts. More than 700 people at 17 councils are employed on the contracts, which allow authorities to hire staff but with no guarantee of work, the BBC has found" (Parker, 2014).

Clearly, the more FOI requests you submit, the more time you will need to compile, combine and compare them. But a little time spent on the preparation of the FOI requests can save an enormous amount of time when the results start coming in. In this chapter I will outline some of the tips and techniques in preparing just such a project. These techniques can make the difference between weeks of work, and hours; between a non-story and a national exclusive. It really is that important.

Is it held centrally?

The first step when tackling such a story is to ask yourself whether you need to make multiple FOI requests at all. If a national or regional picture is required, for example, this can sometimes be obtained by a central authority. Consider the following:

- There are over 200 clinical commissioning groups (CCGs) controlling health spending in England, but they all report to NHS England. A phone call to NHS England may tell you that the data you require is held centrally as well as locally.

- There are dozens of police forces but these must all supply certain information to the Home Office. Likewise, courts and prisons supply certain data on sentencing and reoffending to the Ministry of Justice.

- Hundreds of local authorities - councils - provide information to the Department for Communities and Local Government (DCLG) as well as other agencies. They are also represented by the Local Government Association.

- Universities are subject to the FOI Act but also supply data to the Higher Education Statistics Agency (HESA). Note that the Department for Business, Innovation and Skills (BIS) is responsible for universities, *not* the Department for Education.

- Schools are part of a system that has been particularly complicated in the last few years, as different schools report information to different bodies. Academies and free schools, for example, report directly to the Department for Education, whereas other schools report to their local authority as well, and all schools are inspected by Ofsted.

The key question is the level of *detail* held: the more detail you require, the more likely you will have to submit your request to the bodies closest to it. The majority of information held by a local police force or a school will *not* be passed on to a central body. It is unlikely that the amount paid by NHS staff for parking, or the numbers of staff on zero hour contracts, are collected by central government. But in those cases where it *is* you will save time and money by asking the central authority first. Don't forget that in an increasing number of cases England, Scotland, Wales and Northern Ireland have separate central bodies: NHS England is exactly that. Northern Ireland has its own Environment Agency, and so on. So even if you do find information in one central body, you may benefit from seeking responses from their equivalents in the other nations.

Phrasing the multiple FOI request: ask for spreadsheet format

Once you have decided to submit an FOI request to multiple authorities, you should think carefully about phrasing it so that the responses can be easily combined. Consider the following:

- Exercise your right under the Freedom of Information Act to request data in an electronic format, and spreadsheets specifically

- Submit your request to a few authorities first to 'test the water' and see if responses (either the actual information or their reasons for not supplying it) present problems you could prevent in a better-phrased request

- Request internal codes as well as descriptive or text data so that data can be more accurately matched if needed

- Request data that you will need in order to put the main request into context

- Make sure you specify whether you are asking for figures by financial year (generally April to March, but not for all organisations), or calendar year (January to December) – and you should ask for previous years' figures so you can put it into historical context

- You should also request information on classification systems where relevant. For example, different universities classify many different types of things as a 'complaint', but not all complaints are the same

For example, as part of one investigation into the Olympic torch relay, my collaborative investigations website Help Me Investigate submitted FOI requests to all the police authorities involved to find out how much money was spent on policing it. The Metropolitan Police Service - serving London - spent the most, but this was not surprising, as they have more staff than any other (by some distance) serving a bigger population with a budget to match. Not only that, but the torch relay spent longer in the capital than anywhere else, and was arguably a bigger target for disruption than other parts of the country.

When the spending was divided by the population being served, Gwent police force in Wales turned out to be the biggest spender per capita (Mohammad, 2013). Another option might have been to present those figures as a proportion of each force's total budget. It is always best to ask for the information in the most granular form available. If you are asking for spending, ask for it to be broken down by each type of spending or - better still - ask for every item of spending. If you are asking about complaints, ask for those to be broken down by type of complaint, or to receive a spreadsheet listing all the complaints individually.

'Dirty data'

Dirty data is data that is either inaccurate or inconsistent in some way. In any situation where names are entered manually, for example, it is typical to find typographical errors, unnecessary spaces, and different names for the same thing (for example, Met Police and Metropolitan Police or Jack Smith and J Smith). One member of staff might omit 'Ltd', while another might use an ampersand instead of the word 'And'. When the trade union GMB submitted FOI requests to find out which private landlords were the biggest recipients of housing benefit payments, for example, they only asked for the amount received, and the name of the company. When the *Mirror* newspaper tried to add together payments to companies across more than one authority the journalists hit a problem: they couldn't be certain that companies had been named consistently across each authority. The process of matching companies – 'disambiguation' – would have been helped enormously if the original requests had also asked for a business number, address, phone number or even postcode. Likewise cost codes, incident codes, and similar more consistent pieces of information can make an enormous difference in matching data across more than one spreadsheet.

If you have enough time you might submit a first Freedom of Information request for the organisation's relevant 'data dictionary'. This is a list of the fields used in a particular database, and can help you identify information you might otherwise not have thought of asking for. (You may need to explain what a data dictionary is as part of your request - and be clear that it is just a list of fields rather than the data stored in that database.)

Setting up a spreadsheet to record multiple FOI responses

Before you submit your FOI requests it is a good idea to begin setting up a spreadsheet that will be used to record responses. This will also help ensure you haven't missed anything in your request. Your spreadsheet should be as detailed as possible. Think about some (not all!) of the following columns:

- The name and/or code of the authority responding

- A column for numbers - e.g. incidents, crimes, amount spent, etc

- A column for locations if you are requesting them - these can be split later if you need to but you may want to create more than one column

- A column for postcodes if you are requesting them

- A latitude for each location; and

- A longitude for each location. These are always useful to ask for because it allows you to see if locations are in a particular ward, constituency, county, country, and so on. It also makes mapping results much easier

- A column for categories

- A column for subcategories if you are requesting them

- A column for dates - e.g. date recorded, date spent, or the month or year data is for

- The name of any other party if you are requesting them - e.g. each recipient of money

- A column for your any comments or descriptions included by the respondent

- A column for your own comments

- A column to rate the newsworthiness of each item - a scale from 0 (not interesting) to 5 (shocking) generally works

All of these columns can then be used to **aggregate** or **filter** your information. For example, you could:

- Calculate the grand totals by authority, or all authorities' average figures

- Calculate totals by area, postcode, recipient, category, etc

- Filter to only show only those rows which you have given a 'newsworthiness' rating above 3

- Filter to only show those rows where the respondent has added some explanatory comment

- Chart by date to see whether something is going up or down (you may have to split dates to aggregate by months and years)

Think about what sort of stories you might want to create with your FOI responses. Identifying the authority with the highest or lowest numbers is often just one story - and this is why you want to request data in as detailed a form as possible. Once you've identified one authority you can always drill down to the best and worst locations within that. Or you can shift your attention from authorities to the constituencies with the highest and lowest figures. Or you can look at changes over time. Or you can pick out shocking individual examples of abuse of power, bureaucratic ignorance, or just plain stupidity.

Write out hypothetical headlines so you know what information you will need in your spreadsheet to 'back those up' (Mark Lee Hunter's free ebook *Story Based Inquiry* (Hunter, 2011) provides a comprehensive overview of this process of using hypotheses to direct your investigating). Now you know what to ask for, aggregating numbers by organisation or category can be done quickly in spreadsheets with the pivot table option. It is beyond the scope of this chapter to outline that process, but you can find it detailed - along with advanced filters - in the short ebook *Data Journalism Heist* (Bradshaw, 2013). If more than one person is going to be compiling responses, it is useful to create the spreadsheet in a collaborative tool such as Google Sheets (available as part of Google Drive at drive.google.com).

Using drop-down menus to ensure consistent data entry

Dirty data isn't just a problem with the data you're receiving: you can be guilty of the same inconsistencies and errors in your own data entry. To avoid this, for columns where the data should be predictable - particularly categories and the authority responding - you should learn how to create drop-down menus in your spreadsheet software. This is called **validation**. Validation helps to make sure that you will be able to match the data you're inputting with other data. For example, it will ensure that you name an authority in the same way as it is named in official data, or that your categories are consistently described. You can create drop-down menus in a Google spreadsheet for cells in any particular column as follows:

- Firstly, your spreadsheet workbook will need two sheets: one for the data you are inputting; and a second sheet containing a list of options for your drop-down list: for example, a list of local authorities or police bodies

- In the sheet where you will *input* the data, select the column you want your drop-down lists to appear in (click on A to select column A)

- Click on **Data>Validation...**

- On the window that appears, click on the drop-down menu for *Criteria* and select **Items from a list**

- You can now either type in the list yourself, or select a range of cells that contain the items for your list (*Create list from a range*). It's best to do the latter

- Click on the grid button to the right of this box, go to the sheet containing your 'official' list and select the column or row containing your items. You should end up with a reference that looks like this: SheetName!A:A.

- Click **OK** and click **Save** to apply the drop-down

Back on your data entry sheet each cell in the column you first selected should now have a small drop-down icon to the right. Users can select from this to make sure they're using the same names for authorities as your 'official' list.

When the responses come in: input data at the most granular level

If you're inputting information where different respondents have different categories (as is most often the case), you need to input the data so that this doesn't cause a problem. The simplest way to do this – and also the fastest way

– is to avoid imposing a particular classification system (either one authority's, or your own) onto your data as you're inputting it. Imposing a classification system slows down the inputting process (the user has to make a decision where to categorise each piece of data), can introduce inconsistency (one user makes a different decision to another), and add extra work later on (what if you realise you decide to add a new category halfway through?). It is much simpler to input the data in as basic a fashion as possible. For example, when Help Me Investigate requested information on council spending on the Olympic Torch Relay, instead of having one column per local authority, and having columns for each type of spending, like this:

NAME ———— TYPE1 — TYPE2 — TOTAL

COUNCIL A – 100 ——— 10000 —- 10100

We decided to have one row per item like so:

NAME ———— TYPE — AMOUNT — NOTES

COUNCIL A – Lights –10000 ———— 'Blah blah'

This allows you to add extra columns when required (for example, if a third party contributed funding, or if you want a column for answers to a particular question). It also means you don't have to think about classification now. You can impose this on the data later by, for example, filtering it to look for rows which mention 'light', 'lighting', and other terms you've come across while inputting. However, if you already know that you are looking for particular categories of data, then you may want to add or identify a column which you will use to identify rows that match.

Cleaning up responses: using SPLIT and RIGHT

If you receive a response where the data has been supplied in a Word document, you can paste it into your spreadsheet and use spreadsheet functions to split it up as you need, rather than having to manually input each item separately. Before doing so it makes sense to have your spreadsheet set up in the same order as data is normally provided, i.e. the 'item' and 'cost' columns coming in that order, next to each other, so that these functions work best. The SPLIT function in Google Sheets is particularly useful. This splits the information in any specified cell whenever there is a particular character.

For example, if A1 contains 'Catering £200' then typing this formula in any other cell will grab the contents of that cell and split them into two parts:

=SPLIT(A1," ")

The space between the quotation marks indicates that it should split the cell wherever it finds a space. So once you have written the formula and pressed ENTER, the result will be two cells: one containing 'Catering' and another containing '£200'. The space is removed, by the way.

If the items are *always* only one word (no spaces), followed by a space and the number, you can grab and split them all in one go by repeating the formula for each one. If item and cost are separated by a colon, e.g. 'Starbucks: £1200' then you can adapt it as follows:

=SPLIT(A1,":")

Perhaps most commonly, the SPLIT function can also be used where your costs always begin with a pound sign, like so:

=SPLIT(A1,"£")

You will probably want to delete the raw data once it's been split – but if you do this the formula will stop working (there will be nothing for them to split), so before you do that select all the cells containing the results of your formulae (both columns). Copy the cells. Then click on **Edit > Paste special...** and select **Values only**. This will paste the *results* of your formulae on top of the same cells that previously contained them. That means you can safely delete anything that the now-gone formulae used. Note that the SPLIT function only works like this in Google Sheets. In Excel you can select your pasted data and then use the 'Text to columns' option normally found under the data menu to split that data on every space, or colon, pound sign etc.

There are many other useful spreadsheet functions which can help you with similar problems, particularly the RIGHT, LEFT and MID functions, which will grab a specified number of characters from the right, left or middle of a cell. These functions and others are explained in the ebook *Finding Stories in Spreadsheets* (Bradshaw, 2014).

The big story
The Freedom of Information Act has opened up a raft of possibilities for watchdog journalism, allowing journalists to hold power to account in ways that would have been prohibitively costly or time-consuming previously. Not only that, but use of the Act has coincided with a period when computer power has continually reduced the cost and time required to understand the results. Combining your legal rights with effective planning and information management makes it possible for a single journalist to do in days or hours what would have required a team of researchers decades ago. Careful targeting and phrasing of the initial request; requesting detailed data to enable accuracy and flexibility; and using cleaning techniques to speed up transcription can make all the difference. But it's also about practice: the more experience you gain, the more you will anticipate and prevent problems. You no longer need to be an 'investigative' journalist or part of an investigations team to investigate stories in the public interest. You do not need to be a 'data journalist' to work with numbers. You just need to be curious, and organised, and above all: to want accurate answers to vital questions.

Parts of this chapter were first published on the Help Me Investigate *blog*

References

Bradshaw, Paul (2013) *Data Journalism Heist*. eBook: Leanpub, available at https://leanpub.com/DataJournalismHeist, accessed 15 September, 2014

Bradshaw, Paul (2014) *Finding Stories in Spreadsheets*. eBook: Leanpub, available at https://leanpub.com/spreadsheetstories, accessed 15 September, 2014

Hayward, Stephen (2014) 'Nurses charged almost £200 a month just to park their cars at work,' in the *Mirror*, 12 July. Available at http://www.mirror.co.uk/news/uk-news/nurses-charged-200-month-just-3848184#ixzz3AHr7uCYo, accessed 13 August, 2014

Hunter, Mark Lee (2011) *Story Based Inquiry*. Paris: UNESCO, available at http://unesdoc.unesco.org/images/0019/001930/193078e.pdf, accessed 15 September, 2014

Knight, Christopher (2014) 'Section 11 FOIA and the Form of a Request'. *Panopticon* blog, 1 August, 2014, available at http://www.panopticonblog.com/2014/08/01/section-11-foia-and-the-form-of-a-request, accessed 16 August, 2014

Mohammad, Gesbeen (2013) 'The £6.5m cost of policing the Olympic Torch – get the data,' *Help Me Investigate the Olympics* blog, 2 December 2013, available at http://helpmeinvestigate.com/olympics/the-6-5m-cost-of-policing-the-olympic-torch/ accessed 13 August, 2014

Parker, Ian (2014) 'Hundreds in zero-hours council jobs in the West,' BBC News Bristol, 3 July, available at http://www.bbc.co.uk/news/uk-england-27995729, accessed August 13 2014

Note on the contributor

Paul Bradshaw runs the MA in Online Journalism at Birmingham City University, is a Visiting Professor at City University's School of Journalism in London, and a freelance writer and trainer. He has worked with news organisations including *the Guardian, Telegraph, Mirror* and The Bureau of Investigative Journalism. He publishes the Online Journalism Blog, is the co-founder of the award-winning investigative journalism network HelpMeInvestigate.com, and his books include *Finding Stories in Spreadsheets, Scraping for Journalists, The Data Journalism Heist*, and the *Online Journalism Handbook* (with Liisa Rohumaa).

Too much transparency? Journalists as users of online freedom of information sites worldwide

Savita Bailur and *Tom Longley* discuss the results of research from 27 online FOI sites, which show that while journalists use sites as repositories of information, requests are fewer than anticipated due to lengthy timelines, a leak culture and where the request's audit trail is public, fear of losing a competitive scoop

Introduction

Journalists are often expected to be key users of freedom of information (Hazell et al, 2009; Paterson, 2008; Roberts, 2010). The US FOI Act actively encouraged the role of the media: 'one individual, even a trained researcher, can track down only a limited number of leads upon which to base an FOIA request, while newspapers and television stations… can put teams to work on a problem; they also have the resources to pay for the copying costs of large numbers of documents' (cited in Paterson, 2008). Tony Blair, Prime Minister when the UK FOI Act was passed, was famous for regretting it because it was used by journalists: 'for political leaders, it's like saying to someone who is hitting you over the head with a stick, "Hey, try this instead", and handing them a mallet. The information is neither sought because the journalist is curious to know, nor given to bestow knowledge on "the people". It's used as a weapon' (Blair, 2010: 517).

At the same time, journalists appear to have a complex relationship with FOI. Between May and September 2014, we conducted research on behalf of mySociety on 27 such FOI websites.[1] Although the overall aim of the research was to understand the impact of FOI sites - and assist mySociety and the wider community of interest around online FOI - this chapter focuses on use of such websites by journalists [the broader findings are available from mySociety]. We start by reviewing the relationship between journalists, FOI and online FOI, go on to present our primary data, analyse the findings and draw conclusions and present pointers for future research.

Journalists, FOI and online FOI

Although journalists were expected to facilitate government openness through using and publicising FOI, their use has not been as great as anticipated (see Hazell et al, 2009; Moudgil, 2011; Worthy and Hazell, 2013). First, it has been pointed out that the average 20 to 30-day time limit on FOI means newsrooms working under tight time and resource pressures are likely to look at other means of obtaining information – use is more likely to be by a smaller group of investigative journalists working to medium or long-term deadlines (Hayes, 2009; Hazell et al, 2009; Moudgil, 2011). Secondly, it is suggested that a 'leak' culture still exists where journalists may prefer to use a mutually beneficial arrangement of 'contacts' rather than jeopardise relationships by putting in a formal FOI request, which may seem adversarial (ibid). When formal requests are put in, it may be more of a 'last resort'.

FOI requests tend to concern local issues – the pothole in the road, the local library, a decision to close allotments (Dunion, 2011; Michener and Worthy, 2013; Worthy, 2012) and in many cases there is no strong local press, and local stories do not make national news (Michener and Worthy, 2013). This may mean national media can distort FOI issues by focussing only on the sensationalist aspects (Worthy and Hazell, 2013) – the UK MPs expenses issue was a national / international scandal, but would similar fraud at a local level get as much attention? Of course, this is assuming that the media industry is independent, strong and resource-intensive enough – the *Daily Telegraph* reportedly paid £110,000 for details of MPs expenses, described as 'money well spent in the public interest' (Tryhorn, 2009). Only a few newspapers have the financial capacity to expend such sums. Finally, there is the question of *who* is considered a journalist, as many who use FOI may be bloggers and campaigners (therefore classifying as the general public), which also makes quantifying use more complex.

Where does journalist use of online FOI fit in here? The table below lists FOI sites known to us:

Figure 2: Known FOI sites around the world

Country	Name	URL	Organisation / software
Australia	Right to Know	righttoknow.org.au	CSO/Alaveteli
Austria	FragdenStaat	fragdenstaat.at	CSO/Custom-built
Bosnia	PravoDaZnam	pravodaznam.ba	CSO/Alaveteli
Brasil	e-SIC	http://www.acessoainformacao.gov.br	Government/Custom-built
Canada (Québec)	Je Veux Savoir	jeveuxsavoir.org	CSO/Government/Alaveteli
Chile	Acceso Inteligente	accesointeligente.org/AccesoInteligente/#home	CSO/Custom-built

Chile	Portal de Transparencia	http://www.portaltransparencia.cl/	Government/Custom-built
Czech Republic	Informace pro všechny	infoprovsechny.cz	Individuals/Alaveteli
European Union	AsktheEU.org	asktheeu.org	CSO/Alaveteli
Georgia	Open Data Georgia	opendata.ge	CSO/Custom-built
Germany	FragdenStaat	fragdenstaat.de	CSO/Journalist/Custom-built
Guatemala	Guateinformada	guateinformada.org.gt	CSO/Alaveteli
Honduras	Instituto de Acceso a la Información Pública	http://www.iaip.gob.hn/index.php/solicitud-de-informacion	Government/Custom-built
Hungary	KiMitTud	kimittud.atlatszo.hu	Journalist/Alaveteli
India	Right to Information	https://rtionline.gov.in/	Government/Custom-built
Israel	Ask Data	askdata.org.il	CSO/Alaveteli
Italy	Diritto di Sapere	italy.alaveteli.org	CSO/Alaveteli
Kosovo	informatazyrtare.org	informatazyrtare.org	CSO/Alaveteli
Liberia	iLab	Not yet named	CSO/Undecided
Macedonia	Слободен пристап	slobodenpristap.mk	CSO/Alaveteli
Mexico	InfoMex	https://www.infomex.org.mx/gobiernofederal/home.action	Government/Custom-built
NZ	FYI	fyi.org.nz	Individual/Alaveteli
Romania	NuVaSuparaʔi.info	nuvasuparati.info	CSO/Alaveteli
Serbia	Zajecar Initiative	daznamosvi.rs/sr	CSO/Alaveteli
South Africa	askafrica.org.za	askafrica.org.za	CSO/Alaveteli
Spain	Tu derecho a saber	tuderechoasaber.es	CSO/Alaveteli
Switzerland	Oeffentlichkeitsgesetz	oeffentlichkeitsgesetz.ch	Journalist/ Custom-built
Tunisia	Marsoum 41	marsoum41.org	CSO/Alaveteli
Uganda	Ask Your Gov Uganda	AskYourGov.ug	CSO/Government/Alaveteli

UK	What Do They Know	https://www.whatdotheyknow.com/	CSO/Pre-Alaveteli
Ukraine	Доступ до правди	dostup.pravda.com.ua	CSO/Journalist/Alaveteli
Uruguay	¿Qué Sabés?	quesabes.org	CSO/Alaveteli
USA	iFOIA	www.ifoia.org/#!/	Journalist/Custom-built
USA	Muckrock	www.muckrock.com	Journalist/Custom-built

From the table above, we can see the majority of sites are established by CSOs (although site ownership keeps evolving). The first mySociety FOI site was WhatDoTheyKnow in the United Kingdom, launched in 2008.

mySociety re-engineered WhatDoTheyKnow to create Alaveteli[2] – a free and open source software which can be translated to other languages and adapted to different FOI laws. Using the online form, anyone can put in a request to any public authority, and both query and response are public and searchable. At the time of writing, Alaveteli sites have been set up in more than 20 countries, as well as the EU (in addition to the countries above, it has been implemented in Argentina, Croatia, Indonesia and Norway but the status of these is unclear).

In the scarce literature on online FOI some thoughts emerge that, as with FOI generally, journalists were not as prolific users as expected, particularly of those sites (such as Alaveteli) that publish the entire exchange online, for fear of losing a scoop (Christensen, 2012; Ellis, 2010). Whether responses are made public or not, the leak culture and lengthy response period were still factors in journalists' perceptions of FOI online. In addition, there is no guarantee an FOI query by a journalist will have any better response than one from a citizen – Menapace et al (2013) found that out of 300 emails sent to Italian government departments, journalists (who identify themselves as such) receive a higher proportion of 'mute silence' (70 per cent) to general users (63 per cent). Fumega (2014) finds that between June 2003 and February 2014, media comprise only 12 per cent of InfoMex users (as opposed to 46 per cent academics; 26 per cent companies; and 16 per cent government employees). This figure drops steeply to 0.05 per cent if the majority categories of unreported and 'other' are added. In Brazil, journalists comprise 1.27 per cent of e-SIC requesters since site implementation in 2012 (Fumega, 2014). However, again, we should bear in mind there may be unwillingness/uncertainty in self-reporting as a journalist.

Methodology

Between May and September 2014, we conducted 27 interviews with FOI site implementers (20 Alaveteli-based, 6 based on other software as a control, and one starting in Liberia where the platform was undecided).[3] Although we collected broad statistics on requests and responses (below), we adopted a qualitative approach to interviews (the 'how' rather than the 'how many' approach) which were recorded with permission, transcribed, loaded into a qualitative software analysis tool and analysed.

Findings

On the one hand, we found a lot of support for journalists in our research. Six out of 27 sites were hosted by journalistic organisations (Germany, Hungary, Switzerland, both iFOIA and MuckRock in the United States, and Ukraine). Two of the most used Alaveteli-based websites are hosted by media organisations (Ukraine, Hungary). Four out of the six non-Alaveteli instances are journalist focussed (Switzerland, Germany, iFOIA and MuckRock in the USA). Those organisations *by* journalists for journalists seem to be more successful (success being defined as number of requests). Not all sites kept statistics, but we were provided with the following in September 2014:

Figure 3: FOI online requests and responses September 2014

FOI website homepage	Requests using site	Number successful	Number un-successful	Number un-answered	Country
https://www.whatdotheyknow.com	228,167	138,960	36,841	Not recorded	UK
http://www.opendata.ge	20,400	8,500	1,600	3,400	Georgia
https://fragdenstaat.de	7,269	3,233	1,064	1,274	Germany
http://kimittud.org	3,037	1,305	Not recorded	965	Hungary
https://dostup.pravda.com.ua/	2,109	637	159	1,304	Ukraine
https://fyi.org.nz	1,898	1,036	340	405	NZ
http://www.tuderechoasaber.es	1,531	226	170	864	Spain
http://www.asktheeu.org	1,462	645	85	474	EU
https://www.righttoknow.org.au/	718	190	348	149	Australia
http://daznamosvi.rs/sr	62	16	1	38	Serbia
http://jeveuxsavoir.org	30	15	13	2	Canada/ Québec

We can see that the most used sites are WhatDoTheyKnow in the UK, followed by two non-Alaveteli sites, and then two Alaveteli sites started by journalism organisations. Similarly, TuDerechoaSaber's own study finds that greatest use of Alaveteli sites in 2013 was topped by the UK's WhatDoTheyKnow (77,281 requests), followed by Hungary (1,486) (the Ukrainian site had not started by then), the European Union (844), New Zealand (685), Spain (654), Czech Republic (551), Australia (460), Brazil (283),

Uruguay (144), and Tunisia (117) (TuDerechoaSaber, 2014). A major quantitative drawback was that we were unable to ascertain what proportion of users were journalists as none of the implementers kept details of users.

Qualitatively, the benefits for journalists are seen as being able to manage and track numerous requests (according to Emily Grannis, iFOIA; the Czech Alaveteli) as well as being able to cite the original source document (mentioned by Martin Stoll, Switzerland). Non-journalist Alaveteli sites have tried but not had success establishing partnerships with journalists – mentioned by the Kosovo site with the Balkans Investigative Reporting Network (BIRN), TuDerechoaSaber in Spain, JeVeuxSavoir in Québec and others. Martin Stoll from Switzerland does talk of FOI search fees halved for journalists, perhaps encouraging use. Yet there appears to be a 'not invented here' problem that might explain why FOI platforms run by journalist outfits (eg in Hungary and Ukraine) are more successful than those which are not.

As in the literature review, our findings illustrated the limiting factors of a lengthy response period, a prevailing 'leak' culture in general and losing a competitive scoop. On the time factor, Elena Ignatova (Macedonia) comments: 'the problem is that if they send a written request, the institution in question can answer the request in 30 days which is a long time for journalists.' Gabi Razzano from South Africa states 'as much like to think we [have investigative journalists], we don't; most of them are doing hourly news releases on stuff they see on Twitter.' Stefan from the German FragdenStaat feels 'they don't use FOI law, because it's a bit cumbersome here - you have to wait for a month and it can cost money.'

Second, the 'leak culture': Stefan from Germany says 'the press officer is probably friends with them anyway'. Martin Stoll finds in Switzerland 'decision makers and journalists can sit at a coffee table and they exchange information and so a confrontational request of information is not common. It would be as asking for war. So as a journalist you have to decide do you want to give up the peace [and be independent] or not'. For David Cabo from TuDerechoaSaber:

> *'Basically, investigative journalism doesn't exist in Spain but when it does exist it's based on leaks so the whole ecosystem of politicians and journalists is leaks.... In that environment it's hard to change that method and start using FOI because you're not used to it. And you don't see the point because you can get the answer much quicker just calling your contact.'*

In some cases, it may be a question of bribery to get information, as mentioned by Teemu Ropponen in Liberia. David and Eva from TuDerechoaSaber recount an experience of trying to get congress expenditure for months through FOI, and how easy it was for journalists to obtain it just before they went on air to discuss it.

The particular benefit of online FOI and Alaveteli functionality is the auditing and transparency of the request and response process, yet: 'we discussed this with journalists and they don't want to use JeVeuxSavoir because they want to keep their scoop' (Québec) and 'even like my friends, journalists … say: "ya, come on but everybody will see the reply, and I want to have some of this unique information for me to write an article",' (Alisa Ruban, Ukraine). Michael Morisy of MuckRock voices similar feedback early on and Martin Stoll has evidence in the sense that when Oeffentlichkeitsgesetz moved from visible to closed requests in 2011, the number of requests doubled. A site can effectively be seen as a *competitor* to journalists then rather than a tool (Andrea Menapace, Italy).

Analysis: What is the role of FOI sites for journalists?

A possibility for Alaveteli is for it to follow a semi-closed or closed model similar to MuckRock or Oeffentlichkeitsgesetz. Darko from Bosnia suggests building 'features that would hold the documents for certain periods so that they get their article at the press' (Darko, Bosnia and Herzegovina). However, this would go against the clear 'access to all, publish all' transparency engineering of Alaveteli, be-knighting a particular group rather than seeking as wide a user base as possible. There may be a possibility that most users, whether journalists or not may want to keep their request private, and therefore classify themselves as journalists if there are no checks in place. But how would such checks be introduced, and how should a 'journalist' be defined?

Stefan from Germany counters Darko's suggestion above: 'I expected more journalists to use [FragdenStaat] when we started up, because we also offer the possibility to make the request non-public in the beginning and just publish it later at a later stage. So it could be more attractive for journalists because they can make requests, get the information about a story and then publish a request together with their story. But this hasn't manifested that strongly'.

A different perspective from Bosnia is that there is actually an advantage for journalists to file as 'normal citizens' (Darko Brkan, Bosnia and Herzegovina) - a view reflected in the Italian study mentioned above where journalists received 70 per cent of mute silence, as opposed to the public at 63 per cent (Menapace, 2013). However, most site implementers felt that requests that leveraged the standing, influence – and capacity to take legal action – of CSOs or media organisations were more likely to receive an answer.

Finally, FOI sites could be encouraged for journalists as repositories of requests and responses, for trend analysis and awareness raising – emerging uses mentioned specifically in Georgia, Macedonia and Ukraine. In Québec, Stéphane says the site was encouraged by an ex-journalist minister because even though he knew and understood that journalists would not use JeVeuxSavoir, he understood that using JeVeuxSavoir as a kind of champion to improve the FOI law would help improve the law. Similarly, in South Africa Gabi notes: 'even though media aren't the biggest users they do significantly use the act for headline, profile-grabbing stuff and that's a win. So a big part of our focus is engaging and getting buy in from our media partners, getting them to use it and promote it in their work.'

Limitations, conclusions, future directions

Why should journalists use FOI sites at all? As long as issues are being brought to attention, does the process matter? In some ways, the issue is not just about government transparency but journalistic transparency – that, as Stefan Wehrmeyer from Fragdenstaat says, the process of journalism, citing sources and methods is tightened up. Yet there is also increasing evidence of improvement in the journalistic practices of publishing source documents, whether obtained through FOI or leaks: the UK expenses scandal above is as much a story of the use of FOI as it is of innovation in journalistic practice and support technologies (see Daniel, 2010 and ProPublica amongst others). Further, the critical role journalists play is in advocating for an opening up the FOI process, irrespective of whether they use the sites or not – they can raise FOI awareness and create a 'culture of asking'. In a co-produced, 'we-government' world, the more awareness there is of ways to hold government accountable, the better, and online sites facilitate the process. Methodologically, there are limitations to our research – we focussed on implementer views but in future would like to interview users and non-users (including journalists), and examine how FOI online works by comparison with offline channels. However, our clear finding from this research is that there is such a thing as 'too much transparency' for journalists when it comes to FOI sites.

Notes

[1] https://www.mysociety.org is a UK-based organization, well-known within a field loosely defined as "civic tech". In addition to its FOI work, other projects include TheyWorkForYou, WriteToThem, FixMyStreet and FixMyTransport – see https://www.mysociety.org/projects.

[2] The webiste URL is https://www.mysociety.org/projects/freedom-of-information/alaveteli/

[3] We did want to talk to implementers of e-SIC, InfoMex, and the Honduran and Indian RTI sites but were unsuccessful at initial attempts

References

Christensen, Nic (2012) 'Website to open freedom of information floodgates' *The Australian.* [online] available at https://global-factiva-com.gate3.library.lse.ac.uk/aa/?ref=AUSTLN0020121209e8ca00086&pp=1&fcpil=en&napc=S&sa_from= accessed July 16, 2014

Daniel, Anna (2010) '*The Guardian* reportage of the UK MP expenses scandal: a case of computational journalism' Communications Policy & Research Forum, 15-16 November, 2010, Sydney [online] available at http://eprints.qut.edu.au/38701/2/38701.pdf accessed October 2, 2014

Dunion, Kevin (2011) 'Viewpoint: In Defence of Freedom of Information' *Information Polity*, 16/2, pp 93–96

Ellis, Justin (2010) 'MuckRock makes FOIA requests easy, but will reporters use it?' Nieman Journalism Lab available at http://www.niemanlab.org/2010/10/muckrock-makes-foia-requests-easy-but-will-reporters-use-it/ accessed July 17, 2014

Fumega, S. (2014). *El uso de las tecnologías de información y comunicación para la implementación de leyes de acceso a la información pública*. World Bank/RTA. [online] available at http://redrta.cplt.cl/_public/public/folder_attachment/55/1a/1a3b_6f48.pdf accessed October 2, 2014

Hayes, Jeremey (2009) *Working Paper: A Shock To The System: Journalism, Government and the Freedom of Information Act 2000*. University of Oxford Reuters Institute for the Study of Journalism available at https://reutersinstitute.politics.ox.ac.uk/sites/default/files/A%20Shock%20to%20the%20System.pdf accessed 22 October, 2014

Hazell, Robert, Worthy, Benjamin and Glover, Mark (2010) *The impact of the Freedom of Information Act on central government in the UK: does freedom of information work?*. London: Palgrave Macmillan

Menapace, Andrea, Napolitano, Antonella, Romeo, Guido, Simone, Angela, Darbishire, Helen and Anderica, Victoria (2013) 'Access to information in Italy: Results and recommendations from first national monitoring'

Michener, Greg and Worthy, Benjamin (2013) 'From Fishing to Experimentation: Transparency as Information-Gathering A Typology and Framework for Analysis' *Third Global Conference on Transparency Research, Paris, October 24-26, 2013*

Moudgil, Manu (2011) 'A frenzied media fails to use the RTI Act. The Hoot: Watching the media in the subcontinent' available at http://thehoot.org/web/AfrenziedmediafailstousetheRTIAct/5308-1-1-33-true.html accessed 22 October, 2014

Paterson, Moira (2008) 'The media and access to government-held information in a democracy' *Oxford University Commonwealth Law Journal*, 8/1, pp 3–24

Roberts, Alasdair (2010) 'A Great and Revolutionary Law? The First Four Years of India's Right to Information Act' *Public Administration Review*, 70/6, pp 925–933

Tryhorn, Chris (2009) 'Telegraph paid £110,000 for MPs' expenses data' *The Guardian* available at http://www.theguardian.com/media/2009/sep/25/telegraph-paid-11000-mps-expenses accessed 23 September, 2014

TuDerechoaSaber (2014) 'Silencio masivo de las instituciones en el año de la transparencia: Informe Tuderechoasaber.es 2013' Madrid: Civio. [online] available at http://blog.tuderechoasaber.es/informe2013 accessed 22 October, 2014

Worthy, Benjamin and Hazell, Robert (2013) 'The Impact of the Freedom of Information Act in the UK' in Nigel Bowles, James T Hamilton, David Levy (eds.) *Transparency in Politics and the Media: Accountability and Open Government*, London: L.B. Tauris, pp. 31-45

Worthy, Benjamin (2012) 'Book review: Freedom of Information in Scotland in Practice' *Information Polity*, 17/2 pp 197–199

Acknowledgments
This paper draws on research funded by mySociety on the impact of online FOI sites. Thanks to Tom Steinberg, Paul Lenz and all the mySociety team for their generous support. Thanks also to Ben Worthy for the detailed feedback.

Note on the contributor

Savita Bailur is a researcher (mySociety, World Bank, Commonwealth Secretariat, USAID, and Panos) and has taught at Manchester University and London School of Economics. She has a PhD and MSc from LSE and several publications, most recently *Closing the Feedback Loop: Can Technology Bridge the Accountability Gap?* (World Bank, 2014).

Tom Longley is a human rights and technology consultant with experience in Kosovo, Sierra Leone, Bangladesh, Cambodia, Zimbabwe and others. He consults for Tactical Technology Collective, Global Witness and Open Society Foundations. Tom most recently wrote *Deadly Environment* (Global Witness, 2014)

Section 2:
10 years of FOI in the UK

John Mair

The publication of this seminal collection of essays marks the 10th anniversary of the implementation on the UK FOI Act in 2005. Was it really 'my biggest mistake' as Tony Blair famously claimed or has it led to a journalistic nirvana, transparency and freedom? The report card on the first decade is mixed-some good, some bad, some simply indifferent.

One of the bigger users of the FOI Act, not surprisingly, has been the biggest news organisation in the country – the BBC. Using FOI requests big and small the corporation has been able to find and copper bottom scores, nay hundreds of stories at a local and national level through skilful use of the Act. Martin Rosenbaum is 'Mr BBC FOI' – the go-to man on freedom of information in Broadcasting House. In 'Lessons from the front line: The BBC's experiences of using FOI' he reports on his extensive experience of using FOI and how public authorities have responded, drawing out lessons for media requesters on what works and what doesn't. His advice to ingénues: prepare.

> 'FOI is about accessing material that is actually held by a public authority (and not information that you think they should collate but they don't, or opinions that haven't been written down, or possible responses to hypothetical situations). Successful requesters need to adopt a 'recorded information' frame of mind, focussing on what material would actually be stored in the authority's information system.'

Amanda Geary Pate of the University of the West of Scotland is, or was, more sceptical about the efficacy of the Act In 'The Preliminary Impact of the Freedom of Information Act on the UK Press: the dawn of a new era of newsgathering?' she analyses how, despite the initial scepticism about how 'watered down' the Act was, some journalists have since discovered it was an innovative newsgathering tool:

'The very existence of the Act and the debates it provoked also served to remind journalists of their 'watchdog' role (i.e. of providing checks on a range of public authorities). The evidence from this period showed that there were journalists who were adventurous enough to try to test the Act as an innovative newsgathering tool and, as a result, many were realising its potential and beginning to generate some interesting home-grown exclusives.'

What about when the boot is on the other foot? What is the perspective of those whose professional job it is, day in and day out, to answer FOI requests from the public and from journalists. Are they jumping for joy after a decade? Not exactly. In 'Fishing expeditions or serious investigations? The impact of media Freedom of Information Act requests on local government' Lynn Wyeth of Leicester City Council examines the use of the Freedom of Information Act in British local government by the media and concludes:

'Are journalists making the best use of FOI to hold local government to account? From the anodyne headlines we are still seeing on a weekly basis, it would appear journalists are still not getting the best use from the Act. There is minimal evidence of detailed investigative journalism into local authorities, and there is a considerable lack of originality on subject matter. Such stories are hardly likely to win the Pulitzer Prize for investigative reporting.'

Alan Geere is a well-practiced journalist, newspaper executive and journalism educator. He has been round several tracks several times, and in 'The lazy local journalist's guide to a scoop: FOI it!' he simply reads the papers and assesses the impact of the Freedom of Information Act on local newspaper journalism with examples and a report card story by story. He concludes hacks in the regions have yet to use the Act to its full potential, and in many cases they don't even bother to use it at all. Too often if in doubt FOI It! His advice? More hard work and more fun:

'I'm afraid the FOI report card signs off with "Could Do Better". Too many FOI stories simply regurgitate the facts of the case, and make little attempt to add context or comment. Remember, an FOI is not necessarily a story in itself. It needs work from the journalist to gather more information and opinion to make a rounded story…. Have more fun: I know we are all weary of the "biscuits at the council meeting" style FOI, but why not make a nuisance of yourself? Mine's a Rich Tea.'

Paul Francis is still on the local journalism front line. He is the political editor of the vibrant and successful Kent Messenger Group of newspapers. In "Churnalism' and FOI in local UK newspapers' Francis' position is diametrically opposed to that of Geere. His conclusion:

'Journalists face many challenges in a fast-changing environment in which the 24-hour news agenda often places a premium on breaking stories before anything else any anybody else. FOI is in many ways antithetical to this but considered and intelligent use often produces greater rewards. The challenge, inevitably, is not just finding the right balance

but using FOI in a way that properly holds councils and other public bodies to account for decisions that directly impact on the lives of people they are there to serve.'

Alice Ross, latterly of the Bureau for Investigative Journalism and now at *The Times*, is a digger by training and profession and she never takes no for an answer. In 'Abusing power? Investigating citizen-stripping using FOI' she traces the use of FOI in probing the use (and potential abuse) of anti-terrorism powers and citizen-stripping by the British Government, and uncovers concerns about the arbitrary and unscrutinised nature of this executive power. Her and the Bureau's persistence led to them being labelled 'vexatious' and denied access to information.

> *'Freedom of information requests have been a vital tool in revealing the extent of the Government's use of this secretive power. But it has not proven as straightforward as the Act would suggest: instead, the BIJ has been forced to tread carefully to avoid having this flow of information cut off for the months or even years it could take to appeal the decision to the Information Commissioner. In the absence of official transparency, this negotiated disclosure has helped give the public a sense of the scale of the issue.'*

Tim Crook comes at most journalism issues from the Left Field. His is always an unusual insight in these 'hackademic' tomes. He does not disappoint in this volume. In 'The sealed and emptying chambers of Britain's intelligence history: Why the absolute exception for security sensitive matters is a present and continuing injustice' Crook, of Goldsmiths' College London, re-tells the fascinating tale of Alexander Wilson, the Secret Service spy who wrote novels in his spare time but some of the papers on him are redacted or unavailable for 'national security reasons'. These need reform in his view:

'I would argue that no security body should choke off common law rights and rights to natural justice in the context of this case. Alexander Wilson's encoding of espionage in published novels and his engagements with British intelligence bodies have generated significant public interest controversies. More importantly these events of more than 70 years ago have had a profound and catastrophic impact on the lives of his wives and children and further descendants. There is no doubt that a common law and natural justice argument can be made for the fullest disclosure of all relevant records held about him in the sphere of state intelligence.'

The United Kingdom, like it or not, has been a collection of four devolved nations for the past 15 years. Scotland has been in the van of this devolution and has in any case had its own legal system for more than 300 years. So too its own FOI Act which is also celebrating a decade of implementation. In 'From booze to trews: Perspectives on journalists' use of Freedom of Information in Scotland' Julian Calvert of Glasgow Caledonian University goes directly to the source and talks to Scottish journalists about their experiences of using the Scottish FOI Act. Important differences from the Westminster Act seem to put the media in Scotland at a relative advantage to their counterparts down south. They start from a high point – their initial bulls eye was a good one:

> *"If you've ever tried to impress a guest with a bottle of fine wine, or punished another with a glass of gut rot, you are not alone," was the innocuous first paragraph of a story by Tom Gordon in the Herald on 5 February, 2005. There was more to this than first appeared however; using the Freedom of Information (Scotland) Act which had come into force the previous month, Gordon had discovered the cost and details of all wine served by First Minister Jack McConnell in receptions at Bute House in Edinburgh. "Foreign dignitaries and banking moguls" were served Barolo or Mersault costing £25 per bottle, while the cheapest wine, a white Rioja costing less than £5, had been served to reporters the previous Christmas. The Herald's wine critic was deployed to describe the Rioja as "really pretty ropey".'*

Finally, to another devolved nation, Northern Ireland. Colm Murphy of the University of Ulster scores the report card there in 'FOI in Northern Ireland: Wide ranging FOI requests, sent in by lazy journalists, who will not do any work!' Murphy reports that despite Northern Ireland's journalists using FOI to force the first major UK resignation of a Government minister, Ian Paisley Jnr in 2008, its use has been negligible with reporters increasingly reliant on official releases and other sources:

> *While the Northern Ireland media have shifted their techniques and sources with the evolving political process in the last decade, FOI has not played a role in it. Instead information released by the Executive as part of its public relations has grown in use by journalists. By 2013 it was the source for almost half of all Executive related stories. Political sources had fallen by almost two thirds to just over 10 per cent during the same period.... History, intimidation, resources and often a lack of expertise has hindered FOI's usage.'*

So 10 years on the report card is a Curate's Egg. When used skilfully, and with some journalistic nous and background knowledge, freedom of information requests can reveal a goldmine or a sewer. When dashed off unthinkingly and simply to fill space on slow news days, it is a waste of everybody's time: public body, journalists and worst of all readers. Freedom fighting or lazy journalism – you decide.

Lessons from the front line: The BBC's experiences of using FOI

Veteran BBC journalist and producer *Martin Rosenbaum* reports on his extensive experience of using FOI and how public authorities have responded, drawing out lessons for media requesters on what works and what doesn't

Introduction

Freedom of information can be a valuable tool for journalists, but subject to certain constraints that can make it frustrating. It is often slow and cumbersome, and sometimes doesn't work at all. Yet it does have a unique power to obtain certain material that otherwise could not be squeezed out of reluctant public authorities. My experience of using freedom of information journalistically runs throughout the 10-year period that the law has been in force since January 2005. During this time I've trained hundreds of BBC journalists in using FOI, given advice to many on drafting requests or dealing with replies, blogged on the subject for the BBC News website, and working with a researcher have obtained material via FOI which has been used in hundreds of BBC news stories on TV, radio and online, nationally and locally. (Within the BBC this journalistic usage of FOI is kept entirely separate from the corporate function of responding to requests that come into the BBC as a public organisation). In this decade of FOI I've seen how the media's practical use of the system has developed and become more focussed, and how the public sector has reacted. It's a varied story, given that over 100,000 public bodies are subject to the legislation, but some common themes emerge. This chapter is largely based on my own personal experience.

FOI – the BBC's experience

The stories obtained by the BBC using FOI since 2005 have covered a wide range of topics, showing how far the law reaches into the operations of the public sector (in contrast to some other countries). In the health area, this has included revelations about delays in ambulance response and handover times, staff shortages in A&E departments, regional disparities in the prescription of various medicines, and backlogs in dealing with complaints about nurses. Police-related stories have included the failure of a knife amnesty to cut knife crime, the ageing of the police force, the cost of policing football games, and the extent to which forces boost their detection rates by getting offenders to confess to other crimes. Military stories have included drug taking by soldiers and misconduct on submarines. In the environment field, we've revealed which public buildings had the worst record for energy efficiency. In transport, which makes of cars are most likely to fail MOT tests. In education, how many councils wouldn't meet the government's plans on infant school meals. Then there's the Home Office failing to collect fines imposed on companies employing illegal workers, and how the Foreign Office weakened its safety advice on travel in Thailand partly for commercial reasons. Other stories have included how England tried to use royal links with the Qataris to win the hosting of the World Cup, how officials wrongly dismissed predictions about Eastern European immigration, and the identities of individuals who have turned down honours.

That's only a very small selection, but it's enough to show that FOI has been a very effective device for the BBC on the right topics. Some other FOI-based stories from the BBC have been collated on our website (BBC News, 2013). This provides a very good illustration of the range of FOI, featuring well more than 100 reports from across the UK and covering many different public services. Again, it's only a sample of our FOI journalism. Of course other media organisations have also produced a string of disclosures through FOI. Useful sites for keeping across examples of its wider journalistic use are those run by Trinity Mirror's David Higgerson (FOIFriday, 2014) and FOI Directory's Matt Burgess (FOI Directory, 2014).

One feature of many of these stories, whether BBC or non-BBC ones, is that they contain figures about various aspects of the operation of public services, data about ambulance times or numbers of complaints or staffing levels or energy efficiency ratings or details of public expenditure, and so on. FOI-based stories are often in some sense numerical in nature, possibly identifying the extent of an issue, exploring changes over time, comparing different localities, or collating local data to form a national picture. They may combine an overall assessment of the national situation with a regional focus on the 'best' or 'worst', 'highest' or 'lowest' areas. For the BBC, as a media outlet that combines national and local journalism, this can work particularly well. Recent examples from 2014 include our stories about instances of temporary closures of maternity units and rising numbers of parental fines for children's poor school attendance. Rarer (although still significant) are those stories which are based on quotes or extracts from documents, such as disclosures of internal discussion, records of meetings, exchanges of emails. Before FOI came into force, this was the kind of revelation that I think was widely anticipated – certainly hoped for by many journalists and feared by many officials (as indeed it still is, from my discussions with them). The reality has failed to live up to those hopes and fears.

The nature of what does or does not get disclosed is driven by the scheme of exemptions and the 'public interest' test. This has been at the heart of the UK FOI system, both in the law for England, Wales and Northern Ireland, and in the separate but similar Scottish law. Most exemptions allowing public authorities to withhold information are 'qualified', meaning that the material should be released unless it is against the public interest in all the circumstances of the case. This can be a vague and subjective test. The data commonly featuring in FOI stories generally has to be released because it is not relevant to any exemption or, if it is, it's difficult for authorities to argue that it's against the public interest to disclose it. Many public bodies are happy to accept this, although sometimes some are reluctant. Indeed, thanks to the drive for 'open data', more of such information is being published voluntarily, although not necessarily in a comprehensive or convenient manner.

Then there are some kinds of material where decisions by the Information Commissioner have set precedents that recalcitrant councils have effectively had to follow, for example with warnings about public health. After Bridgend Council was forced by the Commissioner in 2005 to release a food hygiene inspection report on a local hotel, it became clear that councils would have to disclose the results of such inspections. And a summary for most councils is now available as open data on the Food Standards Agency website (Food Standards Agency, 2014).

On the other hand, when it comes to written discussions or records of meetings, decisions taken by the Commissioner and the Information Rights Tribunal point in different directions, some towards openness and some against it. This is not surprising when they have to reflect 'all the circumstances of the case'. They are less significant as precedents (although there are some exceptions on specific legal points), and there is more scope for obstructive public authorities to determine that it is, in their opinion, against the public interest to release material that coincidentally it so happens might be embarrassing for them. Of course if they are later ordered to release it by the Commissioner or Tribunal, that may well be more embarrassing, but not all requesters have the persistence to take their cases to those levels.

The FOI disputes that have reached a Tribunal stage that I have been involved in have tended to concern this kind of material and varied in outcome. The Tribunal ordered the House of Lords Appointments Commission to give me further extracts from its minutes (although it turned out the additional material did not add to the story we had done using the Commission's earlier disclosures to me about it weakening its rules on giving peerages to party donors). In another case the Tribunal rejected my argument for access to briefing papers on government policy on aid to Rwanda. We also had a long-running dispute with the Cabinet Office over our request for documents given to Margaret Thatcher about the Hillsborough disaster, where we settled on a compromise prior to a Tribunal hearing. In the event the material was seen by another BBC journalist and then reported before it was formally released.

In short, under FOI it is often easier to get numbers than words, or at least with words the position is more unpredictable. This is a generalisation and there are circumstances that should clearly favour disclosure, such as when there is evidence of misconduct, and others that will clearly work against it, such as when the policy formulation process is still active. The different system covering environmental information under the Environmental Information Regulations also means it is easier to obtain the text of discussions with outside bodies on environmental matters. In some ways the most unpredictable area of all is how authorities treat requests for what they consider to be personal information. The awkward relationship between FOI and the Data Protection Act makes for a lack of consistency. As a requester it is often hard to assess in advance under what circumstances public authorities, or if comes to it, the Information Commissioner, would consider disclosing personal data to be processing information 'fairly' in terms of data protection, an even vaguer criterion than the public interest test under FOI.

Establishing the pattern

It took some time for the pattern of FOI disclosure to be established. In the first couple of years of FOI, it was unclear what kind of information was likely to be released. I certainly made requests then of a kind that I would avoid now as they would be pointless. I have also learned to write requests in more specific terms, rather than 'catch-all' phraseology that I tried to employ right at the beginning. This uncertainty about how FOI should work was also reflected in the behaviour of public authorities that varied greatly in how they interpreted the new legislation. Some were recalcitrant in adapting to the Act, whereas others I found surprisingly open.

One example of the latter was the Metropolitan Police, particularly what was once called its Special Branch (SB); the unit within the force that monitored what it regarded as subversion. They gave me access to historical papers, which showed how for years they had infiltrated the Anti-Apartheid Movement, which we reported in a radio documentary and online (Rosenbaum, 2005). I was even more surprised to obtain extracts from the Special Branch personal protection file of the former Prime Minister James Callaghan. These papers showed that Lord Callaghan felt his level of protection after leaving office was inadequate, as well as providing an amusing account of the 'embarrassing situation' when a Jehovah's Witness proselytising door-to-door managed to evade the security precautions at his home. However, this kind of access via FOI to old Special Branch documents is now much harder. The Metropolitan Police adopted a new, much more restrictive policy of arguing that SB work was so closely intertwined with the security agencies that SB records should share those agencies' absolute exemption from FOI. This stance was upheld in a decision by the Information Commissioner in 2011 (Information Commissioner's Office [FS50258193/2011]).

In contrast other public bodies have moved in the other direction, from obstructiveness to more openness. One example is the data held by the Vehicle and Operator Services Agency (VOSA), a Department for Transport agency which administered the MOT system, on MOT pass/fail rates for different car makes and models. In 2008 the BBC made an FOI request for these figures. I had first realised this information must be held in a centralised database when I'd renewed my car tax online. But VOSA told us that it would be against the public interest to release the details of pass/fail rates by make, because it would damage the commercial interests of certain vehicle manufacturers. This position struck me as perverse and obstructive. VOSA maintained this case when we complained to the Information Commissioner. But its argument was dismissed by the Commissioner, who ruled that VOSA should supply the information (Office of the Information Commissioner [FS50214210/2009]). VOSA then sent me the material in a 1,200-page PDF document, a rather inconvenient format. Nevertheless it contained the figures I wanted and we published comparative data for popular models. Examining the pass/fail rates showed that, for example, back in 2007 a three-year-old Renault Megane was nearly twice as likely to fail an MOT test as an equally old Ford Fiesta (BBC News, 2010). It took 18 months to extract this information from the agency, but after then VOSA (now merged into the Driver and Vehicle Standards Agency) released the same data voluntarily and regularly (data.gov.uk, 2014), enabling motoring websites to analyse it in detail (Harrison, 2014). We can now expect that this kind of practically useful statistical information will generally be made available to FOI requesters, barring unusual circumstances.

In the early phase of FOI, when asked what score out of 10 I would give to how the new law was operating, I tended to respond, 'about 5 on average – because it some cases it deserves 10 and in some case 0.' Now I'm more likely to say it should score 5 across the board, as the earlier initial extremes of enthusiastic openness and utter obstruction have largely settled down into a middling position.

Efficiency

The FOI performance of public bodies depends not only on their attitudes, but also on their organisational competence. This is very important in practice, to journalists as well as probably to most requesters. The information sought is often time sensitive. And if you're not going to get what you want, it's good to know soon. This has varied widely between authorities and over time. In my experience the Police were probably the best prepared part of the public sector in the initial period of FOI, but the efficiency of some forces (such as the Met) has declined badly since then. The Ministry of Defence was also comparatively prompt and reliable in the early years, whereas the Department of Health was chaotic. The DoH then went through a phase of being very competent and helpful, while the MoD's level of organisation deteriorated. If there is one public body that has been persistently inefficient and slow in my experience, it has to be the Cabinet Office. It is not surprising therefore that it has repeatedly been targeted for special monitoring of its FOI processes by the Information Commissioner's Office, due to its poor performance in handling FOI requests. The impression I have formed is that the variations in effectiveness are influenced both by the overall level of competence of the organisation involved and by the level of prioritisation and resources that it wishes to devote to FOI. Occasionally the incompetence of public authorities can work in favour of a journalist requester, notably when the authority has failed to redact information properly and it is still readable through certain means. The BBC has obtained stories in this way from time to time, such as a report on *The World at One* about how early drafts revealed that a critical National Audit Office report on NHS IT systems had been toned down.

Delay

The main practical problem faced by journalists during much of the first decade of FOI has been delay. A huge backlog of cases built up in the Information Commissioner's Office, which meant that it was soon taking over a year for many complaints to be decided – especially for the trickier issues that media requests often involved. In the worst example I faced, the ICO took four years and three months to consider the case before then ruling in my favour. As the Cabinet Office then appealed fruitlessly to the Tribunal (Information Tribunal [EA/2010/0031]), it took altogether more than five and a half years for me to receive the information I asked for – the minutes of the 1986 Cabinet meeting at which Michael Heseltine had dramatically resigned as Defence Secretary over the Westland affair (gov.uk, 2010).

The enormous delays at the ICO also gave public authorities an incentive to procrastinate themselves – both because it became a simple but effective technique of postponing any embarrassing revelations (possibly until they were no longer relevant), and also because the ICO lacked credibility in criticising the laggard's pace of authorities' decision-making. However matters improved significantly since Christopher Graham became the Commissioner in 2009 and focussed effectively on tackling the backlog. Nevertheless there is still a lot of delay in the system. While authorities are legally meant to reply to requests within 20 working days, there is no legal time limit on their extending this period to assess the public interest test, nor on how long they take to consider an internal review (although the rules are different for environmental information). There is guidance from the Commissioner, but this may be ignored. Just recently, in August 2014, I received from the Treasury a rejection at internal review stage relating to an FOI request I had made 21 months earlier in November 2012. We are still often very far from the legislative requirement that FOI requests should be handled 'promptly' (Freedom of Information Act 2000, Section 10).

Another major practical problem is the issue of assessing what quantity of information can feasibly be obtained within the cost limits. This is often a very difficult question for requesters who are outside an organisation and unfamiliar with its records management systems. One positive change I have seen over the years is the willingness of some authorities to engage in constructive discussion about this. It is in line with their legal duty to provide 'advice and assistance' to requesters. In the early phase of FOI this rarely happened, but ICO decisions have encouraged authorities to take the duty seriously and some have responded well. In the long run it is sensible for all parties, and it saves everyone time and trouble when it's possible for the requester to have a direct conversation with someone who understands how the information is organised.

Lessons learned

The constraints on freedom of information mean that for many daily journalists, FOI has made little if any difference to their working lives. But for those who work to longer timescales, and approach the task of requesting with careful phraseology, with interesting but practical ideas as to what to ask for, and persistence when necessary, it can be a valuable addition to the journalistic toolbox. And in the 10 years of its existence, it has produced many good stories in the public interest, both for us and for other media outlets. So based on my experience, what are the key lessons I've learnt about how journalists should use FOI effectively?

1. FOI is about accessing material that is actually held by a public authority (and not information that you think they should collate but they don't, or opinions that haven't been written down, or possible responses to hypothetical situations). Successful requesters need to adopt a 'recorded information' frame of mind, focussing on what material would actually be stored in the authority's information system. A copy of a blank form can be a useful guide to the categories of data an authority collects for a particular purpose.

2. Don't rush into making FOI requests. Check what information is already published, especially now that more public data is increasingly being proactively released. And if the material you want isn't already out there, a call to the press office might get it more quickly than a formal FOI request would.

3. Be specific. It's crucial to think carefully and rigorously about the phrasing of a request to ensure it covers what is wanted, exactly and unambiguously. Try to use the jargon or phraseology that the authority itself employs to refer to the information concerned.

4. Given the delays that can be involved, bear in mind that FOI is only of benefit for material that would still be of practical use in a few weeks or even months.

5. Before sending a 'round robin' request to a large number of authorities, it is often worth sending a 'pilot' to a few of them to check the questions are sensibly phrased and effective.

6. Make full use of the legal right (under Section 16 of the FOI Act) to advice and assistance from the public body on the best way to make a request (for example, on how to narrow a request to bring it under the cost limit). In practice, some FOI officers will be more helpful than others.

7. Build relationships with FOI officers. Don't shoot the messenger when you get an unwelcome answer. Think of FOI officers not as putting up obstacles, but as providing a pathway to the material wanted. Sometimes they end up arguing the requester's case within the authority to reluctant colleagues - so help them to do that.

References

BBC News (2010) 'Ford leads in MOT failures as figures are revealed' in *BBC News*, available at http://news.bbc.co.uk/1/hi/business/8456116.stm, accessed 13 September, 2014

BBC News (2013) *Freedom of Information Reports*. Available at http://www.bbc.com/news/uk-politics-21768148, accessed 13 September, 2014

Burgess, Matt (2014) *FOI Directory* blog. Available at http://foidirectory.co.uk, accessed 13 September, 2014

Data.gov.uk (2014) 'Anonymised MOT tests and results,' available at http://data.gov.uk/dataset/anonymised_mot_test, accessed 13 September, 2014

Food Standards Agency (2014) *Food Hygiene Ratings*. Available at http://ratings.food.gov.uk, accessed September 13, 2014

Gov.uk (2010) 'Westland Cabinet minute: freedom of information release,' available at https://www.gov.uk/government/publications/westland-cabinet-minute-freedom-of-information-release, accessed 13 September, 2014

Government of the United Kingdom (2000) *Freedom of Information Act 2000*. London: Stationary Office

Harrison, Dan (2014) 'The MOT files, the story behind the data,' available at http://good-garage-guide.honestjohn.co.uk/mot-data-the-mot-files/the-mot-files-the-story-behind-our-mot-data/, accessed 13 September, 2014

Higgerson, David (2014) *FOI Friday* blog. Available at https://davidhiggerson.wordpress.com/tag/foi-friday/, accessed 13 September 2014

Information Tribunal (2010) 'The Cabinet Office v The Information Commissioner' [EA/2010/0031] 31 August, 2010, available at https://www.gov.uk/government/uploads/system/uploads/attachment_data/file/61133/ic-westland-decision.pdf, accessed 13 September, 2014

Office of the Information Commissioner (2009) Decision Notice [FS50214210/2009] 3 December, 2009. Available at http://ico.org.uk/~/media/documents/decisionnotices/2009/FS_50214210.ashx, accessed 13 September, 2014

Office of the Information Commissioner (2011) Decision Notice [FS50258193/2011] 14 March, 2011. Available at http://ico.org.uk/~/media/documents/decisionnotices/2011/fs_50258193.ashx, accessed 13 September, 2014

Rosenbaum, Martin (2005) 'Tracking the anti-apartheid groups' in *BBC News*, available at http://news.bbc.co.uk/1/hi/uk_politics/4285964.stm, accessed 13 September, 2014

Note on the contributor

Martin Rosenbaum, an Executive Producer with BBC Political Programmes, has been BBC News's FOI specialist since the legislation took effect in 2005. He advises and trains BBC journalists on using the law, has produced documentaries for Radio 4 and the World Service on FOI, and blogs for the BBC website on the topic. He has addressed national and international media conferences about journalism and access to information. In 2004 he held a Reuters Fellowship at Oxford University, when he researched how journalists in Ireland and Sweden used FOI. He can be contacted at martin.rosenbaum@bbc.co.uk or via Twitter @rosenbaum6.

The preliminary impact of the Freedom of Information Act on the UK Press: the dawn of a new era of newsgathering?

FOI was initially welcomed by the British press, but the legislation was heavily criticised as 'watered down' by the time it made it into law. Despite this, some journalists discovered the Act was an innovative newsgathering tool, writes *Amanda Geary Pate*

Introduction

Prior to the Freedom of Information Act (FOI) coming into force on 1 January, 2005, much was made by professional bodies, unions and campaigners about the opportunities the new legislation would potentially offer journalists. There was anticipation that it would mark the start of a new era in open government that could have a positive impact on newsgathering opportunities and potentially reinvigorate investigative journalism. Equally there were reservations about the new legislation set against a backdrop of speculation among public authorities about how the Act might be used and how they should prepare themselves in readiness. There were also doubts about the extent to which FOI was going to influence newsgathering practices, as well as how much greater access to information journalists would realistically gain. This chapter provides a historical perspective of the initial impact of FOI on journalism through an examination of speculation by the profession about its effect and also on some of the early experiences of the profession in the period immediately after it came into force.

Anticipation of FOI by the UK Press

The issue of open government had been a hot topic for decades (Oliver, 2003) and despite the debate around the issue in the first few years of the 21st Century, many political scientists still regarded the UK as a 'secretive society' (Austin, 2000: 319). There was a long history of discussion around open government and access to information – both by the press and the general public in the UK. Furthermore, some saw it as a 'human right' that dated back to the UN General Assembly resolution of 1946 (Birkinshaw, 2010). However, in practice journalists found themselves with limited tools for accessing information about central government in particular. Meanwhile at local government level, journalists had greater access to information due to the fact it fell outside the jurisdiction of the Official Secrets Act 1911 (Oliver, 2003; Birkinshaw, 2010). Legislation including the Local Government Act 1933, the Public Bodies (Admission to Meetings) Act 1960, and the Local Government (Access to Information) Act 1985, gave the public – and therefore the press – rights of access to council papers and meetings. The Act therefore was set to supplement several existing laws rather than replace them and this was seen as particularly advantageous by those working at the grassroots of journalism – on local and regional newspapers.

The ability of journalists to access information is a key part of their job and it was clear from an early stage that the lengthy nature of FOIA requests i.e. that it would potentially take 20 working days to elicit a response (Welsh and Greenwood, 2001) put it at risk of being at odds to the time pressures facing most journalists, particularly those covering news. However it was apparent that it had great potential to be a useful newsgathering tool for journalists who were forward-thinking in their approach to generating stories and moreover to gain more exclusives and to encourage investigative journalism.

Debate about FOI within journalism

In the period leading up to the Freedom of Information Act coming into force there was heightened interest in the mainstream media and in the profession's trade press about the issue. From the perspective of journalists, it was hoped that the Act would provide a new and valuable tool for assisting them in their newsgathering by improving their access to information, as well as their ability to gain hard facts and figures that had not been available previously. While in contrast, from the public authorities' point of view, the new law meant that procedures needed to be drawn up and measures put in place in order to deal with any FOIA requests – not only from the media but also from the public – and this led to concerns that the internal information handling systems of many public sector bodies would struggle (Jellinek, 2004).

Discussion over the legislation in the profession had been initiated by the publication of the FOI Bill in 1999. The National Union of Journalists (NUJ) was involved in the consultation about the pending legislation and as a result conducted interviews with a number of its members. Many of them were cynical of the Bill in terms of its potential to be of value to them and concerns raised concentrated on: the exemptions; the limited powers of the Information Commissioner; the extended time to respond to requests for information; and a philosophy that seemed to be at the heart of the legislation that those seeking access to information were viewed in a negative or suspicious light (NUJ, 1999). As a result, the union believed the draft Bill was a retreat from the proposals contained in the earlier White Paper *Your Right to Know* published in December 1997 (for a fuller discussion of the White Paper, see Benjamin Worthy, chapter 2). However, in the immediate run up to the implementation of the Act the NUJ helped to publicise its existence through the publication of several articles in its magazine *The Journalist* in a bid to raise awareness and understanding among its members. By this stage, it feared that journalists may not be ready to use it and the NUJ also raised concerns about 'hard-pressed reporters' having neither the time nor the skills to get into the business of making applications (Brooke, 2004).

The reservations held by the press about the Bill were not just discussed behind the scenes. Many of the national newspapers were quite open in their contempt for the Bill, producing headlines and leaders full of negative comment and referring to it through terminology such as: 'feeble'; 'toothless'; 'deeply flawed'; 'weasel words'; and 'disappointing' (NUJ, 1999). *The Guardian* newspaper had been involved in a campaign about the FOI Bill when it was going through Parliament in 1999 – it too did not feel it was strong enough. The newspaper had led the way by employing a reporter specifically to handle stories generated using FOI's predecessor the *Code of Practice on Access to Government Information*. Editor Alan Rusbridger described how *The Guardian* had been 'investigating and testing the plans for the FOI' and found 'in the run-up to the implementation of the Act, a dismaying catalogue of obstruction, ignorance, delay, and sometimes absolutely brazen contempt for the spirit of freedom of information' (Brooke, 2005: vi). There was also some concern in the industry when Lord Falconer told the Law for Journalists Conference in 2004 that questions asked under the Act would not be guaranteed as exclusive – therefore meaning that scoops could be ruined (Ponsford, 2004). This was alarming for many journalists as an ability to produce exclusives is often regarded as a measure of success. If the process of gaining a story using FOI was going to prove time-consuming due to the nature of the workings of the Act, it was feared that the fact any replies to their requests could be shared with other journalism outlets might put many journalists off using it altogether.

However despite the reservations held by the journalists themselves, several professional organisations strove to promote its use. One such example was the Newspaper Society, in its role representing regional and local newspapers in the UK. Santha Rasaiah, the society's Editorial and Regulatory Affairs Director – who was also on the Lord Chancellor's *Advisory Group on Implementation of the FOI Act* – stated that one of the most useful aspects of the legislation for journalists was that it was retrospective and therefore she encouraged them to use it (Press Gazette, 2005a). Although there were numerous efforts to promote awareness of the legislation among journalists, those who had worked to publicise it could only do a limited amount until it came into force. It would then be down to news organisations and journalists themselves to experiment with it as a newsgathering tool.

Preparing to act on the Act
Prior to the implementation of the legislation, there were some concerns about a lack of knowledge about how journalists could use the Act. These fears were buoyed by a view that the amount of legislation relevant to journalism had

increased tremendously in preceding years, for example with the introduction of the Human Rights Act and the Data Protection Act in 1998. Concerns had reached such an extent that there were suggestions that trainees might need to sit more law exams to ensure their legal knowledge was tested sufficiently (Press Gazette, 2005b). In order to support the pending legislative changes, key law texts studied by trainee journalists were adapted to equip them with knowledge about the background of the legislation, as well as the mechanics of it. The definitive law text *McNae's Essential Law for Journalists* addressed the Act shortly after it went through Parliament in 2000. Welsh and Greenwood (2001) outlined the workings of the Act but were also keen to relate the fact that it had specific potential for journalists with regards to newsgathering. In producing the latest edition of *McNae's*, Welsh and Greenwood (2001) had sought guidance from the *Campaign for Freedom of Information* (CFOI) in terms of specifically addressing its relevance to journalism.

A number of professional organisations including the Society of Editors and the NUJ ran training courses for journalists on FOI, as did several larger individual news organisations such as Trinity Mirror. The aim was to ensure that journalists working at all levels of the media were up to speed on how to apply the legislation and to increase wider understanding about its implications. A study of the use of FOI by journalists undertaken immediately after the legislation came into force showed that almost two-thirds of journalists (64.3 per cent) had received training or guidance on how to apply the legislation for newsgathering purposes during the first three months of 2005 (Geary Pate, 2005).

There were also a number of guides produced about the legislation that were promoted to journalists (Smith, 2004; Wadham, Griffiths and Rigby, 2001; and Brooke, 2005). Attention was given to recent examples where FOI would have been useful for journalists previously, for example whether it could have secured disclosure of what had been regarded as one of the most controversial government decisions of the time: that of the British Government joining the USA in invading Iraq in March 2003 (Bindman, 2004). Prior to the implementation of the Act, efforts by the media to investigate this issue had failed in leading to the publication of the full advice given by the then Attorney General Peter Goldsmith on the legality of the invasion. Indeed in January 2005 it became one of the most common FOI requests made to the Government but was rejected as it came under one of the exemptions of the Act i.e. that of legal privilege (eGovernment News, 2005). Journalists were eventually able to publish the full advice in April 2005, however whether this happened as a result of FOI or its timing was prompted by the imminent General Election remains unclear.

Early experiences of FOI
It was evident that there were plenty in the press who believed the Act could have some impact on the newsgathering activities of journalists, but how was it used initially and how successful were these early requests? It soon became

apparent that journalists were not only using FOI to investigate stories but were also reporting on their own attempts at using the Act to generate copy. During the first months of 2005, publications reported on their own experiences of the Act and it became newsworthy in its own right. A study by Wood (2005) revealed that between 1 January and 15 March, 2005, there were 391 stories about the Act in the national newspapers – spread across the qualities and tabloids – with 23 of these mentioning FOI in the headline; while a further 16 stories in regional and local newspapers referred to the Act in the headline.

The Independent was prominent in its publication of its early experiences and thoughts on FOI and dedicated three pages of an entire edition to the subject in February 2005. It assessed the first month of FOI and revealed that of 70 enquiries it had made, only 10 had been successful. Of the remaining enquiries, half were turned down and the remainder were still awaiting a reply. It used its editorial column to slate the Government for its efforts, as well as the legislation.

> *The worst fears about the Government's Freedom of Information Act have been confirmed. This newspaper, like many others in the media and in Parliament made requests for information to government departments immediately after the long-awaited Act came into force. ..... Today we publish the results of our requests; the results are thoroughly unsatisfactory and make a mockery of claims that the Freedom of Information Act has ushered in a new era in the relationship between the citizen and the state'* (Independent, 2005).

Several regional papers, including the *Bristol Evening Post*, the *Manchester Evening News* and the *Glasgow Evening Times*, also produced overarching reports that summarised their mixed experiences, which not only generated copy but also promoted awareness about the legislation.

FOI and newsgathering in practice

Several themes regularly emerged in reports about FOI in the UK press in the first few months of 2005. Common examples included: the use of FOI as a political tool in the run up to the general election; the Government's refusal to release the Attorney General's advice on the legality of the war in Iraq; the proactive release of information online as a result of requests for information; controversy in the media surrounding deleted and shredded material prior to January 2005; and the release of new health information, examples included MRSA rates and heart surgeons' performance (Wood, 2005). Journalists were therefore using the legislation to some extent and they were also keeping a watchful eye on how others were applying it.

Figures published for January 2005 showed that journalists had made a considerable number of specific requests to the UK Government, being responsible for around half of all the FOI enquiries – 2,000 out of more than 4,000 in total – during its first month (Number 10, 2005). While statistics covering the first quarter of 2005, demonstrated that journalists were responsible for 19 per cent of FOI requests to central government (compared to 31 per cent from individual citizens and 50 per cent from companies) and the press made 23 per cent of requests (compared to 52 per cent from the public and 25 per cent from companies) at local government level (APR Smartlogik, 2005).

In terms of specific publications, there were a number that stood out as being particularly proactive both at national and regional level. *The Guardian* newspaper had taken a pioneering role in its use of FOI and its requests covered a wide range of subjects. For example, it published a special report on the NHS in March 2005 as a result of a two-month long investigation that involved 36 FOI applications being made to NHS authorities simultaneously in a bid to extract data about the mortality rates of heart surgery patients (Boseley, Carvel and Evans, 2005). It also used FOI to generate light-hearted stories, such as the revelations contained in a British embassy report on the clash of cultures that occurred when 1980's pop group *Wham!* performed the first-ever Western pop concert in China in 1985 (Evans, 2005). Other FOI stories run by *The Guardian* related to a range of issues: Whitehall secrets; immigration; education; the miners' strike; and the environment. Regional newspapers also found they were able to put FOI to good use and used it to bring their readers more details of what was going on behind the scenes in local authorities. Journalists reported to the website *holdthefrontpage.co.uk* in February 2005 that newspapers found themselves empowered to uncover details for the first time on topics ranging from school admission policies, hospital waiting lists, restaurant hygiene inspection reports and repairs to council buildings. It also became apparent that some regional publications had put in place special procedures to encourage staff to use the Act, for example the *York Evening Press* set up a FOI task group that met fortnightly to discuss investigations that could provide opportunities for future stories (*HoldTheFrontPage*, 2005).

Early experiences of the Act among journalists had therefore been varied, although possibly it was only the triumphs and failures of the experiences (i.e. the good news and bad news stories) that made it to publication.

Conclusion

The Freedom of Information Act undeniably made an early impression upon the profession. Journalists – particularly those with some considerable experience – tend to be renowned as cynical but this was not shown to be the whole story when it came to the Act. There were those who demonstrated a level of caution in respect of the legislation, but there were also journalists who were curious and willing to be open-minded about its potential and to experiment with it. Possibly any enthusiasm for the legislation during this initial period can be seen partly due to the publicity given to the legislation by industry bodies and the trade press, as well as a result of the training that had been offered to many journalists. However the very existence of the Act and the debates it provoked also served to remind journalists of their 'watchdog' role (i.e. of providing checks on a range of public authorities). The evidence from this period showed that there were journalists who were adventurous enough to try to test the Act as an innovative newsgathering tool and, as a result, many were realising its potential and beginning to generate some interesting home-grown exclusives.

References

APR Smartlogik (2005) *FOI – A Satisfactory Answer*, available online at http://www.aprsmartlogik.com/company/news/item.php?page=1323, accessed on 30 May 2005

Austin, Rodney (2000) 'Freedom of Information: The Constitutional Impact' in Jowell, Jeffrey and Oliver, Dawn (eds) *The Changing Constitution*, Oxford: Oxford University Press, pp 319-371, 4th edn

Bindman, Geoffrey (2004) 'Freedom of what information?' in *British Journalism Review*, 15(6) pp. 53-58

Birkinshaw, Patrick (2010) *Freedom of Information: The Law, the Practice and the Ideal*, Cambridge: Cambridge University Press, 4th edn

Boseley, Sarah, Carvel, John and Evans, Rob (2005) 'Hospitals deny patients facts on death rates' in *the Guardian*, 16 March. Available online at http://society.guardian.co.uk/nhsperformance/story/0,8150,1438602,00.html, accessed 20 July 2005

Brooke, Heather (2004) 'Do you want to know a secret,' in *The Journalist*, September, pp 18-19

Brooke, Heather (2005) *Your Right to Know: How to Use the Freedom of Information Act and Other Access Laws*, London: Pluto Press

eGovernment News (2005) 'Thousands of information requests sent to UK government in January,' 3 February, available online at http://europa.eu.int/idabc/en/document/3840/194, accessed 29 March 2005

Evans, Rob (2005) 'How Wham! baffled Chinese youth in first pop concert,' in *the Guardian*, 9 May. Available online at http://politics.guardian.co.uk/foi/story/0,9061,1479493,00.html, accessed 20 July 2005

Geary Pate, Amanda (2005) 'An analysis of the initial impact of the Freedom of Information Act on the newsgathering activities applied by print journalists in the UK.' Unpublished MA thesis, University of Sunderland

HoldTheFrontPage (2005) 'Evening Press uncovers "stealth tax" on motorists,' *holdthefrontpage.co.uk*, 6 May. Available online at http://www.holdthefrontpage.co.uk/day/foi/050506yor.shtml, accessed 30 May 2005

Independent (2005) Editorial, 2 February, p 28

Jellinek, Dan (2004) 'Pressure grows as deadline looms,' in *the Guardian*, 30 June. Available online at http://www.theguardian.com/society/2004/jun/30/epublic.technology7, accessed on 27 August 2014

NUJ (1999) 'Freedom of Information Bill 1999 – Comments from the National Union of Journalists,' *National Union of Journalists*. Available online at http://media.gn.apc.org/foi.html, accessed 30 May 2005

Number 10 (2005) 'Lord Falconer hails the first month of FOI as a success,' *Number 10*. Available online at http://www.number-10.gov.uk/output/page7044.asp, accessed 13 March 2005

Oliver, Dawn (2003) *Constitutional Reform in the UK*, Oxford: Oxford University Press

Ponsford, Dominic (2004) 'Scoops could be scuppered under FOI,' *Press Gazette*, 2 December. Available online at http://www.pressgazette.co.uk/?t=article&d=Scoops_could_be_scuppered_under_FoI, accessed 15 June 2005

Press Gazette (2005a) 'Making the most of freedom,' in *Press Gazette*, 16 January. Available online at http://www.pressgazette.co.uk/?t=article&d=Making_the_most_of_freedom, accessed 30 May 2005

Press Gazette (2005b) Law guru predicts more exams, *Press Gazette*, 7 July. Available online at http://www.pressgazette.co.uk/article/070705/law_guru_predicts, accessed on 8 July 2005

Smith, Kelvin (2004) *Freedom of Information: A Practical Guide to Implementing the Act*. London: Facet Publishing

Wadham, John, Griffiths, Jonathan and Rigby, Bethan (2001) *Blackstone's Guide to the Freedom of Information Act 2000*. London: Blackstone Press

Welsh, Tom and Greenwood, Walter (2001) *McNae's Essential Law for Journalists*. London: Butterworths, 16th edn

Wood, Steve (2005) 'Editorial: Inaugural Issue' in *Open Government: A Journal on Freedom of Information*, 1(1) pp. 2-6

Note on the contributor

Dr Amanda Geary Pate is a Lecturer in Journalism at the University of the West of Scotland, where her teaching includes both the applied and theoretical reporting of politics. She read Politics at the University of Liverpool and gained a Masters in Journalism from the University of Sunderland where she researched the early use of the Freedom of Information Act by journalists, before gaining a PhD in Journalism. Her research interests include: journalism and gender; and multimedia journalism. Prior to working in academia, Amanda was a reporter for several regional and national newspapers.

Fishing expeditions or serious investigations? The impact of media Freedom of Information Act requests on local government

Lynn Wyeth examines the use of the Freedom of Information Act in British local government by the media and concludes there is minimal evidence of detailed investigative journalism into local authorities, and there is a considerable lack of originality in local journalists' use of FOI

Introduction

In the last 10 years local government has been in receipt of numerous Freedom of Information (FOI) requests, dwarfing numbers sent to other public bodies. Worthy et al (2011) found that FOI requests to local authorities had climbed steeply compared with central government. The research found that 35 per cent of FOI officers questioned believed that larger numbers of requests were due to increased awareness and interest in FOI, 31 per cent thought professional FOI requests (journalists, businesses and researchers) were to blame and 16 per cent believed it to be attributed to media coverage and publicity of FOI. Therefore media has a leading role to play in FOI. This chapter takes a look at the myriad of requests that the media submit to local councils, and the impact that those requests can have on the authority.

Spotting a request from the media

Somewhat controversially, in order to analyse requests from the media, we clearly have to determine which requests they submit. Journalists hate this practice and publish articles indignantly stating that the Act is applicant blind. Undoubtedly there will be authorities that sadly abuse the Act, hoping that the story goes away. (Without research evidence, we will not know how widespread this practice may be.) So why is the requester monitored? Firstly, any decent communications team will want to be ready for any story that may break as a result of a FOI request. Whilst journalists spin negative headlines about the public sector, so will councils monitor requests from the media. Secondly, and most importantly, any journalist asserting that the FOI Act is applicant blind is ignoring exemption provisions under section 12 or section 14. A public authority may need to monitor requests from individuals known to them for potential aggregation of requests, or to assess vexatiousness.

How do local authorities spot a journalist? Some openly put their details in the request or send the request from their work address. Others hide behind a Gmail account, but often blow their cover by using a recognisable template request form that they have acquired on a 'how to submit FOIs for journalists' course. A quick internet search (questionable as this practice may be) can reveal that the requester works in the media. David Higgerson of the Trinity Mirror Group gave tips on ways to avoid being identified as a journalist and a round-robin requester as early as 2001.

Numbers of FOI requests from the media

For many council FOI officers, it can feel like a disproportionate amount of requests are submitted by the media. The reality is sometimes quite different to this perception when statistics are analysed. Journalists can account for a relatively small proportion of requests, especially where a council has a good working relationship with the media. In the last two years the percentage of requests from known media for the following three local large unitary authorities were as follows:

Figure 4: Local authority requests from media 2012 and 2013

Local Authority	% of requests in 2012 from media	% of requests in 2013 from media	Average % of requests from media over last 2 years
Birmingham	14.50	12.40	13.45
Manchester	14.40	13.60	14.0
Leicester	17.0	12.0	14.50
All	15.30	12.60	13.95

Source: www.whatdotheyknow.com and Leicester City Council

This equates, on average, for a local authority such as Leicester City Council to only two FOI requests a week by the media. Not really the excessive and onerous burden that the anti-FOI or anti-media lobby would have you believe.

The media's submission techniques

FOI officers in local authorities can categorise their media 'regulars'. Some media requesters stick firmly to one type, others mix and match, but four types stand out. Firstly, we have the 'direct requester'. Transparent and straight to the point, the direct requester makes no effort to hide their identity. It is often clear from the request which angle the story may take, and such requests often come from regional BBC Radio or TV stations and local printed press.

Secondly, we have the much-derided 'round robin-er'. The requester sends the same FOI request to many public authorities at once, often hundreds at a time, e.g. to all councils, so that results can be compared. As Worthy et all (2011) discovered this was a particular source of frustration with FOI officers. Many officials resented the work as they felt that only a small proportion of the information was ever used, at great cost to public authorities.

Thirdly is the 'piggy back' request, where a journalist asks his local council for information as a result of a national story. As Worthy et al (2011) found, FOI requests can arrive in 'waves' around a particular issue or controversy in the media. 'The Price of Privacy', revealed that Leicester City Council had the most CCTV cameras in the country (Big Brother Watch, 2012). This resulted in local media following up the story, with the BBC running 'Leicester City Council defends CCTV usage' (BBC, 2012) and the *Leicester Mercury* sensationalising with the headline 'Leicester is CCTV capital of UK with city's 2,000 cameras.' (Leicester Mercury, 2012) No context was added to the original report to explain any anomalies. Leicester, a large unitary authority of nearly 400,000 citizens, is one of the few in the country to have retained control of all of its social housing including several high rise blocks of flats. It cannot be fairly compared to a small borough council with no housing stock, no school cameras and no road traffic CCTV cameras (which are operated by its local county council). In light of such press coverage, media requesters should not be surprised if they find councils seeking further dogged clarification to requests in future.

An increasing trend recently has been for the media to use pre-prepared press releases by other organisations. A news release accusing South Tyneside of spending excessive money on flights 'South Tyneside flouts freedom of information obligations' (Taxpayers Alliance, 2012) resulted in stories in the local *Shields Gazette* 'Council bosses spend nearly £50,000 on flights' (Shields Gazette, 2012) and Matthew Elliott's headline 'Free flights for American magicians? Find out how YOUR council tax is being wasted on air travel' (*Daily Mail*, 2012). Trainee journalists should sign up to mailing lists of pressure groups that proactively use FOI. This way of working was defended by investigative reporter Paul Lashmar. In an interview with the *Independent* (August 2008) he said 'Journalists are often now so overstretched that a lot of work that used to be carried out in the newsroom is carried out by groups like the TPA. What you see now is journalists who are grateful for news, which is almost perfectly packaged to go into the paper with a ready top line. In that sense, journalism is becoming very passive'.

The Taxpayers Alliance (TPA) has used this strategy incredibly successfully. Matthew Elliott, its chief executive, told the *Independent*,

> 'Journalists have 101 things to do in their day and don't often have time to read long and dry reports from think-thanks. So we use the Freedom of Information Act and a team of researchers to get fresh figures from government and local councils, which we package up into brief, media-friendly research papers, complete with eye-catching headline figures to give reporters a ready-made top line,' (*The Independent*, 4 August 2008).

Many of these stories can hit the press months after the original question was posed and result in a flurry of media enquiries to the local authority unexpectedly.

Our fourth type of requester is the proactive 'disclosure log reader'. Any ambitious local journalist should read their local FOI disclosure log every day to look for potential stories. Also included in this category is the even smarter journalist that additionally keeps a watching eye on the whatdotheyknow.com website for requests to their local council and picks up on potential stories as soon as the question is submitted.

The press office

Some councils may try to dissuade journalists from using FOI… which sounds like they have something to hide. On the contrary, through experience, some of the most transparent councils positively encourage their local press to communicate with the press team directly. A FOI request may take weeks to answer and may involve redactions; it's a lose-lose for both sides. The media can often receive an un-redacted and timelier response by directly approaching the Council's press office. Worthy et al (2011) noted that 'pre-existing relations seemed to shape how FOI has worked. Some authorities experienced heavy and aggressive use by the media, others none'. The resource impact of FOI on local authorities and the media is reduced greatly if a good working relationship can be established.

Subject matter of media requests

Holsen et al (2007) notes that 'Journalists getting to grips with the Act for the first time were sometimes accused of glamorising relatively anodyne discoveries with a FOI tag'. Almost 10 years on, has anything changed? Many headlines resulting from FOI requests still revolve around repetitive, and yes, anodyne, topics. Let us consider some recent headlines in the media relating to local councils as a result of a FOI request:

> *'Carlisle Council spends £440,000 in airport row.'*
>
> *'FOI reveals City of Edinburgh council spends £36K per year measuring litter.'*
>
> *'Surrey County Council spends £30m to keep schools ship-shape.'*
>
> *'MP blasts council's 150k spend on 'spin doctors brought up from London.'*
>
> *'Aberdeen City Council has spent £1.5million dealing with illegal traveller camps in the past decade.'*
>
> *'Welsh councils attacked over £28k spend on 'civic shindigs' revealed by FOI.'*
>
> *'FOI reveals Yorkshire council spent £250,000 on Harrogate planning blueprint it tore up.'*

All have one word in common… spend. There are also similar stories about costs:

'FOI reveals cash-strapped Midland councils' foreign trips cost £47,000.'

'Removing parking zones will cost Portsmouth taxpayers £90k.'

'Council's failed case over demolition of Humberston Avenue home costs taxpayers £10,000.'

Requests have repeatedly been submitted over the years on expenses of councillors and pay of senior staff. This data is now routinely published under the *Local Government Transparency Code of Practice 2014*. It even results in the publication of the annual 'Town Hall Rich List' by TPA. Worthy and Holsen (2010) reported that at the top of the most requested list was costs and expenses. Little appears to have changed.

Another repeat topic is parking. We see requests on travellers' sites, CCTV, the use of surveillance, expenses, trips abroad... a decade on and it's all still so unimaginative and repetitive. There are sometimes, refreshingly, local stories on more unique topics, such as 'Caught on camera: secret film shows rounding-up ahead of 200 geese cull by Sandwell Council' (not so refreshing for the geese) but these articles seem relatively few and far between. In the very small analysis of British stories over a two-week period for this chapter, were there any stories perceived as positive for the local authority as a result of a FOI request? Yes, just one, in the *Perth Gazette*. 'Mi Perthshire backed by the council to help promote Perth City'. (Perth Gazette, August 2014)

Fishing expeditions?

Jeremy Hayes defined the two styles of FOI journalist:

> *'The fly fisherman knows precisely what information or detail he is looking to secure and uses skill and precision to locate it and extract it. The trawler man on the other hand casts a net in the form of a general request for information relating to a topic area of interest and then sifts the catch to see what comes to light,'* (Hayes, 2009).

Both strategies are encouraged by journalism colleges and trainers. Advice from *The Tab*, an online journalistic website serving 41 UK universities states:

> *'You might just want to use a request as a fishing exercise, for example finding out how much the council is spending on entertainment. Or you might have a story already and want to find out an additional detail,'* (The TAB, 2014).

The political editor of the Kent Messenger Group, Paul Francis (see his chapter in this book), is one of the more inspiring users working with FOI in local media for journalistic purposes. Speaking on journalism.co.uk he justified such use, saying:

> *'I think there are occasions in which, what are derided as fishing expeditions, can throw up information which is important and in the public interest'.*

The trawler man's approach however is essentially a gamble, and journalists have expressed scepticism about its value. An excessive resource is used to cast the net around hundreds of authorities, with absolutely no guarantee of catching a big fish of a story, or indeed having any story to run at all.

Lazy journalism?

Despite the potential workload in terms of hours spent collating information, can the trawler man's technique be classed intellectually as a lazy form of journalism? It has offended some so intensely that one anonymous individual went as far as to identify the 'top three drains on the public purse'. *The Lazy Journalist Index* named Chris Hastings from the *Mail on Sunday*, Jasper Copping from the *Daily Telegraph* and Adam Thorne from the *News of the World* as the top three 'culprits' in 2010. It went on to suggest that at £280 per request, to over 400 authorities per time, it could cost the taxpayer over £80,000 per news story:

> "These journalists no doubt do a very good job and have hunted out some awesome stories but FOIs about biscuits, equality officers and people with climate change in their job title probably don't add up to good value to the public purse!"

wrote the anonymous FOI officer.

The £280 request cost estimation is of course debatable. Every study carried out that puts an estimate on the cost of an average FOI request produces a different amount. In reality the majority of councils do not record time taken. It's complex and a waste of resource in itself. Journalists would do well to beware the stories claiming the cost of FOI to public authorities. What cannot be disputed however, is that round robin requests do produce a sometimes large cost the local authority, and ultimately the taxpayer. The question is, is it a price worth paying for open government?

In an interview with *The Sunday Times* in Scotland, the former Scottish Information Commissioner Kevin Dunion said:

> "There's no doubt, to be frank, that journalists are the group that most disgruntle public officials. One, because of the volume of information they request. And two, because they get the information, decide there's no story and make no use of it whatsoever – so the official thinks that a lot of public expense has gone into finding the information,"
(AllMediaSCOTLAND, 2008).

Conclusion

Are journalists making the best use of FOI to hold local government to account? From the anodyne headlines we are still seeing on a weekly basis, it would appear journalists are still not getting the best use from the Act. There is minimal evidence of detailed investigative journalism into local authorities, and there is a considerable lack of originality on subject matter. Such stories are hardly likely to win the Pulitzer Prize for investigative reporting. Years of openness in local government perhaps means there are less stories to chase, but recent events such as the child abuse scandal in Rotherham would suggest that there most certainly are stories if you know where to look. Local media in particular is still prone to use lazy techniques; happy to piggyback on other stories and use pressure groups pre-prepared stories. Journalists, apart from a handful of experienced trailblazers, still do not appear to have an in depth knowledge of FOI and do not utilise it to its fullest potential. The media continually fails to make use of the Environmental Information Regulations (which quite often will offer up to them much more information that FOI ever will) for local land issues. Budding journalists should familiarise themselves with not just the legislation, but the Information Tribunal and Commissioner key decisions so that they know when they can use an information access request (despite some of the limitations and obstacles) to unlock a potential story.

Journalists argue that their stories are good news for the taxpayer. The use of FOI by the media, regardless of which technique is used, does appear to have uncovered stories that are in the public interest. The impact on local authorities can be evidenced, from no more biscuits or bottled water at meetings to the proactive publication online of the most regularly requested information under FOI. David Higgerson says on his blog's introduction that he believes that the FOI Act is "one of the most powerful tools at our disposal as journalists, and one which should be used more frequently". Some council FOI officers may balk at that sentiment, but some of us fully support it and wish that journalists would work with us and not against us to enable our still relatively young Act to flourish in an open democracy.

References

AllMediaSCOTLAND.com (2008) Article quotes from *Sunday Times* (2007) 'Dunion appeals to journalists to show restraint,' *AllMediaSCOTLAND.com*, March 2008, available at http://www.allmediascotland.com/creative/15064/dunion-appeals-to-journalists-to-show-restraint-on-foi/, accessed 31 August, 2014

Anonymous (2010). *The Lazy Journalist Index*. Available online at http://welovelocalgovernment.wordpress.com/2010/11/09/the-lazy-journalist-index/, accessed 31 August, 2014

Bartlett, R (2014) 'Plaid's fury over "civic shindigs" at time of austerity,' *Wales Online*, 28 July. Available online at http://www.walesonline.co.uk/news/local-news/welsh-councils-attacked-over-lavish-7516745, accessed 31 August, 2014

Bartlett, R (2012) 'How to: Submit a Freedom of Information Request'. Available online at http://www.journalism.co.uk/skills/how-to-submit-a-freedom-of-information-request/s7/a548038/, accessed 31 August, 2014

BBC (2012) 'Leicester City Council defends CCTV usage,' BBC News, 21 February

BBC (2014) 'Carlisle Council spends £440,000 in airport row,' BBC News, 7 August.

Big Brother Watch (2012) 'The Price of Privacy: How local authorities spent £515m on CCTV in four years' Big Brother Watch. Available online at http://www.bigbrotherwatch.org.uk/files/priceofprivacy/Price_of_privacy_2012.pdf#.T0Olbf18Cd4, accessed 31 august, 2014

Brace, H (2014) 'Aberdeen City Council rakes in £5 million in car parking fees in five years,' *Evening Express*, 23 August

Cambridge News (2014) 'As figures reveal Cambridge motorists pay £1 million a year in parking fines, we reveal city's most ticketed streets' *Cambridge News*, 23 August

Daniel, C (2012) 'South Tyneside flouts freedom of information obligations' *Tax Payers Alliance*. Available online at http://www.taxpayersalliance.com/waste/2012/08/south-tyneside-flaunts-freedom-information-obligations.html, accessed 31 August, 2014

DCLG (2014). *Local Government Transparency Code 2014*. Code of Practice. Available online at https://www.gov.uk/government/uploads/system/uploads/attachment_data/file/3081 85/Local_Government_Transparency_Code_2014_Final.pdf, accessed 31 August, 2014

Dunion, Kevin (2010) 'Freedom of information in Scotland and the UK: time to notice the difference' in Chapman, Richard and Michael Hunt [eds] *Freedom of Information: Local Government and Accountability*. Ashgate Publishing Ltd London, pp57-73

Elliot, M (2012) 'Free flights for American magicians? Find out how YOUR council tax is being wasted on air travel,' *Daily Mail*, 15 August

Express and Star (2014a) 'Caught on camera: Secret film shows rounding-up ahead of 200 geese cull by Sandwell Council,' *Express and Star*, 23 August

Express and Star (2014b) 'FOI reveals cash-strapped Midland councils' foreign trips cost £47,000,' *Express and Star*, 26 July

Grimsby Telegraph (2014) 'Council's failed case over demolition of Humberston Avenue home costs taxpayers £10,000,' *Grimsby Telegraph*, 21 August

Hayes, J (2009) *A Shock To the System: Journalism, Government and the Freedom of Information Act 2000*. University of Oxford: Reuters Institute for the Study of Journalism. Available online at https://reutersinstitute.politics.ox.ac.uk/sites/default/files/A%20Shock%20to%20the%20System.pdf, accessed 31 August, 2014

Higgerson, D (2011) 'About' WordPress blog. Available online at http://davidhiggerson.wordpress.com/about/, accessed 31 August, 2014

Higgerson, D. (2011) 'FOI officers hunting round-robin requests? Three ways to reduce that happening' Wordpress blog. Available online at http://davidhiggerson.wordpress.com/2011/01/26/foi-officers-hunting-round-robin-requests-three-ways-to-reduce-that-happening/#more-1127, accessed 31 August, 2014

Holsen, S et all (2007) 'Journalists' Use of FOI' *Open Government: A Journal on Freedom of Information*, 3(1), pp. 1.

Lashmar, Paul (2008) 'How the Taxpayers Alliance is making headlines' *The Independent*, 4 August. Available online at http://www.independent.co.uk/news/media/how-the-taxpayers-alliance-is-making-headlines-884087.html

Leicester Mercury (2012) 'Leicester is CCTV capital of UK with city's 2,000 cameras,' *Leicester Mercury*, 21 February

Matlock Mercury (2014) 'MP blasts council's £150k spend on spin doctors brought up from London,' *Matlock Mercury*, 20 August

Merrill, J (2008) 'How the Taxpayers' Alliance is Making Headlines,' *Independent*, 4 August

Morrison, D (2014) 'Aberdeen City Council has spent £1.5million dealing with illegal traveller camps in the past decade,' *Press and Journal*, 18 August

O'Leary, M (2014) 'Removing parking zones will cost Portsmouth taxpayers £90k<i>,' The News-Portsmouth</i>, 25 August

Perth Gazette (2014) 'Mi Perthshire backed by the council to help promote Perth City,' *Perth Gazette*, 18 August

Shields Gazette (2012) 'Council bosses spend nearly £50,000 on flights', *Shields Gazette*, 14 August, Available online at http://www.shieldsgazette.com/news/council-bosses-spend-nearly-50-000-on-flights-1-4831048

STV (2014) 'FOI reveals City of Edinburgh council spends £36K per year measuring litter,' *STV*, 25 August. Available online at http://edinburgh.stv.tv/155336/ accessed 31 August, 2014

Surrey Mirror (2014) 'Surrey County Council spends £30m to keep schools ship-shape,' *Surrey Mirror*, 25 August

Tax Payers Alliance (2012). *South Tyneside flouts freedom of information obligations.* Available online a http://www.taxpayersalliance.com/waste/2012/08/south-tyneside-flaunts-freedom-information-obligations.html

Tax Payers Alliance (2014). *Town Hall Rich List 2014*. 8th Year. Available online at http://www.taxpayersalliance.com/thrl2014.pdf accessed 31 August 2014

THE TAB, 2012. 'Freedom of Information'. Available online at http://journalism.tab.co.uk/2012/11/16/freedom-of-information-requests/ accessed 31 August, 2014.

Worthy, B and Holsen S (2010) 'Local Government and FOI in England 2005-2007' in Chapman, R and Hunt, M [eds] *Freedom of Information: Local Government and Accountability* Ashgate: Farnham, pp 27-43

Worthy, B, Amos, J, Hazell, R, and Bourke, G (2011) 'Town Hall Transparency? The Impact of the Freedom of Information Act 2000 on Local Government in England'. UCL London: The Constitution Unit

Yorkshire Post (2014) 'FOI reveals Yorkshire council spent £250,000 on Harrogate planning blueprint it tore up', *Yorkshire Post*, 17 July.

Note on the contributor

Lynn Wyeth is Information Governance Manager at Leicester City Council, overseeing the Information Governance agenda including Freedom of Information, Environmental Information Regulations, Data Protection and surveillance. Lynn is the author of two books, *A Practical Guide to Handling Freedom of Information Requests* and *Data Protection: Compliance in Practice* by Ark Publishing. She runs her own information governance training company, and is currently undertaking a PhD at De Montfort University, researching the use of freedom of information in local government by journalists, politicians and pressure groups, and any unintended consequences arising from such use. Email: contact@foiresearch.info

The lazy local journalist's guide to a scoop: FOI it!

Alan Geere **assesses the impact of the Freedom of Information Act on local newspaper journalism, and concludes hacks in the regions have yet to use the Act to its full potential, and in many cases they don't even bother to use it at all**

Introduction

The Freedom of Information Act was hailed as a new investigative reporter in the newsroom for hard-pressed local newspapers. File request, sit back, wait for reply, deliver insightful exclusives. But what has been the reality for journalists on Britain's regional daily and local weekly newspapers? Has the Act proved more useful and meaningful beyond exposing how many biscuits were eaten at the council meeting or revealing the salaries of the great and good?

'Council rakes in money from parking machines that don't give change' – eye-catching local newspaper headline, telling it like it is about an emotive subject that will get everyone talking. And what's the source of this story? Drop down to paragraph three and all is revealed: '...that was more than any other local authority out of the 79 which responded to freedom of information requests made by a national newspaper.' So, hurrah for freedom of information, serving up a front-page lead on a plate. Minimal effort, maximum reward and all on the back of another newspaper's FOI. No credit given, as many community papers still refuse to acknowledge that national newspapers exist. The story has quotes from the AA, TaxPayers' Alliance and the council but no local input from car park users or even council taxpayers.

Whizz 300 miles north and here's a familiar tale: 'Councils make £65k from parking machines, which don't give change'. Yes, same FOI, coyly revealed in paragraph five – 'The figures, released thanks to a query put forward under the Freedom of Information Act' – with the same blunt approach, this time including quotes from two councillors (zzzz) as well as council spokesman. This paper had the good idea to pull in all the local authorities within the circulation area, but again missed out any users i.e. readers. Also neither story had any detail on how much the parking costs and what sort of change people are leaving in the machine. A decent reporter could knock this out in, let's be generous, an hour. It reads well and tells a decent tale so welcome to community journalism 2014-style where digging around for that local element takes time that is at a premium for under-pressure newsrooms.

So, how are local, community newspapers using the Freedom of Information Act and what are the results? This study looks at the output from a sample of newspapers – *Croydon Advertiser, Wales Online* (*Western Mail, South Wales Echo, Wales on Sunday*), *Hull Daily Mail, The Argus* (Brighton), and the *North Devon Journal* – and their websites to reveal these broad areas of interest[1]:

- Stories related to the emergency services, often the police
- Reports of FOI requests from prominent figures, individuals and organisations, including the media
- Stories about local authorities, councils, councillors and officials
- Stories about the Freedom of Information Act and the lengths the media outlet has gone to in pursuit of the story
- Stories about health issues
- Off-beat, 'wacky' stories

Stories related to the emergency services, often the police

Croydon Advertiser, 17 January, 2012

Headline: 'CROYDON RIOTS: Figures show police attended 13 of 500 crimes reported'

Intro: 'OVERSTRETCHED police officers responded to just 2.6 per cent of the hundreds of 999 calls made during the riots, the Advertiser can reveal'.

FOI reveal, paragraph three: 'Figures, obtained via the Freedom of Information Act, provide a unique insight into the events of August 8 and the strain placed on insufficient police resources assigned to the borough. The Advertiser requested details of all emergency calls made to police between 5pm and 5am the following morning.'

Content: Facts, figures, timeline; quotes from disgruntled shopkeeper; quote from police spokesman; list of 'frequently reported roads'; link to 'crimes reported to police during Croydon riots' as a Google fusion table.

Verdict: A comprehensive job of gathering information. The tables are a goldmine of data and presented in a readable manner for the keen enthusiast. The unhappy shopkeeper brought a human dimension to a good follow-up on Croydon's story of the century, but more voices would be welcome.

Wales Online, 18 May, 2014

Headline: 'Police operations at Cardiff City over the current season has amounted to over £140,000 new figures show'

Intro: 'The cost of policing Cardiff City's home matches this season amounted to a staggering £140,000, WalesOnline can reveal.'

FOI reveal, paragraph three: 'Data released under Freedom of Information laws reveals that South Wales Police's costs for keeping order at Cardiff City Stadium during the current season amounted to a massive £140,528 – an increase of £76,226 on 2012/13.'

Content: Just one person quoted, Cardiff City's 'head of operations'. Unnecessary adjective - 'staggering' - in the intro. The word 'data' twice in the story; what's wrong with figures or numbers?

Verdict: Not much effort made to put the numbers in context. As a poster to Wales Online said: 'This averages to less than £7,500 per match. This is Wales On Line [stet] trying to sensationalise some news. It's good value.'

Hull Daily Mail, 19 May, 2014

Headline: 'Ex-Humberside Police officers could face criminal probe over 'paedophile' slurs'

Intro: 'A CRIMINAL investigation could be launched after police branded an innocent teacher a dangerous paedophile.'

FOI reveal, paragraph 15: 'In response to a Mail request under the Freedom of Information Act, the force said…'

Content: Quotes from IPCC spokesman, police spokesman.

Verdict: Someone has done great job to get a decent headline out of long, complicated story.

Wales Online, 2 June, 2014

Headline: 'Cops caught in the act: South Wales Police discipline 127 of their own staff in the past five years'

Intro: 'SOUTH Wales Police disciplined 127 of its own staff over misconduct in the past five years, the *Echo* can reveal.'

FOI reveal, paragraph four: A leading solicitor has called for greater transparency in the wake of the figures, which were released under Freedom of Information law.

Content: Extensive quotes from 'leading solicitor' and 'Policing is complex' explanation from Assistant Chief Constable.

Verdict: Great headline and a good read for the three pars of info from the FOI. Then fast train to Dullsville.

North Devon Journal 10 June, 2014

Headline: 'Happily ever after? Police attend 16 weddings and wakes after fighting breaks out'

Intro: 'Devon and Cornwall Police were called to 16 weddings and wakes last year after fighting broke out between guests - including one incident after a funeral in Barnstaple.'

FOI reveal, paragraph 13: 'The figures were released following a request to the force under the Freedom of Information Act.

Content: Details of where the incidents took place and quotes from police spokesman citing 'emotional and stressful occasions'.

Verdict: Great headline figures, but a missed opportunity to develop story with more views and comments.

Reports of FOI requests from prominent figures, individuals and organisations, including the media

Croydon Advertiser, 18 October, 2012

Headline: 'Ex-MP seeks London brothels list in human trafficking crackdown'

Intro: 'A former MP has asked the Metropolitan Police to hand over the addresses of all known brothels in London, in a bid to help "lift the lid" on human trafficking.'

FOI reveal, paragraph two: 'Anthony Steen, former Conservative MP for Totnes and chairman of the Human Trafficking Foundation, has submitted a Freedom of Information (FOI) request to the Met to reveal the location of all 2,103 brothels in the capital, identified in a 2010 report from the Association of Chief Police Officers (ACPO).'

Content: Details from ACPO report; 'announcement' from ex-MP (not local); lengthy interview with ex-MP (still not local); fact boxes on trafficking and anti-slavery day;

Verdict: Interview is a big plus, but local angle pretty thin

Croydon Advertiser, 19 October, 2013

Headline: 'Croydon to make up to £41m from HS2 railway line'

Intro: 'CROYDON and south London could stand to benefit up to £41 million if a new north-to-south rail link is built.'

FOI reveal, paragraph six: 'Those details were revealed by BBC Two's *Newsnight* programme following a Freedom of Information request.

Content: Details from a KPMG report, no quotes.

Verdict: Generous to name *Newsnight*, but perhaps it's there to lend credibility to a thin story.

Stories about local authorities, councils, councillors and officials

Croydon Advertiser, 24 January, 2011

Headline: 'Croydon spends £850 a day on temporary education chief'

Intro: 'CROYDON Council is spending £850 a day on a temporary member of staff – at the height of the harshest cuts to public spending in living memory.'

FOI reveal, paragraph five: The *Advertiser* uncovered how much Ms Smith was costing the council when it asked, via the Freedom of Information Act, how much she was being paid.

Content: Figures from FOI request; comment from union 'I'm appalled at....'

Verdict: A lot of how we did it – 'Shortly afterwards, the *Advertiser* requested details of her salary as part of an investigation into council profligacy.'

Hull Daily Mail, 12 February, 2014

Headline: 'Hull City Council spends £200k propping up a Beverley Road building it doesn't even own.'

Intro: 'CASH-STRAPPED Hull City Council has spent £200,000 propping up a building it doesn't even own, the *Mail* can reveal today.

FOI reveal, paragraph 12: 'In a reply to a Freedom of Information Act request submitted by the *Mail*, the council said: 'The scaffolding was erected solely to prevent the building collapsing due to the state of internal disrepair that it had fallen into.'

Content: Quote from UKIP'S regional chairman (huh?); Quotes from the council FOI response.

Verdict: Great intro. Interesting to see FOI reveal so low down.

The Argus, 25 June, 2014

Headline: 'Tourism signs cost council £2,772.68 each.'

Intro: 'MORE than £108,000 was spent putting up new signs which are being slammed as "pointless".'

FOI reveal, paragraph 12: 'One sign in Southover Street had been covered with stickers yesterday. Mr Wood asked Brighton City Council under the Freedom of Information Act to reveal the cost of the signs.'

Content: Comment from council with a spokeswoman saying 'the people responsible could not be contacted' but the signs were not paid for from council taxpayers. Quotes from the resident who made the FOI request, which is where the 'pointless' in the intro comes from.

Verdict: An open goal for the *Argus* with someone else doing all the hard work to make the request and provide most of the quotes. What's not to like?!

Wales Online, 10 July, 2014

Headline: 'Revealed: How suspended council boss will receive more than £300,000 in pay by the time he goes on trial for misconduct in public office'

Intro: 'The suspended chief executive of Caerphilly council will have received one third of a million pounds in pay by the time he goes on trial for misconduct in public office next year.'

FOI reveal, paragraph three: 'A disclosure made to Plaid Cymru under the Freedom of Information Act shows that by January 5, 2015, when his trial is due to start at Bristol Crown Court, Mr O'Sullivan will have been paid £333,795 during his period of suspension.'

Content: The FOI was made by Plaid Cymru and their leader gets the quotes as well. Robust defence from council spokesman, forgetting he's supposed to be a speak-your-weight machine: 'This is typical mischief-making by an opposition leader desperate to deflect attention away from his own deputy leader's involvement…'

Verdict: Straightforward story construction - FOI numbers, he said, they said – works well.

Wales Online, 14 July, 2014

Headline: 'How much?! £800k worth of compensation claims for injuries to schoolchildren'

Intro: 'Local authorities in Wales have spent more than £800,000 on damages and legal fees following injuries at schools over the past five years.'

FOI reveal, paragraph eight: 'Neath Port Talbot, responding to a freedom of information request, also confirmed they had paid out almost £12,000 when a child's arm became stuck behind a radiator, while there was also a £14,000 bill after a child ran into a fire exit door.'

Content: A clever sweep around Welsh local authorities to arrive at the total £800k figure. Detail is FOI gold – severed thumb, pupil hit by ball during games, collapsed white board – and while there are no quotes the story probably doesn't need it.

Verdict: No prizes for the top of the intro 'Local authorities in Wales', but generally well written.

Stories about the Freedom of Information Act and the lengths the media outlet has gone to in pursuit of the story

Croydon Advertiser, 10 January, 2012

Headline: 'Information Commissioner forces Croydon Council to reveal regeneration details after Advertiser appeal'

Intro: 'CROYDON Council was wrong to withhold key details of its flagship town centre regeneration project, the Information Commissioner has ruled.'

FOI reveal, paragraph two: 'The *Advertiser* appealed to the Commissioner after figures were redacted from the contract, obtained under the Freedom of Information Act, to protect the interests of developer John Laing.'

Content: Details from Information Commissioner's report; one par from council spokesman

Verdict: Bit too much 'hurrah for us'

Croydon Advertiser, 28 February, 2012

Headline: 'Freedom of Information: Waste of public money or vital democratic tool?'

Intro: 'DEPENDING on which politician you talk to, the council's new headquarters is either a colossal waste of money or the centrepiece of an innovative £450 million regeneration project designed to transform the town centre.'

FOI reveal, paragraph three: 'The Freedom of Information Act has empowered the public, and become an important tool of the press, to uncover such data since it was made law in 2005.'

Content: Interview with local serial FOI submitter; comments from councillor; list of FOIs the paper has done.

Verdict: Self-publicity and an explanation of what FOI can do.

Stories about health issues

The Argus, 28 April, 2014

Headline: 'Royal Sussex "fails to provide safe patient care"'

Intro: 'THE Royal Sussex County Hospital was named among a fifth of hospitals nationwide failing to provide "safe and appropriate care" to patients.'

FOI reveal, paragraph two: 'The Brighton hospital was among the rising number of hospitals failing to hit national standards according to Freedom of Information figures gained by the Labour Party.'

Content: Local take on national FOI. Quotes from union rep and hospital spokesman.

Verdict: Easy meat, low-hanging fruit etc.

Hull Daily Mail, 1 May, 2014

Headline: 'Hull child in rehab at age of 10, figures on alcohol and drug misuse reveal'

Intro: 'A TEN-year-old from Hull is among dozens of under-18s who have been referred to drug and alcohol misuse treatment services.'

FOI reveal, paragraph two: 'According to figures supplied under the Freedom of Information Act, the child drinker is the city's youngest rehab client, while the East Riding has seen children as young as 12 referred.'

Content: The info only amounted to two facts. East Riding Council says it referred 92 under-18s in 2013/14. Hull City Council sent 134 under-19s for treatment. Quotes from health worker; 'public health commissioning lead for Children and Young People's Services' at Council; Citysafe and early intervention manager at Council.

Verdict: Excellent job with not much to go on

Hull Daily Mail, 14 July, 2014

Headline: 'Hospital bosses spend £1m on agency staff due to nursing shortages at Hull Royal Infirmary and Castle Hill Hospital'

Intro: 'HOSPITAL bosses have shelled out almost £1m on temporary workers because of a critical shortage of nurses.'

FOI reveal, paragraph 14: 'The trust spent £700,428 on agency nurses in 2010-11, falling to £578,912 in 2011-12 and then to £558,496 the following year, according to figures obtained under the Freedom of Information Act. From 2013 until this year, the bill soared to £991,736.'

Content: Comments from RCN and union; last par right of reply from Chief Nurse.

Verdict: Well written and neatly put together.

Off-beat, 'wacky' stories

Hull Daily Mail, 22 April, 2014

Headline: 'Thieves steal life-size cardboard bobby belonging to Humberside Police'

Intro: 'A LIFE-size cardboard policeman used to stop people shoplifting is among items stolen from Humberside Police. Bikes, handcuffs and even an old cast iron station lantern have also been taken by thieves in the past two years.'

FOI reveal, paragraph seven: 'Details of the thefts, which date back to the start of 2012, were obtained by the Mail using a Freedom of Information Act request.

Content: Amusing details from the FOI response, detailing just what but also how the items were stolen. 'Thieves even stole a life-size cardboard police officers used in a shop as a deterrent for shoplifters. Valued at £125, the cardboard bobby was taken by a man and a woman, who became abusive to staff after buying an item from the shop. While the shop assistants were distracted by serving other customers, the pair picked up the heavy-duty cardboard model and fled the store.' Used with great pic of cut-out copper.

Verdict: Superb!

The *Argus*, 6 May, 2014

Headline: 'City libraries earn £170 in fines every day'

Intro: 'Libraries in Brighton and Hove collected an average of almost £170 in fines nearly every day last year.'

FOI reveal, paragraph five: 'One woman who complained after receiving a library fine said she was "shocked she could be charged for overdue books as she had not been told this could happen", a Freedom of Information request revealed.'

Content: Quotes from the request response and council spokesman.

Verdict: A cute little FOI that everyone could do. And by calculating the daily fine that annual figure becomes more meaningful and manageable.

North Devon Journal, 8 May, 2014

Headline: 'Dog theft risk high in Devon'

Intro: 'Devon and Cornwall are among the most likely places for dogs to be stolen, according to an investigation.'

FOI reveal, paragraph four: 'In total, 1,468 dogs were reported missing last year, according to the 23 forces who replied to a Freedom of Information Act request.'

Content: Clear attribution to the story source – 'The figures, obtained by the ShootingUK website' – leads on to a reading of the lists plus quotes from MP and a local breeder.

Verdict: A straightforward story from a reliable source, which suffers from numberitis near the top.

Wales Online, 28 May, 2014

Headline: 'The lobsters, the llama, the dogs and the sheep - the animals reported stolen to police across Wales'

Intro: 'When it comes to stealing animals, sheep rustling is perhaps predictably the most common theft in Wales – but last year dozens of chickens, 58 lobsters, a ferret and a celebrity llama also fell foul of thieves.'

FOI reveal, paragraph three: 'The details were revealed as part of a Freedom of Information request to all police forces across the country.'

Content: Quotes from police spokeswoman, owner of Louis the llama and RSPCA spokeswoman. Enticing headline (at least online) and good use of figures.

Verdict: Not sure if this is a knockabout story or a serious piece. And whatever did happen to those lobsters?

Conclusion

So where are we and what do we need to do next? Here are some conclusions:

Work harder: I'm afraid the FOI report card signs off with 'Could Do Better'. Too many FOI stories simply regurgitate the facts of the case, and make little attempt to add context or comment. Remember, an FOI is not necessarily a story in itself. It needs work from the journalist to gather more information and opinion to make a rounded story.

Collaborate: In an extension of my theory of 'Find a Friend Journalism©' there is no issue with getting other people to help out with filing the FOI. Who cares if they are pressure groups, political parties, interested individuals or even pain in the wotsit busybodies? The information that comes back is the same and the party that files the request will be ready with the first quotes.

Localise: Hunt out the national FOI requests, often filed by political parties and organisations like The TaxPayers' Alliance. They will usually publicise the headline figures, which may not be from your patch, so rootle around in the detail and seek out what will work for you.

Monitor: Keep a close eye on sites like https://www.whatdotheyknow.com/ where you can browse requests made to all authorities. Set up your own search to routinely survey what authorities have been up to.

Look in dark corners: Apart from the usual suspects of councils, health authorities and the emergency services there are many other authorities hiding away from public scrutiny. Spend some time looking for the more obscure such as licensing boards; adjudication panels; advisory committees; drainage boards; national and regional parks boards; Safer Roads Partnership. And don't forget individual schools, colleges and universities along with as museums and galleries.

Have more fun: I know we all weary of the 'biscuits at the council meeting' style FOI, but why not make a nuisance of yourself? Mine's a Rich Tea…

Note

[1] Stories accessed via websites. Presentation and content may be different in print.

Note on the contributor

Alan Geere is a journalist, academic and international editorial consultant. He was editorial director of Northcliffe Newspapers (South-East) and, as editor, led the *Essex Chronicle* to two successive Weekly Newspaper of the Year awards. As an editorial executive he worked in the UK, Canada, United States and the Caribbean and his consulting career has taken him into 200 newsrooms worldwide. He was undergraduate journalism course leader at first Westminster and then Worcester, after a spell as senior lecturer on the MA International Journalism programme at City University. Alan ran the new Media, Communications and Journalism undergraduate degree course at Victoria University in Kampala, Uganda and until he moved to Africa Alan was a member of the board of the National Council for the Training of Journalists (NCTJ). Latterly he was head of news journalism at Southampton Solent University.

'Churnalism' and FOI in local UK newspapers

Freedom of information laws are one of the most effective tools journalists have in their armoury and vitally important when reporting on local councils, argues *Paul Francis*

Introduction

Since its introduction in 2005, the Freedom of Information Act has indisputably proved to be one of the most effective – if not the most effective - tools journalists have in their armoury. It has proved particularly potent for journalists working for regional and local newspaper groups and it is a measure of its usefulness that it is rare these days to pick up a paper, or visit an online news site, without seeing stories generated through the FOI Act. In newsrooms, editorial discussions about developing new lines on stories and unearthing previously undisclosed information now routinely lead to the question: 'Can we FOI it?' From health trusts to councils, government departments to quangos, FOI continues to be the centrepiece of the transparency revolution that has provided enterprising journalists with the ability to shine a light on public bodies in ways that were previously not possible. Of course, FOI is not the exclusive preserve of the media and was never intended to be – it is a citizen's right above anything else. That, too, has aided journalists.

A proliferation of bloggers, campaign groups and politicians have also become skilled practitioners of FOI and with the right spirit of co-operation, are often willing – and sometimes too willing - to share their latest discoveries and conspiracy theories with the media. At the same time, public bodies have become considerably more sophisticated in dealing with the legislation, and much more adept at the nuanced arguments around what may or may not be in the public interest. They have done so at a time when local papers have endured a turbulent few years, with newspaper owners forced to respond to the 'perfect storm' of the recession and the surge in online growth. Dwindling staff numbers have inevitably meant even more pressure on newsrooms, faced with producing just as much copy with fewer reporters. So, a decade passing since its introduction, is FOI still being used as effectively as it could be? There is plenty of evidence that it is but against a backdrop of depleted newsrooms, fewer staff and correspondingly less time to fill news pages, the climate for detailed investigations and the opportunities for reporters to pursue off-diary stories are at times inevitably constrained. So, what lessons can journalists draw from the first 10 years about effective FOI requests?

Beyond 'how much' and 'how many'

Many FOI requests to councils from journalists – quite rightly - are inevitably directed at the important issue of how they are spending taxpayers' money. If there is one thing that has been amply demonstrated by FOI, it is that public bodies hold vast and often highly detailed amounts of data, statistics and figures. In some senses, this ought not to be a surprise: without it, councils would not be able to measure the success or failure of policies and be ready to head off or address concerns about varying levels of demand for important frontline services At the same time, councils, who have not always enjoyed the best reputation for managing public money, also have a level of financial detail and data that until FOI was introduced did not often see the light of day unless leaked or, rarely, were the subject of a council report tabled to a committee. Again, this should be no surprise. Councils operate under strict auditing regulations and legislation that requires them to account for every penny that they spend, and can be subject to external auditors' public interest reports where there are claims of unlawful expenditure. The broad budget figures often presented on council committee agendas rarely drill down into the level of macro detail that FOI requests can uncover. So, FOI has been extremely productive in getting authorities and public bodies to account for their expenditure and indeed encouraged greater prudency and care.

Before FOI, disclosures on expenditure on foreign travel by councillors, for example, would have rarely if ever been presented to committees or set out in readily available reports. The notion that a reporter could pick up the phone to the council press office and request all the details of the far-flung corners of the world elected members had travelled to would have been scoffed at. Now, councils know that if they do plan to send officials or councillors abroad for what they like to label 'fact-finding' visits or to attend conferences, they can expect, rightly, to be asked how much the costs were to the public purse. Some authorities have grasped that it is actually better to be up-front about this sort of spending. Kent County Council, which was among the worst offenders, now routinely publishes this sort of information on its website for all to see. The result? A much more modest amount of money is spent each year and a diminishing level of media interest.

For journalists, the ability to get to this kind of information through FOI quite straightforwardly is often where the story begins and ends, when it could lead to more detailed probing. It is one thing to know how many compensation claims over poorly maintained roads a council has dealt with and how much has been paid out. It is another to request more precise detail about individual claims – how many were motorists? How many were cyclists? Is there one particular road, or roads, where more money has been paid out? Have there been any internal reports, notes from meetings, other than council meetings, where officers or councillors considered the safety issue? Where the issue is likely to be politically sensitive, it is worth considering, either as a new request or as part of the initial request, for details of correspondence exchanged between councillors and officers. Resourcefulness and tenacity have always been skills that good journalists have – and in the case of FOI, they are especially useful.

Understanding the public interest arguments

If there is one aspect of FOI that has proved vexing for journalists, it is the application by public authorities of Section 36 – the public interest exemption. As a qualified exemption, the onus on the authority is to demonstrate that disclosure would somehow be prejudicial to the effective conduct of public affairs. The onus on the journalist is to counter this with compelling arguments that trump those of the authority. This is not as easy as it might seem, particularly when the process can be time-consuming with no guarantee of success.

As a general rule, the application of this catch-all veto should, to the journalist, indicate that the odds are probably tilted towards there being a decent story to be had. Often underlying the deployment by councils of these catch-all exemptions is the hope and sometimes expectation that by kicking the issue into the long grass of the appeals process, the requester will simply give in and not pursue it. Often, authorities will cite Section 36 in formal responses that posit some generalised arguments about the possible harm that disclosure might lead to. It is less common for the exemption to be justified in a way that is directly related or tailored to the information sought – good journalists can usually tell when there has been some adroit cutting and pasting from a council's FOI template.

The difficulty here is that there is no definition of what might or might not be in the public interest. The guidance from the Information Commissioner's Office (ICO) reflects this ambiguity, saying 'the public interest can cover a wide range of values and principles relating to the public good, or what is in the best interests of society' (ICO, 2014). While this might prove awkward for reporters, it is worth keeping in mind that the authority has to provide credible evidence that there could be harm, not just make an untested assertion that it would as the basis for a rejection. This is as useful to councils but equally, it is as useful to journalists who, when challenging refusal notices should bear in mind that arguments in favour can be as simple as the general principle of enhancing accountability and openness, or exposing the specific impact of new government legislation.

At times, councils have used and continue to use Section 36 in ways that can only be described as creative or imaginative. In 2008, Kent County Council sought to argue that releasing details to The Kent Messenger Group of sites it was considering for a huge lorry park for 3,000 HGVs would 'create anxiety and uncertainty' among those who lived nearby. In a ruling overturning this decision in 2010, the ICO said there was a stronger public interest in disclosing information that would inform public participation and debate around an issue about that 'there is clearly considerable concern and anxiety' (Information Commissioner, 2010). It is a moot point whether the council would try to fall back on such a justification today. But it is probably less likely. Indeed, in September, 2014, the council published a new strategy for lorry parks, which clearly stated its preferred locations and invited views under a public consultation.

Not a substitute for old-fashioned reporting

The contraction of the local newspaper industry has seen countless titles closed, newsrooms pared back to the minimum and the emergence of the dubious phenomenon of 'user generated content'. Inevitably, this has led some to bemoan the ability of the established local media to hold to account public bodies; and that bloggers and so-called 'citizen journalists' – often with their own agendas – are replacing the trusted voice of the local paper. True, there are fewer local government specialists but this does not mean tumbleweed is rolling around the press bench of town hall committee rooms and council chambers.

On the other hand, FOI is just one tool in the journalist's box and can sometimes seem to be regarded as the start and end of holding elected politicians to account. FOI requests have the virtue of being relatively quick to frame for reporters and there is nothing wrong with using it as a stand-alone tool. But in my experience, the best FOI ideas often spring from attending council meetings, sometimes from the obscure nugget buried deep into a report; sometimes through the unguarded remark from a politician or officer. As the key-decision making body, attention will naturally focus on the cabinet, but there is often as much to get from the more obscure but no less important scrutiny meetings.

One interesting development in recent years is that a growing number of councils are abandoning cabinet government in favour of a return to the traditional all-party committee system, arguably more fertile territory for FOI stories as, unlike cabinet government, all parties are represented. One area often overlooked by journalists is the wealth of potential material that, under the government's transparency revolution, is now routinely published by councils detailing how they are spending taxpayers' money. Councils now publish thousands of invoices and data transactions each month, detailing any expenditure above £500. Some have chosen to go even further, lowering that threshold to £250. While Communities Secretary Eric Pickles, whose zeal for openness is commendable, proclaimed that this would lead to an army of armchair auditors, the evidence is decidedly mixed. This is partly because the data is voluminous, with larger councils publishing thousands of invoices each month, with little or next to no context, rendering it impregnable to any kind of meaningful analysis.

In 2012, The Kent Messenger Group requested data from 12 district and borough councils and Kent County Council about the number of FOI requests each had received about invoices. Seven replied that they had none, three said they had just one while Kent, which on average publishes 18,000 such invoices a month, had five. While the thought of ploughing through endless spreadsheets may be daunting, it can produce results. The first step is to ask – through FOI if necessary – what each of the numerical codes used by the authority relates to. Some of these may be obscure. A code that equated to the costs of external room hire turned out in the case of Kent County Council to be money that was spent on hiring rooms in hotels for meetings. Adding the sums up over a year showed the bill ran into several thousand pounds. The underlying point here is that while FOI in isolation is useful at one level, it can often be effectively harnessed to other transparency rights.

Journalists face many challenges in a fast-changing environment in which the 24-hour news agenda often places a premium on breaking stories before anything else any anybody else. FOI is in many ways antithetical to this but considered and intelligent use often produces greater rewards. The challenge, inevitably, is not just finding the right balance but using FOI in a way that properly holds councils and other public bodies to account for decisions that directly impact on the lives of people they are there to serve.

References

Information Commissioner's Office (2010) 'Complainant V Kent County Council' [FS50217563/2009] 19 December 2009

Information Commissioner's Office (2014) 'The Public Interest Test' available online at http://ico.org.uk/for_organisations/guidance_index/~/media/documents/library/Freedom_of_Information/Detailed_specialist_guides/the_public_interest_test.ashx accessed 1 December 2014

Note on the contributor

Paul Francis is political editor of The *Kent Messenger* Group and has been a journalist for 18 years. He is a three-time winner of the Kent Journalist of The Year Awards and associate lecturer at the University of Kent's Centre for Journalism. He is a member of the NCTJ's Public Affairs Board.

Abusing power? Investigating citizen-stripping using FOI

Investigative journalist *Alice Ross* traces the use of FOI in probing the use (and potential abuse) of anti-terrorism powers and citizen-stripping by the British Government, uncovering concerns about the arbitrary and unscrutinised nature of this executive power

Introduction

On the afternoon of 21 January, 2012, a US unmanned drone fired missiles at a vehicle travelling on the outskirts of Mogadishu, Somalia. The strike killed a senior commander in the armed Islamist group al Shabaab, named as Bilal al Berjawi. It soon emerged that Berjawi had strong links to the UK. 'At around 1400 (1100 GMT), a US drone targeted our mujahideen. One foreigner, a Lebanese with a British passport died,' an al Shabaab spokesman told reporters shortly after the attack (Sheikh and Omar, 2012). But the UK Foreign Office denied that Berjawi was a British citizen (Pflanz, 2012). The following day, *the Guardian*'s Ian Cobain reported that Berjawi was born in Lebanon, but moved to London as a baby and became a British citizen (Cobain, 2012). But Cobain reported the Government had stripped his citizenship, using little-known powers in the British Nationality Act 1981 that allow the Home Secretary to use an executive order to revoke the nationality of individuals who she believes threaten national security. *The Guardian* added that on the day of Berjawi's death, his wife gave birth to a son in London, and he called her to congratulate her. His family suspected the phone call helped pinpoint his location, raising the disturbing prospect that the British Government had shared intelligence leading to his death.

The reports caught the attention of Chris Woods, a reporter at the Bureau of Investigative Journalism (BIJ), a non-profit journalism organisation based at City University London. At the time, Woods ran a major project monitoring US drone strikes occurring outside declared hostilities, in Pakistan, Yemen and Somalia. Curious to know more about Berjawi's loss of British citizenship, Woods found an article published by Cobain in August 2011 (Cobain, 2011).

Cobain told me in August 2014 that he explored the area because 'I had a theory that with the exception of the Russian spy, Anna Chapman, the only people who were losing their citizenship were British Muslims, and I decided to ask about this through FOI. The Home Office responded in a way that was difficult to know anything at all about how they were using the power.'

Under these executive orders, the Home Secretary can strip an individual of their British citizenship with little notice. The only way to contest an order is through retrospective appeal, in court processes that can leave the individual stranded abroad for years. The only restriction on the Home Secretary at that point was that she could not use it to make someone stateless - so in practice it could only be used on dual-nationality citizens. The process has been compared by human rights lawyer Gareth Peirce to 'medieval exile, just as cruel and just as arbitrary' (Woods and Ross, 2013). Cobain's FOI revealed that since coming to power in May 2010, the coalition government had used the powers to revoke the nationality of an increasing number of people. Cobain reported that nine people had lost their nationality under the Conservative / Liberal Democrat coalition, compared to four cases in seven years of Labour government. Any indication of who these people were, or what they were believed to have done, was blocked on data protection grounds – although, as he noted, officials had previously briefed reporters on at least two cases.

Cobain appealed to the Information Commissioner, trying to get information on the reasons for the orders. 'At the tribunal, one of the witnesses was a senior official from the UKBA and the whole purpose of his evidence was to bolster the Home Office's claim,' said Cobain. 'He blurted out during his evidence that the deprivation cases only included one spy, so he more or less confirmed that which I was seeking in the process of giving evidence to prevent me from getting it.' Cobain's experience of obstruction would later be echoed repeatedly by those attempting to investigate the Government's escalating use of this power. The Home Office has consistently refused to discuss its use of the law, insisting that journalists and other researchers resort to FOI for even outline statistics. It issues nothing more as explanation than an oft-repeated statement that 'citizenship is a privilege, not a right'.

As the number of people losing their citizenship grew, the Home Office reduced the information it would release - and at one point sought to ban all BIJ staff from requesting further information on citizenship-stripping. Following the reports of Berjawi's death, Woods approached the Home Office for more details on the citizenship-stripping process, and with questions specifically on Berjawi. 'We approached the press office, but it declined to release any information. That forced the BIJ into its first FOI,' Woods said. He was told information on Berjawi could not be released, under data protection rules. In his request, Woods pointed out that since Berjawi was now dead, data protection law did not apply.

The Home Office took over three months to respond to Woods' request, but eventually, in September 2012, it released figures showing that 12 people had now lost their citizenship under the coalition Government. But it still refused to release information relating to Berjawi, or to the others who had lost their citizenship, now citing sections 23 (1) and Section 31 (1) of the Freedom of Information Act. Section 23 (1) exempts authorities from having to provide information that has been provided - directly or indirectly - by intelligence agencies, while Section 31 (1) protects information that could jeopardise law enforcement (FOI, 2000a; FOI, 2000b; MOJ, 2012). The Home Office did release the other nationalities of those affected, as it had done previously for Cobain. Woods and the author of this chapter set about trying to find out what had become of others who had lost the protections of British citizenship under this arbitrary and secretive power.

Selective disclosure

Some information was already in the public domain. David Hicks, an Australian-born fighter held in Guantanamo, managed after a lengthy court case to claim British nationality through his British-born mother. But on the day he was granted citizenship, then-Home Secretary John Reid revoked it. 'David is the only detainee who has ever received a fax in Guantanamo Bay. He had his citizenship for five hours. The next fax for him came saying, "We are going to take citizenship away",' his lawyer Major Michael Mori told Australian newspaper *The Age* (Crabb, 2006a; Crabb 2006b; EWCA, 2006). He was later returned to Australia. Anna Chapman, the Russian spy, was stripped of British citizenship in July 2010. Chapman, who was unmasked as a spy in the US, had been married in her early 20s to a British citizen. After she was outed, a Home Office spokesperson told the BBC: 'The Home Secretary has the right to deprive dual nationals of their British citizenship where she considers that to do so would be conducive to the public good. This case is under urgent consideration' (BBC, 2010). The BBC reported that her lawyers had been sent a letter revoking her British nationality. But nothing was known about others who had lost their citizenship under the coalition government. 'There's a contradiction in the Home Office's approach - they will discuss cases like Hicks and Chapman but they won't disclose anything about other cases,' said Cobain. 'It's a very extreme, coercive power that's exercised as an executive power. In that context it's even more important that there should be scrutiny by the media.'

Secret courts

Where a deprivation of citizenship order is on national-security grounds, appeals must be made to the Special Immigration Appeals Commission (Siac), a tribunal that can exclude even the appellant and their lawyers from the court when sensitive material is discussed, leaving specially vetted lawyers to argue on the appellant's behalf. The BIJ's team scoured Siac judgments and identified eight further cases, including an entire family, all born in the UK, who were stranded in Pakistan and claimed to be in danger after the father and three adult sons lost their citizenship (Woods, Ross 2013). Cases in Siac are usually anonymised to protect the identity of the appellant – but despite this, and the concerns over data protection cited by the Home Office, the judgments frequently contained key details that allowed us to identify the individuals.

'The Home Office talks about the need to protect identities, but we found details such as full addresses and family names - including in one case where it was claimed the family was at direct risk,' said Woods. 'We were incredibly careful not to breach court orders or allow for jigsaw identification in our reporting.' The records showed how, time and again, people were losing their citizenship with only the barest indications of the allegations against them. The order to revoke was almost always made while the individual was abroad, leaving them unable to return to the UK. But where individuals had not appealed to the court, information was far harder to come across.

During his inquiries about Berjawi's case, Woods learned that a friend of Berjawi's named Mohammed Sakr, who was of Egyptian origin, had also lost his nationality. In February 2012, the month after Berjawi's death, a drone again attacked a vehicle in Somalia. An unnamed 'senior intelligence official' told Reuters (Sheikh, 2012) the dead included a 'very senior Egyptian' militant. But, Woods established, this 'Egyptian' was actually a 27-year-old man, born in London to Egyptian-British parents. Berjawi and Sakr lost their citizenship within months of one another, in 2010. Less than 18 months later, each died in separate US drone strikes. As we started to piece this worrying picture together, something puzzling occurred.

Mystery cases

An online campaign in autumn 2012 claimed another young Londoner, Mahdi Hashi, had been stripped of his citizenship, then disappeared. Hashi was originally from Somalia, but grew up in London. From his mid-teens onwards, he claimed he was the subject of harassment from MI5 agents demanding he work as an informant on the Islamic community (Verkaik, 2012). He returned to Somalia in 2009, and in June 2012 the Home Office sent a letter to his father's home in London informing him that he was to lose his citizenship. Shortly after receiving this news, Hashi disappeared. A man contacted the family soon afterwards saying he had been held alongside Hashi in a jail in Djibouti, the tiny country immediately to the north of Somalia that is home to a large US military base. Hashi's family feared he would be taken by the US, and went public with his story. But this was the puzzle: in the FOI we had received at the end of August, the list of alternate nationalities held by the former Britons did not contain a Somali. It turned out that the information released by the Home Office was only correct up to the date of the request, three months earlier, so even though Hashi had lost his citizenship 10 weeks before we received the data, his case did not appear.

Realising our figures were more out-of-date than we had thought, we contacted the Home Office's press office for more current statistics. The previous response had created a precedent for releasing the information, we argued, so it should now be released to journalists through the press office.

Resorting to FOI would create delay for us and impose costs and statutory obligations on the Home Office. But the press office refused to release the information, directing us to use FOI. Reluctantly, we did so. This time we asked how many orders had been issued in each year since 2006, when the citizenship laws were rewritten, along with information about the alternate nationalities of those affected, again broken down by year, and a list of all appeals lodged to date. We also highlighted our objection to being forced to use FOI, saying we found it obstructive and created a risk of FOI being used as a delaying tactic, particularly in light of the long delay of our previous request.

Again, the request exceeded its time limit, despite us contacting the Home Office repeatedly as the request lapsed into being overdue. At the BIJ, we started publishing reports on deprivation of citizenship, starting with the case of Mahdi Hashi. The author interviewed Hashi's father, Mohamed Hashi, in December 2012, about his fears that he was in secret US custody somewhere in east Africa, and was vulnerable to mistreatment (Ross, 2012a). The Friday before Christmas, Mahdi Hashi reappeared in the most unexpected place: in downtown New York, where he appeared in a courtroom charged with belonging to al Shabaab (Ross, 2012b). He had undergone rendition to the US and was held in secret for over five weeks (ibid). The interview and follow-up news report were the first of what would eventually be over three dozen BIJ pieces on the Government's use of citizenship-stripping.

Two months later, we were nearly ready to publish our full findings, highlighting the cases of Berjawi, Sakr and Hashi - former British citizens who had found themselves at the sharp end of US counter-terrorism operations. We had identified nearly all of the 12 citizenship-stripping orders under the coalition of which we were aware. But days before we published the first phase of the investigation in late February 2013, we received the response to our latest overdue FOI, revealing that Theresa May had revoked a further five people's citizenship. The number of cases under the coalition had grown by a almost third since the previous FOI response, six months earlier. The BIJ's investigation into citizenship-stripping was a front-page story in the *Independent* (Woods and Ross, 2013). Following publication, we continued to dig into the stories of those affected. We met lawyers and family members, and sat through days of hearings in Siac's brightly-lit basement courtroom.

What we found raised concerns about the arbitrary and unscrutinised nature of this executive power. In one case, the Home Secretary was advised by the security services that the risk posed by an individual would be best managed by returning him to the UK and monitoring him. But after consultation with 'senior Cabinet colleagues', Theresa May rejected this advice and revoked his nationality (Ross, 2013a). The courts are supposed to provide scrutiny - but we know only one instance when someone has successfully challenged an order made on national security grounds, fighting all the way to the Supreme Court. And three weeks after the court overturned the Home Secretary's order, she issued a fresh order stripping his newly restored nationality again (Ross, 2013b).

An arbitrary power

During 2013 we continued to submit regular FOIs asking for numbers and alternate nationalities. We also asked for the grounds on which citizenship was revoked. In addition to national security grounds, the Home Secretary can also revoke an individual's nationality if they acquired British citizenship by fraud. There is a difference between removing the citizenship of someone who you find lied to get it in the first place, and using what is effectively banishment as a counter-terrorism tool. So we asked the government to provide separate figures showing how many cases were on grounds of being 'not conducive to the public good' - usually national security grounds - and how many were on fraud grounds. The Home Office refused to provide this, saying that combining statistics with information in the public domain would allow others to identify individuals. Eventually it did release some figures – but bizarrely said that where there were fewer than five people in a category it would not be more specific than saying there were 'fewer than five'. Again it cited data protection. That remains its position to this day.

Eventually, the Home Office attempted to sever even this limited flow of information. In December 2013, it revealed in an FOI response that 20 people had lost their citizenship that year - more than triple the highest number for any previous year. Accompanying this was a further surprise. 'We wish to advise you, after careful consideration, that we have decided to treat any further requests from yourself or colleagues from the Bureau of Investigative Journalism that relate to matters of deprivation of citizenship, as vexatious,' the letter added, citing section 14(1) of the Freedom of Information Act. It said BIJ staff had submitted 10 FOIs on the topic. In mid 2013, some months before this notice was sent, the Information Commissioner issued guidance on vexatious requests. This stated: 'we would suggest that the key question the public authority must ask itself is whether the request is likely to cause a disproportionate or unjustified level of disruption, irritation or distress' (ICO 2013).

The Home Office decision would have significantly impeded the BIJ's investigation, at a moment when it appeared ever larger numbers of people were affected. The BIJ's requests were not aimed at causing 'disruption, irritation or distress' - instead, they were the only way to access key information about a national security power, and clearly in the public interest, as they informed the public about a function of government. The BIJ appealed against this decision through an internal review with the Home Office - an onerous process that involved working with a lawyer to identify each grounds on which the Home Office might judge requests to be vexatious, and making counter-arguments. Our key argument was that FOI played a central role in a major journalistic investigation when there was a continuing refusal to release information through other routes. The appeal was lodged as an internal review with the Home Office, and while we waited for a response we were unable to lodge further requests to probe the new findings.

Eventually - two months after we were first told we were to be treated as vexatious in future and a month after submitting our appeal - the internal review found that future requests should be handled on a 'case by case basis'. It agreed there was a public interest in publishing the figures. On the threat to judge all future requests as vexatious, the review found: 'The wording used here was intended as a warning, but was rather heavy handed.' It advised that in order to avoid future requests being judged as vexatious, we should submit requests no more frequently than every quarter or six months. So the BIJ has retained its access to outline statistics, but this is in jeopardy. This door could be slammed shut at any time - not only to the author, but to the entire organisation. Requests on other counter-terrorism areas have been refused on the grounds that I had recently asked for further citizenship-stripping figures. And where fewer than five cases have been reported, the Home Office continues to decline to provide exact figures.

To date the BIJ is aware that at least 54 people have lost their citizenship. And thanks to figures provided to parliament, it is aware that there has been a steep rise in the number of people losing their nationality on fraud grounds. But its refusal to provide more detail means that at this point we do not know exactly how many people have been stripped of their citizenship, let alone who most of these individuals are or what they are alleged to have done. 'The Home Office is behaving as if it doesn't want anybody to know what it's doing and how it's depriving people of their citizenship. I don't know why they can't be more open about it if they think it's the right thing to do,' says Ian Cobain.

Abuse of power?
Freedom of information requests have been a vital tool in revealing the extent of the government's use of this secretive power. But it has not proven as straightforward as the Act would suggest: instead, the BIJ has been forced to tread carefully to avoid having this flow of information cut off for the months or even years it could take to appeal the decision to the Information Commissioner. In the absence of official transparency, this negotiated disclosure has helped give the public a sense of the scale of the issue.

References
BBC (2010) 'Russian spy Anna Chapman is stripped of UK citizenship' BBC online 13 July, available online at http://www.bbc.co.uk/news/10620352, accessed 21 August, 2014

Cobain, Ian (2011) 'Home Office stripping more dual-nationality Britons of citizenship' *the Guardian* 15 August, available online at http://www.theguardian.com/uk/2011/aug/15/home-office-law-dual-citizenship, accessed 21 August, 2014

Cobain, Ian, (2012) 'British "al-Qaida member" killed in US drone attack in Somalia' *the Guardian* 22 January, available online at http://www.theguardian.com/world/2012/jan/22/british-al-qaida-suspect-drone-somalia, accessed 21 August, 2014

Crabb, Annabel (2006a) 'Law strips Hicks of UK citizenship in hours' *Sydney Morning Herald* August 20, available online at http://www.smh.com.au/news/world/law-strips-hicks-of-uk-citizenship-in-hours/2006/08/19/1155408075077.html, accessed 21 August, 2014

Crabb, Annabel (2006b) 'Hicks cast out after day as British citizen' *Sydney Morning Herald* 27 August, available online at
http://www.theage.com.au/articles/2006/08/26/1156012790201.html?from=top5, accessed 21 August, 2014

EWCA Civ 400 (2006) 'Secretary of State for the Home Department v David Hicks' In the Supreme Court of Judicature Court of Appeal (Civil Division) 12 April, available online at http://eudo-citizenship.eu/caselawDB/docs/UK%2012%20April%202006%20original.pdf, accessed 22 August, 2014

FOI (2000a) Section 31: Law Enforcement. Freedom of Information Act 2000 , available online at http://www.legislation.gov.uk/ukpga/2000/36/section/31, accessed 22 August, 2014

FOI (2000b) Section 23: Information supplied by, or relating to, bodies dealing with security matters. Freedom of Information Act 2000, available online at http://www.legislation.gov.uk/ukpga/2000/36/section/23, accessed 22 August, 2014

ICO (2013) Dealing with vexatious requests (section 14) Information Commissioners Office 14 May, available online at
http://ico.org.uk/~/media/documents/library/Freedom_of_Information/Detailed_specialist_guides/dealing-with-vexatious-requests.pdf, accessed 21 August, 2014

MOJ (2012) Exemptions guidance Section 23: Information supplied by, or relating to, bodies dealing with security matters. Ministry of Justice March, available online at http://www.justice.gov.uk/downloads/information-access-rights/foi/foi-exemption-s23.pdf, accessed 21 August, 2014

Pflanz, Mike (2012) 'US drone strike in Somalia kills Britain-linked al-Qaeda agent' *The Daily Telegraph* 22 January, available online at
http://www.telegraph.co.uk/news/worldnews/al-qaeda/9031127/US-drone-strike-in-Somalia-kills-Britain-linked-al-Qaeda-agent.html, accessed 21 August, 2014

Ross, Alice K (2012a) 'British-Somali man's family fears US is secretly holding him' Bureau of Investigative Journalism 21 December, available online at
http://www.thebureauinvestigates.com/2012/12/21/british-somali-mans-family-fear-us-is-secretly-holding-him/, accessed 21 August, 2014

Ross, Alice K (2012b) 'Missing British-Somali man reappears in New York court' Bureau of Investigative Journalism 22 December, available online at
http://www.thebureauinvestigates.com/2012/12/22/missing-british-somali-man-reappears-in-new-york-court, accessed 21 August, 2014

Ross, Alice K (2013a) 'Theresa May overruled security services in citizenship-stripping case' Bureau of Investigative Journalism 14 November, available online at
http://www.thebureauinvestigates.com/2013/11/14/theresa-may-overruled-security-services-in-citizenship-stripping-case/, accessed 21 August, 2014

Ross, Alice K (2013b) 'Home Secretary strips man of UK citizenship - for the second time' Bureau of Investigative Journalism 2 December, available online at http://www.thebureauinvestigates.com/2013/12/02/home-secretary-strips-man-of-uk-citizenship-for-the-second-time, accessed 21 August, 2014

Sheikh, Abdi (2012) 'Four foreign militants killed in Somalia missile strike' Reuters 24 February, available online at http://in.reuters.com/article/2012/02/24/somalia-conflict-idINDEE81N0C820120224, accessed 21 August, 2014

Sheikh, Abdi and Omar, Feisal (2012) 'Somalia's Shabaab says air strike kills foreign fighter' Reuters 21 January, available online at http://uk.reuters.com/article/2012/01/21/uk-somalia-kenya-idUKTRE80K0RI20120121, accessed 21 August, 2014

Verkaik, Robert (2009) 'Exclusive: How MI5 blackmails British Muslims' *Independent* 21 May, available online at http://www.independent.co.uk/news/uk/home-news/exclusive-how-mi5-blackmails-british-muslims-1688618.html accessed 21 August, 2014

Woods, Chris & Ross, Alice K (2013) 'Former British citizens killed by drone strikes after passports revoked' The Bureau of Investigative Journalism 27 February, available online at http://www.thebureauinvestigates.com/2013/02/27/former-british-citizens-killed-by-drone-strikes-after-passports-revoked/, accessed 21 August, 2014

Note on the contributors

Alice K Ross is a journalist based in London. She is a graduate of the MA Investigative Journalism programme at City University London, and worked for three years at the Bureau of Investigative Journalism, a non-profit journalism organisation based at the university. During her time at the BIJ, she worked on and eventually ran two projects: one tracking citizenship-stripping, and the BIJ's three-year investigation into the CIA's use of drone strikes outside of officially recognised battlefields. With her colleagues Chris Woods and Jack Serle, she won the Martha Gellhorn Prize for Journalism in 2013, for their work on CIA drones.

The sealed and emptying chambers of Britain's intelligence history: Why the absolute exception for security sensitive matters is a present and continuing injustice

Tim Crook re-tells the fascinating tale of Alexander Wilson, the Secret Service spy who wrote novels in his spare time, and argues that blanket exemptions in the UK's FOI Act for the security and intelligence services are far too draconian and need reform

Introduction

Mike Shannon was nine-years-old when he was told his father Alexander Wilson died at the Battle of El Alamein. His mother Dorothy became angry if he asked too many questions about him. When she died in 1965, he found a copy of one of his father's spy novels *Wallace Intervenes* abandoned in a chest of drawers. When 73-years-old, in 2005, he came to me with a poorly labelled photograph album of his parents in British India in the 1920s, the well thumbed book published in 1939 by Herbert Jenkins and the memory of his father taking him to the German Embassy in the Spring of 1938 where there was a meeting with Joachim Ribbentrop and another mysterious rendezvous with a man at the Savoy Hotel where German was only spoken (Crook, 2010: 13). Mike was a veteran actor and poet who wanted to know more about an affectionate father who could enchant him with improvised stories, *joie de vivre*, but was tragically taken away from him by world war.

I therefore became a humanitarian researcher on behalf of a friend and established that Alexander Wilson had constructed at least a double identity by varying his middle names. Mike's father turned out to be a man who lived several lives across four multiple marriages some of them bigamous (ibid: 268-294). Between 1928 and 1940 he published 24 novels and several academic books arising out of his role as a Professor of English and university college principal in Lahore in present day Pakistan. His fiction was very well reviewed in the national and international press (ibid 6-8). He originated and developed a series of nine Sir Leonard Wallace Chief of the British Secret Service novels. Some expressed British imperial assessments of risks that were not widely represented in mainstream media (Crook 2010:10 & Wilson 1940). Wallace appeared to be based on the first 'C' of MI6, Captain Mansfield Smith Cumming.

The Wallace character first appeared in print in 1928 (Wilson, 1928) when Wilson headed the prestigious Islamia College of the University of Punjab, educating the sons of the Muslim elite and raising half a company of officer cadets for the British Indian Army (Hussain, 2009: 86-107). Descriptions of the real 'C' did not appear in the media and published books until from about 1930 onwards (Crook, 2010: 342-366). Wilson's fictional representation of Wallace had several resemblances with Smith Cumming. They included grey eyes (less than 3 per cent of the population); a wooden false limb (Smith-Cumming's leg / Wallace's arm); London and country homes (West End & Hampshire); and wives' names beginning with 'M' (ibid). The investigation resulted in the publication of *The Secret Lives of a Secret Agent*, the biography of Mike Shannon's father in 2010. Mike died three months later. He had gained four half-brothers, a half sister and scores of relatives he had no previous knowledge of. He had also learned that his father and mother had cruelly deceived him by making him falsely grieve for his father as a 9-year-old child. Alexander Wilson was not killed in action in 1942 but died in 1963 (ibid: 287-294).

His third wife Alison wrote a memoir, when she was alive, describing meeting Mike's father at the Secret Intelligence Service in 1940 where they worked in a unit covertly listening to the telephones of embassies and diplomatic legations. His nickname was 'Buddha' on account of his wisdom and background in British India (Wilson, 1991: 13-14). His War Office file included the annotation 'S.S.' on one of the documents (Crook, 2010: 446). 'S.S.' was a civil service acronym for the Secret Service at this time. (Jeffery, 2010: 475). The blurb of his last published novel *Chronicles of the Secret Service* in 1940 stated: '...Major Alexander Wilson probably knows as much about the Secret Service as any living novelist' (Wilson, 1940: 2).

The need for intelligence agency disclosure

Mike and his newly discovered family wanted answers to what was a mysterious and disturbing story. What was the true nature of his career in intelligence? When did it start? Did he work for other agencies apart from MI6/SIS? Why did he begin writing spy novels in British India with an apparent representation of the first 'C' from 1927? What was the connection between the spying and his multiple and parallel marriages with children? How could a bankrupt with a background of jail sentences for theft in Vancouver 1919 and London 1948 and wearing a false uniform and medals in 1944 succeed in working for the secret service?

Wilson's third wife Alison reported that her husband explained away their poverty and social misfortune from the end of 1942, and his prosecution two years later, as intelligence operations though he would not explain their purpose (Wilson, 1991: 24). The Alexander Wilson story was and is fundamental to the identity, origin, background and wellbeing of his surviving children, and the growing number of his grand children and great grand children. It could be argued that this was a strong case for an exception to be made of the statutory exemption under section 23 of the UK Freedom of Information Act applying to security bodies (Freedom of Information Act, 2000). There is a 'neither confirm nor deny' provision so that MI5 and MI6 can avoid being put in a situation of revealing information by denying or admitting that it was held. The 'NCND' acronym is an unshakeable shield vectoring the past, present and future. As a result of making a detailed presentation of questions to MI6 I received the written declaration that they could neither deny nor confirm they held any records on Alexander Wilson. The Security Service, MI5, did not respond in any way even though they received a detailed briefing and questionnaire. The requests went up to the level of Director General.

Why excessive secrecy and the FOI security body exclusion is unfair and discriminatory

Intelligence history in terms of the release of files to the National Archives is wholly in the control of the state intelligence bodies. They decide what to retain, shred, destroy and release into the public domain. Officially sanctioned histories such as Christopher Andrew's *The Defence of the Realm: The Authorized History of MI5* (2010) and Keith Jeffery's *MI6: The History of the Secret Intelligence Service 1909-1949* (2010) are heavily vetted. The scholars do not have free reign to quote and publish from the material they are allowed to view. Sometimes senior retired intelligence personnel are given privileged access to classified files. For example the award-winning author Alan Judd was able to write a biography of the first 'C' and access Smith-Cumming's diary as well as other documents not available at the National Archives (Judd, 2000).

I have never worked in the intelligence field and I am not blessed with the sources and contacts that inform so powerfully the handful of recognised espionage and intelligence historians. Interpretation and research continues to be searching while blindfold. Alexander Wilson's life is like that of a constantly conjuring magician manipulating convex and concave mirrors that distort, obscure, project and contort information and its context. The apparently shameful 1944 prosecution for posing as a Colonel with false decorations is contradicted by the fact that a prosecution claim he was actually entitled to wear World War One medals was false. He was writing from the Author's Club in the West End when he was supposed to be in Brixton prison serving his sentence (Crook, 2010: 185-6).

He was a successful Professor of English Literature and principal at an Indian University for six years, awarded an honorary fellowship and was also falsely claiming an Oxford degree, Distinguished Service Order, and knighthood (ibid: 319). He was a respected linguist interpreting in Arabic, Persian and Hindustani for the Foreign Office and at the same time falsely claiming a Cambridge degree in modern languages and the identity of a Manchester Grammar School teacher also called Alexander Wilson, also a commissioned officer in the Great War and who also had a father called Alexander Wilson (ibid 131).

FOI applications proved slow but fruitful in the jurisdiction of British Columbia where I managed to navigate section 25 of the state's Freedom of Information and Protection of Privacy Act, 1996. As a result of obtaining Wilson's Oakalla Prison Farm inmate record it was possible to link his fictional writing of travelling the world by ship with his actual round the world service as a purser in the merchant navy (ibid: 172-3). The detailed description by Canadian jailers of many visible shrapnel scars across his body correlated with his fictional description of being blown up in an air-raid in France. Yet his War Office file of service in the Great War referred only to a knee injury. One file stated he had served overseas, but another denied him a medal on the basis he was not stationed anywhere overseas (ibid: 322).

Alexander Wilson and the case of the Egyptian ambassador

In May 2013, the Foreign and Commonwealth Office released a second tranche of intelligence related files comprising 463 pieces covering the period from September 1939 to 1951 as well as 17 files from 1903 to 1913. I prepared to start looking. Fortunately an intelligence historian based at the Public Record Office at Kew, Phil Tomaselli, recognised that the redacted subject of file FO1093/263 'Case of the Egyptian Ambassador' was likely to be Alexander Wilson (Tomaselli, 2011: 14). The file does not explicitly identify Wilson. At one point it is possible to detect the top of the 'l' as the third letter in a reference to Wilson in the annotated longhand of Sir Alexander Cadogan on the first page of the correspondence from 'C' Sir Stewart Menzies to the Director-General of the Security Service dated 18 June 1943. In addition the spaces left in relation to each redaction throughout the file match a combination of 'Wilson', 'Mr. Wilson' and 'Alexander Wilson.'

Documents in the file reveal that Alexander Wilson was dismissed from SIS in October 1942 because he faked a burglary and had been in serious trouble with the police. MI5 officer Alex Kellar was tasked to investigate Wilson's Section X 'Special Material' reports indicating the Egyptian Ambassador in London and his staff were intelligence gathering against the interests of Great Britain and her allies. Kellar concluded Wilson had fabricated the reports.

The chief civil servant at the Foreign Office, Sir Alexander Cadogan, the then Director General of MI5, and the Chief of MI6, known as 'C,' condemned Wilson as a serious public danger, a 'master of fiction' who had produced 'pure invention.' The third 'C' Sir Stewart Menzies said: 'I do not think it at all likely that we shall again have the bad luck to strike a man who combines a blameless record, first rate linguistic abilities, remarkable gifts as a writer of fiction, and no sense of responsibility in using them!' (FO1093/263, 1943: 10).

The justification for full disclosure

I would argue the *omertà* style 'neither confirm nor deny' policy relating to Alexander Wilson has no operational, legal, or constitutional validity. The Egyptian Ambassador's file is a blatant release of detailed information about Alexander Wilson in a public domain context when anybody with any knowledge of him would be able to recognise him as the redacted subject. Mr Tomaselli was able to do so. The inefficient redacting means that his identification is now beyond doubt. Yet the FOI request for the release of the withheld MI5 report by Alex Kellar was denied on the grounds of security sensitivity (Burton, 2014: 1). Two requests for a Foreign Office internal review received no response after several months and the next step at the time of writing is to appeal to the Information Commissioner. I will be arguing that the Foreign Office has misdirected itself by claiming that exemption is absolute with no application of a balancing public interest test (ICO, 2013). There is a public interest test when it is clear that files exist and relate to more than 30 years ago. The historical information is in fact at least 70 years old (ICO, 2012; TNA, 2012). There are clearly compelling public interest reasons to release Alex Kellar's report and all files relating to Alexander Wilson's involvement with MI5, MI6, Metropolitan Police Special Branch and intelligence bodies while he was in British India.

Evidence supporting Alexander Wilson's reports on the Egyptian Ambassador

Alex Kellar's report may be inaccurate and wrong on the basis of other files released into the public domain and available at the Public Record Office. The files FO 371/23372, HW 1/1341 and HW 1/1376 demonstrate that the Egyptian Ambassador, Hassan Nachat Pasha, was intelligence gathering with his staff in establishing contacts and obtaining information from the Ministry of Information, discussing post war alignment with the Soviet Union's Ambassador in London, and obtaining information from foreign correspondents based in London about the Allied leaders' war conference in Casablanca. The file FO 371/41392 demonstrates that in the early part of 1944 Nachat [in documents his identifying name is presented as 'Nashat'] was recalled to Cairo and in only a matter of weeks was plotting an overthrow of the pro-British (described as Anglo-maniacal) regime.

The British ambassador in Cairo, Sir Miles Lampson, (later Baron Killearn) sent to Sir Alexander Cadogan intelligence reports of Nachat's mischief and urged Cadogan to engineer Nachat's recall to London: 'Nachat is being a political nuisance and his early return to London would be a blessing' (FO 371/41392, 1944: 6). Killearn reported Nachat's intention 'eventually to become Prime Minister' (ibid: 3). He observed: 'It will be remembered how effectively in 1925 Nachat organised the absolutist regime for King Fouad not only against the Wafd but against the Liberals and democratic independents. It was only our intervention which brought about the removal of Nachat, and the end of his attempt to establish Palace rule in the country' (ibid: 3-4).

Hassan Nachat Pasha had been described as Egypt's Rasputin in the 1920s and was strongly associated with Anti-British imperial political elements (Von Weigand, 1925). He was Egyptian Ambassador in Berlin for 10 years before taking up the post in London in 1938. He was said to have had an affair with a German Princess, entertained the Nazi elite lavishly, (Almeida, 2008: 174) and although diplomatically polite and courteous to the British when in London, part of an Egyptian elite that hoped for Axis Power victory and allied defeat in North Africa.

A secret declassified FO file indicates his counterpart in Tehran, Zulficar Pasha, was in secret negotiations and intelligence gathering for Nazi Germany (FO 371/27488, 1941). A United Nations file in 1948 reveals German intelligence and Foreign Office files proving the Egyptian diplomatic service was playing a double game with the British even after the defeat of Rommel at El Alamein in 1942. (Nation Associates, 1948: 27). Plans were discussed to smuggle King Farouk into exile in Berlin; and bomb Tel Aviv (ibid 3). Hitler and Ribbentrop exchanged secret overtures of support and hopes for British defeat in Egypt with King Farouk's governments and diplomats (ibid: 5-7).

Major AW Sansom of Egyptian field security in Cairo published his memoirs in 1965 and stated that the majority of the Egyptian elite and armed forces were pro German and Italian; actively working against the British (Sansom 1965:22). Prior to 1942 'Under an almost openly pro-German Prime Minister Aly Maher Pasha, for nine months the Egyptian government gave our enemies all the aid it possibly could' (ibid 24). Egyptian forces had to be withdrawn from Allied operations in the desert in 1940 on the order of Winston Churchill because they were known to be reluctant to fight for their effective military occupiers (ibid: 30).

At the end of 1940 General Sir Henry Maitland Wilson, examining papers captured in the Italian HQ in Libya, was surprised to find a complete set of British plans for the defence of the Western Desert. They had been supplied by Egyptian Army Chief of Staff, General Aziz el Masri (ibid: 57). Sansom described forcing a plane carrying General Aziz el Masri to crash land on take off in 1942. It was being flown by Egyptian Air Force Squadron Leader Hussein Zulficar Sabri to Rommell's headquarters (ibid: 68). There was a plan to establish a 'Free Egyptian Army' on German occupied territory. The Germans had been in contact for the previous two months and this was his third attempt to escape after previous attempts by U-boat and German plane disguised with RAF markings (ibid 74). The British forced King Farouk to dissolve a pro-Axis power government in 1942 by surrounding his palace with tanks and deposing the Prime Minister, to be replaced with pro-British Egyptian politicians (Herf, 2010: 94-96; Sansom, 1965: 93).

The need for greater disclosure is exacerbated by the fact that the memoir by Wilson's third wife, Alison, contradicts the information disclosed by 'C' Sir

Stewart Menzies in file FO 1093/263. She reported that there had been a burglary at their flat in late 1942, but that did not include any suspicions or recollection of the police investigating her husband for faking the burglary and indeed 'being in serious trouble with the police,' at that time (A Alison, 1991: 20). Furthermore, public reports of his later prosecutions made no mention of these matters (Crook, 2010: 642-646).

The need for a new legal approach

The last major challenge to the blanket exemption for security bodies under section 23 of FOI in relation to historical matters concerned Dr Vincent Frank-Steiner who in 2007-8 wanted confirmation and release of documents about his uncle Paul Rosbaud said to have been the spy codenamed 'The Griffin' during the Second World War. A book published in 1986 had speculated that he remained in Germany as the editor of an academic journal and was able to supply unique intelligence while usefully positioned at the heart of the Nazi scientific establishment (Frank-Steiner v SIS, 2008: 1-4).

The Investigatory Powers Tribunal ruled in favour of the unshakeable SIS policy to neither confirm nor deny. But I would argue that this cannot be indefinite. The statute allows a public interest test after 30 years. The Foreign Office has conceded that they have files on Alexander Wilson through their release of the file on the case of the Egyptian Ambassador in May 2013. Its release into the public domain in the context of his published biography in 2010 was an indirect confirmation. The failure to redact his name properly is a direct confirmation. In addition I believe the UK Supreme Court ruling on 26 March 2014 in Kennedy (Appellant) v The Charity Commission (Respondent) Hilary Term [2014] UKSC has broken down statutory exceptions to freedom of expression public interest balancing exercises. The effect of this case is that English common law separately holds a public interest remedy in relation to the freedom to receive and impart information and ideas without interference by public authority.

I would argue that no security body should choke off common law rights and rights to natural justice in the context of this case. Alexander Wilson's encoding of espionage in published novels and his engagements with British intelligence bodies have generated significant public interest controversies. More importantly these events of more than 70 years ago have had a profound and catastrophic impact on the lives of his wives and children and further descendants. There is no doubt that a common law and natural justice argument can be made for the fullest disclosure of all relevant records held about him in the sphere of state intelligence.

References

Books

Almeida, Fabrice de (2008) *High Society in the Third Reich*. Cambridge: Polity

Andrew, Christopher (2010) *The Defence of the Realm: The Authorized History of MI5*. London: Allen Lane

Crook, Tim, (2010) *The Secret Lives of a Secret Agent: The Mysterious Life and Times of Alexander Wilson*. Essex: Kultura Press

Herf, Jeffrey, (2000) *Nazi Propaganda For The Arab World*. New Haven & London: Yale University Press

Hussain, Syed, Sultan, Mahmood (2009) *56 Years of Islamia College Lahore 1892-1947*. Lahore: Izharsons

Jeffery Keith (2010) *MI6: The History of the Secret Intelligence Service 1909-1949*. London: Bloomsbury Publishing

Judd, Alan, (2000) *The Quest for C: Mansfield Cumming and the Founding of the Secret Service*. London: HarperCollins

Sansom, Major AW (1965) *I Spied Spies*. London: George G. Harrap & Co

The Nation Associates (1948) *The Record of Collaboration of King Farouk of Egypt with the Nazis and Their Ally, The Mufti: Memorandum Submitted to the United States*. New York: The Nation Associates.

Wilson, Alexander (1928) *The Mystery of Tunnel 51*. London: Longmans & Green

Wilson, Alexander (1928) *The Devil's Cocktail*. London: Longmans & Green

Wilson, Alexander (1939) *Wallace Intervenes*. London: Herbert Jenkins

Wilson, Alexander (1940) *Chronicles of the Secret Service*. London: Herbert Jenkins

Legal guides, Statute and Case Law

Freedom of Information Act 2000, Section 23, http://www.legislation.gov.uk/ukpga/2000/36/section/23, accessed 10 August, 2014

ICO (Information Commissioner's Office), Security bodies (section 23) Freedom of Information Act, 20130226, Version: 2.0. http://ico.org.uk/for_organisations/guidance_index/~/media/documents/library/Freedom_of_Information/Detailed_specialist_guides/security_bodies_section_23_foi.ashx, accessed 2 September, 2014

ICO (Information Commissioner's Office), The public interest test, Freedom of Information Act, 10130305, Version 2.

http://ico.org.uk/for_organisations/guidance_index/~/media/documents/library/Freedom_of_Information/Detailed_specialist_guides/the_public_interest_test.ashx, accessed 2 September, 2014

TNA (The National Archives), Access to public records, July 2012. http://www.nationalarchives.gov.uk/documents/information-management/access-to-public-records.pdf, accessed 4 September, 2014

Vincent C Frank-Steiner v The Data Controller of the Secret Intelligence Service, Case no. IPT/06/81/CH, Investigatory Powers Tribunal, Judgment, 26 February 2009, available at http://www.ipt-uk.com/docs/Steiner%20Judgment%20FINAL%20for%20publication.pdf accessed 4 August, 2014

Kennedy (Appellant) v The Charity Commission (Respondent) Hilary Term [2014] UKSC. http://supremecourt.uk/decided-cases/docs/UKSC_2012_0122_Judgment.pdf accessed 10 July, 2014

Archives

Burton, Clare, 'Freedom of Information Act 2000 Request- Ref: 0140-14' decision by letter to Tim Crook, 4 March, 2014

Von Wiegand, Karl H, 'Khedive's Aid Death Suspect', *The Milwaukee Sentinel*, 16 December, 1925

Wilson, Alison (1991) *Before*, private memoir in the possession of the Alexander Wilson Estate.

The National Archives, Kew.

FO 371/23372/4242, Complaint made by Egyptian Ambassador, 1939

FO 371/27488, Activities of Egyptian Ambassador at Tehran, 1941

FO1093/263, 'C', Chief of the Secret Intelligence Service (SIS): report on the Egyptian ambassador, 25 May – 2 July 1943

FO 371/41392, Activities of Hassan Nashat, Egyptian Ambassador in London, 1944

HW 1/1376, Egyptian ambassador, London: discussion with Soviet ambassador on Feb 11 on attempts to pressurise Egypt into aligning herself with Soviet Union and China, 17 February, 1943

HW 1/1341, Egyptian ambassador, London: rumours of German peace proposals discussed at Casablanca, 29 January, 1942

Online

Tomasseli, Phil, 'Alas a dreadful book' Review and comment trail 11 May 2011 to 22 February, 2014 http://www.amazon.co.uk/Secret-Lives-Agent-Mysterious-Alexander/dp/0954989986/, accessed 24 August, 2014

Note on the contributor

Tim Crook is a long-standing journalist and academic currently employed as Head of Radio and Media Law & Ethics at Goldsmiths, University of London, where he holds the post of Reader in Media and Communication. He is also Visiting Professor of Broadcast Journalism, to the faculty of Media, English and Performance at Birmingham University. His publications include *International Radio Journalism* (1997); *Radio Drama* (1999); *Comparative Media Law and Ethics* (2009); *The Sound Handbook* (2011); and *The UK Media Law Pocketbook* (2013) all by Routledge; *The Secret Lives of a Secret Agent: The Mysterious Life and Times of Alexander Wilson* (2010) by Kultura Press; and forthcoming *Writing Audio Drama*, also by Routledge; and *George Orwell on the Radio* by Ashgate.

From booze to trews: perspectives on journalists' use of freedom of information in Scotland

Julian Calvert goes directly to the source and talks to Scottish journalists about their experiences of using the Scottish FOI Act, 10 years after its introduction. Important differences from the Westminster Act seem to put the media in Scotland at a relative advantage

Introduction

'If you've ever tried to impress a guest with a bottle of fine wine, or punished another with a glass of gut rot, you are not alone,' was the innocuous first paragraph of a story by Tom Gordon in the *Herald* on 5 February, 2005 (Gordon, 2005). There was more to this than first appeared however; using the Freedom of Information (Scotland) Act which had come into force the previous month, Gordon had discovered the cost and details of all wine served by First Minister Jack McConnell in receptions at Bute House in Edinburgh. 'Foreign dignitaries and banking moguls' were served Barolo or Mersault costing £25 per bottle, while the cheapest wine, a white Rioja costing less than £5, had been served to reporters the previous Christmas. The *Herald*'s wine critic was deployed to describe the Rioja as 'really pretty ropey'.

This was one of the best known early uses of FOI legislation in Scotland, and later that year Gordon's colleague Paul Hutcheon had made headlines across the UK when Scottish Conservative leader David McLetchie was forced to resign after his expenses were revealed following an FOI appeal (BBC, 2005). Few issues since then have had quite such an impact outside Scotland, but journalists have continued to use the Scottish Act to break and research a wide range of national and local news, while the legislation itself shows important differences from the Westminster Act which seem to put the media at a relative advantage.

At first glance the Freedom of Information (Scotland) Act 2002 (widely known as FOISA) seems very similar to the legislation covering the rest of the UK; the types of public authorities covered by the legislation are consistent with those 'south of the border'; they are given 20 days to respond and use of the legislation has been widespread among both the media and the wider public.

Two other laws apply in Scotland alone: the Environmental Information (Scotland) Regulations 2004 and the INSPIRE (Scotland) Regulations 2009, which gives a right to discover and view spatial datasets held by Scottish public bodies. The UK equivalent of FOISA also applies in Scotland for UK-wide public bodies such as the BBC and Ministry of Defence, while the Data Protection Act 1998 applies to the whole of the UK including Scotland.

The Act, which was drawn up by the then Scottish Executive and took effect on 1 January, 2005, has had a significant effect on the work of journalists but this has been the subject of a relatively low amount of academic study in comparison to the UK legislation. Several articles make only passing mention of the Scottish legislation (Birkinshaw 2010; Hayes 2009; Hazell and Worthy 2010) or discuss the UK without making any mention of Scotland at all (Bindman 2004; Worthy 2010; Glover et al 2006), while discussion of particular news stories tends to focus on the McLetchie case. This study will analyse the importance of differences between the Scottish and UK Acts and use interviews with working journalists, the head of communication at a large public body and the Scottish Freedom of Information Commissioner to indicate strengths and weaknesses of the legislation, as well as considering a variety of news stories which have come about through use of the Act.

Journalists at work with FOI

Four journalists were interviewed: Paul Hutcheon, investigations editor at the *Sunday Herald*; Rob Edwards, environment editor of *Sunday Herald* and correspondent for the *New Scientist* and *the Guardian*; Roisin McGroarty, editor of the *Irvine Times*; and Drew Cochrane, who has just completed 40 years as editor of the *Largs and Millport Weekly News*. All have used FOI applications to research news stories, McGroarty and Cochrane at a local level in North Ayrshire, Hutcheon across Scotland and Edwards covering Scotland and the entire UK. They have used it to uncover information ranging from iPads being stolen from schools to nuclear incidents at military bases.

Hutcheon is one of the few Scottish journalists whose use of FOI has attracted comment outside Scotland, with Hayes (2009: 60) saying that at one point 'he accounted for 40 per cent of all requests under FOI in Scotland' and crediting his 'hours of forensic examination in the search for the killer detail' (ibid). Hutcheon's own account gives a rather lower figure of 49 appeals to the Commissioner's office and five or six requests per week being entered into his database and he stresses that the vast majority of his stories come from contacts and sources while only about 10 per cent have an FOI element. Most of his current FOI inquiries are to the Scottish Government:

> *'Obviously I've got a lot of requests at different stages – at review stage, at information commissioner's office stage, so … it's just something I've built into the job. The most important thing obviously in journalism is contacts and sources, so it's just another club in the golf bag really,'* (Hutcheon, 2014).

It was Hutcheon whose FOI inquiry in 2005 started the David McLetchie affair; he appealed to Kevin Dunion, the first Scottish Freedom of Information Commissioner, after expenses information was withheld by the Scottish Parliament. The appeal was upheld, revealing that McLetchie had been claiming for taxi journeys between the Parliament building and his law practice. McLetchie subsequently repaid £250, which had been wrongly claimed for a flight to Bournemouth, as well as the cost of a trip to Selkirk. (BBC, 2005). The expenses details had been withheld on security grounds, but Dunion analysed 800 taxi journeys and concluded there was no way that they could be used by a third party to predict McLetchie's movements (BBC, 2005). Hutcheon says that before this incident the Scottish Parliament had been 'terrible' in dealing with FOI requests, despite being the body, which introduced the legislation, and the story was important not just because of the resignation but in the precedent it set for Parliamentary expenses, a precedent that was later followed by Westminster:

> *'I think that that sort of opened the floodgates to a massive change in how expenses were dealt with at Holyrood. That was a big one, obviously it had a knock-on with Westminster as well because they looked to Holyrood when they had their own expenses scandal they imported that model of putting everything online,'* (Hutcheon, 2014).

Cochrane pointed to the appointment of Kevin Dunion, formerly a campaigner rather than a civil servant or lawyer, as being an important first sign of commitment to FOI and paid tribute to Dunion's early work in liaising with editors' organisations (Cochrane, 2014), while McGroarty said FOI use was an important part of the news coverage which had seen her newspaper achieve a circulation increase in 2014 – one of only eight weekly newspapers in the UK to do so. Stories where her staff had used FOI requests included the cost of accommodation for travellers; the extent of infestation in newly built schools; and assaults on teachers by pupils and binge-drinking children (McGroarty, interview, 2014). Figures revealing computer equipment stolen from schools followed a short article written by pupils for their regular 'class chat' section of the newspaper saying they were upset after four iPads were stolen (ibid).

The current Scottish Information Commissioner, Rosemary Agnew, said FOI requests often worked best at a local level, where they were 'really focussed on what's happening in a particular town, region, city' (Agnew, 2014). In contrast, she said that at a national level there were still stories that were government-focussed or about issues of the day, however increasingly FOI itself was becoming the story:

> *'Instead of commenting on a particular government policy on X, what we now get is the story that runs for a few days if not weeks on the efforts that the organisation took to withhold the information,'* (ibid).

She quoted the example of First Minister Alex Salmond's 'tartan trews', where the story became not their cost, but efforts to conceal their cost. In December

2011 the First Minister charged the taxpayer £259.40 for a pair of tartan trousers on a visit to China (Johnson, 2014). In March 2013 the *Daily Telegraph* submitted an FOI request to disclose the purchase, then appealed after the Scottish government failed to respond. Two weeks into the Commissioner's investigation, Mr Salmond repaid the amount he had claimed.

A question of timescales

In Scotland public authorities have 20 working days to respond to a request for information, as is the case with the rest of the UK. The Scottish Act however also sets the same timescale for the public body to review its original response. All journalists said that the first 20-day period in Scotland was effectively seen as a minimum rather than a maximum response time for authorities. Edwards and McGroarty both said that authorities rarely acted in the spirit of the FOI Act, that the information should be made available as soon as possible and the 20-day period was the maximum rather than a standard. McGroarty said in dealing with councils, Strathclyde Police and health trusts she had never known a single request which was fully answered within the 20-day period (McGroarty, 2014), while Edwards noted similar problems with the Ministry of Defence and government departments (Edwards, 2014). The 20-day turnaround for appeals in Scotland was seen as the most important difference by Hutcheon, who said that the system in the rest of the United Kingdom allowed public bodies to 'stonewall' journalists for an undefined period of time, while the Scottish system was more robust. Edwards concurred; arguing the absence of a second 20-day deadline was exploited by public agencies in England (Edwards, 2014). Agnew, meanwhile, said that the Scottish system gave greater clarity with timescales, while admitting there were still problems:

> *'[The UK system] seems very open-ended and especially when you consider that even under the Scottish rules you can wait months and months and months for information. It's a good differential for us,'* (Agnew, 2014).

Despite this stipulation, the Scottish system can still lead to journalists waiting many months to receive information. Hutcheon described the review stage as 'a waste of time' with bodies 'flouting the Act because there is no financial penalty'. He suggested sanctions, if not fines then 'naming and shaming,' citing the Scottish government as the worst offender (Hutcheon, 2014).

Hutcheon was interviewed four weeks before Agnew produced a special report, *Failure to Respond to FOI requests: extent, impact and remedy*, (Agnew, 2014) which was laid before the Scottish Parliament in August 2014, stating that a quarter of appeals to her office during the last three years had been because of failures by Scottish public bodies to respond to at all or on time; 50 per cent of these appeals related to just five bodies, and *the Guardian's* Scotland correspondent Severin Carrell had to wait 471 working days for information about nuclear power and nuclear power stations from Scottish ministers. Agnew also sent press releases to all major news organisations in Scotland and her report included tables of the top 10 authorities for failure to respond to appeals between 2012 and 2014, with the Scottish government topping the league table. Local authorities such as Edinburgh and Dundee City Councils were praised for improved performances after taking action following poor figures in previous years. In 2013/14 the media accounted for 14 per cent of all appeals and 22 per cent of failure to respond appeals, while 12 of the 20 failure respond appeals were from two journalists (Agnew, 2014: 13-15).

Interviewed after the report's publication, Agnew said she personally did not support fines as the public purse would be involved for both parties: 'I think the public censure is a sanction in itself and by using my powers in this way I think the name and shame is a sanction in itself.' She stressed that the problem was concentrated in 'pockets' and the emphasis should be on helping authorities to 'get it right first time' (Agnew, 2014).

Other cross-border differences

In addition to the clearly defined review period, there are four other elements that distinguish the Scottish Act from its Westminster counterpart, firstly relating to the public interest test. In the UK if the public interest applies the timescale can be extended - although the code of practice states authorities should aim to reach the decision within 20 days, they can issue a notice extending it to something they think reasonable, whereas in Scotland's legislation the public interest test is a clear cut-off point, part of that 20 days. The appeal process in Scotland is also different, with the process going from request to review, commissioner and then finally the Court of Session. Again Agnew argues that this is faster than the UK equivalent: 'The tribunal system can add a long time to that, and I think it puts a very different responsibility on requesters as well,' (Agnew, 2014). Edwards (2011) describes it as 'a daunting experience' when he took a Ministry of Defence case relating to nuclear safety to the Information Tribunal in 2010. Although he was successful, he said it was 'too daunting, too intimidating, too scary. Scotland's funding system for FOI is also different from the rest of the UK; rather than a grant in aid system Agnew's office is funded through the Scottish Parliament, which Agnew again believes is an advantage. The final noticeable difference from a journalist's perspective is perhaps the most telling one: despite some journalists feeling that the current SNP Government is not in favour of FOI, a Ministerial veto has never been applied.

A hammer or a scalpel? Advice on using the Act

All the journalists interviewed for this study agreed that good communication with the public body concerned was important for effective use of freedom of information legislation. Agnew suggested that failure to respond to requests was most common when there were wider problems between the organisation and the journalist. Requests can be refused if it is likely that they would cost more than £600, but Hutcheon said experience had taught him how to avoid these problems:

'The first couple of years lots of requests went in, it was a learning experience, it was a learning curve, not every request I put in was perfect. Looking back I wouldn't have put in every single request that I did do, but I think it's got better, I don't think any journalist wants to waste a public servant's time, and FOI is not my first port of call. If I want information I always ask myself, do I know someone in the organisation who can help me. If the answer is no, and if there is no other way then I'll try and draft an FOI in the tightest way possible,' (Hutcheon, 2014).

Public bodies in Scotland have a duty to provide advice and assistance when someone is making a request, so they should work with individuals asking for information so that it can be refined or narrowed down, avoiding the potential cost problem. Agnew said that wherever possible, journalists should call the public body to establish the best way to frame the inquiry, although she acknowledged that staffing pressure for both journalists and civil servants might make this more difficult.

Colin Edgar, head of communication and service development at Glasgow City Council, described the act as 'immensely frustrating and a bit of a pain in the backside' but acknowledged 'that doesn't make it a bad thing.' He stressed that FOI legislation was simply another method of obtaining data and drew attention to occasions when a national issue was taken up locally and reporters submitted FOI requests to all 32 of Scotland's councils:

'Now I don't think it's lazy to do that rather than pick up the phone 32 times and have a conversation with 32 council press offices, you just send out a single FOI to each and every one of them and this is where you've got this issue where it's a hammer but they think it's a scalpel,' (Edgar 2014).

He cited a case when a BBC journalist covering the disposal of babies' ashes asked for information via FOI about what happened to four categories of babies that had died. Eventually the information was supplied, at a cost of more than £9,000 after an appeal had gone to Rosemary Agnew, who ruled that the council was not obliged to comply with the request but had not provided reasonable advice and assistance about how it could be reduced in scope. He said FOI requests from journalists were usually run past him or someone in his office so that 'explanatory context' could be added to avoid data being misunderstood, as in a case when the *Scottish Sun* had asked for the total spend on catering in schools and the total number of schoolchildren.

'When we gave them those numbers we said expressly, we are giving you X and we are giving you Y, however be aware that if you divide X by Y that will not give you the cost of a school meal and you should understand that that is not what that is because Y, the number of children in schools in Glasgow, is a substantially bigger figure than the number of children who take school meals in Glasgow, so if you divide X by Y it gives you a very small number,' (ibid).

Despite this the newspaper ran a story using the phrase 'Cheaper than Chum', saying the meals cost 32p per head. The council took the case to the Press Complaints Commission and the *Scottish Sun* published a retraction acknowledging they had been told in advance that the actual cost was between 95p and £1.05.

The future - more openness ahead?

The Scottish Act covers a wide range of bodies, but some organisations which were previously open to public scrutiny are currently exempt. Notable among these are housing associations, which have taken over the management of housing stock from councils and are not covered by FOISA. Hutcheon described it as 'incredible that the biggest housing association in Europe has not been added to the list'. Agnew pointed out that the Environmental Information (Scotland) Regulations applied to some bodies that are not covered by FOISA, including housing associations, and said that if resources permitted she planned to submit another special report before January reflecting on the scope of FOI and the public bodies that are covered:

> *'I think housing associations are a very good example, for me, I think they should be covered because when they were departments within councils far more people had access to far more information that I think is of a nature that the Act meant, that they no longer have access to,'* (Agnew, 2014).

Some of the 'arm's length organisations' that have been formed across Scotland in recent years are already covered by FOISA – these include Glasgow Life, which now runs the city's museums and art galleries; ferry operators Caledonian MacBrayne are also subject to the Act. In September 2013 Scottish ministers used their power to 'designate' further organisations including other trusts which had been created by councils, including Edinburgh Leisure, Inverclyde Leisure and the Festival City Theatres Trust (Scottish Information Commissioner's Office, 2014), so there are grounds for hope that the scope of the Scottish Act will continue to be broadened in coming years.

References

Agnew, Rosemary (2013) 'Decision Notice 270/2013 Stephen Magee and Glasgow City Council.' St Andrews: Office of the Scottish Information Commissioner

Agnew, Rosemary (2014) *Special Report. Failure to respond to FOI requests: extent, impact and remedy*. St Andrews: Office of the Scottish Information Commissioner

BBC (2005) *McLetchie resigns as Tory leader* Available at http://news.bbc.co.uk/1/hi/scotland/4393622.stm accessed on September 15 2014

Bindman, Geoffrey (2004) 'Freedom of what information?' *British Journalism Review* 15(4) pp 53-58

Birkinshaw, Patrick (1997) 'Freedom of information and open government: The European community/union dimension' in *Government Information Quarterly* 14(1), pp27-49.

Birkinshaw, Patrick J (2000) 'Freedom of Information in the UK: A progress Report' *Government Information Quarterly* 17(4) pp 419-424.

Birkinshaw, Patrick J (2010) 'Freedom of information and its impact in the United Kingdom' *Government Information Quarterly* 27(4) pp 312-321

Cherry, Morag, and McMenemy, David (2013) 'Freedom of information and 'vexatious' requests—The case of Scottish local government' *Government Information Quarterly* 30(3) pp 257-266

Edwards, Rob (2011) *Freeedom of Interest Appeals: The requester's perspective.* Available at: http://www.robedwards.com/2011/10/freedom-of-information-appeals-the-requesters-perspective.html?cid=6a00d8341c091653ef015392741a58970b (Accessed 4 August 2014)

Edwards, Rob (2014) *Environmental news and comment (2014)* Available at http://robedwards.typepad.com/about.html Accessed August 4 2014

Glover, Mark et al (2006) *Freedom of Information: History, experience and records and information management implications in the USA, Canada and the United Kingdom.* Kansas: Arma International Educational Foundation Endowment Fund

Gordon, Tom (2005), *Status by the bottle* Available at http://www.heraldscotland.com/sport/spl/aberdeen/status-by-the-bottle-for-the-bute-house-dinner-guests-mcconnell-wreaks-revenge-on-the-press-1.63754 accessed on 12 August 2014

Hayes, Jeremy (2009) 'FOI: Whitehall strikes back' in *British Journalism Review* 20(3) pp 57-62

Hazell, Robert, and Ben Worthy (2010) 'Assessing the performance of freedom of information' *Government Information Quarterly* 27(4) pp 352-359

Johnson, Simon (2013) *Alex Salmond's secrecy battle over £250 tartan trews.* Available at http://www.telegraph.co.uk/news/uknews/scotland/10359238/Alex-Salmonds-secrecy-battle-over-250-tartan-trews.html Accessed September 1 2014

McClean, Tom (2010) 'Who pays the piper? The political economy of freedom of information' *Government Information Quarterly* 27(4) pp 392-400.

Nam, Taewoo (2012) 'Freedom of information legislation and its impact on press freedom: A cross-national study' *Government Information Quarterly* 29(4) pp 521-531

Press Complaints Commission (2007) *Report 74* Available at http://www.pcc.org.uk/news/index.html?article=NDMwMw== accessed on 2 September 2014

Scottish Information Commissioner's Officer (2014) *FOI law in Scotland* Available at http://www.itspublicknowledge.info/Law/Legislation.aspx Accessed September 1 2014

Scottish Information Commissioner's Officer (2014) *Who can I ask?* Available at http://www.itspublicknowledge.info/YourRights/WhocanIask.aspx#authority Accessed September 1 2014

Worthy, Ben (2010) 'More Open but Not More Trusted? The Effect of the Freedom of Information Act 2000 on the United Kingdom Central Government' in *Governance*, 23(6) pp 561–582'

Interviews

Rosemary Agnew, St Andrews, 12 August 2014

Drew Cochrane, Irvine, 8 August 2014

Colin Edgar, Glasgow, 15 August 2014

Rob Edwards, Edinburgh, 5 August 2014

Paul Hutcheon, Glasgow, 22 July 2014

Roisin McGroarty, Irvine, 8 August 2014

Note on the contributor

Julian Calvert is a senior lecturer in journalism at Glasgow Caledonian University. He started his career as a trainee reporter in 1988 and went on to spend 13 years as a newspaper editor in Scotland and England. He is chair of the Society of Editors (Scotland) and a member of the International Society of Weekly Newspaper Editors.

FOI in Northern Ireland: Wide ranging FOI requests, sent in by lazy journalists, who will not do any work!

Despite Northern Ireland's journalists using FOI to force the first major UK resignation, its use has been negligible with reporters increasingly reliant on official releases and other sources, writes *Colm Murphy*

The Troubles and threats to journalists

Investigative journalism has found it hard to find its feet in Northern Ireland. Despite only having a population of 1.8 million, the country is very well served by media outlets. It benefits from receiving the London and Dublin-based media as well as that produced locally. Despite 30 years of civil war up to 1998, which left 3,568 dead and 47,541 badly injured, no journalist was killed in Northern Ireland intentionally. In addition the constant flow of news relating to the Troubles meant that there was little capacity or demand for newsrooms to develop investigative stories. But with so many armed and dangerous groupings it was also very dangerous for journalists. But many who attempted investigations in this period or were covering events were threatened by paramilitaries and several left for their own safety with their families. The Sunday World tabloid, which investigated extensively the paramilitaries' links to organised crime, was particularly targeted, and its Belfast bureau chief Jim Campbell was shot by paramilitaries in 1982. A decade later loyalist gunmen left a bomb in the newspaper's office and staff had to walk over it to escape. Although generally in the propaganda war of the so-called Troubles it was not in the main paramilitaries interests to target the media.

Given the situation the main British television networks did not want to take the risk. Instead programmes like Thames Television's 'This Week', the 'Cook Report' and BBC's 'Panorama' would fly-in a team from England to make the investigative documentaries rather than risk local journalists. Well-known journalists like Jeremy Paxman, Robert Fisk and Martin Bell honed their reporting skills in Northern Ireland.

But with the ceasefire in 1998 and peace process many paramilitary gangs branched further into crime including drug dealing, smuggling, fraud and counterfeit goods. But the post ceasefire move by journalists into more investigative areas was met with greater threats from paramilitaries who no longer feared the negative propaganda-risk. This culminated with the shooting dead of *Sunday World* reporter Martin O'Hagan in front of his wife Marie in 2001 by a breakaway loyalist paramilitary group the Loyalist Volunteer Force. He had been writing stories about their alleged involvement in drug dealing.

The targeting of journalists involved in investigations increased significantly even after this. In addition to this the pool of investigative journalists reduced considerably with the withdrawal and cutback of news media outlets from Northern Ireland once the Troubles had ceased and due to the downturn in the print media.

It has meant that most investigative journalism is done by only a handful of journalists in a few outlets including BBC Northern Ireland's *Spotlight* programme, and theDetail.tv – an online philanthropic project founded to fill the void in investigative journalism in Northern Ireland which is part-funded by American philanthropist Chuck Feeney. Some investigative work is also undertaken by the two largest indigenous selling daily newspapers, *The Irish News* and the *Belfast Telegraph*. The Northern Ireland editions of *The Sun* and the *Daily Mirror* are the biggest selling dailies in Northern Ireland but rarely use FOI for local stories. This has meant that the Northern Ireland media's use of freedom of information to break big news stories and exposés has been relatively weak. The pattern has been a few sensational headlines on one side and annual statistical stories on the other. There is little investigative journalism to accompany the information the FOI request has provided to the journalist, often due to a lack of newsroom resources.

Belfast newspapers' use of FOI
Northern Ireland's three Belfast-based newspapers have adopted different approaches to use of FOI. The *Belfast Telegraph* uses FOI the most and has unearthed several big stories since 2005. Most are the annual lists got through FOI – revealing politician's expenses, crime figures or health statistics. Annual examples range from welfare benefit cost figures and public sector overtime costs to hospitality costs at the Northern Ireland Assembly. These types of stories often command a front page headline and a two-page feature inside. The newspaper has also been successful in breaking some major investigative stories through FOI. David Gordon, then an investigative reporter with the *Belfast Telegraph*, uncovered information about lobbying and other ties between Ian Paisley junior and a property developer. These contributed to Paisley junior's resignation as a junior minister in February 2008. The son of the former First Minister, the late Ian Paisley senior, he was the first UK government minister to resign due to information released through FOI (Gordon, 2008).

The story surrounded Mr Paisley's relationship with one of his constituents, a Co Antrim developer Seymour Sweeney and his denial of such a relationship, which later transpired following FOI requests by David Gordon (Gordon, 2007). The allegation was that Mr Sweeney had undue influence in the processes of government after he was granted planning permission for a controversial visitor attraction centre at the Giant's Causeway, Northern Ireland's key UNESCO World Heritage site. UNESCO threatened to remove this status if the development went ahead. Despite initial denials the *Belfast Telegraph* unearthed through FOI widespread lobbying by Mr Paisley junior on Mr Sweeney's behalf across government for several projects over a number of years.

Paisley senior was also mentioned in a letter obtained under FOI and in response criticised in the Northern Ireland Assembly in October 2008 'wide ranging FOI requests, sent in by lazy journalists, who will not do any work' (Hansard, 2007). However, as the revelations continued, the *Belfast Telegraph* uncovered that Paisley's parliamentary constituency office was rented from a company, which Mr Sweeney was a director of.

Interestingly, journalists only began pursuing the connection between the Paisleys and Mr Sweeney following an FOI request from Jim Allister, the leader of Traditional Unionist Voice, who had broken away from the Paisley's Democratic Unionist Party. As Mr Allister asked under FOI about a DUP 'wish list' which they had negotiated as part of the 2006 St Andrew's Agreement. Allister's original FOI initiated interest in the Seymour Sweeney relationship as it revealed lobbying by Mr Paisley at that point for major land purchases, which Mr Sweeney was at the centre of.

The Irish News and to a lesser extent the Belfast *News Letter* tend to use FOI to highlight scandals or bring new information to the public's attention. It is often used to embarrass a Stormont executive minister or department or raise awareness of perceived injustice. The 'Jet-set NHS' series by *The Irish News* health correspondent Seanin Graham revealed that senior health officials were flying first class and staying at expensive hotels to attend courses at the taxpayers' expense at a time of huge waiting lists for operations (2010a; 2010b).

In broadcast terms BBC Northern Ireland, which has the second largest TV market share after commercial station UTV, occasionally uses FOI material. The *Stephen Nolan Show*, one of the country's most listened to radio programmes, uses FOI stories from other media as a basis for debate. The level of absenteeism due to sickness in Northern Ireland's large public sector, for example, is often a big source of contention with private sector workers. The BBC's flagship current affairs television programme in Northern Ireland, *Spotlight*, has on occasion also made significant use of FOI to investigate a range of issues, from housing to organisational management in the public sector to the legacy from the Troubles.

Despite having only five full-time journalists the online news website, theDetail.tv has also demonstrated how FOI requests can be utilised for quality journalism in Northern Ireland. In a series of in-depth investigations the website's journalists have regularly used FOI to uncover perceived injustices across state services in Northern Ireland in relation to a number of issues such as education, the justice system and health provision.

Disappointingly, however, the 53 weekly local newspapers in Northern Ireland that comprise the largest amount of the country's print readership barely use FOI. Some have written follow-up pieces on the back of FOI-based items in Belfast-based papers, but these papers tend to use local Assembly Members' question responses on issues in their area rather than FOI.

The years since 2008 have produced a more mixed picture of FOI usage. The recession coupled with the rapid decline in print sales has seen newspaper's resources shrink. The daily newspapers' FOI usage has shifted largely to requests annually for known data, which is then turned into a story with comment from experts. In 2013 the Northern Irish media evolved a step further under devolution when an exposé by BBC NI's flagship *Newsline* programme led to the eventual resignation of an up-and-coming Assembly Member Conall McDevitt of the moderate nationalist Social Democratic and Labour Party (SDLP). The BBC's reporter Tara Mills revealed how information contained on the assembly member's expenses register at Stormont did not tell the full extent of costs (BBC News online, 2013). The BBC's probing showed that office expenses he claimed were not fully listed and in fact a range of costs were paid to his wife's company JM consulting in 2011. Initially the register was corrected, however, after a month of political and media pressure Mr McDevitt resigned his seat as MLA for South Belfast (Clarke, 2013). This was the first time the media had forced the resignation of a sitting assembly member and evidence of the on-going political evolution of the media in Northern Ireland under the devolved institutions of government. But that said, this is an example of how the media simply used information, which is already published rather than FOI.

Co-incidentally, the introduction of the United Kingdom's *Freedom of Information Act* in 2005 has part overlapped with the latest period of devolution of political powers from the UK parliament in Westminster to a parliament and government in Northern Ireland. The institutions of the Northern Ireland Executive and Assembly were re-instated in May 2007. This brought a greater change in political reporting than FOI. The emphasis changed from covering Westminster to the Northern Ireland Assembly. The volume of government press releases doubled in tandem with their increased use by journalists as a story source.

Conclusion

So while the Northern Ireland media have shifted their techniques and sources with the evolving political process in the last decade, FOI has not played a role in it. Instead information released by the Executive as part of its public relations has grown in use by journalists. History, intimidation, resources and often a lack of expertise has hindered FOI's usage. But experiments like the award-winning theDetail.tv have shown that there are plenty of areas in Northern Ireland where journalistic FOI usage can produce important stories.

References

BBC News Online (2013) 'Conall McDevitt from SDLP quits politics over payment', 4 September, available at http://www.bbc.co.uk/news/uk-northern-ireland-23963979 accessed 14 August 2014

Clarke, Liam (2013), 'Conall McDevitt resignation: He didn't live up to standards he demanded of others' in *Belfast Telegraph*, 5 September

Gordon, David (2007), 'Paisley embroiled in cronyism furore' in *Belfast Telegraph*, 4 October

Gordon, David (2008), 'First major casualty of the right to know legislation'

The Independent, London, 7 March.

Graham, Seanin (2010a) 'The Jet-Set NHS' in *The Irish News*, 15 November

Graham, Seanin (2010b) 'Six-day, £3k US trip for health chief despite ban by Minister' in *The Irish News*, 16 November

Hansard (2007) Record of Dr Ian Paisley's statement in the Northern Ireland Assembly, on 8 October 2007. Available at http://archive.niassembly.gov.uk/record/reports2007/071008.htm#5 accessed 16 October, 2014

Mills, Tara (2013), 'Conall McDevitt's assembly expenses paid to wife's company' BBC Newsline, 6 August

Note on the contributor

Dr Colm Murphy is Head of School of Media, Film and Journalism at Ulster University, Northern Ireland. He pioneered the use of the Freedom of Information Act in Ireland using it to develop the annual *The Sunday Times* university and secondary school league tables. He is author of *Policymaking for Digital Media Growth* and is a non-executive director of the UK's industry accrediting body for journalism qualifications, the National Council for the Training of Journalists.

Section 3:
International perspectives on freedom of information

Tom Felle

International perspectives on freedom of information, as they appear in the following chapters, are somewhat of an enigma in a book originally designed to examine the operation of the Freedom of Information Act in the UK, 10 years after its introduction. It soon became clear to us as editors that FOI does not respect borders and the issues of concern to journalists in the UK in relation to how FOI was operating were shared by journalists worldwide. The following, so, is a collection of essays examining the operation of freedom of information legislation worldwide, in various forms, and under various titles. The chapters break roughly into two, the first set are from contributors in what we might classify as advanced democracies including the US, Canada, New Zealand, Australia and Ireland; and the second from fragile democracies such as South Africa; states with limited freedoms including Malaysia and Singapore; and states with little or no democratic credentials such as China and Zimbabwe.

The first essay is by the distinguished Dean of the Henry W Grady College of Journalism and Mass Communication at the University of Georgia, Charles N Davis. He argues that FOI is in disarray in the US because of a range of problems, including the cost of lawsuits to access documents; lethargy (groups that were once vocal have lost their voice); and stone-walling by public bodies. The three biggest problems facing the US FOIA, as it is known, are the citation of invalid exceptions; lack of response or delayed responses; and unreasonable fees. Davis, who himself served as director of the highly respected National Freedom of Information Coalition, concludes that it is time for a new generation of data journalists to step up to the plate and continue the fight:

'Data-driven reportage fuelled by FOI offers great promise for creating the next generation of FOI advocates in the United States. Coupled with government's embrace of 'proactive disclosure' and self-service data sets for citizens to engage with, this new generation of requesters could transform FOI law, but only if the two movements — data journalism and FOI — join forces.'

Brant Houston of the University of Illinois writes that the slow drip toward secrecy continued under Obama despite promises of openness. Houston takes the reader through America's FOIA history with an overview from Watergate through 9/11 to the present day. Houston too argues that the legislation is being manipulated by vested interests in public bodies, with delays; excessive fees; and the over-use of classification all too commonplace. In some cases requests are not replied to at all; and in a rather humorous anecdote, he retells the story of a fee request of more than $1bn (£630m) from a public body following a FOIA request. Despite the problems, FOIA continues to be a powerful tool for investigative journalists if used properly.

Despite delays, lengthy negotiations, and initial denials, citizens, attorneys, researchers and journalists submit hundreds of thousands of requests a year and hundreds of thousands of those requests result in complete or partial releases of information. At the US government's FOI site, it said its sample of federal agencies showed more than 700,000 requests made in 2013. In a partial analysis, it said that roughly 238,000 requests were released fully in that year, 203,295 had partial releases of information and 41,380 were denied fully.'

Michael Foley of the Dublin Institute of Technology charts Ireland's relationship with FOI from the legislation's enactment in 1997, to its filleting in a 2003 amendment act, to its recent restoration in 2014 legislation that extends the law to cover the Irish police and financial oversight bodies. Ireland's attachment to official secrecy can be in part attributed to its colonial past and violent birth with a war of independence and a civil war in the 1920s, but the Irish government continued a policy of official secrecy extending and strengthening the Official Secrets Act and prosecuting journalists who broke it. Though prosecutions were rare, Foley argues that the legislation had a chilling effect. FOI in Ireland is viewed as largely positive, but battles have been hard fought:

Time and time again stories are obtained using FOI and the refrain, 'according to information released under the Freedom of Information Act' is increasingly heard on the broadcast news. After the initial teething problems of journalists not knowing how to use the Act, using it for trivial stories or going on massive trawling exercises, to many journalists today using FOI has become a routine. However, state and public bodies are still fighting access to information. The Information Commissioner received many objections to forcing the publication of judges' expenses, for instance, which has happened. Getting information relating to the government's handling of the economic collapse and the bank bailout and bank guarantees has been a long battle.'

Dean Jobb, of the University of Kings College, Halifax, Nova Scotia, writes that Canada's freedom of information laws played a key role in exposing a scandal that brought down a national government. The country's access to information laws have proven indispensable for journalists investigating government activities and important public issues, however delays, fees, political interference and stonewalling are making the laws less effective. Jobb offers a useful overview of how's Canada's Access to Information Act, and assesses the threats posed by pervasive tightening of the rules by the Canadian government.

> *'Despite these successes – or, more accurately, because of them – Canada's access regime is under threat. Politicians and bureaucrats, the public officials that freedom of information laws are designed to hold accountable, have mounted a determined and highly successful counterattack to evade requests and frustrate applicants. It can take months and sometimes years for access requests to work their way through the system. The legislation exempts records from disclosure to protect cabinet secrecy, advice given to ministers in confidence, personal privacy and similar interests, and public officials have become adept at using these exemptions to justify withholding information that should be made public.'*

Canada's 'FOI Warrior' Ken Rubin has worked as a professional agitator for and as an experienced and astute user of access to information for more than three decades. His chapter recounts the days before Canada's access to information laws were introduced, his own role as a campaigner, and he charts how the laws have been used by the media – and by him as an investigative researcher. Many of his disclosures have been of significant public importance, as he writes, including uncovering Canada's deceitful role in funding promotion of asbestos exports aboard while denying its lethal impact. And there have also been some lighter moments, as he recalls:

> *'Records can reveal the lighter side of government follies and faults resulting in one-day "hits". They do at least help poke fun at and ridicule government actions. One such example is the government's preparation to meet well-known international celebrities. In one case, records showed that then Canadian heritage minister, Sheila Copps, herself with a journalistic background, was funding a Toronto celebrity Walk of Fame. One access briefing note release included details of plans to meet with the Rolling Stones while they were in Canada. The notes included her scripted dialogue with inductee Mick Jagger. Too bad she never got a chance to use her briefing note as the Stones stood her up and were a no-show.'*

Australian lawyer Peter Timmins writes about the importance of key journalists in the early years following the introduction of the legislation in Australia in the early 1980s. FOI experts like Jack Waterford were forerunners and broke the mould, he argues, but over time the use of FOI by the media became commonplace. Unfortunately, like in a number of other similar countries with a long history of moves toward openness, the current Liberal government in Australia has regressed back toward secrecy in recent years, and this is having an impact on legitimate journalism, and journalists' use of FOI. Staggeringly the government there plans to abolish the office of its Information Commissioner.

'The federal Abbott government – elected in August, 2013 – has acquired a reputation for excessive secrecy, and has shown little interest in leading on improvements in FOI law and practice. On the contrary, a decision announced in May 2014 to disband the Office of Australian Information Commissioner by the end of the year is a retrograde step, despite widespread disappointment with the Commissioner's office, in particular with the slow pace of review of agency decisions…. Journalists still have many justified grumbles about delays in processing; exorbitant charges; inappropriate exemption claims; and an unhelpful run around instead of assistance from some agencies.'

Staying in Australia where researchers David Blackall and Jolyon Sykes examine the story of the 'Trio Capital' fraud as a case study in FOI failure. A complex web of deceit in a ponzi scheme across several countries led to the eventual collapse of the company, and convictions for some of its senior managers. Financial and news journalists in Australia failed to examine the scheme adequately. Now victims of the scheme are finding FOI almost impossible to navigate in their search for answers, and for justice. Few journalists have as yet taken up the cause.

'The public has a need to know how derivatives are capable of destroying what appear to be sound investments. Journalists must understand this market and use FOI effectively to scrutinise government regulators. This is crucial to investigative journalism education. If citizen journalism… delivers FOI outcomes where mainstream news media fail, then journalism educators are obliged to respond accordingly.'

To neighbouring New Zealand, where journalism academics Greg Treadwell and James Hollings warn there is trouble in paradise, arguing that the reputation of New Zealand as a Mecca for FOI has a thin veneer. The two recount the recent scandal of brazen, whole-scale political abuse of FOI for tactical gain, where government ministers were complicit in giving preferential treatment to FOI requests from a right-wing attack blog, in order to smear political opponents. The scandal has spoiled that image of a South Seas information-paradise. They rightly argue that while New Zealand society has gone through radical change since the legislation was first introduced in the 1980s, the Act has barely changed, and is (like many similar laws in other countries) hopelessly out of date.

'FOI in New Zealand is increasingly shown up for its shortcomings and that significant abuse of the Official Information Act has become relatively common. Not only has a worldwide tendency back towards state secrecy taken root in the post-9/11 era, but in New Zealand, and in other countries, significant programmes of privatisation have moved much public spending beyond the gaze of FOI legislation. In addition, the New

Zealand Ombudsman – the main route of appeal against denials of FOI requests – is now overloaded with rapidly increasing numbers of complaints of state secrecy.'

In South Africa some 20 years after the end of apartheid, the country is still a fragile democracy. Corruption, nepotism and cronyism have dogged the ruling African National Congress (ANC). Investigations by journalists have uncovered many stories, including lavish spending on the President's private residence, funded by taxpayers. An attempt to enact a secrecy bill, although fiercely opposed by the media and opposition parties and eventually significantly watered down, was tantamount to a slow drip back toward a securocrat state, writes Anusharani Sewchurran of the University of KwaZulu-Natal in Durban. She also theorises on issues including communication and information. She writes:

'It is clear that under the guise of state security, very repressive control mechanisms are being promoted in relation to the 'right to know' in South Africa. The Secrecy Bill even in its revised format promotes parallel information regimes reminiscent of the apartheid past. The revised bill still criminalises any use of classified information without the inclusion of a public interest defence. This will effectively close the public sphere in South Africa if the revised bill is signed into law. It will also extend the state security minister's powers to regulate oversight bodies like the Public Protector's Office (South African Ombudsman), including what access and use can be made of classified information.'

To India, where two chapters by two Indian academics examine India's Right to Information Act, which also celebrates its 10th birthday in 2015. The legislation is similar in structure to Western laws, and is in operation at the federal as well as the state and local levels. While India has a history of democracy, extreme poverty and high levels of corruption impact on the effectiveness of its institutions and public services. Kiran Prasad, Professor of Communication and Journalism at Sri Padmavati Mahila University, Andhra Pradesh, writes that the legislation acts as bulwark against corruption, and there have been many notable uses of the act to expose corrupt practices by officials in the different Indian states. Despite this, low levels of literacy in many parts of India (and little or no understanding of the legislation as a corollary) as well as poor administrative practices by Indian public bodies are hampering the act's effectiveness. She writes:

'The right to information law could be the tentative beginnings of a more inclusive and just development process – what Amartya Sen (1999) describes as 'a momentous engagement with the possibilities of freedom'. The right to information embodies the struggles for survival and justice in India and will be an important instrument in the journey for equitable and sustainable development of its people.'

Meanwhile Sudeepta Pradhan of IFHE Hyperbad discusses the legislation in detail and also examines a number of important cases. What is interesting in the Indian context is that it is often local community groups and NGOs that have taken action using the legislation, in seeking records to expose corrupt practices, or for public health reasons. Civil society groups, rather than the media, appear to be most active in using the legislation in the public interest, and as a tool to expose and fight corruption. Worryingly, however, this has come at a price as investigators have been attacked and murdered, with demands that the Indian government needs to do more to protect activists.

> *'Despite its extraordinary benefits, the Act has its own inherent risks. RTI activists have increasingly been threatened and attacked, with several casualties. Over the years, numerous activists were assassinated throughout the country, leading to widespread fear within civil society groups. The victims were investigating abnormalities in highly corrupt sectors like land, mining and local elections. Organisations therefore demanded the government take measures to protect the RTI activists. While activists debate whether the RTI has reduced corruption in India, it is generally agreed that the legislation plays a crucial role in promoting transparency'.*

Sankaran Ramanathan of the Mediaplus Research Consultancy discusses the wider issue of democratic rights and 'freedom' of information and expression in Singapore and Malaysia, both former British colonies, and both largely single-party states where individual freedoms are limited. While there are some limited FOI type laws in Malaysia, there are no such laws in Singapore. In both states the flow of information is tightly controlled, and the media in both countries is largely influenced by the state, with licencing requirements in Singapore. However in Malaysia the internet has proved impossible to control, with blogs criticising opposition policies now commonplace, and social networking sites flourishing, giving voice to alternative views and opinions not aired on traditional media. This has also occurred in Singapore, though to a lesser extent:

> *'The Singapore media environment remained unchanged in 2012 and 2013, with few developments in the areas of freedom of the press or expression that attracted international attention. Social media sites and other internet-based sources of news continued to grow but also drew scrutiny from government authorities, with several bloggers forced to retract postings and one jailed for inciting violence. While opposition parliamentarians have repeatedly called for an FOI Act, leaders of the ruling PAP have rejected this, and ask media to be more socially responsible.'*

China can hardly be considered democratic, nevertheless even the rulers of that communist regime realise they cannot rule without the will of the people. Demands from Chinese citizens to know who was benefitting from land rezoning and compulsorily purchases of farms and other properties forced limited disclosure, in the form of ROGI – the Regulations on Open Government Information. Chinese academic Yongxi Chen traces the history of the ROGI, and discusses its impact, albeit limited, on public bodies and the workings of the Chinese administration. Requests for information that are of a personal nature are usually answered, but the system clamps down whenever requests start to stray toward quizzing how the state – and the party – is making decisions. While appeal to the courts is allowed, the courts have been slow to overturn rulings and order disclosure. He writes:

> *'Because of the ROGI, Chinese journalists as well as other citizens enjoy, for the first time in history, a statutory right to access government information. While the ROGI has led to increased disclosure of non-sensitive information, it has yet to secure disclosure of information with democratic implications, i.e. enhancing government accountability and promoting civic engagement, as shown by data concerning request handling and judicial review.'*

Finally, to another non-democratic state, Zimbabwe, which also offers limited information rights to its citizens via the Access to Information and Protection of Privacy Act. Bruce Mutsvairo of the University of Northumbria in Newcastle discusses the Zimbabwean legislation, and concludes that despite its provisions offering limited access to information, the law is not what it seems. The law has been heavily criticised as it included provisions that force journalists and media organisations to register and be licenced by the state. Some journalists and newspapers refused, citing the law as an attempt to control the press.

> *'Zimbabwe is uniquely difficult when it comes to access to information. This is because while perhaps only a minority of the nation's 12 million people know how to access information from public bodies, in a country where some are facing starvation and millions are jobless, this may not be a high priority. Besides, for journalists, a real predicament awaits: criticise the government and be prepared to face severe consequences or avoid politically sensitive topics but then perhaps no one will know you exist.'*

What is surprising is the uniformity with which many of our contributors voice concerns regarding the operation of FOI in advanced democracies, and the 'gaming' of the Act especially when it comes to requests by journalists. Political interference, delays, refusals on increasingly dubious grounds and in some cases even legislative changes to exclude government deliberations, are all impacting on the work of journalists. As alluded to in the preface to this book, there are some green shoots in that FOI type laws are also having an impact in countries such as Zimbabwe and China, where bottom up demands for accountability are forcing the regime to be more transparent, especially when it comes to citizen rights, though in both countries requests that may expose the state to embarrassment or criticism are routinely denied. Indeed even in liberal democracies, increasing refusals and 'gaming' of FOI requests may well be directly linked to protecting state actors from embarrassment or criticism also.

The right to information is under threat around the world. The freedom fighting civil society groups, advocates and journalists who are at the coalface, and whose stories are told in the following pages, need to be protected, and deserve our support.

The sorry state of FOI

The USA's Freedom of Information Act offers a lot for journalists but media use is in decline because of structural weaknesses in FOIA and public officials 'gaming' the system, writes *Charles N Davis*

Introduction

The freedom of information movement in the United States offers the paradox of great promise and great peril, on a variety of fronts. As digital democracy offers avenues to transparency the founding generation of FOI could only have dreamt of, it simultaneously threatens legal orthodoxy, challenging long-held notions of access and propriety, of privacy and personal dominion.

Further complicating matters, the critical gap between the letter of the law and its implementation – the space between the law and how it responds to requests on the ground, in the clerk's office – faces challenges of both the volume of requests (increasing annually) and of a systemic lack of enforcement and meaningful penalties for non-compliance.

Greater still is the threat posed by lethargy, as the once-vocal FOI movement that nurtured the emergence of state and local watchdog institutions finds it ever more difficult to battle highly organised, well-financed forces in favour of secrecy. The digital revolution reshaping the mass media in the United States is as much to blame for this phenomenon as anything else, as it has created deep financial challenges for many of the players that fuelled the openness movement. From dwindling support for state FOI groups to the diminishing threat of media-led FOI litigation, the evidence points to erosion of hard-earned access rights if a course correction fails to emerge in the short term.

Each of these issues merits further exploration. Let us begin with what has become a symptom of the general stagnation of FOI law in the United States – the structural weaknesses of the laws themselves. It is worth noting at the outset that the FOI ecosystem in the United States originates from a patchwork quilt of statutes at the federal, state and local level. Nothing about this is remarkable –

174

the law of access reflects the federal-state-local trifecta – but it adds to the complexity and difficulty of modernising the law.

Structural weakness in the FOIA

The laws vary widely from state to state, but share a lack of meaningful enforcement mechanisms, with the vast majority of statutes placing the burden of initiating most enforcement action on the requester rather than calling on the state itself to assert the power of the law enforcement establishment in the event of legally dubious denials. The dominant statutory form is one of permitting, but not requiring official response, with rare exceptions such as in Connecticut, with its admirable administrative arm dedicated to FOI, and Texas, where the state Attorney General, empowered by state FOI law, provides legal response to any denial of access under its law. More typical is the approach of Illinois, to pick one state, which states that 'any person denied access to inspect or copy any public record by a public body may file suit for injunctive or declaratory relief' (5 ILCS 140/11(a) (2013)).

Oregon joins a handful of states offering some modicum of relief for requesters, as its statute outlines a precise method for responding: 'If a records request is denied by a state public body, appeal is made to the Attorney General. If the denial is made by a public body, the appeal is made to the district attorney for the county where the public body is located. If the denial is made by an elected official, however, any appeal must be taken directly to court (ORS 192.450 (2013)).

In 2007, the Better Government Association and the National Freedom of Information Coalition (NFOIC) studied all 50 state public records laws to evaluate the process the requesting party must undergo to gain access to public records. No state earned better than Nebraska's and New Jersey's 14 out of a possible 16 total. A stunning 38 states earned F ratings, with the rest scattered between C and D. Such procedural roadblocks frustrate requesters and make it easier for government agencies to simply stonewall them until they go away. If a dogged requester sees their request through to litigation, things do not improve much. The questions of whether petitioners are entitled to attorney fees and court costs in the event they prevail in their action and to what extent also reveals systemic weakness in state FOI laws. The importance of attorney's fees awards in citizen-driven FOI litigation cannot be overstated. First, they assure petitioners that their expenses will be covered in the event they are successful in their appeal, encouraging people to challenge an agency's denial. Second, awarding fees and costs to the prevailing petitioner provides a deterrent to agencies and promotes compliance with the law.

Language is critical here. For example, the use of the single word 'may' in a statute means that fees and costs are to be awarded at the judge's discretion, while 'shall' means that fees and costs must be awarded to the prevailing petitioner. A statute that states fees and costs 'shall' be awarded will be stronger than a statute that provides fees and costs 'may' be awarded. There also is a major difference between 'prevail' and 'substantially prevail' in terms of recovering attorney fees. 'Prevail' refers to a situation wherein the petitioner wins on all points, and is given access to all the records requested, while 'substantially prevail' refers to a situation wherein the petitioner wins on only some points, loses on other points and is only given access to some of the requested records. States awarding fees and costs to petitioners that only substantially prevail will be stronger than those that require the petitioner to completely prevail in order to get fees and costs. Yet those states are rare, with the vast majority of requesters facing the much higher prevailing standard. The gap between the letter of the law and its practical implementation perplexes FOI advocates, and breeds cynicism amongst requesters.

Media use in decline

Equally threatening are anecdotal signs that FOI use and advocacy are slowing, especially media usage of the laws. NFOIC's 2013 joint study with the New York-based Media Law Resource Centre found a substantial decline during the last two to five years in the amount of resources devoted by media organisations to FOIA and open government issues. Additionally, the survey suggests there is a greater inclination among government officials for gaming the system to avoid compliance, and that legislative changes that harm transparency far outweigh legislative attempts to improve the laws (NFOIC, 2013). Some 46 per cent of the surveyed media attorneys said media organisations had decreased those resources substantially; 26.2 per cent of media attorneys said that intervention in FOI issues has decreased substantially in the last two to five years; while 27.9 per cent said such intervention has decreased slightly (ibid).

The media attorneys and NFOIC members agreed that the three most common obstacles presented by the government in accessing information are: the citation of invalid exceptions; lack of response or delayed responses; and unreasonable fees.

While it remains difficult to quantify the slowdown in FOI activity industry wide, it stands to reason that the resultant decline in 'boots on the ground' would have a negative effect on FOI activity. From 2003 to 2012, the American Society of News Editors documented a loss of 16,200 full-time newspaper newsroom jobs while Ad Age recorded a decline of 38,000 magazine jobs, which includes all jobs for the entire consumer magazine sector (Jurkowitz, 2014). That collapse also has made itself felt in terms of support for the non-profit state associations that rally for, and work to improve, access legislation, in terms of talent, time and treasure.

Digital re-birth?

All is not lost, however. The emergence of new digital journalism outlets in the United States – many focused on watchdog reporting and data journalism – signals a partial rebirth of the editorial sector, and is filled with just the sort of journalists who rely heavily upon FOI laws to do their work. The Pew Research Center made a first effort to put a number on the shifting journalism landscape by using interviews and multiple databases to account for editorial staffing at 30 major digital news organisations and 438 smaller ones. Those 468 outlets—the vast majority of which started in the past decade—have produced almost 5,000 full-time editorial jobs (ibid). Data-driven reportage fuelled by FOI offers great promise for creating the next generation of FOI advocates in the United States. Coupled with government's embrace of 'proactive disclosure' and self-service data sets for citizens to engage with, this new generation of requesters could transform FOI law, but only if the two movements – data journalism and FOI – join forces. The data-reliant, digital-first outlets must realise that FOI creates the operating system for their work, and rush to protect it, filling the gap left by the disruption of traditional journalism.

References

Elliott-Engel, Amaris (2013) '2013 NFOIC/MLRC open government survey showed troubling trends for transparency' in *National Freedom of Information Coalition* online, available at http://www.nfoic.org/2013-nfoic-mlrc-open-government-survey-showed-troubling-trends-transparency, accessed 13 September, 2014

Jurkowitz, Mark (2014) 'The growth in digital reporting' in *Pew Research Journalism Project* online, available at http://www.journalism.org/2014/03/26/the-growth-in-digital-reporting/ accessed 13 September, 2014

Note on the contributor

Charles N Davis, PhD, is the Dean of the Henry W Grady College of Journalism and Mass Communication at the University of Georgia. Prior to his appointment as Dean in 2013, he served as a professor of journalism at the University of Missouri School of Journalism, specialising in FOI law. From 2005-2010, he served as executive director of the National Freedom of Information Coalition, the organisation for state freedom of information groups.

Government in the sunshine? The problems and practices of journalists' use of the US FOIA

America's democratic pedigree, enshrined the First Amendment to the Constitution, acts as a beacon to millions worldwide. It was the first Western democracy to introduce modern FOI laws in the 1960s, with far-reaching openness and transparency guarantees. Despite this, many problems remain for journalists investigating and reporting in the public interest, writes *Brant Houston*

Introduction

Barack Obama began his presidency in 2009 with a pledge of transparency and deep support of the US Freedom of Information Act. Indeed the US government's Freedom of Information Act website currently declares:

> *President Obama and Attorney General Holder have directed agencies to apply a presumption of openness in responding to FOIA requests.... President Obama has pledged to make this the most transparent Administration in history* (FOIA.gov, 2014).

As part of his pledge, Obama issued a memorandum to that point, thus reversing an infamous memorandum issued by the Bush administration. The Bush administration memo in 2001 advised agencies that they did not have to have a presumption of openness and would be supported if they initially said 'no' to freedom of information requests. Despite his goals, Obama's administration has been sharply criticised by advocates of openness and by the news media for being one of the least open and most difficult administrations since the Freedom of Information Act (FOIA) was signed into law in 1966. Among the many organisations saying the administration has not met its goals on openness is the Electronic Frontier Foundation, a non-profit advocate of civil liberties:

> *Unfortunately, the Obama administration has fallen far short of the goals stated in the January 2009 memo, and in many ways has made the government more secretive.*

178

Agencies have either been slow to implement changes, and in some cases, they've been outright ignored. The exemptions the President vowed to curtail have been used more than the Bush administration. Classification is also at an all-time high' (Electronic Frontier Foundation, 2014).

The foundation cited a Bloomberg News story in 2012 that tested the administration's FOIA practices and found that 19 out of 20 agencies failed to respond to requests in the time required by law. Also in 2012, the Transactional Records Access Clearinghouse at Syracuse University, which collects and analyses government databases, found that there were more court complaints asking federal judges to force the government to abide by the Freedom of Information Act during the first term of the Obama administration than there were in the last term of President Bush. It reported that a 28 per cent increase freedom of information related lawsuits were filed during last two years of first term of President Obama (720) than were filed in the second term of President Bush (562) (Freedom of Information Project, 2012).

Furthermore, the OpentheGovernment.org, a coalition vowing to make the 'federal government a more open place,' said there was still 'a governmental predisposition towards secrecy, especially in the national security bureaucracy'.

A history of struggles and changes

The US law, commonly known as FOIA, was signed into law in 1966 by President Lyndon B Johnson, who really was not in favour of it. Although Sweden and Finland had open records laws before that signing, the US law was the most sweeping in the kinds and numbers of records it said should be open. But over the past four decades it has been amended significantly several times. In 1974, after the Watergate scandal, Congress strengthened the law, overriding a veto by President Gerald Ford made partly on the advice of Richard Cheney and Donald Rumsfeld, White House staffers who later held high positions in the Bush administration. (National Security Archives, 2014)

Congress acted in 1974 after hearing of bureaucratic resistance to requests, the charging of excessive fees and excessive delays that dissuaded journalists from using the law to obtain information – problems that are still cited today about the law. The amendments, however, did require that agencies respond in a timely fashion to requests and litigation; allowed for recovery of reasonable attorney fees and costs; required annual reporting on handling of FOIA requests; and expanded the definition of an 'agency'.

In 1996, after years in which it was apparent that many documents had become digitised, the law was amended to include electronic records, thus quelling arguments that a document was not a public record because it was not on paper. At the same time another law restricted release of health documents. Known as the Health Insurances Portability and Accountability Act (HPPA), it privatised previously public health records and has been used by officials to limit, sometimes wrongly, the release of medical records.

After the terrorist attack on the World Trade Towers in 2001, the law was amended to prohibit access by foreign governments and organisations to national security documents. During the same time, the Critical Infrastructure Information Act was passed. It permitted officials to deny access to records about facilities the officials deemed as potentially vulnerable. That law led to sometimes absurd decisions by some officials to shut down access to data that could actually be used to protect the public. For example, the US Army Corps of Engineers stopped releasing the National Dam Inventory, which contained information on the locations and inspections of dams and what threat they could pose to human life if they collapsed. Yet much of that information could be found with Google searches, Google Earth, at archived government sites and at the state level.

Ironically, as President Bush was leaving office, he signed a bill strengthening the FOI – the so-called Open Government Act of 2007. Among the changes, the law forbids agencies from charging fees if it misses FOIA deadlines – such as having to respond to requests within 20 business days. That part of the law had its own shortcomings because it lengthened the time period from 10 days to 20 days. The Act also created more mediation on requests and better monitoring of how requests are handled. Another important part of the law was that it required agencies to make the raw statistical data used in its reports available electronically. The law still does not apply to Congress or the federal court system, although those two branches of the US government have their own disclosure policies that allow for information to be open. Also, many non-US citizens and journalists do not realise the law permits them to make requests unless the information falls under the umbrella of national security and they are deemed a 'foreign agent'. The ability to make requests under the US FOIA has allowed foreign journalists and citizens to often obtain information about their countries after their own countries have denied the information.

In addition, the 50 states of the US have enacted similar freedom of information laws that not only lead to the release of documents and data about those state governments, but also frequently result in the release of federal government information that has been shared with them.

Exemptions and other roadblocks

Currently, there are nine broad exemptions written into the freedom of information law. The exemption often cited as especially onerous is the one that allows documents to be withheld if they concern national security or are classified. Repeated studies show that many documents are inappropriately labelled as classified. Other exemptions include personnel files; documents containing trade secrets or potentially damaging commercial information; certain law enforcement files; and certain files on regulation of financial institutions. Geological information such as the location or maps of wells is specifically exempted.

The broad exemptions leave much room for discretion by officials and lead to appeals, court battles, and ingenious methods by journalists of getting the information through other requests and agencies. For example, the US Small Business Administration (SBA) routinely denies information about which borrowers are delinquent on billions of dollars in government-backed loans. Yet, reporters can simply research court records to show that the agency fails to disclose businesses that are not only delinquent but have entered bankruptcy or have closed – and obviously are no longer paying back their loans.

In addition to exemptions, officials continue to use the traditional tactics of making denials not allowed by the law, creating long delays and charging high fees. In 1994, a group of journalists came up with 38 ridiculous excuses used by officials when denying access to government data, many of which are still used. Typical excuses are that a request is too broad and the officials did not understand it; that the need to redact information created a new record and officials were not required to create new records under the law; that they did not have the staff to do the work to collate and send material requested; that it would be too expensive to find the records; or they had given their data to a contractor and thus it was private.

Such excuses create more delays and increase the need to negotiate for information. But some of the delays can become laughably long. In 2007, the non-profit, nonpartisan National Security Archives requested information on how long some FOIA requests had been pending. The Department of State reported 10 requests that had been pending for more than 15 years. In 2011, the Knight Open Government Survey, conducted by the National Security Archive, found 'the Obama administration is only about halfway toward its promise of improving freedom of information responsiveness among federal agencies'. Although it found improvement from 2010 when only 13 out of 90 agencies had actually made concrete changes in their FOIA procedures, it still found that the number was only 49 agencies out of 90. (National Security Archive, 2011)

In its survey, the National Security Archive said FOIA requests were acknowledged, but never acted upon, by 17 agencies. 'Under law, a response is required within 20 business days. Yet, the survey noted that 117 business days had passed since the FOIA requests were submitted.' Four agencies had still had not responded at the time the report was released. Again, the study found long-standing requests, this time with one as old as 18 years. The survey found that 'marooned FOIA requests . . . remain a key obstacle to transparency'.

Overall, there is a considerable backlog of pending requests that Obama pledged to significantly reduce. In 2008, the government said there were more than 130,000 pending requests in a sample of federal agencies. The backlog dropped to 70,000 at one point but had risen to 92,000 in 2013. (FOIA.gov, 2014)

Another barrier is the tendency of agencies, despite the law, to levy ridiculously high fees in the thousands and sometimes the millions of dollars. Any fees or costs are supposed to be fair and reasonable, but an agency knows that a high fee can dissuade a requester from seeking information or result in delays while the agency and requester argue about the fee. One of the most egregious examples of using a fee to prevent a release of information was one set by the US Justice Department. The fee was more than £1.23bn (US$2bn) for a database from the department. The fee was in response to a request by the National Institute for Computer-Assisted Reporting, a non-profit organisation that provides and analyses government data for journalists. The Justice Department came up with the fee by saying it would print out the database of millions of records, redact certain parts of the records by hand and then re-enter the information by scanning each record back into the database. It was a task that could be quickly performed electronically.

Still useful

In 2001, US Senator Patrick Leahy issued a statement on the 35th anniversary of the signing of FOIA into law. 'FOIA may be an imperfect tool, but as one foreign journalist observed, "in its klutzy way, it has become one of the slender pillars that make America the most open of modern societies",' Leahy stated. He went on to note that:

> *'Records released under FOIA have revealed the government's radiation experiments on human guinea pigs during the Cold War, the evidence that the Food and Drug Administration had about heart-valve disease at the time it approved the Fen-Phen diet drug, the Federal Aviation Administration's concerns about ValuJet before the 1996 crash in the Everglades, radiation contamination by a government-run uranium processing plant on nearby recreation and wildlife areas in Kentucky, the government's maltreatment of South Vietnamese commandos who fought in a CIA-sponsored army in the early 1960's, the high salaries paid to independent counsels, and the unsafe lead content of tap water in the nation's capital,'* (Congressional Record, 2001).

In the awards archives of Investigative Reporters and Editors (IRE), many winners cite the use of freedom of information laws as critical to their revelations and one of IRE's awards is for exemplary use of FOIA. In 2013, the non-profit investigative newsroom ProPublica won the FOI Award from IRE for an investigation that used federal prescription data to show dangers in the prescriptions and wasted government money. The award citation said:

> *'After filing a FOIA request with the Centers for Medicare and Medicaid Services for data on prescriptions doled out through the Part D drug program, reporters labored for a year negotiating with the agency. Some officials opposed disclosing the identities of doctors and providers, but the information was ultimately released, scoring a precedent for all future requests. ProPublica used the data on prescriptions written over five years by 1.6 million doctors to conduct a nationwide review on questionable practices,'* (Investigative Reporters and Editors, 2014).

Despite delays, lengthy negotiations, and initial denials, citizens, attorneys, researchers and journalists submit hundreds of thousands of requests a year and hundreds of thousands of those requests result in complete or partial releases of information. At the US government's FOI site, it said its sample of federal agencies showed more than 700,000 requests made in 2013. In a partial analysis, it said that roughly 238,000 requests were released fully in that year, 203,295 had partial releases of information and 41,380 were denied fully (FOIA.gov 2014).

But use by journalists continues to be a problem. In a 2005 study, the Coalition of Journalists for Open Government looked at a sample of 6,439 requests to 11 agencies. It said 60 per cent of the requests came from commercial interests, particularly data brokers, others from private citizens, and only 6 per cent from the media. As in 1974, many reporters said it took too long to get information from FOIA requests for the stories they were working on (Coalition of Journalists for Open Government, 2005).

Many groups ready to assist

Yet there is plenty of help for journalists and practically a non-profit industry at work in the US to help both journalists and citizens make more effective use of FOIA. Many of them provide training and assistance on their websites. Among the non-profits – many of which are cited in this article – that provide guidance on how to use the law are the American Civil Liberties Union; the National Security Archives; the National Freedom of Information Coalition; the Reporters Committee on Freedom of the Press; OMBWatch; OpentheGovernment.org; the Federation of American Scientists; the Electronic Privacy Information Center; and the Society of Professional Journalists.

Investigative Reporters and Editors, an association of 5,000 US and international members, offer constantly updated tip-sheets on how to use FOIA for stories. All those entering the annual IRE awards are asked to fill out a form that includes a question on whether reporters used FOIA and, if they did, how they used it. Those filled-out forms are available to journalists who join IRE. Even the US government itself provides advice and guides on filing FOIA requests at the FOIA.gov website; at the FOIA section on most government agencies' websites; at the Federal FOIA Ombudsman website; and the Office of Government Information Services. Several websites offer sample letters and automated forms to assist in writing FOIA letters. The Reporters Committee on the Freedom of the Press has a whole section on its website that generates automated letters and lets requesters keep track of requests under a website known IFOIA. A new, independent project, the 'FOIA Machine', also provided automated assistance with software intended to streamline the FOIA process.

There are also very practical guides by journalism organisations, journalists, and Congress on how to successfully request information. The US Congress continues to update its own 'Citizen's Guide to Using on Using FOIA' on its website (House Oversight, 2014) and it is linked to by the Federation of American Scientists. 'The Art of Access' (2011) by journalism professors David Cuillier and Charles N Davis (see his chapter in this book) is a particularly good compendium of advice and tips gathered from their and other journalists' experience. While their intended audience is journalists, it can be used by anyone. They echo the basic steps developed over the years by journalists in effectively using the FOIA and in negotiating for documents and data. Those steps reflect the necessary research and 'social engineering' that is the reality of making good use of the law.

For example, a large government bureaucracy is fragmented and agencies often live in their own silos, not communicating with other agencies. Thus, the same FOIA request to several agencies or departments within the agencies can result in different disclosures. In one case, *The Washington Post* obtained documents on prescription drugs from bureaus of the US Food and Drug Administration (FDA) while the home office of the FDA still was denying them. Also, many of the guides note that sending an FOIA request to a federal agency and state FOIA to a state agency at the same time can elicit information that the federal agency might not release.

Most of the guidelines on FOIA can be distilled into a series of tips:

- Simply ask for information
- Search an agency's website before filing an FOIA. Many agencies lose track of what is on their own websites
- Actually read and know the law
- Look at the agencies' own FOIA logs of releases to see if the information has been released before and thus a precedent of release has been established
- Be prepared to negotiate over redacted information
- Follow up on the request and be prepared to appeal a denial
- Make requests as early as possible since an agency can easily take months to release the information
- If the information is in a database, know what kind of data format it is in and how the data are organised.
- Know what fees can be charged and how they are calculated

The struggle continues

Meanwhile, another effort is being made in the US Congress to improve the law's performance. The FOIA Oversight and Implementation Act of 2014 intends to make it easier and faster to request and receive information, according the Congressional Research Service. The bill would require the Office of Management and Budget to create a single FOIA website for people to use to make FOIA requests and check on the status of their request. The bill would also create a Chief FOIA Officers Council charged with reviewing compliance and recommending improvements. The introducer of the bill, Representative Darrell Issa, said the bill 'shifts the burden of proof from the public requestor seeking information about a government agency... to the government being open and transparent unless it has a good reason to withhold.' The bill was passed by the House in the spring of 2014 and is poised to be acted on by the US Senate, but at the time of this writing had not been voted on.

References

Congressional Record, Leahy statement, FOIA Turns 35, available at http://www.gpo.gov/fdsys/pkg/CREC-2001-03-15/html/CREC-2001-03-15-pt1-PgS2383-2, accessed 19 September, 2014

Cuillier, David, and Davis, Charles N, (2011) *The Art of Access: Strategies for Acquiring Public Records*. CQ Press: Washington DC

Electronic Frontier Foundation, History of FOIA, available at https://www.eff.org/issues/transparency/history-of-foia, accessed 19 September, 2014

FOIA Project, (2012) 'FOIA Lawsuits Increase During Obama Administration' available at http://foiaproject.org/2012/12/20/increase-in-foia-lawsuits-during-obama-administration/ accessed 19 September, 2014

FOIA.gov http://www.foia.gov/

Ginsberg, Wendy, (2014) *The Freedom of Information Act (FOIA): Background, Legislation, and Policy Issue*. The Congressional Research Service: Washington DC

House Oversight Committee, *Citizen's Guide on Using FOIA*, available at http://oversight.house.gov/wp-content/uploads/2012/09/Citizens-Guide-on-Using-FOIA.2012.pdf accessed 19 September, 2014

Houston, Brant, and IRE, (2009) *The Investigative Reporter's Handbook*. Bedford/St Martin's: New York. 5th Edn

Lathrop, Daniel, and Ruma, Laurel, (2010) *Open Government: Collaboration, Transparency and Participation in Practice*. O'Reilly Media Company: Sebastopol, CA

National Security Archives, (2011) *The Glass Half Full*. Knight Survey, available at http://www2.gwu.edu/~nsarchiv/NSAEBB/NSAEBB338 accessed 19 September, 2014

National Security Archives, *History of FOIA*, available at http://www2.gwu.edu/~nsarchiv/nsa/foialeghistory/legistfoia.htm accessed 19 September, 2014

OpentheGovernment.org

Reporters Committee on Freedom of the Press, available at https://www.ifoia.org accessed 19 September, 2014

Note on the contributor

Brant Houston is the Knight Chair in Investigative Reporting at the University of Illinois, where he teaches journalism and oversees an online newsroom. An award-winning journalist, he was an investigative reporter at US newspapers for 17 years. For more than a decade, he served as executive director of Investigative Reporters and Editors, a 5,000-member association at the University of Missouri School of Journalism, where he also taught investigative reporting, computer-assisted reporting and how to use freedom of information laws. He is co-founder of the Global Investigative Journalism Network (gijn.org) His email is brant.houston@gmail.com

Keeping the State's secrets: Ireland's road from 'official' secrets to freedom of information

The introduction of the Freedom of Information Act in Ireland in 1997 was a profound change for a state, a civil service and political system far more comfortable with official secrets. It has had a transformational effect on relations between citizen and the state, and has been useful for journalists despite many challenges, writes *Michael Foley*

From 'official' secrets to FOI

It was probably the most profound and radical change in Irish political history when the Dáil (Ireland's lower house of parliament) enacted the Freedom of information Act, ending a culture of secrecy that went back to the foundation of the state. Prior to the introduction of the Act in 1997, Ireland was easily the most secretive state in Western Europe, even more so than the UK. The Official Secrets Act, which some saw as a relic of the British Empire was no such thing, it had been hardened up in 1962 by a Fianna Fail government, a political party that was, in 1997, the major party in a coalition government that was now seeking to turn on its head 70, or so, years of secrecy to 'let in the light' on the workings of government, to quote the then Taoiseach (prime minister), Albert Reynolds.

After the Official Secrets Act was amended everything that emanated from government was assumed to be secret unless deemed otherwise. The original Act was passed by the British parliament in the early years of the century in the lead up to the First World War and brought into Irish law upon independence. However, that highly restrictive piece of legislation was not enough for some Irish politicians, so in 1962 the then Minister for Justice, Charles Haughey amended the legislation. His legislation ensured it was government ministers who decided what was and was not secret and that the courts could not challenge such decisions. Under the 1962 Act disclosure became the exception rather than the rule. It gave civil servants and politicians a major role in suppressing information. Commenting on minister Haughey's legislation, the journalists Ronan Brady and Patrick Smyth said: '...he overrode important principles of human rights and substituted ministerial discretion for the traditional role of the courts in deciding what is, and what is not to be secret' (Smyth and Brady, 1994: 3).

Under that legislation, should a minister or state authority classify any 'sketch, plan, model, article, note, document, or information' as secret then it was illegal to divulge it. It was said even the restaurant menu in Leinster House, the seat of the Irish parliament, was covered by the Officials Secrets Act. The lowliest of civil servants, including students working for the post office on the Christmas postal rush, had to sign it.

Birth of the 'Free State'

In 1922 Ireland, or at least what became the Irish Free State, gained independence, following a struggle that went back hundreds of years, but can probably be dated in its modern context to the post Famine period of the mid-19th Century. While much of that struggle was fought out in the chamber and committee rooms of the British Houses of Parliament, it was also the result of clandestine work of a revolutionary nature. As Ronan Fanning points out:

> '*Although the republican rebellion of 1916 registered as no more than a blip against such a cataclysmic backdrop (the Great War), its legacy – the Irish Republican Army's guerrilla war for independence – was the key determinant of British policy between 1920 and 1922*' (Fanning, 2013: 1).

Ireland's independence, therefore, was won by men and women who understood, violence, secrecy and the taking of oaths. And if the new state was a democracy it was a fragile one in a world where democracies were not the norm. The new state was borne out of a violent war of independence, followed by a civil war, which probably convinced anyone who needed convincing to keep in place the secrecy that was already part of the British regime in Ireland prior to 1922.

Following the civil war and the establishment of Fianna Fail, the political party that came out of the losing republican side of the conflict, it took time to ensure there were clear divisions between constitutional politics and a guerrilla movement. The Free State, which Ireland was called until the declaration of a republic in the late 1940s, established strict censorship during the Second World War, with the Emergency Powers Act, 1939, which allowed for wholesale censorship of media and mail. It was rescinded in 1949, though strangely, the Emergency was not ended until 1976.

While the authorities appeared neutral towards the Allies, it was felt there were those, including some elected to parliament, who might have liked to see British lose the war on the basis of my enemy's enemy is my friend: especially as some believed a German victory would mean the end of partition and the country unified. Censorship was necessary, it was believed, for a neutral Ireland to tread a delicate diplomatic path, along with widespread draconian powers that affected nearly every aspect of Irish life.

There was another factor, the Roman Catholic Church. Much is often made of the links and even control the Church had over civic life in Ireland until recent times. There were tensions and the Church did not always get its own way. Censorship is possibly one of those areas, where Catholic organisations, such as the Catholic Truth Society and the Knights of Columbanus pushed for far greater censorship than was brought in. As the historian, Diarmaid Ferriter said:

> *The idea of two warring factions in relation to censorship – Catholic organisations such as the Catholic Truth Society and the nights of Columbanus, versus liberal intellectuals such as Yeats, Shaw, O Faoláin and Frank O'Connor – is superficially appealing. But it is highly unlikely that either elite presented the concerns of the general population, or was intimately connected to the reality of Irish life,'* (Ferriter, 2005: 341).

There is no doubt some within the Catholic Church were seeking a far stricter censorship regime, including the banning of British newspapers, but while that was seen as a step too far, the idea of censorship was something both Church and state favoured.

Ferriter notes that the Catholic Church tended to agree with Republicans that moral corruption was to do with English influence and with independence an internal cause had to be found and dealt with. In 1927, just five years after independence, a pastoral letter from the Catholic hierarchy said:

> *The evil one is ever setting his snares for unwary feet. At the moment his traps for the innocent are chiefly the dance halls, the bad books, the motion picture, the indecent fashion in female dress – all of which tend to destroy the virtues characteristic of our race,'* (quoted in Ferriter, 2005: 336).

The Church would work with the state on the books and the cinema and would, itself, look after the other moral dangers. Despite the immense popularity of cinema going in Ireland the Censorship of Film Act passed quietly only a year after independence, in 1923. The Censorship of Publications Act took a little longer. In 1929, following a report from the wonderfully named Committee on Evil Literature, upon which sat three laymen, and representatives from the Catholic and Protestant churches, the Act was passed and the Censorship of Publications Board was born.

Such seeming obscurantism was not unique to Ireland, though without doubt the struggles for independence, the land reforms and the aftermath of a famine that had reduced the population by half as well as the decline in the speaking of Irish made Ireland a special case. However, the Official Secrets Act remained on the statute books in the United Kingdom, as well as in Ireland, and the Lord Chancellor was still banning plays in England, while in the US, the Motion Picture Code, known as the Hays Code, look remarkably like Irish film censorship. It was a period of particular militancy in the Catholic Church, one commentator described the motion picture code in the US as: 'a Jewish owned business selling Roman Catholic theology to Protestant America'. The comments in the Bishop's pastoral, which was matched by comments from senior Catholic clergymen in other countries, showed the deep fear the Church had with the new popular culture and with democracy itself.

Strengthening 'official' secrets

Ireland entered its post-colonial phase as the inheritor of official secrecy, as a fragile democracy, following a civil war and with a dominant church forced to find the source of moral corruption inside the Irish state, rather than in England, as had been the case until heretofore. That was the context, a highly centralised state, that felt it safer to rule with caution and secrecy fearing enemies within and without. As the political scientist Tom Garvin noted,

> '...*a certain tendency towards authoritarian law-enforcement and censorship in the name of keeping public order and also as a way of furthering state policy has persisted in Irish public life and detracts somewhat from the republican character of Irish political institutions,*' (Garvin, 1992: 226).

And so, as already alluded to, at the height of the Cold War in 1963, the then justice minister, Charles Haughey, decided to strengthen the Official Secrets Act. There were a number of reasons cited, international espionage, fear of a possible resurgent IRA, and weirdly, the leaking of the schools Leaving Certificate examination by an apprentice printer the previous year. At the time of intense anti communism in the world of Irish official secrecy, a stolen schools' examination paper was on par with leaking to the KGB.

As far as journalists were concerned the main threats to an open media were the libel laws, possibly the most draconian in Europe and not reformed until the Defamation Act of 2009: the official Secrets Act: and Section 31 of the Broadcasting Act. What all three did was engender a culture of secrecy. There was some investigative journalism, Joe MacAnthony's investigation of the Irish Hospital Sweepstake or Susan O'Keefe's programme on scandals in the beef industry and investigations in child abuse of children in care, especially that of Mary Raftery.

Despite Haughey's enthusiasm, the Act was actually rarely used; The *Irish Independent* was once fined for publishing a police identikit photograph in an investigation into the disappearance of the racehorse, Shergar. A crime correspondent, Liz Allen, was found guilty of an offence under the Act in the District Court, the equivalent of the Magistrates Court, for publishing the contents of a police bulletin. But it was never the number of prosecutions that was the issue, but the chilling effect the legislation had on journalists and journalism. The elite were defended by defamation law, once Northern Ireland blew up after 1968 the broadcasting ban kept 'subversive' voices, including Sinn Fein, off the airwaves; and the Officials Secrets Act allowed ministers to decide what was secret secure in the knowledge that no civil service would leak or blow the whistle.

Toward freedom of information

So why did the Irish government agree to introduce freedom of information? There had been some opening up before the Freedom of Information Act; the National Archives Act, which came into effect in 1991, gave historians, journalists and others access to public records over 30-years-old – other than when information relating to state security is withheld. An Ombudsman had been appointed in 1984 and much of the censorship of publications and films had been relaxed throughout the 1970s, 1980s and 1990s. There had been some individuals who were proposing freedom of information. A former senator, Brendan Ryan, wrote *Keeping Us In The Dark*, a study of censorship and freedom of information. There had been a private members bill and a campaign was run named 'Let in the Light', which united mainly journalists, academics and others. It organised a highly successful conference, with a list of speakers that included Salman Rushdie, then in hiding following a fatwa, the journalist Carl Bernstein, Anthony Lewis of *The New York Times* and others. The number of people who turned up at the two-day conference, and the subsequent sales of the book of the conference, was testament to a groundswell favouring legislative changes, openness and transparency.

However, the biggest single contributory factor in the drive for FOI was probably the Beef Tribunal, a hugely expensive judge-led inquiry into practices within the highly valuable beef industry, and the relationship between it and the political establishment. It made a number of disturbing findings about certain ministers and their departments in relation to the beef industry, including giving favourable treatment to some operators at the expense of others and of the taxpayers. Inexplicably, the journalist, Susan O'Keefe, who exposed the corruption, was the only person ever to appear in court, when she was charged with contempt having refused to reveal her sources. She was acquitted.

During the early part of the tribunal in January 1992 its chairman, Mr Justice Liam Hamilton, said: 'I think that if the questions that were asked in the Dáil (Irish parliament) were answered in the way they are answered here, there would be no necessity for this inquiry and a lot of money and time would have been saved,' (quoted in Foley, *The Irish Times*, 2 January, 1997). The tribunal continued hearing evidence until June 1993 and reported in August 1994. Costing some £30m, it was the longest, most expensive, and most controversial inquiry in the history of the state until then – there have been longer and more expensive inquiries since. It caused a general election; gave rise to three Supreme Court cases; led to an investigation by a parliamentary committee and a disciplinary hearing of the Bar Council; and led to the introduction of freedom of information legislation. Its impact on Irish politics was immense. (For more on the Beef Tribunal see O'Toole, 1995).

Following the 1992 general election, which returned a Fianna Fail/Labour coalition, both parties committed to introducing FOI laws and ethics in public office legislation in its programme for government. The tribunal had opened the door on the workings of the state just a fraction, but enough to make it difficult to close it fully again. It was the tribunal that made it possible for freedom of information to be added to the Programme for Government in 1993. That Fianna Fail / Labour coalition collapsed, partly due to tension arising from the Beef Tribune report, and was succeeded by the so-called 'Rainbow' coalition of three parties. That government also committed itself to enacting freedom of information legislation. The same junior minister, Eithne Fitzgerald, remained responsible for preparing the legislation. The proposed legislation was modelled very closely on FOI laws already in place in Australia and New Zealand.

Ms Fitzgerald did not have an easy task. As memory of the Beef Tribunal dimmed so did the commitment to openness and transparency. The legislation was nearly lost inside the Department of Justice, where the strategy seemed to be to delay as long as possible and it would fall with the government when a general election was called. Compromises were made. The right of public servants to blow the whistle on what they believed was a wrong doing was not included in the Act, though it had been included in earlier drafts. Also the police, An Garda Síochána, were to be included as a public body under the Act, but that was dropped, though provision to be added later was in the final legislation. The law also included a certification system, whereby ministers could issue a certificate deeming some information 'secret' under three categories - security of the state; law enforcement and international relations. These certificates were subject to regular review at the most senior governmental level. This system is similar to one operating under the FOI legislation in New Zealand and Australia. It was, according to one civil service source, more a 'security blanket.'

There were some criticisms of the Act from journalists. The 30- day response limit was seen by many as too long; that the Act did not specifically mention journalism and its role in society; and that as the bill made its slow journey through Parliament and its committees' it had become much more about the individual right to information rather than one based on the public interest (for more on journalists' criticism of FOI see Foley, 1997).

FOI and its legacy

More or less the Act has had a positive impact on Irish society. Since April 1998 people in Ireland have had the right to seek access to any information held; the right to correct information held that might be wrong; and the right to see how decisions relating to one self were taken. For members of the public they can see where they are on the housing list; see why the Arts Council turned down their application for a performance art project; and access their medical files.

For journalists it has meant having access to politicians' expenses, after an appeal to the courts; information on the use of the government jet and other expenditure; and also information held by the Department of Education on schools, which has led to a plethora of controversy over school league tables. It has also allowed access to reports on nursing homes; hospitals; schools; prisons and other public bodies, including the public service broadcaster, RTÉ; and state funded universities. Former inmates of so-called industrial schools, many of whom suffered appalling abuse, were able to access their records using FOI when making claims under a redress scheme. Journalists have been able to inspect how regulatory bodies are working; get details of hospital waiting lists; or the details of public procurement. Discussions between the Department of Education and the Catholic Church on issues relating to the governance of new model primary schools were also accessed. However, what has also happened is that increasingly records are released as a matter of course, without journalists always having to use FOI to force disclosure.

Time and time again stories are obtained using FOI and the refrain, 'according to information released under the Freedom of Information Act' is increasingly heard on the broadcast news. After the initial teething problems of journalists not knowing how to use the Act, using it for trivial stories or going on massive trawling exercises, to many journalists today using FOI has become a routine. However, state and public bodies are still fighting access to information. The Information Commissioner received many objections to forcing the publication of judges' expenses, for instance, which has happened. Getting information relating to the government's handling of the economic collapse and the bank bailout and bank guarantees has been a long battle.

The former minister Eithne Fitzgerald fought for FOI every step of the way. After it was passed she commented that it would change, forever, the way public business was done and would herald a quiet revolution in the public service. Unfortunately, she lost her seat in the next election and parliament lost its most articulate FOI champion. For journalists, it was hoped FOI would mean an end to the days of the reputed 'no comment' and 'don't quote me' responses to queries. That probably did happen, and there is evidence that suggests more official information is now routinely placed in the public domain than was the case.

The Act amended

The 1997 Act was predicated on the notion of what best serves the public interest. It was welcomed by civil service unions, by the courts, journalists and the public in general. Its radical nature is possibly best understood when in 2003 it was amended by the then government in what the then Information Commissioner, Emily O'Reilly, described, in an understated way in a publication to mark the first 10 years of the legislation, as 'a step back from the commitment to openness, transparency and accountability which was the key factor in the enactment of the 1997 Act' (Office of the Information Commissioner: 2008: 13).

The 2003 amendment was a severe setback to openness in Ireland. The then government, led, ironically, by Fianna Fail – the party that in opposition had argued the act had not gone far enough. That government, which included the Progressive Democrat party, was a centre right government and it is believed the impetus to amend FOI came from the Fianna Fail's Minister for Finance, Charlie McCreevy, later a European Commissioner.

The amendment brought in charges for making requests; extended the time when access to the records of government was available to 10-years rather than five; gave full protection to communications between ministers concerning matters before government; and so on. One reason for this was that Fianna Fail had been in government since 1997 and still in government in 2003 with a term due to run until 2007, when files relating to 1997, when it came into office, would be available for public scrutiny. The new Act followed a review, which was held in secret (yes, really) and did not seek any contribution from the Information Commission. It was then pushed through parliament by the government.

The fees, which were extraordinarily high, especially for journalists involved in major investigations, were clearly responsible for a dramatic fall off in FOI usage since 2003 and that fall-of was particularly evident in the use of FOI by journalists. When the cost of accessing a record and the hourly cost of searching and retrieving were combined, the average cost of an FOI request was about €200 (£160). Only a year after the amendments were enacted the use of the Act by journalists fell by 50 per cent (*The Irish Times*, 17 May, 2004).

A new government elected in 2011 included the Labour Party, which had brought in the original Act, committed itself to restoring the Freedom of Information Act to its pre 2003 state. The Fine Gael and Labour Party Programme for Government, 2011-2016 stated:

> *We will legislate to restore the Freedom of Information Act to what it was before it was undermined by the outgoing Government, and we will extend its remit to other public bodies including the administrative side of the Garda Síochána, subject to security exceptions. We will extend Freedom of Information, and the Ombudsman Act, to ensure that all statutory bodies, and all bodies significantly funded from the public purse, are covered. We will introduce Whistleblowers legislation. We will put in place a Whistleblowers Act to protect public servants that expose maladministration by Ministers or others, and restore Freedom of Information,* (Programme for Government 2011).

In October, 2014, the Government did as promised and the Freedom of Information Act, 2014 was passed. The new legislation extends the Act to all public bodies, including the police, (An Gárda Síochána), the Central Bank and public financial bodies, including the National Assets Management Agency, which has been involved in a long legal case with a journalist attempting to ensure it is not defined as a public body. All new public bodies will automatically come under the Act, unless an exemption is made or if some of its work is exempted. It also abolishes the €15 application fee, caps the search and retrieval and gives the first five hours searching free. The abolition of the fee was, at the end of the day, undertaken with some reluctance, with a number of ministers voicing support for its retention, even though some of them had opposed it in 2003. The period during which government records are exempt was also restored to five years.

References

Fanning, Ronan (2013) *Fatal Path: British Government and Irish Revolution 1910 – 1922*. London: Faber and Faber

Ferriter, Dermot (2005) *The Transformation of Ireland, 1900-2000*. London: Profile Books

Foley, Michael (1999) 'What the Freedom of Information Act does not Provide: a Journalist's View' in Donnelly, Joseph and Doyle, Mary (eds) *Freedom of Information: Philosophy and Implementation*. Dublin: Blackhall Publishing

Foley, Michael (1997) 'Information Bill Offers limited Scope to Investigate Workings of Government' in *The Irish Times*, Dublin, January 22

Garvin, Tom (2005) 'Democratic Politics in Independent Ireland' in Coakley, John and Gallagher, Michael (eds) *Politics in the Republic of Ireland*. Galway: PSAI Press, pp 222-233

O'Reilly, Emily, (2008) *Freedom of Information: the First Decade*. Dublin: The Office of the Information Commissioner

O'Toole, Fintan (1995) *Meanwhile Back At the Ranch: The Politics of Irish Beef*. London: Vintage

Government of Ireland (2011) *Programme for Government*, available at www.per.gov.ie/wp-content/.../ProgrammeforGovernmentFinal.pdf *accessed Oct 20th, 2014*

Smyth Patrick and Brady Ronan (1994) *Democracy Blindfolded: The Case for Freedom of Information*. Cork: Cork University Press

Note on the contributor

Michael Foley, PhD, is a lecturer in journalism at the Dublin Institute of Technology, Ireland. He is a member of the editorial board of the *Irish Communications Review*, the advisory board of the journal, *Index On Censorship*, and a member of the NUJ's Ethics Council. He is a former reporter with *The Irish Times* and was that newspaper's media correspondent and covered the introduction of the Freedom of Information Act in Ireland and wrote extensively about it and its initial impact. He has worked extensively in media development in Eastern and South Eastern Europe, the Balkans, Central Asia and Africa, working with the BBC, IREX and UNICEF. His email is michael.foley@dit.ie

Deny, delay, deter, defeat: promise and reality in Canada's access regime

Canada's access to information laws have proven indispensable for journalists investigating government activities and important public issues, however delays, fees, political interference and stonewalling are making the laws less effective, writes *Dean Jobb*

Introduction

Canada's freedom of information laws played a key role in exposing a scandal that brought down a national government. Daniel Leblanc, a reporter with the Toronto-based *Globe and Mail,* one of the country's major newspapers, applied for access to the records of a little-known program created to promote national unity. The federal Department of Public Works poured hundreds of millions of dollars into advertising and sponsorship campaigns to persuade residents of the predominantly francophone province Quebec, who had narrowly voted against a proposal to seek independence, to stay in Canada. How much money was earmarked for the program? Where was it going? And how was the money being spent? Leblanc's initial access request yielded few details but follow-up requests and further investigation, with the assistance of newsroom colleague Campbell Clark, revealed that money had been funnelled to private advertising firms with close ties to the ruling Liberal party. One firm received a CAD$615,000 (£344,000) contract to assess its own performance while another was paid CAD$550,000 (£307,000) to produce a report that was never submitted (Greenspon, 2004).

Federal Auditor General Sheila Fraser, who reviewed the sponsorship initiative in response to the *Globe and Mail's* revelations, filed a 2004 report that depicted a CAD$330m (£184m) program shrouded in secrecy and riddled with waste and mismanagement. These findings, in turn, prompted Prime Minister Paul Martin, who inherited both the program and the scandal from his predecessor, Jean Chrétien, to order an inquiry. Justice John Gomery, the retired Quebec judge appointed to lead this wider investigation, held public hearings that produced new revelations of corruption and kickbacks to federal officials and Liberal fundraisers. Martin's government was reduced to minority status in a 2004 election, in large measure due to public outrage over the sponsorship scandal, and was voted out of office less than two years later. The *Globe and Mail* and reporters Leblanc and Clark received Canada's most prestigious journalism honour, the Michener Award for Meritorious Public Service Journalism, for their part in bringing the scandal to light.

Canada's access laws have been used to expose countless other instances of wrongdoing in high places, abuses of power and the misuse of public money. The legislation that launched the *Globe and Mail*'s investigation of the sponsorship scandal, the Access to Information Act, covers the national government and its institutions and has been described as having 'more potential than any statute to harass, embarrass, distract and annoy the government of the day' (Information Commissioner of Canada, 1994A: 23). Similar laws apply to provincial and local governments and journalists have used them to investigate the training of police tactical teams; poor hygiene and food-preparation standards in restaurants; and whether government agencies are vigilant in their inspections of mines and other workplaces. A Canadian Broadcasting Corporation investigative team obtained data on adverse reactions to medications that exposed lax procedures for monitoring the safety of drugs approved for use in Canada. Andrew McIntosh, a reporter for the *National Post* newspaper, used access laws to probe former prime minister Chrétien's role in securing federal grants and loans for businesses in the Quebec riding he represented in parliament. And media demands for details about the Canadian soldiers responsible for the beating to death of a Somali man during a peacekeeping mission exposed an elaborate military cover-up.[1]

A regime under attack

Despite these successes – or, more accurately, because of them – Canada's access regime is under threat. Politicians and bureaucrats, the public officials that freedom of information laws are designed to hold accountable, have mounted a determined and highly successful counterattack to evade requests and frustrate applicants. It can take months and sometimes years for access requests to work their way through the system. The legislation exempts records from disclosure to protect cabinet secrecy, advice given to ministers in confidence, personal privacy and similar interests, and public officials have become adept at using these exemptions to justify withholding information that should be made public. Since requests from journalists are likely to generate negative publicity for governments and public bodies, these applications are flagged and subjected to additional scrutiny and delay. Exorbitant search and processing fees, sometimes reaching into the tens of thousands of dollars, have been levied to block disclosure and deter applicants. Duff Conacher, a director of the advocacy group Democracy Watch, has suggested it would be apt to change the name of the Access to Information Act to the 'Guide to Keeping Information Secret Act' (Gillis, 2014).

This official backlash has transformed Canada, once a leader in providing and promoting government openness, into a global laggard (Tromp, 2008). A comparison of the scope and provisions of access laws in effect as of 2013, compiled by the Centre for Law and Democracy, relegated Canada's freedom of information regime to 56th spot on a roster of 98 countries, sandwiched between Mongolia and Malta and far below India (second), the United Kingdom (27th) and many developing countries (CLD, 2013). That year, the organisation Canadian Journalists for Free Expression decried the 'sorry state of access to information' at the national level and took to task the Canadian government for its failure to reform and modernise its legislation. The right to demand and receive government information in Canada, it concluded, has become 'a hollow right' (CJFE, 2013: 3).

A patchwork of laws

Canada was an early convert to open government laws, with the province of Nova Scotia leading the way in 1977. The federal Access to Information Act became law for the national government in 1983 and, by 2002, all provinces had adopted similar legislation (even Canada's thinly-populated northern territories have access laws). Provincial governments, in turn, have enacted legislation to make cities, towns and other local governments subject to access laws.

The scope of this access regime is broad, at least on paper. The premise of the federal law, for instance, is to facilitate public access and all government records are subject to disclosure with 'limited and specific' exemptions to protect sensitive and confidential information. The Act's definition of the kinds of records subject to release is also generous, encompassing any 'book, plan, map, drawing, diagram, pictorial or graphic work, photograph, film, microform, sound recording, videotape, machine readable record, and any other documentary material, regardless of physical form or characteristics.' And the legislation applies to a wide array of public institutions, including all federal government departments and agencies; the Canadian military; the national police force and prison system; and publicly owned corporations such as the post office and the Canadian Broadcasting Corporation.[2]

This patchwork of laws is the product of Canada's federal structure, which includes a national government, 10 provincial, and three territorial administrations, each with its own access legislation and practices. It can make the legislation difficult to use – as journalists and other applicants can struggle to determine which level of government holds the records being sought; whether those records are subject to disclosure; and the procedures for filing a request. While there are many similarities in the provisions and scope of this legislation, access sometimes varies depending on the government involved. To cite two examples, most records that would reveal the secret deliberations of the federal cabinet – the executive branch of the national government – are exempt from disclosure for 20 years. But each province has its own cabinet and Nova Scotia makes these records available after just 10 years, and discloses some records as soon as the decision on an issue or policy has been made public.[3] Another discrepancy is that not all provinces include hospitals, school boards, universities and colleges within their access regimes, and at least one province, British Columbia, has extended its legislation to include self-governing societies that regulate lawyers, doctors and other professionals.[4]

An annual freedom of information audit conducted on behalf of Newspapers Canada, an organisation that represents the country's daily and weekly press, has exposed inconsistencies in how government agencies interpret their legislation. Information readily available in one jurisdiction may be heavily censored, released after a long delay or withheld entirely in another (Beeby, 2014). These jurisdictional differences also become apparent when applicants seek to challenge a public agency's refusal to release records. While all applicants have the right to file a court action and ask a judge to order the release of records, each jurisdiction appoints an information commissioner or similar official to conduct an independent review of decisions to withhold information. In five provinces, these officials have the power to order governments to release records if they conclude there are no grounds for withholding them. Information watchdogs in the remaining provinces and their federal counterpart, however, can only recommend that information be released; government decision-makers may find such rulings persuasive and release additional records, but they are under no legal obligation to comply (Roberts, 1998: 58-9).

Broad access in theory

Canada's courts have underlined the importance of access laws. 'The overarching purpose of access to information legislation,' Canada's Supreme Court ruled in 1997, 'is to facilitate democracy.... It helps to ensure first, that citizens have the information required to participate meaningfully in the democratic process, and secondly, that politicians and bureaucrats remain accountable to the citizenry.'[5] Justice Gomery, in the 2006 report of his inquiry into the federal sponsorship program, described a strong and effective access to information regime as 'an essential element of modern public administration.' The secrecy that surrounded the sponsorship program, he concluded, 'made it possible for some individuals to subvert management processes and bypass lines of accountability' (Gomery, 2006: 177, 179).

Court rulings have also enhanced the scope and effectiveness of access laws. 'Access should be the normal course,' observed one judge who interpreted the federal law. 'Exemptions should be exceptional and must be confined to those specifically set out in the statute.'[6] Courts in at least two provinces have ruled that media reports based on records obtained in response to freedom of information requests enjoy qualified privilege. This is of tremendous importance to journalists because such reports have the same immunity to libel actions as news coverage of court testimony and parliamentary debates.[7] The Supreme Court of Canada also has ruled that the federal government does not have the final say on whether records are exempt from disclosure on the grounds of cabinet confidentiality, and applicants have the right to challenge such claims in the courts (Makin, 2002).

Access to information in the possession of Canadian governments, however, is not a constitutional right. While the *Canadian Charter of Rights and Freedoms* guarantees freedom of expression as well as 'freedom of the press and other media of communication,' the Supreme Court of Canada ruled in 2010 this provision 'does not guarantee access to all documents in government hands.'[8]

Targeting journalists

A former federal minister of justice once dismissed access legislation as a tool of 'mischief-makers' intent on using the information they unearthed to 'embarrass political leaders and titillate the public' (Roberts, 2006: 87). The minister put into words the antipathy many Canadian politicians and bureaucrats have toward freedom of information laws and those who file access requests, especially journalists. At the federal level in Canada, many departments and agencies single out requests from the media and government critics for special treatment and additional scrutiny. The process, known in some departments as 'amber lighting,' usually results in longer-than-usual delays in producing records and gives officials time to prepare the government's response to the publicity expected to arise from the revelations (Roberts, 2006: 89-91).

Canadian Journalists for Free Expression has criticised this practice and warned that the access system is becoming politicised as partisan appointees assigned to some federal departments and agencies have begun to usurp the traditional role of civil servants in processing requests (CJFE, 2013: 4). In a 2014 report Canada's information commissioner, Suzanne Legault, warned of 'systemic interference' with applications for access after concluding that three political appointees had been involved in decisions on whether requested information should be made public (Canadian Press, 2014).

Misuse of statutory exemptions

John Reid, Canada's former information commissioner, has warned of a culture of secrecy that has developed within the federal government and its bureaucracy, and of a 'deep distrust' of access legislation 'at all levels in government' (Deveau, 2005). This distrust is most evident in the over-reliance on statutory exemptions to withhold information, even though the legislation calls for the 'limited' use of exemptions and the courts deem them exceptions, and not the rule, when decisions are made on access requests. Too many officials deliberately apply exemptions to records that should be released or err on the side of caution and refuse to disclose information.

An exemption for records that would reveal advice and recommendations provided to a cabinet minister or the head of a public body, for instance, is often given a broad interpretation and used to deny access. The federal legislation's protection of cabinet secrets has been dubbed the 'Mack Truck clause' for creating a loophole large enough for a truck to pass through (Information Commissioner of Canada, 1994B: 7). A 2014 media report accused the

Conservative government of Prime Minister Stephen Harper of using the cabinet secrecy rule to block access to reports, briefing notes and other information that had been routinely released in the past. The list of newly minted cabinet secrets included why a plan to buy new armoured vehicles was cancelled; Canada's stance on the proliferation of chemical weapons; and the safety of rail transport in the wake of a deadly 2013 derailment. 'Cabinet confidence is invoked so often,' an opposition critic complained, that 'everything is secret, including the colour of the minister's dress on any given day' (Brewster, 2014).

Limiting the scope of access laws

Governments also have been hesitant to extend disclosure obligations to public institutions that operate outside access regimes and to new entities as they are created. The federal legislation, for instance, does not apply to records in the possession of members of parliament, cabinet ministers or their staff, or to the prime minister's office, which wields enormous power in the Canadian political system. And when the federal government created new agencies to manage the storage of nuclear waste; provide air traffic control services at airports; and oversee the collection and distribution of donated blood, these entities were not made subject to the Access to Information Act. This prompted one access advocate to accuse federal authorities of engaging in 'a low-level campaign of attrition' to shield national bodies from public scrutiny (Roberts, 2003: 5). The federal government appeared to respond to such concerns in 2006 by extending access coverage to several government-operated corporations and foundations and the offices of the auditor general, privacy commissioner and information commissioner. Canadian Journalists for Free Expression, however, estimates that at least 100 other federal agencies and institutions are not required by law to disclose their records, and the list is growing (CJFE, 2013: 8-9). At least one jurisdiction has rescinded established rights of access. In 2012 the government of Newfoundland and Labrador, Canada's easternmost province, amended its legislation to block the release of cabinet records previously accessible to the public. The list of newly excluded records included materials prepared for cabinet even if this information was never discussed at the cabinet level (Antle, 2012).

Delays and fees

Perhaps the most serious barriers to using freedom of information laws – and major deterrents for journalists – are the time and money required to pursue many access requests. The legislation establishes a token application fee (as low as CAD\$5 (£2.77)) but government officials can charge much more – sometimes thousands of dollars in additional research and preparation fees. Access laws typically stipulate a 30-day deadline for responding to requests, but governments have the right to extend the response time if a request is considered complex or involves a large number of records.

In 2009 then-information commissioner Robert Marleau issued a report warning that delays permeate the federal access system. Few access requests are completed within the 30-day deadline set out in the Access to Information Act, he noted, and response times for some departments and agencies can be up to four months. 'Canadians,' he wrote, 'expect and deserve far greater efficiency and accountability from their government.' The solution, he added, is better record-keeping practices, more staff to handle access requests and political leaders willing 'to guide a cultural change away from a tendency to withhold information' (Jobb, 2009).

A Challenge for journalists
Successive governments, however, have demonstrated little of the leadership and political will needed to improve Canada's access laws. Prime Minister Stephen Harper's Conservative government, which held power at the time of writing, was elected in 2006 on promises to improve openness and accountability at the federal level. Harper's platform included proposals to give the federal information commissioner the power to order the government to release records and reforms that could have seen the public interest trump other barriers to releasing documents. Once elected, however, his government shelved these proposals as well as plans to require officials accustomed to doing business verbally or using mobile devices (rather than creating a paper trail that would be subject to an access request) to document their actions and decisions (Jobb, 2006).

Delays, fees, government stonewalling and other barriers have deterred many Canadian journalists from using freedom of information legislation. Between April 2009 and March 2010, journalists accounted for about 3,700 access requests filed with the federal government, barely one in 10 of all requests submitted – a drop from 14 per cent the previous year. Corporations submitted almost half of the requests and members of the public filed in excess of 12,000 applications, more than triple the number originating with the media (McKie, 2011). Kirk Lapointe, a former bureau chief for the Canadian Press newswire service in the national capital, Ottawa, has dismissed access laws as a 'last resort for reporters' and a 'better tool of history than of journalism' (Information Commissioner of Canada, 1994A: 16). Canadian Press reporters continue to make effective use of the laws to probe government decisions and policies, however, and the news service's stylebook encourages journalists to file applications that can 'shed new light on key issues and developments' and add depth to important stories that may have faded from the headlines (McCarten, 2103: 73).

Despite these shortcomings, access laws have proven indispensable as journalists investigate government activities and important public issues. One study identified more than 100 major stories published between 2006 and 2010 that were based on information obtained using the Access to Information Act. The stories tackled an array of public-policy issues – health and safety; the environment; national security; policing; foreign policy; lack of government accountability; waste of tax dollars – and demonstrate that journalists can overcome 'barriers of bureaucratic and political resistance to produce valuable results' (Tromp, 2010). David McKie, an investigative reporter with the Canadian Broadcasting Corporation, has argued that important stories such as these need to be told – and often can only be told by journalists willing to exercise their access rights and devote the time and effort needed to pry records from a reluctant bureaucracy. 'Going through the process is not for the faint of heart. But neither is being a journalist facing a federal government bent on spin and obfuscation,' he added. 'There's too much at stake for journalists to be on the wrong side of a downward trend' (Lacey 2011).

Notes

[1] See David Pugliese, 'Armed and Dangerous – SWAT, You're Dead,' *Media*, Summer 1999, p 14; Robert Cribb, 'Dirty Dining,' ibid, Summer 2001, pp 12-3; Dean Jobb, *Calculated Risk: Greed, Politics and the Westray Tragedy*, Halifax, NS: Nimbus Publishing, 1994; 'Faint Warning,' *CBC News Online*, available online at http://www.cbc.ca/news2/adr/index.html; Andrew McIntosh, 'Into the Rough' *Media*, Summer 2000, pp 6-7; and David McKie, 'The General's Mea Culpa,' ibid, Fall 1996, pp 5-6, 23-4

[2] Access to Information Act, ss. 2(1) and 3, and schedule 1, available at http://laws.justice.gc.ca/en/A-1/index.html

[3] Access to Information Act, s. 69 (3); Freedom of Information and Protection of Privacy Act, SNS, s. 13(2), available at http://nslegislature.ca/legc/statutes/freedom%20of%20information%20and%20protec tion%20of%20privacy.pdf

[4] Freedom of Information and Protection of Privacy Act, RSBC 1996, c. 165, schedule 3, available at http://web2.gov.mb.ca/laws/statutes/ccsm/f175e.php

[5] Dagg v. Canada (Minister of Finance), [1997] 2 SCR 403 at para. 61

[6] Canada (Information Commissioner) v. Canada (Minister of Employment and Immigration), [1986] 3 FC 63 at para. 69 (TD)

[7] Fletcher-Gordon v. Southam Inc. et al. [1997], 33 BCLR (3d) 118 (SC). This ruling was endorsed, for portions of news reports drawn directly from records obtained using access legislation, in Hodgson v Canadian Newspapers Company Limited et al. [1998], 39 OR (3d) 235

[8] Ontario (Public Safety and Security) v. Criminal Lawyers' Association, 2010 SCC 23, [2010] 1 SCR 815 at para. 30

References

Antle, Rob (2012) 'NL Law to Clamp Down on Access to Information,' *CBC News Online*, 11 June, available at http://www.cbc.ca/news/canada/newfoundland-labrador/n-l-law-to-clamp-down-on-access-to-information-1.1178488, accessed 17 September, 2014

Beeby, Dean (2014) 'Freedom of Information audit singles out Federal Government as "Among the Worst",' *The Star* (Toronto), 4 June, available at http://www.thestar.com/news/canada/2014/06/04/freedomofinformation_audit_singl es_out_federal_government_as_among_the_worst.html, accessed 10 September, 2014

Brewster, Murray (2014) 'Soldiers on Viagra part of a list of secrets held by Harper Government,' *The Star*, 14 September, available at http://www.thestar.com/news/canada/2014/09/14/soldiers_on_viagra_part_of_a_list _of_secrets_held_by_harper_government.html, accessed 17 September, 2014

Canadian Journalists for Free Expression (CJFE) (2013) *A Hollow Right: Access to Information in Crisis*. Available at https://cjfe.org/resources/features/new-report-hollow-right-access-information-crisis, accessed 12 September, 2014

Canadian Press (2104) 'Conservative Staffers Interfered in Access to Information, Commissioner Finds,' *The Star*, 10 April, available at http://www.thestar.com/news/canada/2014/04/10/conservative_staffers_interfered_i n_access_to_information_commissioner_says.html, accessed 17 September, 2014

Centre for Law and Democracy (CLD) (2014) *Global Right to Information Rating - Country Data*. Available at http://www.rti-rating.org/country_data.php, accessed 16 September, 2014

Deveau, Scott (2005) 'Access to information not always accessible,' *Globe and Mail*, 6 June

Gillis, Wendy (2104) 'Canadians' rightful access to public information being blocked, experts say,' *The Star*, 27 April 27, available at http://www.thestar.com/news/gta/2014/04/27/canadians_rightful_access_to_public_i nformation_being_blocked_experts_say.html, accessed 17 September, 2014

Gomery, Justice John (2006) *Commission of Inquiry into the Sponsorship Program and Advertising Activities, Second Report: Restoring Accountability*, available at http://www.cbc.ca/news2/background/groupaction/gomeryreport_phasetwo_full.html, accessed 17 September, 2014

Greenspon, Edward (2004) 'Four years of dogged digging unravelled sponsorship scandal,' *Globe and Mail*, 14 February

Information Commissioner of Canada (1994A) *The Access to Information Act: 10 Years On* Ottawa: Information Commissioner of Canada

Information Commissioner of Canada (1994B) *The Access to Information Act: A Critical Review* Ottawa: Information Commissioner of Canada

Jobb, Dean (2006) 'Stephen Harper's cult of secrecy,' *Winnipeg Free Press*, 14 May. Available at http://www.winnipegfreepress.com/historic/31705239.html, accessed 2 September, 2014

Jobb, Dean (2009) 'The sorry state of access to information,' *The Lawyers Weekly*, 27 March, available at http://www.lawyersweekly.ca/index.php?section=article&articleid=885, accessed 2 September, 2014

Lacey, Dana (2011) 'Fewer journalists requesting access to information,' *J-Source*, 5 January, available at http://j-source.ca/article/fewer-journalists-requesting-access-information, accessed 18 September, 2014

Makin, Kirk (2002) 'Tenets of cabinet confidentiality upheld,' *Globe and Mail*, 12 July

McCarten, James (2013) (ed) *The Canadian Press Stylebook: A Guide for Writers and Editors.* Toronto: Canadian Press, 17th edn

McKie, David (2011) 'Fewer journalists are using Access to Information,' *CBC News Online*, 4 January, available at http://www.cbc.ca/newsblogs/politics/inside-politics-blog/2011/01/fewer-journalists-are-using-access-to-information.html, accessed 17 September, 2014

Roberts, Alasdair (1998) *Limited Access: Assessing the Health of Canada's Freedom of Information Laws*, Kingston, Ont.: School of Policy Studies, Queen's University

Roberts, Alasdair (2003) 'The Politics of Open Government' in *Fraser Forum*, May, pp 5–6

Roberts, Alasdair (2006) *Blacked Out: Government Secrecy in the Information Age.* New York: Cambridge University Press

Tromp, Stanley (2008) *Fallen Behind: Canada's Access to Information Act in the World Context*, available at http://www3.telus.net/index100/report, accessed 10 September, 2014

Tromp, Stanley (2010) *Notable Canadian News Stories Based on ATIA Requests, January 30, 2006 to March 20, 2010*, available at http://www3.telus.net/index100/atiastories1, accessed 17 September, 2104

Note on the contributor

Dean Jobb is an award-winning author and journalist and an associate professor of journalism at the University of King's College in Halifax, Nova Scotia, Canada. His textbook *Media Law for Canadian Journalists* (2nd edn, 2011) is used in newsrooms and journalism programs across Canada. Dean filed numerous freedom of information requests in his years as an investigative reporter and chaired an independent review of Nova Scotia's access legislation. His articles and commentaries have appeared in Canada's major newspapers, including the *National Post, Globe and Mail* and *Toronto Star*, and in the *Chicago Tribune* and Northern Ireland's *Belfast Telegraph*. His website is www.deanjobb.com

Tales from the front line: Canada's FOI warrior

Ken Rubin has battled FOI officers on behalf of the media, citizens and other clients for more than 30 years. He advises weary investigative reporters to keep testing the legislation, and the decision makers

Promises and realities in the world of FOI

The media's expectations for FOI were high when Canada first introduced its Access to Information Act a little more than 30 years ago. But the use of the legislation since then has come up against the brutal limitations of what's provided or not and made me into a battle-hardened FOI warrior. As the Canadian national public broadcaster CBC recently found out, even the most public of events can become secret under FOI releases. Records from the Privy Council Office concerning British Prime Minister Cameron's trip to Ottawa back in 2012 were two years late and continually blanked out PM Cameron's name as 'personal information' (Fitz-Morris, 2014). The following chapter recounts some of those battles.

The making of an FOI warrior

My background is as an independent researcher with five decades of exploring all kinds of issues. Interest in public policy issues came from working with all types of community and citizen groups from civil liberty to environmental groups. I'd usually be the one who wanted to know what's behind the scenes and what power structure was making life difficult for causes... and trying to get information and yes, the media's attention. So it was perhaps a logical extension that in the early 1970s, along with others, I began to press for the public's right to know more about the issues of the day. The lobby group I joined, called ACCESS, spent a decade helping to get Canada's 1982 Access to Information Act passed. Along the way, I prepared for ACCESS a survey of parliamentarians' own none-too-successful attempts to get government information (Rubin, 1997).

From the start, I became an 'access junkie' and began testing the system and filing FOI requests even before the formal July 1, 1983 kick-off date. Since then,

I've filed thousands of requests at all levels of Canadian governments, becoming a kind of expert and critic of all things too secret. Mine has been as a day-to-day foot soldier using FOI as a legal weapon battling for the release of information. I've had to deal with thousands of government officials, many client groups, gone to the courts, and seen hundreds of my research efforts grace the front and inside pages and reports of media outlets, thanks to the stories journalists did. You don't have to go to a J School to be curious and regularly search for data. You do have to be persistent, skilled, and committed however to practice the black art of FOI queries successfully – whether in Canada or elsewhere.

For pursuing hard to get data, I've been called a 'pain in the neck' (MP Perrin Beatty, 1984) and by others an information ambulance-chaser costing government a bundle of bucks to respond (Fine, 1997). But no one has called me a frivolous or lazy FOI user to be expelled or intimidated from asking for relevant data. Some officials have even used my FOI services to get information from rival bureaucracies. When I found hidden government studies on toxic bathroom moulds, other officials confided in me that they actually were shocked that their government wasn't releasing and telling them about something that affected their daily lives. Being a persistent and constant FOI user means your motivations are bound to be queried as, after all, the game being played by officials is to protect their ministers. That's despite some records revealing for instance, excessive and irregular spending and inspection violations.

Associating with the media

The journey for data has taken me much closer to the media but still places me at a distance as an outsider. I've frequently been given credit for bringing data forward for many news stories, and I've seen the backrooms of many media outlets. At one point, I was hired to coordinate one outlet's access work by its journalists. But it's rarer nowadays that media outlets ask me to file access requests on their behalf because they now usually have someone on staff who is very capable of this.

Bringing a cutting edge piece of data out in the open is not as simple when you're not a media employee or it's not related to the events of the day. Not all of my access research brought to the media is accepted, and remuneration for material used is minimal. Having many 'scoops' does not place you in line for the regular media awards, invitations or events nor grant you media privileged access if that's what counts. Media outlets however will remind me when I do not come to them first with a hot news story before their rivals. Most media on the whole have been supportive of my investigations and services should a good story be revealed by government documents. Some outside and inside government do perceive me as being part of the 'media'. Some government agencies label me as fitting in the 'business', 'research', or 'public' user category. Certainly, the code of silence applies to me too when I try and get officials talking. It can be beneficial that government cannot pin me down as coming from one group or working at times for particular clients. In many instances, I am following my own public interest instincts and analytical abilities to dig out hard-to-get data.

As one who is a users' user, working at times with unions, corporate trade and professional associations, individuals, and public interest groups, I have a broad appreciation of the struggles of many, including journalists. Put a different way, government agencies and their law, security and corporate allies, possessing more resource and communication staff, readily outnumber and outgun most users in the uphill battle to get and use government data. One reason that I may be perceived as being 'media' is because I've been a regular commentator on FOI and for the last 15 years have had an 'Open Government' column in Ottawa's parliament hill publication, *The Hill Times*. Writing columns gets you a platform, but it means being timely, checking facts, wanting to be read and being knowledgeable. Cutting through the thick fog of so-called bold 'transparency' initiatives can make your columns critical, cutting, and occasionally being checked by libel lawyers. Maybe too, it can make you part of the media 'establishment' and into a fifth estate know-it-all if you let it happen rather than a seeker of what's really going on behind the scenes.

Getting stories via FOI and seeing them published is a three-part battle. A third of the battle is getting the data; a third is getting the media interested in doing the story; and a third is having the readers and larger public pay attention and use the sought after data to generate public understanding, debate and action. Having received many calls from journalists for advice and presenting FOI workshops for the media and others, I know over the years I have assisted and encouraged journalists and the public to use FOI. My eye on getting newsworthy data on public issues has made me a kind of 'citizen' journalist. Dean Beeby, Deputy Bureau Chief, Canadian Press, called me 'a government gadfly for more than three decades... a frequent source of blockbuster stories ...having extracted embarrassing documents from reluctant departments' and one who 'has stuck to his profession and principles through thick and thin for many years' (Beeby, 2011).

The Media and FOI

Journalists like to think that they are the best and most motivated users of FOI, but are they? They account, at least in Canada, for only one in 10 requests with the corporate world putting in well over half of all queries. The inquiry rate has been very low at 20,000 to 40,000 a year, with correctional inmates, immigrant queries and frequent users accounting for many of the requests (Rubin and Kozolanka, 2014: 198).

Not all journalists are FOI oriented, with a research or investigative bent, preferring to rely on their sources and interviewing skills. But that's not enough in today's information environment. Journalists have little choice but to use this FOI request channel with attendant delays, exemptions and the creative avoidance that accompanies such requests. Whether FOI is used or not, it's not easy getting answers when reporters have to go through media relations folks, are not able to talk with most officials and have to report on what at times is self-serving information. Editors are not always willing to pay fees for requests, and publishers rarely want to spend the investigative time and money FOI can take, especially now with less resources, and cutbacks. Operating under tight deadlines, journalists hate the delays in response the most, and tend to be impatient with the rather dull government record replies. Reporters in one media outfit rarely operate systematically as a team together in using FOI, and many media outlets tend to go after the same FOI material. Government politicians, bureaucrats, corporate third parties, security and law enforcement agencies with a vested interest in the outcome of FOI requests tend to loath reporters. Journalists are targeted and 'amber lighted' with defensive media lines being prepared and occasionally, the spin includes bullying editors (Rubin, 1996). Yet without journalists' probing, many stories would not have been published, had FOI not been used.

The story of Canada's 30 plus FOI years

Canada's Access to Information Act was hardly an *avant-garde* piece of FOI law making when it was first introduced in 1983. It gave Canadians limited access to specific government agencies' records after paying a CAD$5 (£2.77) fee, with provisions for further charges. It included a long list of exceptions - both mandatory and discretionary - including policy advice, commercial material, personal information, national security, and law enforcement. Cabinet files were excluded for a 20-year period. Replies were supposed to be completed within 30 days with provisions for time extensions for consultations and voluminous record requests. The legislation was complimented with privacy laws, and the provinces and territories have their own legislation. The review process for those denied records or experiencing lengthy delays or excessive fees was to complain to an Information Commissioner. That government appointed official, approved by Parliament for a seven-year term, could make recommendations on the release of records to government agencies. If complainants wanted to still pursue matters further, they could go to the federal courts, which could order the release of denied records. The legislative flaws became apparent pretty quickly as much of the material that was of interest to journalists – policy advice and the background to contentious government decisions – was exempt. The access process was cumbersome with fee and time delay barriers and there were no public interest override or proactive disclosure provisions to enable greater release of information.

In that vein, Canada's access legislation was hardly a bold initiative, even though it was one of the first to actually incorporate a review officer called an Information Commissioner to check on what government officials released. In reality, the legislation was put in place not so much out of a desire for greater openness, but rather to avoid leaks to the media and codify government records with layers of exemptions. If that was not apparent, the first PM to feel the full brunt of a limited access act, Brain Mulroney, had enough when his own travel accommodation expenses in Paris and the Far East were revealed – showing lavish spending on hotels and flights (Poirer, 1986). As a result, he and his officials set up an early warning system to avoid embarrassing releases (Rubin, 1996). His government also rejected any changes that an unanimous, non-partisan House of Commons committee suggested in the first and only statutory review of Canada's access act. That Committee suggested time restrictions to exemptions being claimed by officials; ending the exclusion of cabinet records; broadening the number of agencies covered; and having regular reviews of the legislation.

Lest anyone think PM Mulroney's administration was unique, they were not. His predecessor, PM John Turner, for one, stopped producing cabinet discussion papers that had become publicly available much earlier than the 20-year cabinet confidences exclusion protection deadline. The current PM Stephen Harper is an information control freak, doing nothing to order agencies to stop increasing delays to FOI responses, and denying the public even more information. Encountering such a centralised information messaging machine lowers FOI expectations. Harper's further contribution includes eliminating meaningful quality record systems like the mandatory long-form census, cutting back on the maintenance of historic records, and downgrading putting resources into effective record retrieval. In an age of spin, record dressing and downplaying, official records are what governments want them to be.

No regime to date has put forward and passed meaningful access to information reforms, although in opposition or on the election trail they periodically promise that accountability measures will be forthcoming. For a further analysis of Canada's FOI, the reader is referred to *Managing Information: Too Much Publicity, Not Enough Public Disclosure* (Rubin and Kozolanka, 2014). Benchmark events reviewed include an unwillingness to provide information about government waste and irregularities; the perks received by top brass; an overreaction to classifying records under 9/11 security needs; and a desire to hide scandals. As a consequence, Canada's federal, provincial, territorial and municipal FOI systems have become even more institutionalised and messy but users have become more sophisticated and aware of the pitfalls they will encounter.

FOI war stories re-told

Using FOI legislation, I have helped report on misspending, scandals, health and safety gaps and mishaps, environment degradation, international asbestos sales agent work, perk and pork-barrelling practices, aboriginal mistreatment, income inequalities and tax evasion among others. On the serious long-term investigative side, exposing Canada's role in asbestos promotion and export has required a determined 25-year plus effort. The records fought for and obtained showed how successive Canadian governments sided with the asbestos industry to find overseas markets and fend off efforts to ban asbestos as a hazardous product. The government poured millions of dollars into an asbestos lobby group and used embassies and international forums to prevent asbestos from being declared a hazardous product. Countries like Russia agreed to higher priced Canadian asbestos exports just so long as Canada continued, until recently, to fund international pro-asbestos lobby efforts (Rubin, 2011).

It is frustrating that such health and safety stories do not get quick action. Such was the case in 2000 when it emerged there were severe problems with drinking water on many First Nations reserves (Laghi, 2000). Canada, as 2002 External Affairs records show, was the only country to vote against a UN resolution making access to clean drinking water an international right (Blanchfield, 2003). Back in 1987, exposing the many locations having naturally occurring radon gas that can cause lung cancer hardly got action despite there being simple remediation solutions (Munro, 1987). Just recently an electronic mapping of some of the continued hazardous radon gas locations was reported, again after a FOI reply (Loiero, 2014).

Sometimes, too, records reveal surprising data. This was the case in 1997 when released Agriculture Canada records showed that federal scientists since at least 1980 had been involved in trying to raise the addiction level of nicotine in cigarettes (*Globe and Mail*, 1997). That benefited tobacco companies. Meanwhile, Health Canada was running programs trying to get people to quit smoking. Other troublesome tactics can be used to prevent public release of data. For instance, meat inspection records fought for and reported on revealed inadequate safety at meat packing plants. But these reports have been done away with (Curry, 2008).

Records too can reveal the lighter side of government follies and faults resulting in one-day 'hits'. They do at least help poke fun at and ridicule government actions. One such example is the government's preparation to meet well-known international celebrities. In one case, records showed that then Canadian heritage minister, Sheila Copps, herself with a journalistic background, was funding a Toronto celebrity Walk of Fame. One access briefing note release included details of plans to meet with the Rolling Stones while they were in Canada. The notes included her scripted dialogue with inductee Mick Jagger. Too bad she never got a chance to use her briefing note as the Stones stood her up and were a no-show (Cobb, 2000 A1-2). In another instance, documents indicated how PM Harper and his fisheries minister were going to try and counter ex-Beatle Sir Paul McCartney on his visit in opposition to the east coast seal hunt. Accessed optional communications lines that went all the way to PM's handlers on a high alert basis tried none too cleverly to contain Sir Paul's anti-clubbing beliefs (Rubin, 2006).

Sometimes news cannot be entirely reported because it is retrieved with the consent of individuals who the information is about. In one case, a national television program used records obtained on a failed breast implant product, but certain sensitive photographs were not. In another case, the story of a fired researcher responsible for re-evaluating the history of early Arctic settlement was aired but not all the personal details of management's dismissal. A most demanding and well-publicised case was that of Maher Arar, a Canadian citizen originally from Syria. He allegedly had been associating with others accused of terrorism and was forcefully sent in 2002 by US law and intelligence forces to Syria's notorious prison system where he was tortured and held for months. This 'rendition' was done with the knowledge of Canadian law and intelligence forces. Dozens of Access to Information and Privacy requests on he and his wife, Monia Mazigh's, behalf were filed (Rubin, 2004). Some of the data received was highly personal. Some of the data helped to push for a public inquiry that eventually exonerated him and resulted in him receiving government compensation. Data retrieved complemented the inquiry's own investigation.

What you don't know can hurt you: Concluding thoughts of an FOI warrior

I encourage even those most frustrated to keep testing FOI legislation. It is both an art and a science to help paint a picture of hidden government operations and dynamics. For example, it can reveal the clout a large corporation like Monsanto had in pressing ahead in Canada and abroad with genetically modified crop testing and sales (Gorrie, 2001). The FOI process can be tough, even taking seven long years to pry out a report on the post-accident safety deficiencies of airplanes operated by Nationair, a report done after its 1991 fatal airline crash in Saudi Arabia (Mittstaedt, 1998). It would be great to think there can be easy over-the-counter access to information laid out for inspection in government reading rooms and on the internet. But even then there still would be the need for those like the iconic US journalist Izzy Stone, whose Vietnam exposés were accomplished largely by ploughing through official records. The challenges remain to drastically reverse the pro-secrecy emphasis of existing Canadian FOI legislation. This means drastically cutting exceptions to release; broader coverage; a duty to document; tougher enforcement provisions; and aggressive pro-active disclosure of health, safety, environment and consumer information.

So does Britain with 10 year's FOI experience and all the more recent countries adopting FOI have much to look forward to? With more countries, more journalists entering the fray and international civil society efforts at getting regional and world bodies to become transparent, that's good news. A positive development has been the growing movement for news media associations doing annual audits in their countries of how FOI is working. In 2011, Associated Press very ambitiously tackled a case-by-case international evaluation of some countries' responses to FOI queries. Another positive trend has been civil society's quest for greater transparency in such international bodies as the World Bank and NATO.

Initiatives by international campaigners to have more data on extractive resource industries' payments, and on clinical drug trials to be made public, are also underway. Other bodies have been rating the effectiveness of countries' FOI legislation. Internationally, journalists and advocates need better interaction to bring to light stories on pending military acquisitions like the F35 fighter plane or drug companies' influence and product safety problems. FOI users around the world are being more than frustrated and in some cases, intimidated, maimed, imprisoned or killed for their efforts. We need to give concrete support to FOI users under attack or to their next of kin, similar to what is done for journalists and political prisoners.

I've briefly explored FOI as an outsider and independent 'warrior' researcher with a penchant for muckraking. Fighting the too often-entrenched culture of secrecy means I've always operated on the basis of fervently believing 'what you don't know can hurt you'.

References

Beatty, Perrin (1984) House of Commons-Senate Regulations and Other Statutory Instruments Joint Committee Proceedings, May 17

Beeby, Dean (2011) Letter to Ken Rubin, January 10. Personal correspondence

Blanchfield, Mike, (2003) 'Our "painful" vote against clean water' *Ottawa Citizen*, September 21, p A4

Canadian Press (1997) 'Effort to boost nicotine in cigarettes linked to federal scientists' *Globe and Mail*, March 17, p A4

Cobb, Chris (2000) 'The day Mick Jagger stood up Sheila Copps' *Ottawa Citizen*, April 3, p A 1-2

Curry, Bill (2008) 'Ottawa wanted US to accept more lenient meat inspection regime' *Globe and Mail*, August 29, p A1, 9

Fine, Sean (1997) 'A mission to embarrass the bigwigs' *Globe and Mail*, December 3, p A2

Fitz-Morris, James (2014) 'David Cameron's 'top-secret' visit to Canada revealed' CBC News, May 14

Gorrie, Peter (2011) 'Taxpayers fund biotech food giant' *Toronto Star*, February 11, p A1, 15

Laghi, Brian (2000) 'Studies reveal depth of native water crisis' *Globe and Mail*, December 22, p A1, 7

Loiero, Joseph (2014) 'High radon levels found in Health Canada tests across country' CBC News, June 3

Mittstaedt, Martin (1998) 'Major charter airline flew illegally, review says' *Globe and Mail*, February 6, p A3

Munro, Margaret (1987) 'Health officials reluctant to act on radon that's killing Canadians' *Ottawa Citizen*, January 7, p 1, 2

Poirer, Patricia (1986) 'Requests for information about PM must be cleared, departments told' *Globe and Mail*, December 3, p 1

Rubin, Ken (1977) *The Public's Right to Information Act in the Federal Government as viewed by Cabinet Ministers, Members of Parliament and Senators*. Ottawa: Access Citizen Group

Rubin, Ken (1996) 'Early warning system undermines access requests: Access or Early Warning' *Hill Times*, November 4, p 1, 4 and 5

Rubin, Ken (2001) 'Research data on asbestos exposure hidden' *Toronto Star*, May 18

Rubin, Ken (2004) 'Struggle to get at the facts in Maher Arar case' *Hill Times*, August 8, p 8

Rubin, Ken (2006) 'Amber alert: access to information users targeted as the bad kids on the block' *Hill Times*, October 2, p 7

Rubin, Ken (2006) 'Countering and presenting images: inside PCO's and Fisheries' attempts to deal with Sir Paul McCartney' *Hill Times*, November 6, p 11

Rubin, Ken and Kirsten Kozolanka (2014) 'Managing Information: Too Much Publicity, Not Enough Public Disclosure' in *Publicity and the Canadian State*. Toronto: University of Toronto Press, p 195-214

Note on the contributor

Ken Rubin is an Ottawa-based investigative researcher and citizens' advocate. He has filed and analysed thousands of requests for public and personal information, resulting in hundreds of media stories. He has acted as an access consultant to a variety of media, public interest groups, political parties, labour unions, research groups, trade associations, and individuals. Many of his Federal Court actions for freedom of information are referred to as benchmark cases. He has published many articles and reports on government secrecy, writes a column on open government and promoted improvements in freedom of information and privacy protection legislation. For nearly five decades, he has been involved in a wide range of regional and national public actions that include food and air safety, health and environmental protection issues and telecommunications. His website is www.kenrubin.ca, where a case history of stories, articles, presentations and interventions can be found.

From 'skippy burgers' to WMDs: An Australian perspective on FOI

Australian journalists were slow to embrace Freedom of Information opportunities when the Federal Government enacted the law in 1982. But a number of stand-out journalists came to be experts, donning the title 'FOI editor' and challenging rejection slips through the courts all the way to the High Court of Australia, writes *Peter Timmins*

Introduction

On 1 December, 1982, Australia's Freedom of Information Act - providing the right to access documents held by federal government ministers and agencies - commenced operation. Jack Waterford, a journalist with *The Canberra Times* was well prepared. Waterford had watched government dither for 10 years over the form and content of the law, all the while keeping a list of FOI applications ready when the day finally came. One sought access to an unpublished appendix to a Royal Commission report into a scandal surrounding the substitution of horse and kangaroo for beef in Australian meat exports. The scandal emerged in 1981 when a food inspector in California came across imported Australian beef that looked 'darker and stringier' than the real thing. Tests showed it was horse meat and it got worse from there. Kangaroo meat was identified giving rise to jokes about 'skippy burgers' long before Australians, let alone others, acquired the taste. A Royal Commission was established to investigate, and reported in September 1982.

Waterford's application was not refused but 'deferred' meaning a formal decision on access would be made at a later time. The Prime Minister's department advised that disclosure would be premature in the light of continuing police investigations and possible prosecutions. Waterford had plenty to keep him otherwise occupied but raised the issue to no effect on several occasions over the years. In 2012, by this time editor at large, he reminded the department that he was still waiting for a formal decision. After more than 16 months of further consultations the document was released, arriving on Waterford's desk exactly 29 years, 11 months and two weeks after he lodged the application. The previously secret appendix revealed Americans weren't the only ones eating substitutes for the real thing. And it wasn't limited to horse and kangaroo. The Royal Commission received evidence that Australians unwittingly had been fed donkey meat, goat, and maggot-ridden offcuts by some of the country's leading meat producers. One company trimmed off the dye legally required on pet food and sold it for human consumption.

Stricter standards were in place in 2013 and Australia's standing as an exporter of certified quality beef had been long restored. However the document gave Waterford and *The Canberra Times* an opportunity to muse over the longest running application in Australia's 30 year FOI history under eye catching headlines 'Thirty years in the deep freeze', 'Skippy meat scandal became global joke' and 'How they fed us donkey burgers" (Waterford, 2012).

The 30-year delay was not typical of the way FOI applications were handled by government agencies initially or any time since, and may have been caused in part by the hap-hazard follow up by Waterford himself. However delay and obfuscation had been a common experience and an on-going concern as *The Canberra Times* observed:

> *"The fact that it has taken three decades for this information to be revealed is in itself a scandal, and highlights not only the importance of freedom-of-information laws, but the difficulties faced by those trying to use them... Yet despite the lofty statements of many federal, state and territory leaders about the importance of accountability and accessibility of government information, many of the holders of that public information continue to obfuscate, delay or redact details that should be freely available to the public,'* (Canberra Times, 2012)

Jack Waterford: the FOI pioneer

The meat scandal was just one of Waterford's many FOI jousts. At one stage he was managing around 200 live requests with 20 or more active appeals underway in the external review tribunal. Waterford's deep interest in, use and frequent success in FOI was the exception rather than the rule among journalists for many years. With a law degree to back him up he didn't take no for an answer and challenged government decisions where reasons given for refusal of access didn't stack up. A challenge to refusal of another of those first day requests went all the way to the High Court of Australia.

Waterford lodged a request to the Department of the Treasury for access to documents relating to projections in the 1982-1983 Budget papers and subsequently referred to in a ministerial press release, regarding the estimated number of persons who would receive unemployment benefits. The request unearthed a large batch of documents including some that passed between officers and the government's legal advisers in another agency. Access was denied on grounds of legal privilege. The case was the first involving interpretation of the Freedom of Information Act to come before the High Court. In 1987, by a 3-2 majority the court rejected Waterford's principal argument that the legal professional privilege exemption in the FOI Act did not apply to communications between an agency and a salaried government lawyer (High Court of Australia [1987/HCA25]).

Waterford was named the 1985 Graham Perkin Australian Journalist of the Year for his work on Freedom of Information. In 2007 he was Canberra Citizen of the Year and honoured as a Member of the Order of Australia (AM) for services to journalism, particularly as a commentator on national politics, the law, ethical issues and public sector accountability.

Others slow on the uptake

But he was a pioneer. Most journalists had little knowledge of freedom of information and showed limited interest in using the laws even as freedom of information legislation extended through the 1980s and 1990s and beyond the national government sphere to all states and territories. Waterford in 1999 said the 'surprising thing really is that few journalists even understand their rights under the Act, have even a passing idea of how a request might be framed, what sort of documents might be available and what they might expect' (Waterford, 1999). His observations about limited use of FOI laws by journalists were borne out by other studies during the first 20 years. One review identified a tendency among journalists to rely on the FOI activity by civil society groups and piggyback on the results (Waters, 1999).

FOI is cumbersome for journalists when compared to a hand out, leak or friendly contact with an insider. However Waterford showed it could pay off for those who had a good knowledge of how government operates and what documents might exist, who had time and experience to craft an application so as to enhance the prospect of success, and who operated with an accommodating deadline given the process could take weeks and often longer. This wasn't the newsroom familiar to most journalists, particularly those who had daily deadlines. Even less so in today's 24/7 news cycle.

Over time, freedom of information has provided access to information about day-to-day operations of government. References to documents released under FOI appeared with increasing frequency in media reports about health, education, the environment, transport and other areas of government activity. However FOI applications for information on matters that involved ministers and senior public servants, particularly politically sensitive information likely to cast government in a poor light, were a different matter and often ran into difficulties. As did attempts to get beneath the surface regarding national security, international relations and law enforcement. Government attempts to manage information flows through tight controls and 'spin' mean that applications of this kind could be delayed and more often than not denied. Cost, legal technicalities and the absence of speedy external review of decisions contributed to the generally gloomy view of FOI among journalists. Not improved by reports about political interference in FOI decision-making and behind the scenes efforts by senior public servants to thwart requests.

Australia's FOI legislation, before improvements in 2010, came in for heavy criticism. The federal government had ignored more than 100 recommendations for change by the Australian Law Reform Commission in a 1996 report. Ten years later Waterford wrote that 'FOI legislation has been rendered so complicated and expensive - and so subject to novel and arbitrary exclusions, such as the need to protect a minister from possible embarrassment - that it now plays almost no role in the accountability system' (Waterford, 2006).

Most journalists, lacking in knowledge and experience in the dark arts of the bureaucracy and unfamiliar with a complex law found themselves up against experts on the government side who know their FOI backwards and are not above gaming the system from time to time. Investigative journalists, at least on occasion not subject to daily deadlines, have come to use FOI as one of the tools of trade, with patchy results. Some including Michael McKinnon and Matthew Moore came to see opportunities along the trail blazed by Waterford.

Michael McKinnon: the FOI 'guided missile'

In far north Queensland in 1990 while working for the *Townsville Bulletin* Michael McKinnon first resorted to FOI when, as part of a routine assignment, he noticed soldiers from a nearby army base training in a disused power station that he knew was contaminated with asbestos. McKinnon accessed documents that revealed the soldiers had not been given advice about the possibility of exposure to asbestos or the precautions that should be taken. His articles drew the attention of army top brass. Notations were added to the medical records of thousands who had trained there over the years, ensuring possible exposure to asbestos during the course of service would be noted for the future.

McKinnon subsequently went to Canberra where he worked for News Limited in the press gallery at Parliament House covering national affairs. He describes his five years there as mostly routine reporting on parliament, government and politics, carried out below the lofty heights where press gallery stars were afforded privileged access, and insider accounts. However McKinnon started to push the boundaries, finding leads for FOI applications in agency annual reports, media releases, parliamentary committee proceedings, public service news, audit reports, speeches and anything else he could get his hands on. He also learned the importance of crafting an FOI application in a way that improved the prospects of at least some success. McKinnon was working in a system where spin-doctors eked out news selectively to journalists seen to be reliable, 'on side' and likely to stay there if the titbits kept coming.

Rocking this boat through use of FOI could come with risks attached, a point brought home to McKinnon after he lodged an FOI application for the list of wines stored in the Prime Minister's cellar - for entertainment purposes only of course. The Prime Minister's press secretary told him resort to this tactic would be the end of his hopes for 'drip feeds.' McKinnon replied that as someone at the lower end of the food chain, he had never been on the drip in any event. When McKinnon left Canberra and joined the *Courier Mail* in Brisbane, he and

Editor Chris Mitchell came up with the idea of a specialist position. McKinnon was appointed FOI co-ordinator, the first such appointment in Australia. He immersed himself in government operations and the federal and Queensland laws, becoming an expert in both fields, breaking many stories and taking a refusal of access as a green light to challenge decisions.

McKinnon has been at it now for 25 years, following Mitchell to the national broadsheet *The Australian* in 2002 where he served as national FOI Editor until 2007, then taking up that role in another first, this time in television news at the Seven Network. In early 2014 McKinnon was appointed FOI Editor at the Australian Broadcasting Corporation (ABC). McKinnon's bosses, Mitchell at the *Courier Mail* and *The Australian*, and Peter Meakin at Seven Network, both saw freedom of information as help to build a reputation in the news business, and to provide the basis for, or assist along the way with breaking news.

In 2009 McKinnon won the Walkley Award for Leadership for his role in Freedom of Information. Commonwealth Ombudsman at the time Professor John McMillan said McKinnon has played a 'pivotal role in the transformation of Australian FOI law and practice' by drawing public attention to the cause. 'He has shone a light on many government actions that would otherwise be buried from public scrutiny, on matters such as asbestos contamination, tax administration, Treasury forecasts, weapons safety, grant schemes, bulk billing and Reserve Bank decision making.' McKinnon that year also shared the Investigative Journalism Award for a story that exposed widespread police corruption in Queensland. In 2012 he shared the Walkley Award for Television News Reporting for a series of stories that revealed the NSW Government went against its own advice to support the ethanol industry, who were significant donors to the governing political party.

McKinnon has made hundreds of applications to Federal and state agencies and lodged more than 80 review applications, most of which he has won or settled satisfactorily - he puts his success record in the 80 to 90 per cent. His experience is that preparedness to challenge a decision on access invariably results in additional access. Faced with a determined, knowledgeable applicant, agencies often concede something more as external review looms.

Like Waterford, McKinnon also had his day in the High Court of Australia. He too lost, contesting a 'conclusive' ministerial certificate issued by the Treasurer that withheld requested documents on grounds that disclosure on balance was contrary to the public interest (High Court of Australia, [228/CLR/423/2007]). The media and open government advocates had hoped the High Court would fully explore the issue of the public interest and provide a helpful precedent to countermand a growing trend to more secrecy, less disclosure within government, and in FOI decisions in the courts and review tribunal. The decision disappointed but had the effect of putting excessive government secrecy and FOI on the front pages, prompting widespread discussion and debate and spurring lobbying efforts for reform. *The Canberra Times* editorialised that 'FOI is now effectively a dead letter whenever ministers want to conceal information from the public,' while the *Sydney Morning Herald* posited '... Australia's democracy is diminished by the Court's decision' (McMillan, 2006).

In May 2007 Australia's leading media organisations established a coalition - *Australia's Right to Know* - and commissioned an independent review of freedom of speech in Australia to catalogue FOI and other problem issues concerning access to government information (Moss, 2007). The coalition subsequently led a campaign that pushed the issue on to the agenda during the federal election and led to federal and state FOI reforms in Queensland, NSW and Tasmania in the period 2007-2010. Notably the case proved to be the death knell of conclusive ministerial certificates. At the national level over a 10-year period 14 certificates had been issued, four in 2006, and most to head off applications by McKinnon. They were abolished in 2009.

Matthew Moore: like a dog with a bone

Matthew Moore was an experienced journalist when he returned to Sydney in 2005 after four years in Jakarta. Prior to his posting to Jakarta, Moore had been state political correspondent, chief of staff, national editor and between 1998 and 2000 the Olympics editor for the *Sydney Morning Herald*. In the first of these posts and just after the New South Wales Freedom of Information Act commenced in 1989, Moore took on then Premier (the state's governor) Nick Greiner over access to information about involvement of a government minister in a land rezoning issue only to be blocked by a conclusive certificate of the kind that McKinnon later battled in the High Court. The scandal that followed led to the sacking of the minister for administrative services, Matt Singleton, for pressuring a fellow minister to lift a zoning restriction on land in which Singleton had a substantial undeclared financial interest.

Moore had limited success in seeking access to the secret contract between the International Olympic Organising Committee and the state government entity established to prepare for the games. The government had granted the Sydney committee a complete exemption from the FOI Act, but Moore battled with other agencies subject to the Act that may have held a copy. As the games in Sydney grew closer, Moore lodged other FOI applications that led to disclosure of a scandal involving preservation of reserved seat tickets that the public had been led to believe did not exist. A majority of tickets had been withheld for sale by special arrangement, contrary to the public claim that tickets for every event at every venue could be obtained by participating in a ticket lottery.

In 2005 as investigations editor of the *Sydney Morning Herald*, Moore made a pitch for a new role: FOI Editor, to write about failures as well as successes. He had heard of something similar in New Zealand where a columnist wrote 'what they won't tell you'. For the next two years Moore used FOI effectively but reserved a Saturday column to name and shame those responsible for knockbacks that seemed unjustified. Often they read like a 'Yes Minister' script.

For example Moore was initially refused FOI access to the names and street addresses of businesses and individuals fined by Sydney council for breach of restaurant hygiene standards on grounds that disclosure 'would breach the Privacy Act'. He had great mileage out of a long running campaign on the issue of secrecy that made no sense. He was able to reveal that a sushi factory had been found to be infested with rats, the source of food poisoning, and fined 11 times. Two years after the secrecy was brought to light the government decided to publish fines and other compliance information about restaurants and food hygiene standards online in a public register.

The FOI editors club

Other FOI editors have followed Waterford, McKinnon and Moore. In addition to managing multiple applications at any one time, the editors have all played important roles in acting as in house mentor and adviser to others in the news room on how to use FOI to good effect. While legitimate causes for concern remain about Australia's access to information laws and the way they are implemented, the editors have shown that expertise, experience and time to ply their FOI trade pays off. Notable names include Kelvin Bissett (Nine Network); Sean Parnell (*The Australian*); and Alison Sandy (Seven News).

Conclusion

FOI receives more attention from journalists these days than when Waterford was almost alone digging for gems and fighting the good fight. Awareness is high, and skills have improved. Reports that refer to FOI disclosures by federal, state and local government agencies appear daily in print and on television, going beyond the mainstream writers into online and in specialty publications. Award-winning investigative journalists including Marian Wilkinson and Linton Besser of ABC *Four Corners* and Nick McKenzie and Richard Baker of *The Age* know how and when to resort to FOI to help with a developing story. However often the really interesting material from a journalist's perspective is closely guarded.

The federal Abbott government – elected in August, 2013 – has acquired a reputation for excessive secrecy, and has shown little interest in leading on improvements in FOI law and practice. On the contrary, a decision announced in May, 2014, to disband the Office of Australian Information Commissioner by the end of the year is a retrograde step, despite widespread disappointment with the Commissioner's office, in particular with the slow pace of review of agency decisions.

Australia's federal Freedom of Information Act ranked 48 of 93 national laws surveyed in 2013, with 84 points out of a possible 150 (Centre for Law and Democracy, 2013). Journalists still have many justified grumbles about delays in processing; exorbitant charges; inappropriate exemption claims; and an unhelpful run around instead of assistance from some agencies.

More government information than hitherto is proactively published including data sets that attract the interest of data journalists including Nick

Evershed at the *Guardian* Australia, Edmund Tadros at the *Australian Financial Review*, Craig Butt at *The Age* and Conrad Walters at the *Sydney Morning Herald*. There is still a long way to go however for access as a matter of routine to data sets and other information in machine readable open formats. The FOI editors club is at the forefront and the battle continues.

References

The Canberra Times (2012) 'Editorial: Officials not so free with freedom of information,' *The Canberra Times*, 17 November, available at http://www.canberratimes.com.au/federal-politics/officials-not-so-free-with-freedom-of-information-20121117-29jbw.html#ixzz3CJR0vcRX, accessed 1 September, 2014

Centre for Law and Democracy (2013) *Global Right to Information 2013*, available at http://www.rti-rating.org/news, accessed 21 September, 2014

Devine, Frank 'Freedom confronting the curse of Sir Humphrey' in *The Rathouse* blog, available at http://www.the-rathouse.com/guestroom/FD_FOI.html, accessed 1 September, 2014

High Court of Australia (1987) 'Waterford v the Commonwealth of Australia' [HCA25/163/CLR/54] 24 June 1987

High Court of Australia (2006) 'McKinnion v Secretary, Department of the Treasury' [228/CLR/423] 6 September, 2006

McMillan, J 2006 'The FOI landscape after McKinnon' Australian Institute of Administrative Law, Canberra, October. Available at http://www.ombudsman.gov.au/files/October_2006_The_FOI_landscape_after_McKinnon.pdf, accessed 3 September, 2014

Moss, Irene (2007) *Report of the Independent Audit of into the State of Free Speech in Australia*. Sydney: Australia's Right to Know. Available at http://www.smh.com.au/pdf/foIreport5.pdf, accessed 5 September, 2014

Podger, Andrew (2009) *The Role of Departmental Secretaries*. Canberra: Australian National University Press

Timmins, Peter (2008) 'The power of the FOI exclusive' in *Open and Shut* blog, 16 December, available at http://foi-privacy.blogspot.com.au/2008/12/power-of-foi-exclusive.html#.VBXs1kuDOvJ, accessed 1 September, 2014

Timmins, Peter (2009) 'FOI features in journalism's Walkleys' in *Open and Shut* blog, 27 November, available at http://foi-privacy.blogspot.com.au/2009/11/foi-features-in-journalisms-walkleys.html#.VA5exEh4IUk, accessed 2 September, 2014

Tomazin, Farrah (2012) 'FOI architect blasts political interference' in *The Age, 18 November*, available at http://www.theage.com.au/victoria/foi-architect-blasts-political-interference-20121117-29j25.html, accessed 3 September, 2014

Waterford, J (2012) '30 years in the deep freeze' *The Canberra Times*, 18 November, available at http://www.canberratimes.com.au/act-news/skippy-meat-scandal-became-global-joke-20121117-29jp2.html#ixzz3C36IZ7J4, accessed 1 September, 2014

Waterford, Jack (1999) 'Journalists, Freedom of Information and Investigative Journalism' speech at University of Queensland, 7 October. Available at https://espace.library.uq.edu.au/eserv.php?pid=UQ:11234&dsID=jwfoi.pdf, accessed 2 September, 2014

Waterford, Jack (2006) 'By all accounts the government that can' in *The Canberra Times*, 4 July

Waters, N (1999) *Print Media use of Freedom of Information laws in Australia*. Sydney: Australian Centre for Independent Journalism

Note on the contributors

Peter Timmins is an Australian lawyer and consultant with a long history of involvement in information access and related issues. He writes the *Open and Shut* blog, now in its ninth year. Peter graduated with Arts and Laws (Honours) degrees from the University of Sydney, and is a Fellow of the Australian Academy of Law. He was deputy chair of the *Independent Audit of Free Speech in Australia*, commissioned by Australia's Right to Know (2007); a member of the Australian Law Reform Commission Advisory Committee for its reference on secrecy laws (2008-2009); and a member of the New South Wales state government's Information Advisory Committee.

The Trio Capital fraud and its victims: A study in freedom of information legislation failure

David Blackall and *Jolyon Sykes* examine the story of the largest superannuation fraud in Australian history, and how FOI has failed to help its victims

Introduction

Openness and accountability are important qualities to which democratic governments must aspire. A well functioning freedom of information (FOI) system encourages public participation in the political process and builds trust via transparency (Lidberg, 2014). When Australia's FOI legislation was introduced into the Federal Parliament in 1981, the responsible minister said: 'A document is not exempt merely because it relates to the internal working of a department; to justify refusal, disclosure must cause some detriment to a specified public interest' and 'there is a statutory duty on agencies to assist applicants to make requests in a form which will enable them to be dealt with' (Hansard, 1981). In 2013, the Centre for Law and Democracy (CLD) released a report comparing FOI legislation in 89 countries. Australia's rating was average (CLD, 2013).

> '*Australia's access law is problematic on several fronts. Foremost is its limited scope... The Act also lists several exceptions which are not harm tested, provides a very weak public interest override, [and] allows other legislation to provide separate exemptions* (ibid).

Johan Lidberg's submission to the Australian 2009 FOI Amendment Bill begins: 'In the last decade it has become abundantly clear that the current federal FOI regime in Australia is dysfunctional. It does not deliver on the promises made in the objects part of the 1982 FOI Act,' (Lidberg, 2009: 3). Effectiveness of FOI legislation ultimately depends on the level of commitment to it by political leaders and senior bureaucrats. This chapter explores this statement in an Australian context, using a large international fraud as a case study. The fraud, referred to as Trio, was committed across a number of jurisdictions, was planned by overseas financial operators, and is believed to have stolen AUS$192m (£104m) from the Australian superannuation system.

The 'Trio' scheme

According to the US Federal Bureau of Investigation (FBI), the term 'securities fraud' covers a wide range of illegal activities, all of which involve the deception of investors or the manipulation of financial markets. The type of fraud practiced by Trio was a Ponzi scheme, where returns to investors are paid from funds obtained from new investors, rather than from profit (FBI, 2014). Trio Capital's eventual collapse, like that of all Ponzi schemes, was inevitable. The fraud targeted investors in the Illawarra region of Australia, was premeditated and may have been planned as early as November 2003 (APJC 2012: xix). A central character was Shawn Richard, a young and unassuming CEO of one of the two funds that purported to amalgamate a number of other funds into Trio Capital. Trio's founder, Matthew Nguyen Littauer, was murdered in 2004. Littauer's business partner was Hong Kong resident and US citizen, Jack Flader, and it was Littauer who introduced the inexperienced Shawn Richard to hedge fund management. Flader was the ultimate controller of the Trio Capital Group and associated entities, while Richard arranged the transfer of Australian investors' money from Trio Managed Funds in Australia, to overseas funds controlled by Flader. The money was used to purchase shares at inflated prices from foreign companies controlled by Flader, realising significant profits. From November 2006, Trio's investment committee became concerned and decided to cease its exposure to a particular Flader-controlled fund, but Richard helped to create new funds, all of which were controlled by Flader (Garling, 2011: 7).

In late 2009, Australian Securities and Investments Commission (ASIC) began investigating certain Trio funds and, two years later, ASIC and the Australian Prudential Regulation Authority (APRA) accepted undertakings from 13 people associated with Trio, precluding them from activity in financial services for periods ranging from three years to life (APJC, 2012: 36). By September 2009, ASIC was alerted to Trio's suspiciously smooth returns despite the turbulent financial environment. Trio went into liquidation on 22 June, 2010, leaving investors with significant financial losses. Richard was convicted on two charges of dishonest conduct in the course of carrying on a financial services business. While he was only the 'local foot soldier of the scheme' (APJC, 2012: 21), 'Shawny-cash' Richard's role was central to the operation in Australia in moving funds out of Trio and then offshore. He admitted to a third charge of making false statements in relation to financial products (Garling, 2011: 8). Richard was released from jail in 2014 after serving a reduced two-and-a-half year term. At the time, he was the only person to be convicted on two counts of engaging in dishonest conduct in relation to a financial product or service (S1041G(1) of the Corporations Act).

The parliamentary inquiry

In 2012, a parliamentary inquiry found that the collapse of Trio was the largest superannuation fraud in Australian history, affecting 6,090 investors. It confirmed Justice Garling's finding that Jack Flader, head of Global Consultants and Services Limited (GCSL), was behind the fraud (APJC, 2012: 58). GCSL provided administration services to EMA, a special purpose vehicle under Richard's control, established to facilitate the movement of Trio funds offshore (APJC, 2012: 27). Richard moved money through Trio Capital into two other hedge funds, Astarra Strategic and ARP Growth, which directed at least AUS$176m (£90m) to obscure Caribbean-based tax havens to the apparent benefit of Flader (APJC, 2012: 17). The inquiry was critical of the financial regulatory regime, particularly the time taken to commence investigating Trio and take action. While APRA had conducted five prudential reviews since 2004, it was unable to obtain from Trio a valuation of its assets. This lack of basic information was not communicated to ASIC. ASIC likewise had not communicated its concerns about Flader's involvement (APJC, 2012: pxx).

These shortcomings may have their origin in Trio describing itself as a hedge fund. Hedge funds appear in various forms and are derivatives: investments whose value derives from the movements in value of underlying entities such as commodities, interest rates or currencies. Hedge funds are able to operate with greater flexibility because they are generally not sold to the public and many of the regulations designed to protect investors do not apply (Lhabitant, 2007). Consequently, they are less strictly regulated than some of the entities on which their value depends, such as stock prices (equities) and mortgages (debt), and are often traded privately in so-called over the counter dealings. Trio avoided many of the warning signs that the FBI says can help identify fraud: the investment returns did not appear too good to be true; high-pressure sales tactics were not used; and investors were not solicited (FBI, 2010). The regulators, ASIC and APRA, may have simply accepted Trio as an entity not requiring the surveillance applied to ordinary retail investments.

The parliamentary inquiry also commented adversely on ASIC's level of risk communication, which led to many investors believing that the regulators were protecting them against fraud, when largely, the reverse applied. Despite the reality that deliberate criminal activity was specifically exploiting deficiencies in the Australian financial and superannuation systems, ASIC and APRA failed to alert the market. Documents presented to the inquiry proved the regulators had negative information on Trio from 2008, and so were obliged to advise investors. Many investors were unaware that their investments would be deemed self-managed superannuation funds (SMSFs) and therefore excluded from compensation arrangements enjoyed by other superannuates. The ASIC publication, *Investing between the flags*, does not advise investors that they could be regarded as self-managed, even if they invest through an agent or advisor, and that they may be denied compensation (ASIC, 2012). People told the inquiry that they had no knowledge or warning that they were unprotected by compensation, otherwise provided to APRA-regulated funds. Underlining this criticism, ASIC published a factsheet in 2013, which clarifies the situation (ASIC, 2013b). However, at the time of Trio's collapse, no information about investment fraud or the effect of Part 23 of the Superannuation Act was available (See SIS, 1993: 439-40).

The parliamentary inquiry demonstrated that investors were unaware their investment had slipped from APRA's jurisdiction and was subject only to the supervision of the Australian Tax Office, which was more concerned with tax compliance than prudential matters (APJC, 2012: 13). Investors remained unaware until Trio's collapse and Richard's conviction. There were four factors contributing to this risk: the reduced regulatory vigilance applied to hedge funds; the legislative exemption for SMSFs; ATO's lack of prudential supervision; and the lack of information provided by the regulators.

FOI rewards and frustrations

Wollongong Trio victims created an association, Victims of Financial Fraud Incorporated (VOFF), with the aim of discovering what happened and who was responsible, to assist in bringing the perpetrators to justice, to recover members' losses and to prevent a recurrence (VOFF, 2014: 1). Using FOI legislation, VOFF is attempting to access information from government agencies such as the Treasury Department, APRA, the Australian Transaction Reports and Analysis Centre (AUSTRAC), the Australian Federal Police (AFP), Australian Tax Office (ATO), and ASIC. At the time of writing, VOFF had lodged 250 separate FOI applications, with limited success.

While some Australian bureaucrats administer the Act fairly, Ricketson and Snell found it disturbing to read successive reports by the Australian Law Reform Commission in 1996 and the Commonwealth Ombudsman in 1999, complaining of a prevailing ethos of secrecy (Ricketson and Snell, 2002: 151). If there had been greater scrutiny of Trio by journalists before, during and after the 2008 global financial crisis (GFC), it may not have been as catastrophic for VOFF – they may have had warning to make adjustments to investments and the AFP may have had evidence to prosecute.

VOFF first sought FOI access to documents from Flader's corporation, GCSL. This was encouraged by the critical findings of the APJC, but ASIC refused access, citing a section of the FOI Act dealing with international relations (Sect 33b) and the *Multilateral Memorandum of Understanding Concerning Consultation and Cooperation and the Exchange of Information 2002*. After pursuing various avenues of appeal over the next 10 months, the FOI application stalled. To VOFF, Flader's activities seemed irrelevant to international relations and, as the MMOU provided a public interest exemption, VOFF is considering another appeal (VOFF, 2014: 2).

VOFF's second application related to compensation. The victims and many commentators believe ASIC is obliged to not only bring perpetuators before Australian courts but also to ensure restitution for victims of the fraud. In 2012, the former minister for superannuation, Bill Shorten, labelled Trio as a superannuation matter rather than one affecting all managed investment. This limited the government's liability for compensation. Self-funded retirees are specifically denied compensation and this differentiation between normal investors and self-funded retirees seemed arbitrary, so VOFF inquired on the basis of the minister's decision. At the time of writing this application is pending (VOFF, 2014: 5).

Another FOI application sought copies of the five prudential reviews by APRA of Trio (Astarra), which the inquiry mentioned. APRA failed to either act on these reviews or communicate Trio's failure to provide valuations of its assets to ASIC. This FOI was refused on the ground that it would unreasonably divert the APRA's resources. After extensive correspondence, including a revised application, negotiations continue at time of writing. APRA is citing the confidentiality provisions in the FOI Act as the reason for refusal, while VOFF argues that the use of these provisions should be restricted to individual documents and not used as a blanket refusal of access to - by APRA's estimate - 3,600 pages of documents.

Yet another FOI application by VOFF on 21 April, 2014, sought 'ASIC's preparation material and key contributors in finding extent of losses incurred in Trio Capital and the losses due to fraud and the losses due to market conditions' (VOFF, 2014: 115). It yielded Richard's 46-page sworn court statement, confessing his illegalities (Richard, 2010). VOFF regard this document as a significant breakthrough, as it was previously listed as confidential. In it, Richard confirmed that he had knowingly deceived Trio's investment committee, of which he was a member. From July, 2004 onwards, Richard told investors that he controlled funds that were actually controlled by Flader. Richard arranged the transfer of investors' monies from managed investment schemes and superannuation funds, for which Trio was responsible, to overseas funds controlled by Flader. In August 2006, Trio's investment committee banned further investment in one of the funds controlled by Flader, the Exploration Fund, but Richard then helped create three new offshore funds controlled by Flader and directed investment to them instead. He did not disclose to the committee his conflict of interest or the fact that new investments, rather than actual earnings, were funding the dividends (Richard, 2010: 3).

The regulators' reactions

Despite a few successes, such as Richard's statement, VOFF is of the opinion that access to information through FOI processes is near impossible. One, or a combination, of the following Sections of the FOI Act are being used to refuse access:

- the Act requires applicants to provide sufficient information about a document to enable a responsible officer to identify it (Sec 15 (2)(b));

- if edited copies with exempt or irrelevant matter deleted are required, then it must be reasonably practicable for the agency to prepare the edited copy (Sec 22(1)(c));

- a request may be refused if the work involved would substantially and unreasonably divert the resources of the relevant agency (Sec 24AA(1)(a));

- documents affecting national security, defence or international relations or that would divulge any information or matter communicated in confidence by or on behalf of a foreign government, an authority of a foreign government or an international organisation to the Government may be exempt (Sec 33(a) and (b)) as may be documents affecting enforcement of law and protection of public safety (Sec 37);

- documents to which secrecy provisions of other government Acts apply (Sec 38) and documents containing material obtained in confidence (Sec 45);

- documents whose disclosure would be contempt of Parliament or of court (Sec 46) or have a substantial adverse effect on the proper and efficient conduct of a government agency (Sec 47E (d)).

ASIC is not only a regulator; it is also a corporate entity making profit in its own right. In 2012, *Sydney Morning Herald* writer Ian Verrender suggested this is a structural conflict in that the law enforcement division of ASIC is disadvantaged by government motivation for expediency (Verrender, 2012). Bank statements dated 2010, containing ASIC's stamp, show Trio had AUS$75m (£41m) remaining in Australia, yet these funds were not frozen and eventually they too disappeared (VOFF 2012). Regardless of conflict of interest, Government regulators have a responsibility to bring all criminals to justice. ASIC in particular is failing to police financial fraud adequately. This finding of the APJC indicates that ASIC is in breach of its obligations under the *ASIC Act* 2001. On a page headed *What we do*, ASIC's web-site states its roles include 'to enforce and give effect to the law' and 'to make information about companies and other bodies available to the public as soon as practicable' (ASIC 2014).

Officials from ASIC and APRA are continuing to blame financial planners who directed clients to Trio, rather than accepting a share of the responsibility. The collapse of Trio coincided with the GFC, enabling government officials and politicians to claim that Trio was also a victim of the GFC (APJC 2012: 146). Irresponsible media spin from politicians also shifted blame from regulators and criminals to victims by saying that self-managed superannuation investors were 'swimming outside the flags' (Hasham, 2011). This referenced an Australian metaphor on surf-beach water safety, operating outside of regulations, and an ASIC publication on superannuation (ASIC 2012a).

Transnational enquiries

While actually a Ponzi scheme, Trio purported to operate as a type of hedge fund but its funds were ephemeral, and therefore its activities qualified as fraud under the United Nations Convention against Transnational Organized Crime (CTOC, 2000):

a) 'Organized criminal group' shall mean a structured group of three or more persons, existing for a period of time and acting in concert with the aim of committing one or more serious crimes or offences established in accordance with this Convention, in order to obtain, directly or indirectly, a financial or other material benefit (CTOC: 1).

b) 'Serious crime' shall mean conduct constituting an offence punishable by a maximum deprivation of liberty of at least four years or a more serious penalty (CTOC: 1). To this, the Organisation for Economic Co-operation and Development (OECD) adds the need for an international dimension, meaning that the criminal dealings must occur through at least two countries (Miraglia, 2012).

Since Australia is signatory to the OECD convention on transnational organised crime, it is required to report such crime to the OECD. VOFF made two separate FOI applications (13a to ASIC and 13b to the Australian Treasury) seeking the report that Australia was obliged to submit on Trio's activities. Both FOIs produced the negative assertion that no such document exists, suggesting that Australia did not meet its treaty obligations to the OECD (VOFF, 2014: 15ff).

ABC News investigates

Charles Provini, president of Paradigm Global Advisors, was Astarra's US asset consultant, in Wall Street, New York. Astarra was one of the hedge funds that comprised Trio. Provini advised US Vice-President Jo Biden's company, which also worked with Richard, (VOFF 2014: 60). Provini knew Richard and was named on Astarra's website (Lagan 2014: 5). While not directly involved in the Trio fraud, he remains an excellent starting point for journalistic enquiry. The Australian Broadcasting Corporation's (ABC) current affairs program, *7:30 New South Wales*, in collaboration with one of the writers of this chapter, produced a television current affairs program on the Trio fraud, broadcast 15 February, 2013. Journalists telephoned Provini and asked, in a recorded telephone interview, if ASIC, APRA, or the AFP had ever contacted him in respect to Trio. Provini replied: 'No' (Blackall, 2013).

On 5 June, 2012, 30 months after Trio's liquidation, ASIC confirmed it had yet to provide information about Flader to the AFP and the Australian Crime Commission, despite alleging Flader was the ultimate controller of the Trio group (ASIC, 2012b). The following year, on 29 October, 2013, ASIC announced that, despite its efforts and those of the AFP and its overseas regulatory counterparts, there was insufficient evidence to prove Flader had breached Australian law: 'ASIC is now finalising its investigation into Mr Flader' (ASIC, 2013a). VOFF has said it found this unacceptable after Justice Garling's finding that Flader was both architect and controller of the fraud (Garling, 2011: 10).

Culture of corruption

The Trio fraud exemplifies the risks posed by the reduced prudential supervision of trade in derivatives and hedge funds. This was at the centre of the 2008 GFC, and increasingly, non-transparent high-frequency-trading in derivatives will drive the so-called 'Dark Pool' money markets and 'Shadow banking' (Patterson and Hope, 2014). Derivatives are increasingly integral to economies, as confirmed in an analysis by the US Federal Reserve Bank of New York (FRBNY, 2012). The credit risk equivalent of derivative contracts is estimated at AUS$3.3 trillion (£1.8 trillion) (Liu and Lejot, 2013: 343).

Due to their opacity, crime syndicates find derivatives and hedge funds irresistible. The Australian superannuation sector alone is now valued at AUS$1.8 trillion (£970bn), second in size only to that of the Netherlands, yet journalistic exposure about its on-going vulnerability to such trade is virtually non-existent. The reality is that transnational organised crime successfully penetrated Australian superannuation, yet government regulators failed. This is exacerbated by the sophistication and speed of the market, despite the *Corporations Legislation Amendment (Derivative Transactions) Act 2012*. The public has a need to know how derivatives are capable of destroying what appear to be sound investments. Journalists must understand this market and use FOI effectively to scrutinise government regulators. This is crucial to investigative journalism education (Ricketson and Snell, 2002: 155). If citizen journalism, as practiced by VOFF, delivers FOI outcomes where mainstream news media fail, then journalism educators are obliged to respond accordingly.

References

APJC (2012) *Inquiry into the collapse of Trio Capital*, Australian Parliamentary Joint Committee on Corporations and Financial Services, available at http://www.aph.gov.au accessed 30 July, 2014

ASIC (2012a) *Investing between the flags: A practical guide to investing*, available at http://www.moneysmart. gov.au/media/173788/investing-between-the-flags.pdf, accessed 13 August, 2014

ASIC (2012b) *12-116MR ASIC provides update on Trio*, available at http://www.asic.gov.au/asic/asic.nsf/byheadline/12-116MR, accessed 28 August, 2014

ASIC (2013a) *13-294MR Update on Trio investigation*, available at http://www.asic.gov.au/asic/asic.nsf/byheadline/13-294MR, accessed 31 July, 2014

ASIC (2013b) *Self-managed super: Factsheet June 2013*, http://www.moneysmart. gov.au/media/ 421665/smsf-factsheet.pdf, accessed 14 August, 2014

ASIC (2014) *What we do*, available at http://www.asic.gov.au/asic/asic.nsf/byheadline/Our+role?open Document, accessed 14 August, 2014

Blackall, D (2013) 'Camera journalism - ethical and legal hazards', *Precedent* No.117 July/August: 34–39, available at http://ro.uow.edu.au/cgi/viewcontent.cgi?article=1930&context=lhapapers, accessed 14 August, 2014

CLD Australia (2013) spread sheet, available at www.law-democracy.org/wp-content/uploads/2011/09/Australia1.xls, accessed 14 August, 2014

CLD (2013) *RTI Rating Data Analysis Series: Overview of Results and Trends*, available at http://www.rti-rating.org, accessed 23 July, 2014

FBI (2010) *Securities Fraud Awareness & Prevention Tips*, available at http://www.fbi.gov/stats-services/publications/securities-fraud accessed 23 July, 2014

FOI (2013) *Freedom of Information Act 1982, No. 3, 1982* as amended, includes amendments up to *Act No. 146*, available at http://www.austlii.edu.au/au/legis/cth/num_act/foiaa2010371/ accessed 11 June, 2014

FRBNY (2012) *Staff report No. 458, Shadow Banking*, Federal Reserve Bank of New York, available at http://www.newyorkfed.org/research/staff_reports/sr458.pdf accessed 30 July, 2014

Garling, J (2011) Regina v Shawn Darrell Richard [2011] NSWSC 866, 12 August

Hansard (1981) Parliament of Australia House of Representatives, 18 August, available at http://parlinfo.aph.gov.au/parlInfo/search/display/display.w3p; accessed 9 June, 2014

Hasham, Nicole (2011) 'Trio fallout: DIY investors 'swimming outside flags', *Illawarra Mercury*, April 13, available at http://www.illawarramercury.com.au/story/634981 accessed 2 September, 2014

Lagan, Bernard (2014) 'Inside the Offshore Fraud: The Villains and Victims of Australia's Biggest Pension Scam', *The Global Mail*, 17 January, http://www.theglobalmail.org/feature/ accessed 19 April, 2014

Lhabitant, François-Serge (2007) *Handbook of Hedge Funds*. Chichester: John Wiley & Sons

Lidberg, Johan (2009) 'Submission on the Exposure Drafts: Freedom of Information Amendment (Reform) Bill', available at https://www.dpmc.gov.au/consultation/foi_reform/pdfs/PDFs15.pdf, accessed 31 August, 2014

Lidberg, Johan 2014, 'Transparency trade-off means FOI will get more expensive', *The Conversation*, 16th May, available at https://theconversation.com, accessed 21 July, 2014

Liu, Qiao and Paul Lejot (2013) 'Debt, derivatives and complex interactions', in *Finance in Asia: Institutions, Regulation and Policy*. New York: Routledge

Miraglia, Paula, Rolando Ochoa and Ivan Briscoe (2012) *Transnational organised crime and fragile states*. Paris: Organization for Economic Co-operation and Development

Patterson Scott and Bradley Hope (2014) 'Exchange seeks $200m for life in the slow lane', *The Wall Street Journal*, May 27, http://www.theaustralian.com.au/business/wall-street-journal/ accessed 2 June, 2014

Ricketson, Matthew and Rick Snell (2002) 'FOI: Threatened by governments, underused by journalists – still a sharp tool' in Tanner, Stephen [ed] *Journalism investigation and research*. French's Forest, NSW: Pearson Education Australia

SIS (1993) *Superannuation Industry (Supervision) Act 1993*. Canberra: Office of Parliamentary Counsel

VOFF (2014) *Summary of FOI applications by Victms of Financial Fraud Inc to 1st August 2014*, Unpublished draft given to the writers by VOFF

Verrender, Ian (2012) 'See you later, regulator: ASIC too slow for its own good, or ours', *Sydney Morning Herald*, August 4, available at http://www.smh.com.au/business/ accessed 3 September, 2014

Note on the contributors

David Blackall is a senior lecturer in journalism at University of Wollongong. He is a camera journalist and documentary filmmaker. His 1995 broadcast documentary on freedom of information, in collaboration with investigative journalist Brian Toohey, is available in two sections on YouTube at https://www.youtube.com/watch?v=ycc6IX4Lsdw and https://www.youtube.com/watch?v=HLd-Kzfo8T0

Jolyon Sykes is a journalism researcher and is treasurer of the Journalism Education and Research Association of Australia. He works on funded research projects, in public journalism; in journalism practice when dealing with psychologically traumatised sources; in the treatment of vulnerable sources; and in an investigation into news media role in community recovery after major bushfires.

An increasingly secret paradise

New Zealand was once viewed as a paragon of open government. But no one ever asked its journalists if it was true. Now a new narrative – capped off by recent revelations of skullduggery at the highest levels – has emerged, write *Greg Treadwell* and *James Hollings*

Introduction

There could scarcely be a more interesting time to write about freedom of information (FOI) in New Zealand, generally thought to be among the least corrupt, most transparent societies. But a period of political turmoil shortly before the 2014 general election has turned out to have FOI and issues of transparency at its very heart, spoiling that image of a South Seas information-paradise. Five weeks out from polling, a book claiming that high-ranking government ministers have been quietly complicit in the smear campaigns of right-wing attack blogs – including feeding them sensitive intelligence information by giving preference to their FOI requests – hit the election like a grenade. Politicians and public-relations agents hoping to manage the electoral news agenda found themselves sucker-punched by the biggest political story in decades.

These disclosures became the strongest evidence yet that New Zealand's reputation as a country of openness is an exhausted narrative already rather late for bed. For decades, policy and legal analysts have proclaimed New Zealand's FOI regime to be virtually without comparison and its citizens among the freest in the world. But New Zealand, like all societies, has undergone radical and far-reaching change since the Official Information Act (OIA) was enacted in 1982. The Act itself, in contrast, has hardly changed at all. It is our argument here that FOI in New Zealand is increasingly shown up for its shortcomings and that significant abuse of the Official Information Act has become relatively common. Not only has a worldwide tendency back towards state secrecy taken root in the post-9/11 era (Roberts, 2002: 152), but in New Zealand, and in other countries, significant programmes of privatisation have moved much public spending beyond the gaze of FOI legislation. In addition, the New Zealand Ombudsman – the main route of appeal against denials of FOI requests – is now overloaded with rapidly increasing numbers of complaints of state secrecy (Ombudsman, 2013). This is both evidence of a public frustrated in its desire for information and often a blockage itself in the rightful transfer of information the law was meant to ensure. On top of this, despite celebrated cases of whistleblowers performing a critical role in its democracy, the legislation aimed at protecting them from retribution is ineffective and almost unused. There is, indeed, trouble in paradise.

But let's start with the book. What has been dangerously opaque about the highly popular National-led government (which has held power since 2008), argues Nicky Hager in *Dirty Politics: How Attack Politics is Poisoning New Zealand's Political Environment*, is that behind the nice-guy, centre-right image of Prime Minister John Key and the National Party has been another type of politicking altogether – a strategic partnership between government, powerful public relations practitioners and vicious attack blogs. This co-operation has seen opponents discredited with character assassinations, sex scandals and other hate-filled attacks. In particular, the story has centred on the supply of information from officials as high as the Prime Minister's press secretary to an openly vindictive blog called Whale Oil, through which its publisher, Cameron Slater, has relentlessly pursued his political enemies (usually on the left, and including the popular mayor of Auckland). Having been given thousands of emails and other messages hacked from Slater's computer, Hager used those he deemed in the public interest to weave a detailed picture of a covert and bullying blog culture working in the government's interests and also as a paid attack dog for selected businesses (among other things, Whale Oil has launched attacks on behalf of the tobacco and dairy industries, describing breast-feeding campaigners as the 'breastapo'). Most shocking, and captured in fine detail in the book, are the two-way political connections that the blogger has had as high as the cabinet table.

Hager's book paints a picture of a vindictive culture at ease with its immoral self, intent on maximising personal damage to opponents at every opportunity. The prime minister had earlier admitted he spoke regularly with Slater (Hager, 2014: 123) and critics cried that he must have known about the dirty politics, because some of the dirtiest, including digging around inside a Labour Party computer and accessing private information, had been coming from his own close adviser Jason Ede (Hager, 2014: 35). The top echelons of the administration, says Hager, must have been aware that this type of politics was being conducted in its interests. Certainly, Slater's close friendship with former justice minister Judith 'Crusher' Collins has been at the heart of the scandal. Collins, who was forced to resign when implicated in a campaign to undermine the chief executive of the Serious Fraud Office (an enforcement agency within her own ministry), admitted to arguably worse behaviour just days before when she acknowledged she had sent Slater the name and details of a civil servant she erroneously believed to be the source of a leak. The Whale Oil blog had then viciously attacked the man, who subsequently received a death threat. It was an ugly attack, based on false information and apparently enabled by the minister herself.

Not bad for a pizza delivery

If the dualistic nature of this approach to politics – where the electable, public faces of the party are kept well clear from a subterranean world of personal, damaging and often scandalous attacks on opponents – would be enough to strike fear into the heart of transparency lovers everywhere, worse and more concrete news was still to come. At the middle of the maelstrom is increasing evidence of serial abuse of the Official Information Act, including preferential treatment of Whale Oil in order to fuel the blog's negative politics. In one instance, Collins is said to have granted an official information request from Slater in just 37 minutes. Labour Party MP Grant Robertson told TV3's *The Nation* it was 'pretty much unheard [of]' to receive an OIA response so quickly. 'It's a good time for a pizza delivery - 37 minutes - but you'd never expect that from an OIA' (Fisher 2014a).

At the centre of another case, now to be the subject of an urgent high-level inquiry by the Inspector General of Intelligence and Security, was the release by the Security Intelligence Service (the SIS is New Zealand's equivalent of Britain's MI5 and MI6) of information directly to Whale Oil, again surprisingly within just a few days. The SIS is the most secret part of the New Zealand state, dealing as it does in matters of national security. Journalists used to month-long waits for relatively trivial information from non-security agencies are now shaking their heads at the speed with which the SIS information was declassified and provided to a blog that used it to embarrass the then-leader of the opposition, Phil Goff. It is alleged that in one email exchange, leaked later by the original hacker of Slater's computer, the minister of justice and the blogger discuss the imminent release of the SIS information. Slater is shown responding: 'Well hopefully I will get my reply to my OIA on Monday. Then we will see what happens.'

Collins: 'Oh dear. All this open government thingy.'

Slater: 'twewwible' (Fisher, 2014b).

The Official Information Act 1982

How did we get here? Like many countries, New Zealand took a dramatic step in its development as a liberal democracy in 1982, when it passed legislation that turned on its head a long-held presumption of the government's right to keep secrets from its people. There had been deep rumblings, a 'long period of public concern and criticism about the lengths to which the government went to preserve secrecy' (Aitken, 1998: 4). The government's response to this growing pressure for a disclosure regime was the formation of the Official Information Committee, a body not of politicians (who might fear openness) but government officials (who would have to facilitate it and would not want something unworkable), which recommended an 'Official Information Act' under which all information held by the government would become available to anyone in New Zealand (unlike many regimes around the world, rights to information are not restricted to citizens and residents) unless there was good reason for withholding it. It would be based on a clear articulation of the principle of availability (Liddell as cited in Snell, 2000: 577). Media law researcher Steven Price has it that:

> *'[e]ssentially . . . we, the public, own the information that's held by government. And we're entitled to see it on request unless there's good reason to withhold it. "Good reason" isn't just any old reason the government thinks is justified. There is a careful list of "good reasons" for refusing to give you information in the OIA (such as prejudice to national security or international relations). If the government can't find a good reason from that list, it has to give you the information.'* (n.d.a)

Indeed, information could still be withheld from the public if it met certain strict and narrow criteria. But situations demanding such secrecy were now defined in law and restrained principally to matters of state and crown security, commercial privilege, 'free and frank' advice to ministers, and the privacy of natural persons. In global terms, New Zealand's list of justifications for withholding information was comparatively short. Further boosting its reputation was that information considered secret still had to pass an over-riding public interest test if it was to be withheld – that is, while there may be reasons for withholding information, it could still be released if that was more in the public interest. Adding further to the act's reputation as a game-changer was the lack of any prescription to what form 'official information' took. There was no requirement that the information sought had to have been aggregated in a document of any sort. Well-known investigative journalist Nicky Hager applauds this as one of the act's strengths. As a New Zealand requester of information 'you request "information", not documents: answers to questions, lists of data and so on, whether or not they are contained in a document' (Hager, 2002: 1).

Five years after it was passed, the OIA's principles were extended to local government through the Local Government Official Information and Meetings Act, 1987 (LGOIMA). Together, the two acts were celebrated as the core of one of the most permissive and successful FOI regimes on the planet, especially since now FOI was increasingly acknowledged as a prerequisite for the achievement of other, perhaps all, human rights. In late 1999 the country's then Chief Ombudsman, Sir Brian Elwood, was happy to declare that New Zealanders' right to know was, as far as he knew, 'unmatched' (Elwood, 1999). In 2005 Privacy Commissioner Marie Shroff told the FOI Live conference when the UK finally enacted its own FOI law that New Zealand had 'one of the freest FOI regimes in the world' (2005: 1). Britain appeared to be readying itself for the storm that must surely follow such a radical increase in access, but Shroff assured delegates that New Zealand was some 23 years ahead and that she had come from the FOI future to assure them that 'it works' (Shroff, 2005: 1). New Zealand appeared very pleased with itself.

An emergent narrative

But a broader, deeper understanding of FOI issues in New Zealand has emerged. Informed more by journalists than its utopian predecessor, this narrative describes a generally uninterested public (which still tends to rely on journalists to 'use' the OIA on its behalf), obstructive officials ignorant or dismissive of their legal obligations, an increasingly privatised world of state-funded services, and an Ombudsman's office drowning in complaints.

Research by Price (n.d.a) recorded deep ambivalence on the part of information requesters, some of whom were journalists, about the OIA. While none would voluntarily return to the days before the Act, those interviewed for the project were sceptical of officials' and ministers' motives and knowledge of the OIA. The requesters said officials wrongly believed that OIA requests must be written down – or that the request must specifically mention the Act; if not, the officials believe they can choose whether or not to release the information. Sometimes officials offer requesters a trade-off, requesters said, along the following lines: 'You will have to put that request under the OIA, which will take time to process – or else I could just give you this [less important] information right now.'

The requesters had all experienced frustrating delays in the processing of requests, particularly when they sought controversial or sensitive material. They listed what they saw as common stalling tactics used by officials:

- transferring requests between agencies;
- seeking clarification of the request, then treating this as a new request with a fresh 20-working day time limit;
- insisting they are 'working on it' or 'conducting consultations';
- claiming that the person processing the request is away or sick or that it is 'on the minister's desk' awaiting final approval;
- waiting for weeks and then refusing the request;
- losing or simply ignoring requests;
- [creating delays] when the Ombudsman becomes involved; and
- brazenly not releasing information immediately even after agreeing to do so following an Ombudsman's investigation. (n.d.a: 11-12).

Hager acknowledges the OIA is a powerful tool, but says he regularly finds himself 'held up or blocked' (2002: 1) by officials. At least half his requests end up with the Ombudsman and he almost always then gets more information.

> *'[This] means that, at least with my requests, officials are – regularly and routinely – being more considerably more restrictive with official information than they should be if they followed the Act properly. It should not be necessary to complain to the Ombudsman to get information'* (ibid).

Structural pluralism and FOI

Another problem is that the Act has some major exemptions. These include the courts; the Police Complaints Authority (which investigates complaints against police); and Parliamentary Services (which manages MPs expenses and other all other parliamentary business). Despite a recommendation from the New Zealand Law Commission (June 2012) that the OIA should be rewritten from scratch (and in the process be extended to cover the business of parliament), very little has changed about the act since the 1980s. New Zealand society, on the other hand, has changed dramatically. Elected in 1984 at a time of economic crisis, [the Labour Party] embarked on a radical response, a programme of social and economic reform that reached deep into New Zealanders' lives (Walker, 1989). Critical to the reforms was the idea of smaller government and over the past three decades many of the services once provided by government – from passport photos to prison services – have been moved to the private sector.

> *The transformation of the architecture of the public sector over the last two decades has caused confusion about the applicability of disclosure laws, most of which were drafted with the purpose of improving transparency within government agencies staffed by government employees. As work left government departments – to go to contractors, privatised utilities, and non-profit organisations – the principle of access to government documents began to break down* (Roberts, 2006: 152).

Roberts is writing about economic liberalisation in Western democracies generally. But it is a movement New Zealand was famous for leading and here, as much as anywhere, the socio-political context of 2014 is very different to that in 1982 when the OIA was drafted. Now significant amounts of public money are being spent by private organisations outside the watchful eyes of those who monitor the state. Some of these services have high levels of public interest attached to them – private prisons and charter schools, for example. As the provision of these services shift to the private sector, the public loses sight of them to varying degrees, despite being the primary funders of the service and often having a strong interest in it beyond that funding.

Overlooked in the rush to privatisation is the threat posed to public access to governmental records. Records long open to public inspection now are being created, maintained, and controlled by private businesses often at odds with the very purpose of public records laws (Bunker and Davis, 1998: 464). The transparency created so effectively under the OIA has started to become strangely opaque in places. We should not have to go far down that road before asking if today's world simply is not the governance structure for which the OIA was envisioned.

Protected disclosures

A lack of meaningful protection for whistleblowers in New Zealand remains a significant constraint on freedom of speech, and press freedom in particular. Whistleblower protection is supposed to be guaranteed by the Protected

Disclosures Act 2000 (amended 2009). The PDA protects an employee who discloses information about their employer from retaliation. It was introduced mainly as a response to a high profile case in which an employee of a mental health service was sacked for leaking information to the news media about a dangerous paedophile's release on parole, despite advice that he was still a risk to children. However, the act has been criticised as ineffective by whistleblowers (Scholtens, 2003). The major problem is that it sets a high threshold before employees qualify for protection – there must be 'serious wrongdoing' i.e. actions that would pose a serious risk to public safety or maintenance of the law; unlawful, corrupt or irregular use of funds or resources; or corrupt management or negligence.

The employee must also believe 'on reasonable grounds' that the wrongdoing allegation is true, and must believe 'on reasonable grounds' that it is about serious wrongdoing. They must also have attempted to follow internal procedures. If they are frightened of doing this, they can disclose to 'an appropriate authority' – but the list of who these are is limited. For example, it doesn't include journalists. Employees of the intelligence services *must* disclose *only* to the inspector general of intelligence and security, the appropriate minister, or the prime minister. Furthermore, the employee has no protection if the disclosure is 'known to that person to be false' or he or she acts in bad faith (but it doesn't say how or who decides this), or if the information is protected by legal professional privilege.

The act was amended in 2009, following a review by Queen's Counsel Mary Scholtens (Scholtens, 2003). The review concluded that where the act's procedures had been properly embedded in an organisation, it had worked well. It recommended greater involvement of the Ombudsman's office to support people, which the 2009 act provided for, as well as extending protection to people who volunteer supporting information.

Despite these improvements, the act is still barely used. The Office of the Ombudsman noted in its 2012/2013 annual report that it gets an average of 10 requests a year for guidance and assistance and expressed puzzlement that the number was so low:

> It is not clear why the PDA is not used more often. It could be due to a lack of awareness of the act, or a perception that the protections it provides are inadequate. It may also be a reflection of the fact that New Zealand enjoys such low levels of corruption (Ombudsman, 2013: 47).

The real reason for the lack of use of the act can be found in Scholten's report. She talked to a number of whistleblowers that had tried to use the act, and found their experiences were all negative. The act was cumbersome, difficult to apply, and unlikely to protect the discloser against publicity or retaliation. None of these concerns seem to have been reflected in Scholten's recommendations for changes to the act, and none seem to have found their way into legislation. Add to this an increasing use of gagging clauses in employment contracts, and the climate of freedom of speech appears to be getting worse.

The Ombudsman

When your FOI request fails in New Zealand, your recourse is to the Ombudsman, a celebrated back-stop for government accountability. Indeed, one of the strengths of NZ's FOI laws so admired by commentators around the world is the informality of – and easy, inexpensive, access to – an appeals process. However, the figures in the Office of the Ombudsman's 2012/13 report (Ombudsman, 2013) make for arresting reading. In it, the office acknowledged it had received 2,374 complaints that year, which was up 92 per cent on the previous year. While 1,012 were from one complainant about school boards of trustees, if one excludes that complainant, complaints were still up 26 per cent on the previous year. During the year the office had 'completed' 1,913 complaints, which was a 78 per cent increase on the number it had completed the previous year, a sign of both improvement in processing of complaints but also a key indicator of the submersion in complaints the office had been experiencing.

Perhaps of greater interest to journalists is the increasing and worrying tendency for complaints to the Ombudsman to be about not refusals but *unreasonable delays* in the provision of information, a political tactic often seen by journalists to be about punishing them for their requests.

> '...there was an 18 per cent increase in delay complaints this year. This continues to be a worrying trend, after a 34 per cent increase in delay complaints in the previous year. As a result, we will be including the issue of timeliness in our upcoming wider administrative improvement investigation of official information policy and practice in selected government agencies* (Ombudsman 2013: 42).

Conclusion

The unique and successful characteristics of the OIA – an open and flexible view of information, a concrete principle of availability and a successful appeal mechanism – have meant it has been lauded by those who appreciate a great piece of law or policy. But a new narrative has emerged now that, over decades, the views of journalists and journalism scholars have been included. While not all policy studies projects are cheerleaders for the efficacy of the regime (eg, White, 2007) and not all legal scholars think the OIA is perfect law (eg, Price n.d.a), the perspective of arguably the most influential of all so-called requesters under the act is only now being woven into the discourse. Journalism's interest in FOI goes to the very heart of both FOI and journalism. Nicky Hager's book *Dirty Politics* has confirmed what many journalists suspected. The reputation the New Zealand government has for transparency is a thin veneer indeed.

References

Aitken, Judith (1998) 'Open government in New Zealand' in McDonald, A and Terrill, G (eds) *Open government: Freedom of Information and Privacy*. London: Macmillan

Bunker, Matthew and Davis, Charles (1998) 'Privatized government functions and freedom of information' in *Journalism and Mass Communication Quarterly*, 75(3)

Elwood, Brian (1999) 'The New Zealand model - the Official Information Act 1982'. Paper presented at the *FOI and the Right to Know* conference, Melbourne, Australia, available at http://www.humanrightsinitiative.org/index.php?option=com_content&view=article&id=841:member-states-laws-a-papers&catid=48:mandate, accessed 21 September, 2014

Fisher, David (2014a) 'Hacker releases new Collins conversations,' *New Zealand Herald*, 1 September, available at http://www.nzherald.co.nz/nz/news/article.cfm?c_id=1&objectid=11317385, accessed 21 September, 2014

Fisher, David (2014b) 'Collins grants blogger's request in just 37 minutes,' *New Zealand Herald*, 23 August, available at http://www.nzherald.co.nz/nz/news/article.cfm?c_id=1&objectid=11313041, accessed 21 September, 2014

Hager, Nicky (2002) 'A researcher's view of New Zealand's Official Information Act'. *International Symposium on Freedom of Information and Privacy*, available at http://www.nickyhager.info/a-researcher%E2%80%99s-view-of-new-zealand%E2%80%99s-official-information-act-international-symposium-on-freedom-of-information-and-privacy/, accessed 21 September, 2014

Hager, Nicky (2014) *Dirty politics: How attack politics is poisoning New Zealand's political environment*. Wellington: Craig Potton Publishing

New Zealand Law Commission (2012) *The public's right to know: review of the official information legislation*, available at http://www.lawcom.govt.nz/project/review-official-information-act-1982-and-local-government-official-information-act-1987?quicktabs_23=report, accessed 21 September, 2014

Ombudsman (2013) <i>Annual Report 2012/2013</i>. Wellington: Office of the Ombudsman, available at http://www.ombudsman.parliament.nz/system/paperclip/document_files/document_files/708/original/annual_report_2012_-_2013.pdf?1381799341, accessed 21 September, 2014

Price, Steven (n.d.a) *The Official Information Act 1982: A window on government or curtains drawn?* Available at http://www.medialawjournal.co.nz/?page_id=17, accessed 21 September, 2014

Roberts, Alasdair (2006) *Blacked out: government secrecy in the information age*. New York: Cambridge University Press

Scholtens, Mary (2003) *Review of the operation of the Protected Disclosures Aft 2000: Report to the Minister of State Services*, available at http://www.beehive.govt.nz/Documents/Files/ACFF62C.pdf, accessed 21 September, 2014

Shroff, Marie (2005) *The OIA and privacy: New Zealand's story*, available at http://privacy.org.nz/news-and-publications/speeches-and-presentations/the-oia-and-privacy-new-zealand-s-story-june-2005/, accessed 21 September, 2014

Snell, Rick (2000). 'The Kiwi paradox: A comparison of freedom of information in Australia and New Zealand,' available at http://heinonline.org/HOL/LandingPage?handle=hein.journals/fedlr28&div=34&id=&page=, accessed 21 September, 2014

Walker, Simon (1989) *Rogernomics: reshaping New Zealand's economy*. Wellington, NZ: GP Books

White, Nicola (2007) *Free and frank: Making the Official Information Act 1982 work better*. Wellington: Institute for Government and Policy Studies

Note on the contributors

Greg Treadwell is a former journalist, photographer and newspaper editor. He is now a senior lecturer in journalism at AUT University in Auckland, New Zealand. His doctoral research is on structural pluralism and freedom of information in New Zealand.

Dr James Hollings was a journalist in both print and radio. He is now a senior lecturer in journalism at Massey University, Wellington, where he specialises in investigative journalism. His research interests include whistleblowers and the decision-making process of the reluctant, vulnerable witness.

An elephant in sheep's clothing? South Africa's experience of FOI

Anusharani Sewchurran **theorises the relationship between information, communication and power before examining the fragile access to information regime in South Africa**

Introduction

The freedom of expression paradigm traditionally involves the debate around censorship, i.e. between the press acting as the fourth estate and the conditions under which government can be allowed to impose censorship. The paradigm has evolved to include political economy perspectives; where media scholars became concerned with ownership and its controlling effects on journalism, later clarified as 'market censorship' or 'market capture'. Post-convergence the media environment has grown to be riddled with complexity and the clear divisions that previously existed have only limited application. Therefore when one takes up the question of freedom of information, the net cast is necessarily a rather wide one. In this chapter, the freedom of expression paradigm will be explored as it is shaped by the digital, mobile environment. Of concern is the digital infrastructure increasing users' visibility in particular ways. Surveillance theorists invoke the idea of the *panopticon* as analogous of the changing nature of power in a digital world (Lyon, 2006; Monahan, 2006; and Jensen and Draffan, 2004). In the industrial (Victorian) age, productive power was manifest in machines of industry augmenting physical labour. In the current age dramatic shifts in the communication industry have resulted in important shifts of power (Leadbeater, 2004). The new productive power is signified by information, an increasingly important category that has redefined the fault lines of productive relations (Masuda, 2004). The chapter first introduces the *information category* and then moves on to describe the *panopticon* historically and its application to current informational infrastructures of power and control. The final discussion includes a review of the South African press and the arising tensions with freedom of expression/information.

The information category

It is unequivocal that information as a category developed traction post world war two. This may be attributed to the advances in communication technology as well as in the mathematical and allied scientific fields. In 1948-9 Claude Shannon wrote *The mathematic theory of communication* in which he outlined that information was the quantitative measure of communicative exchanges, clarifying further that information was the resolution of uncertainty created by distortions as messages were transmitted over communication hardware of the era. This radical redefinition of the concept of information (as compared to the pre-existing meanings) took firm root in the communication industry when new networks of communication were being developed as the primary occupation was the measurement of communication, or bits of information, which had to then be matched to appropriate bandwidth with enough carrying capacity. Adding the market factors of cost and efficiency to the mix perhaps accounts for why this redefinition of information retained such influence, dominating the discourses around information ever since. Ascribing an economic indicator to the category of information also developed during this era; however at the inception post-industrial writers viewed information as a resource with certain intrinsic qualities which purportedly conferred an economic status. 'The information resource in short, is different in kind from other resources.... Not subject to the laws of thermodynamics, information is expandable, compressible, substitutable, transportable, leaky, shareable.' These inherent characteristics, Cleveland argues, 'divulge the vital clue to information's mounting economic importance,' (Cleveland in Schiller, 2007: 7).

The contradictions arising out of viewing information with certain intrinsic qualities (thereafter) layered with economic value are numerous. Schiller indicates that ascribing an intrinsic quality is problematic as it extends the connotation to being natural and eternal (Schiller, 2007: 7-9). Hence what remains unaddressed is why information became in-vogue in economic theory only after the Second World War; and also how information gained its economic value and status at this particular juncture in history. Innis (1950: 3-9) asserted an almost causal link between communication and power, indicating that communication revolutions like literacy and the Gutenberg press resulted in a reorganisation of society with declining old power blocs giving way to new systems and hierarchies of power (ibid). In this sense Innis maintained that systems of communication were always linked to historical processes and power. Schiller reasserts this idea by asking, 'What if, however, we suppose that information in not inherently valuable? What if only a profound social reorganisation can permit information to become valuable?' (Schiller, 2007: 7) He proceeds to explain that information ideologues in economic theory created a supposedly new field and with it an analytical distance from history or the contested terrain of lived experience. In this sense information as a post-industrial economic category was reified with the scientific accents of value neutrality, the promise of progress and endowed with technological determinism

(Schiller, 2007: 7 – 28). Schiller offers a way into and out of this space via the idea of *commodity*.

Information as a commodity

Schiller, among other information studies theorists, makes a case for information's location. Following on from neo-Marxist thinking, he argues that when information is taken on as a commodity form, it necessitates the inclusion of historical context; material culture and individual experience; basically all the things *post-industrial information* excludes. Information as a commodity generates a review of productive relations involved in its very creation, and hence unearths hidden power relations. For the purpose of this chapter it is not necessary to delve any further into *information as commodity*. It is important to note the binary opposition between the different notions of information. Post-industrial notions of information are defined in two tongues; as open, progressive and potentially sublime (Mosco, 1996: 28-32). These notions of information are further captured by market forces that are neoliberal in nature, conveying naturalness, value neutrality, and presented as non-negotiable. On the other hand, information as a commodity form comes into being as a contested concept, inclusive of historical context, material and individual culture. Information as commodity frames enquiry not in terms of the economic, but the political economic and so includes important questions around ideology, power and productive relations.

These two ways of seeing information delineate the fracture in approaches to freedom of expression / information debates. Having outlined this variance in the dominant understandings of information, the chapter will next explore the panopticon as it relates to the modern informational infrastructure.

The panopticon

The panopticon, emerging from Jeremy Bentham's moral reformist thinking in late 1700s, was energised by Michel Foucault (2001) who extended Bentham's original idea of moral reform to modern hierarchies and infrastructures of control. While Bentham's design was strictly architectural; Foucault's was infrastructural. Bentham conceived of a prison structure in the round, many cells packed next to each other, above and below, with the only illuminating feature being the guard house (or controller's space) in the centre. The lights illuminating the central controller's space are meant to render any prisoners vision of it hazy and indistinguishable. As a result, prisoners would only ever be able to assume the presence of an all seeing eye (the guard) as opposed to actually perceiving the guards. Bentham's idea was to create certain psychological conditions of self-regulation without the added cost of too many extra guards. Nothing really came of Bentham's designs until Foucault resurrected it for modern application. Foucault (Rabinow, 2001: 451) argues for the trap of visibility, i.e. where modernist preoccupations were with capital expansion to the global markets; post modernism sought to rationalise the modern nation state – especially the control of its citizenry. Current surveillance theorists argue that the trap of visibility is created by informational mechanisms of hardware; software and hegemony. The current panopticon is digital in nature; end users occupy and populate their individual devices that are connected to centralised hierarchies of power. There are possibilities for scrutiny of individuals' digital activities from within the hierarchies of power, but no possibility of individuals to return the gaze. Scrutiny takes the form of locating consumers or dissenters; the former perhaps more benign than the latter, which unequivocally embodies the threat of force.

Whitaker (1999) argues that intelligence gathering has been going on for centuries (the second oldest profession), in the pursuit of nation states, monarchies and governments would gather information covertly about bordering nations' intentions, arms and ammunitions etc. Whitaker argues further that the outward 'intelligence' gathering gaze of nation states has now turned inward partly as a result of the digital infrastructure affording it these possibilities. There has never been the possibility of having access to an entire nation state until the birth and evolution of informational infrastructures. Information or intelligence no longer needs to be covertly sought. Ironically it is tacitly, most willingly surrendered by end users. While this intelligence is more robustly used by marketing companies seeking more consumers and sometimes a better understanding of consumptive practises; citizens are also subject to infringements by power brokers in different ways. In the next section, the case studies of South Africa are offered as means to tease out the complexities arising out of a digital panopticon as it confronts notions of freedom of information.

As to the origins, it appears a proverbial chicken-egg question. While it is questionable whether the nation states (in particular the north Atlantic nations) sought to deliberately set up intelligence networks via the existing technological infrastructure; or whether technological advances simply made more types of surveillance possible. No current surveillance theorist answers the question satisfactorily but all agree that one needs to approach the resultant with some caution.

The South African context

In the film, *A scanner darkly* (2006) the absurdity of national surveillance reveals a nexus of power (the State; the police via intelligence agencies; and industry) working together to generate hegemonic relations and manage the citizenry through surveillance and force when necessary. South Africa has an intimate memory of the suffocating and oppressive effects of such nodes of power during apartheid years. In a way the abuses during this era provided a tremendous impetus for comprehensive provisions for freedom of information in the post 1994 constitution as one of the pillars of good governance enabling transparency.

The South African constitution, when passed into law in 1996, was saluted as one of the world's most progressive constitutions. The legislation around freedom of expression is dealt with in section 16 of the Bill of Rights detailing the list of freedoms; i.e. of the press and other media; to receive or impart information and /or ideas; of artistic creativity; academic freedom and freedom of scientific research (South African constitution, 1996). The limitations to freedom of expression typically deal with propaganda for war; incitement of imminent violence; and advocacy of hatred that is based on race, ethnicity, gender or religion and that constitutes incitement to cause harm. The constitution also details allied freedoms; such as freedom of assembly (section 17); freedom and right to security (section 12); and access to information held by the State (section 32) (Berger, 2007: 99-104). However, a little under two decades since adoption, South Africa remains a legislative democracy facing serious threats to these key constitutional freedoms.

An elephant dressed as a sheep

The Secrecy Bill formally known as the 'Protection of State Information Bill' emerged in 2010, when public hearings were held for debate on the bill (Staff reporter, 2010a). It drew widespread condemnation from all walks of South African life. In its original form the Secrecy Bill sought government latitude in classifying information deemed in the interests of protecting national security (*Mail and Guardian*, 29 October, 2010). The bill further criminalised any infringements of said classifications without any protective provisions for weighing up public interest against what was a matter of national security. Simply put this amounted to the possibility of wholesale classification as 'secret' any information the government did not want released into the public domain. There were even provisions for municipalities to classify information. When first proposed the bill was referred to as an elephant dressed up as a sheep. Sole (2010: 27) explores the multitude of problems with the bill.

> *'The Bill allows commercial information held by the state to be easily classified, which will mean tender processes and the activities of state-run enterprises are likely to be shielded from public scrutiny. This will have a negative impact on competitiveness and accountability in the government and will promote corruption...The Bill makes members of the public or journalists as guilty as those who disclose classified information. The possessor and the publisher are as guilty and the "leaker",'* (ibid).

Vuuren and Nkomo (2010: 17) add that the bill could impose harsh sentences (up to 25 years) on whistle-blowers, criminalising even the leaking of information in the public interest. Ironically such whistle-blowers and journalists could face longer prison sentences than officials who deliberately hide information that is in the public interest, and that ought to be disclosed. The bill would trump the Promotion of Access to Information Act, which its detractors have claimed is unconstitutional, as the Act provides for citizens' rights to have access to state information. A further clause in the bill sanctions banning the release of any state security matter (Clause 49) (Witness reporters, 2012). A most troubling inclusion is the veil drawn over the work of intelligence services, preventing public scrutiny of potential abuses of power and violations of human rights.

Contested terrain

The Secrecy Bill has been strongly contested by opposition parties; civil society; NGOs and public intellectuals. The official opposition, the Democratic Alliance (DA) amongst others raised objections to the bill in parliament comparing it to apartheid style laws, stating that 'the opposition parties would continue in their efforts to not back down in the face of this assault in democracy' (SAPA, 2013). Following public hearings on the original version of the bill in 2010, a civil society coalition formed to stop the bill and its damaging effects on freedom of expression in South Africa, and the troubling knock-on effect on levels of corruption. The coalition was named the Right2Know (R2K) campaign, garnering support from other organisations, famous South Africans and ordinary citizens, who mobilised to voice their opposition to the Secrecy Bill (*Mail and Guardian*, 27 October, 2010). R2K embarked on a week long campaign of raising awareness and protest, climaxing on 27 October, 2010, when thousands of South Africans marched to Parliament and the main streets of the other major cities, giving visual voice to the protest against a repressive 'apartheid-style bill'. R2K had the support of 400 organisations and collected 14,000 signatures in a petition (*Mail and Guardian*, 29 October, 2010).

The civic protest, which included the support of major labour unions, and the prolific publicity around the bill forced a rethink resulting in a revised version appearing before the national assembly in 2013 (SAPA, 2013). In the revised version, the Secrecy Bill no longer trumped the Promotion of Access to Information Act; Clause 49 originally banning the release of information relating to state security was removed; and the provision extending power to municipalities to classify information were also withdrawn (Witness reporters, 2012). The revised bill, though still contentious, gained a majority vote and at time of writing awaits President Zuma's signature to be passed into law. The limbo in relation to the bill is good news for South Africans as it could be testament to the vigorous protest raised against it. However it could also be that 2014 was an election year and the ruling party did not wish to chance any unpopular moves. The public sphere continues to reflect the R2K debate on the bill, revealing problematic issues in relation to freedom of information and democratic norms the new South Africa.

Conclusion

It is clear that under the guise of state security, very repressive control mechanisms are being promoted in relation to the 'right to know' in South Africa. The Secrecy Bill even in its revised format promotes parallel information regimes reminiscent of the apartheid past. The revised bill still criminalises any use of classified information without the inclusion of a public interest defence. This will effectively close the public sphere in South Africa if the revised bill is signed into law. It will also extend the state security minister's powers to regulate oversight bodies like the Public Protector's Office (South African Ombudsman), including what access and use can be made of classified information.

Under these conditions the South African public would not have been made aware, for example, of the exorbitant spending of public money on President Zuma's home (Nkandla); as Nkandla is defined as a 'national key point'. National key points are another throw back to apartheid times, used to define sites of 'national security'. National key points have increased from 118 in 2006 to 344 in 2013. (Hunter, 2014) Apart from a private home, the public service broadcaster (SABC); the national energy regulator and several petrochemical firms are listed as national key points.

The former president, the late Nelson Mandela once said, "The administrative conduct of government and authorities are subject to the scrutiny of independent organs. This is an essential element of good governance that we have sought to have built into our new constitutional order…It was, to me, never reason for irritation but rather a source of comfort when these bodies were asked to adjudicate on the actions of my government and judged against,' (*Mail and Guardian*, 15 November, 2013). This slow drift back toward secrecy represents sinister efforts towards creating a securocratic state, one where democratic principles are adjusted and modified until democracy is all but gone leaving behind a bureaucracy of surveillance and force, in the service of a small political and financial elite.

References

Berger, G (2007) *Media legislation in Africa. A comparative legal survey.* Grahamstown: UNESCO.

Crotty, A (2010) 'Secrecy bill could be written for institutions,' *Business Report*, 11 August

Editorial (2013) Secrecy destroys accountability, *Mail and Guardian*, 15 November. Available online at http://mg.co.za/print/2013-11-14-secrecy-destroys-accountability, accessed on 14 September 2014

Foucault, M (1977) *Discipline and punish: the birth of a prison.* New York: Pantheon

Freedom of Expression Institute, (2014) Internet freedom and the freedom of expression in South Africa. Braamfontein: Raith foundation

Hunter, Murray (2014) Securocrats choke flow of information, *Mail and Guardian*, 12 September. Available online at http://mg.co.za/print/2014-09-11-securocrats-choke-flow-of-information, accessed on 14 September 2014

Innis, HA (1950) *Empire and communications.* Oxford: Claredon Press

Jensen, D and Draffan, G (2004) *Welcome to the machine. Science, surveillance and the culture of control.* Vermont: Chelsea Green Publishing

Leadbeater, C (2004) 'Living on thin air,' Webster, F (ed) *The information society reader.* London: Routledge, pp 21-31

Linklater, R (2006) *A Scanner Darkly.* Film.

Lyon, D (2006) *Theorizing surveillance. The panopticon and beyond.* Devon: Willan Publishing

Masuda, Y (2004) 'Image of the future information society,' in Webster, F (ed) *The information society reader*. London: Routledge, pp 15-21

Monahan, T (2006) *Surveillance and security*. New York: Routledge.

Mosco, V (1996) *The political economy of communication*. London: Sage.

Rabinow, P (2001) *Essential works of Foucault 1954-1984*. New York: The New Press

SAPA (2013) 'Parliament sends secrecy Bill back to Zuma again,' *Mail and Guardian*, 12 November. Available online at http://mg.co.za/print/2013-11-12-secrecy-bill-to-be-sent-back-to-zuma-again, accessed on 14 September 2014

Schiller, D (2007) *How to think about information*. Chicago: University of Illinois Press

Shannon, C (1949) *The mathematical theory of communication*. Chicago: University of Illinois Press

Sole, S (2010) 'Not in the national interest,' *Mail and Guardian*, 16 July

South African constitution (1996). Available online at http://www.gov.za/documents/constitution/1996/a108-96.pdf, accessed on 31 August 2014

Mail and Guardian (2010) 'Right2Know Campaign is marching to Parliament today, 27 October. Available online at http://mg.co.za/print/2010-10-27-right2know-marches-to-parliament, accessed on 14 September 2014

Mail and Guardian (2010) 'Right2Know Campaign shows impact,' 29 October. Available online at http://mg.co.za/print/2010-10-29-right2know-campaign-shows-impact, accessed on 14 September 2014

Vuuren, H and Nkomo, P (2010) 'Cloud of secrecy hides the rot,' *Mail and Guardian*, 3 September

Witness reporters (2012) 'Info Bill: ANC gives in,' *The Witness*, 30 August

Note on the contributor

Anusharani Sewchurran is a lecturer at the Department of Media and Cultural Studies - University of KwaZulu-Natal, South Africa. She is currently completing a PhD in the field of telecommunications in South Africa. Her interests range from the regulation of media and new media technology to religion and the mediation of religious identity via the new and social media. She enjoys cooking most though.

The right to information in India: A journey from survival to social justice

India's 'Right to Information' Act, introduced in 2005, acts as a bulwark against corruption, however low levels of literacy and poor administrative record- keeping hamper its effectiveness, writes *Kiran Prasad*

Introduction

Many developing countries, including India, are crippled by corruption that has had a considerable impact on the provision of basic needs and services – with the most serious impact on the lives of the poor. It took India 77 years to transition from an opaque system of governance, legitimised by the colonial Official Secrets Act, to one where citizens can demand the 'right' to information. The enactment of the Right to Information Act in 2005 marked a significant shift for Indian democracy. It is interesting that in 2015 both India and the UK will be completing a decade since the passage of right to information legislation. In India, it is the citizens, voluntary organisations and social activists, who have widely used the legislation to seek information on issues of public interest and also to uncover corruption. Journalists have also used the legislation in investigative reporting in specific cases but have supported citizen journalism to actively pursue the right to information for greater transparency and accountability in public life.

The right to information (RTI) campaign in India

Article 19(1) of the Constitution provides for a fundamental right of speech and expression. The right to information is included in the constitutional guarantees of freedom of speech and expression has been recognised by Supreme Court decisions challenging governmental control over newsprint and bans on the distribution of newspapers. The right to know has been reaffirmed in the context of environmental issues that have an impact upon people's very survival. Several High Court decisions have upheld the right of citizens' groups to access information where an environmental issue was concerned. Although this provision is meant to facilitate citizen input, in fact it is too limited and

251

environmental groups have had to go to the courts to get more complete disclosure until the RTI law was enforced from 2005

Efforts to bring in legislation to release information in the public interest go back to the time when India was newly independent. There were objections to the Official Secrets Act ever since 1948, when the Press Laws Enquiry Committee recommended certain amendments so that the application of the Act would be confined, as the Geneva Conference on Freedom of Information recommended, only to matters that must remain secret in the interests of national security. In 1977, a working group was formed by the government to look at amending the Official Secrets Act. Unfortunately, that group did not recommend change, as it felt the Act related to the protection of national security. In 1989, a parliamentary committee was set up that recommended limiting the areas where government information could be hidden, and opening up of all other spheres of information. But no legislation followed from these recommendations.

The Press Council of India drew up the first major draft legislation on the right to information in 1996. The draft affirmed the right of every citizen to information from any public body. Significantly, the term 'public body' included not only the state, but also all privately-owned undertakings, non-statutory authorities, companies and other bodies whose activities affect the public interest. Under their proposals, information that could not be denied to parliament or state legislatures could not be denied to a citizen either. The draft also provided for penalties for defaulting authorities.

The Press Council of India's draft was followed by the Consumer Education Research Council (CERC) draft, by far the most detailed proposed freedom of information legislation in India. In line with international standards, it gave the right to information to anyone, except 'alien enemies', whether or not they were citizens. It required public agencies at the federal and state levels to maintain their records in good order, to provide a directory of all records under their control, to promote the computerisation of records in interconnected networks, and to publish all laws, regulations, guidelines, circulars related to or issued by government departments and any information concerning welfare schemes. The draft provided for the outright repeal of the Official Secrets Act. This draft didn't make it through parliament either.

Finally in 1997, a conference of chief ministers resolved that the central and state governments would work together on transparency and the right to information. Following this, the Indian government agreed to take immediate steps, in consultation with the states, to introduce freedom of information legislation, along with amendments to the Official Secrets Act and the Indian Evidence Act, before the end of 1997. The central and state governments also agreed to a number of other measures to promote openness. These included establishing accessible computerised information centres to provide information to the public on essential services. The Right to Information Bill, finally introduced in Parliament on 22 December 2004 came into force as the RTI Act from 13 October 2005.

Social audit

The word 'information' evokes an immediate response in the form of information technology (IT) from most people but very few even among the highly educated would raise the issue of a right to information (RTI) (Sen, 2001). The Magsaysay awardee and the guiding spirit behind the right to information campaign, Aruna Roy, emphasised that 'the RTI law is a basic entitlement for the effective use of other laws and rights. Denial of the right to know underlies the denial of all rights. It is therefore a part of all campaigns and basic to any demand for democratic and civil rights' (Roy in Sen, 2001).

The path breaking experiment in social audit had its genesis nearly 10 years ago where a mass organisation of workers and peasants - Mazdoor Kisan Shakti Sangathan (MKSS), founded by Aruna Roy in 1990, made use of the public right to scrutinise official records at the village level and uncovered a massive fraud of Rs.50 lakh (more than £5,000) over a period of six years in Janawad, Rajasthan. This campaign is striking and worthy of emulation in poorer parts of the world, especially since it was the illiterate and oppressed rural folk who spearheaded it and not the urban, politically aware and educated people (Prasad, 2008).

The MKSS compelled the administration to release details of specific development projects and then conducted *jan sunwayis* (public hearings) in 1994. The *jan sunwayis* were so successful in unmasking corrupt officials that they had to endure public humiliation and even return the money taken, back to the villagers (Bhaumik, 1996; Basu, 1997). The state that was the first in India to implement the *Panchayati Raj* system (local governance), Rajasthan, was the base selected by the MKSS for its campaign on the right to information. On 6 April, 1996, the Rajasthan government was forced to issue an order allowing inspection of records and copying by hand but not the crucial right to photocopy (Bhaumik, 1996). But in an illiterate society the right to photocopy is essential, without which the order loses its teeth.

The sustained campaign by the MKSS attracted countrywide attention and support of NGOs, citizens, media groups, the Press Council of India, and the Press Institute of India, encouraging the MKSS to be broad-based as the National Campaign Committee for People's Right to Information (NCCPRI) (Basu, 1997). The struggle for the right to information in Rajasthan converged with many other mass-based struggles to rehabilitate those displaced by big dams and the movement protesting violence against women. The campaign brought awareness to the people that their survival depends on the right to information (Prasad, 2011).

National campaign for people's right to information (NCPRI)

The National Campaign for People's Right to Information (NCPRI) was founded in 1996. Its founding members included social activists, journalists, lawyers, retired civil servants and academics, and one of its primary objectives was to campaign for a national law facilitating the exercise of the fundamental right to information. As a first step, the NCPRI and the Press Council of India formulated an initial draft of a right to information (RTI) law, which was sent to the government of India in 1996. The government finally introduced the Freedom of Information Bill in parliament, in 2002. This was a very watered down version of the bill first drafted by the NCPRI and others in 1996. Meanwhile, the NCPRI was also working to promote awareness and broadening and deepening the campaign. The first national convention was held at Bewar, Rajasthan, in 2002, and was attended by over a thousand delegates, from all parts of the country. The second convention was held in Delhi in 2004, and was attended a similar number. More than 30 workshops were organised as a part of the convention to discuss the use of RTI in different areas of work and governance.

In August 2004, the NCPRI forwarded to the National Advisory Council (NAC) a set of suggested amendments to the Freedom of Information Act 2002. The NAC endorsed most of the suggested amendments and recommended them to the prime minister of India for further action. These formed the basis of the subsequent Right to Information Bill, introduced in parliament on 22 December, 2004. However, this bill, as introduced in parliament, had many weaknesses. Most significantly, unlike the NCPRI suggestion, it did not apply to the whole country but only to the central government. The consequent outrage from civil society groups, including the NCPRI, forced the government to review the changes. The bill was referred to a standing committee of the parliament and to a group of ministers. The standing committee asked several NCPRI members to give evidence before it, and ultimately endorsed the stand taken by the NCPRI in most matters.

The Right to Information Act, 2005
The RTI Act that came into effect all over India from 13 October, 2005, aimed to empower every citizen with the right to obtain information from the government. The Act describes the obligations of public authorities [S.4 (1)]; designation of public information officers and assistant public information officers [S. 5(1) and 5(2)]; constitution of the central information commission (S.12 and 13); constitution of the state information commission (S.15 and 16); the non-applicability of the Act to intelligence and security services (S.24); and the power to make rules to carry out the provisions of the Act (S.27 and 28). The Act extends to the whole of India except the state of Jammu and Kashmir.

Information means any material in any form including records, documents, memos, e-mails, opinions, advices, press releases, circulars, orders, logbooks, contracts, reports, papers, samples, models, data material held in any electronic form and information relating to any private body, which can be accessed by a public authority under any other law for the time being in force [S.2 (f)]. Every citizen has a right to know how the government is functioning. That 'right' to information empowers every citizen to seek information from the government, inspect any government document and seek certified photocopies thereof. Some state laws also empower citizens to inspect any government work or to take a sample of material used in any work. The people have a right to know how they are being governed and how their money is being used. Right to information laws provide the machinery for the use of this right. The right to information laws provide for forms in which one can apply, where one can apply, in how many days one should get information, and what to do if a requester is refused access.

Limitations of the Act

The most scathing indictment of the Act has come from critics who focus on the sweeping exemptions it permits. Restrictions on information relating to security, foreign policy, defence, law enforcement and public safety are standard. The poor flow of information is compounded by two factors - low levels of literacy and the absence of effective communication tools and processes. In many regions, the standard of record-keeping is extremely poor. Most government offices have stacks of dusty files everywhere; providing an easy excuse for refusing access to records stating that they have been 'misplaced', though the rapid growth of information technology has indirectly contributed to an improved flow of information.

The appointment of members of the Indian Administrative Service (IAS), or the country's bureaucracy, to the Information Commission in charge of implementing India's Right to Information Act could hamper the effectiveness of a law that is supposed to ensure transparency and accountability in governance. In fact, it was to guard against a commission stacked with civil servants that one of the changes suggested to the original RTI Bill was to allow for the appointment of people from other fields. Since the RTI Act was passed in May 2005, several civil servants have been appointed as chief information commissioners of states. Proponents of the RTI argued that having on board representatives from other fields would make the information commission independent enough to discharge its role as the appellate authority that adjudicates disputes between the government and the citizen on whether a certain type of information could be disclosed or not. Thus, the appointment of IAS officers everywhere as chief information commissioners violates the spirit, if not the letter, of the RTI Act.

Shaping citizen journalism

The newspapers and television channels that do not have reporters in many rural and remote regions of the country have now provided their media platforms to voice public opinion and narrate stories that exploit the poor or expose corruption through the right to information. Citizen journalist shows on television regularly feature issues such as poor amenities like safe water, sanitation, proper roads, and lighting, which the local administration often fails to provide. For instance, social activists demanded a right to governmental information regarding health schemes to stem the maternal mortality rate;

measures to control violence against women and children; while environmental activists demanded information on the costs and benefits of development projects like big dams, which directly concerned the survival of local people.

The Right to Information Act gave a fillip to the nationwide anti-corruption people's campaign led by veteran social activist Anna Hazare, who fasted for 13 days in August, 2011. Hazare broke his fast only after both houses of the Indian parliament agreed to consider the draft of a bill proposing an ombudsman with legal powers to act against corruption. The movement for a stringent anti-corruption law across India saw a convergence of social movements, new media, and civic engagement never witnessed before in the country (Prasad, 2012; Prasad 2013). While people from all walks of life staged sit-in protests at designated venues, led marches, and took part in relay hunger strikes, the mass media in the country gave considerable support to and coverage of the movement to spur people's participation. The movement created awareness by holding candlelight vigils, fasting in support of Anna Hazare, giving media interviews, sending e-mails, tweeting, forming online forums, and sending mobile clips on the protests organised across the country and even abroad (Saxena, 2011: 46-48).

On-going struggle

As Aruna Roy and Nikhil Dey (2006), RTI activists wrote: 'For the energetic and rapidly growing right to information movement in India, the major challenge is to see whether we can protect this nascent fundamental democratic right from being undermined'. In the space of less than a decade, the burgeoning movement for the right to information in India has significantly sought to expand democratic space, and empower the ordinary citizen to exercise far greater control over the corrupt and arbitrary exercise of state power (Mander and Joshi, 2000). There is still a long way to go before the right to information can strike firm roots among the people. However the silver living is that the rural poor are clearly ahead in spearheading the right to information and anti-corruption challenge. For the law to be truly effective, it will need the active participation of the community at large, including non-government organisations and the mass media, which will need to simplify and disseminate the possibilities under the law to citizens.

The demand for the right to information about all development projects through the mass media and other channels to the people will establish the right of ordinary people to protest against corruption, monitor use of funds and become part of the governance structures of the state. The right to information law could be the tentative beginnings of a more inclusive and just development process – what Amartya Sen (1999) describes as 'a momentous engagement with the possibilities of freedom'. The right to information embodies the struggles for survival and justice in India and will be an important instrument in the journey for equitable and sustainable development of its people.

References

Basu, S (1997) 'Unknown Faces, Determined Minds' in *The Hindu*, 27 July

Bhaumik, SN (1996) 'Robbing the poor' in *India Today*, 15 November, pp 156-163

Mander, Harsh And Joshi, Abha (2000) *The Movement for Right To Information in India: People's Power for the Control of Corruption.* Available online at http://www.rtigateway.org.in/Documents/References/English/Reports/12.%20An%20article%20on%20RTI%20by%20Harsh%20Mander.pdf accessed 15 August, 2014

Prasad, Kiran (2008) *Communication for Development: Reinventing Theory and Action*, Volume 1 & 2. New Delhi: BRPC

Prasad, Kiran (2011) *Media Law in India.* The Netherlands: Kluwer Law International

Prasad, Kiran (2012) 'E-Governance Policy for Modernizing Government through Digital Democracy in India' in *Journal of Information Policy*, 2, pp 183-203

Prasad, Kiran (2013) 'New Media in Modernizing Government: Digital Democracy and People's Participation' in Prasad, Kiran (ed) *New Media and Pathways to Social Change: Shifting Development Discourses*, New Delhi: BRPC

Roy, Aruna (2001) quoted in 'The Right to Know' in *The New Sunday Express*, 26 August (by Ashish Sen)

Roy, Aruna and Nikhil Dey (2006) 'Taking the life out of the right to information' in *The Hindu*, 24 July

Sen, Amartya (1999) *Development as Freedom.* New York: Alfred. A. Knopf, Random House

Sen, Ashish. (2001) 'The right to know' *The New Sunday Express*, 26 August

Sharma, Kalpana (1997) 'Lalu and our right to know' in *The Hindu*, 3 July

Saxena, Payal (2011) The Protest Party, *The Week*, 4 September, pp 46-48

Note on the contributor

Kiran Prasad is Professor of Communication and Journalism at Sri Padmavati Mahila University, Andhra Pradesh, India. She was Commonwealth Visiting Research Fellow at the Centre for International Communication Research, University of Leeds, United Kingdom and Canadian Studies Research Fellow at Carleton University, Canada. She is recipient of several national awards for academic excellence and has published 20 books including *Transforming International Communication: Media, Society and Culture in the Middle East* (2014); *New Media and Pathways to Social Change: Shifting Development Discourses* (2013); and *Media Law in India* (Kluwer Law International, 2011).

India's Right to Information Act: A work in progress?

India introduced its Right to Information Act in 2005. The Act has had many successes in exposing corruption, but 10 years later problems still remain to be ironed out, writes *Sudeepta Pradhan*

Introduction

September 28 is celebrated as the 'Right to Know Day' worldwide, focusing on the importance of the citizen's right to access information held by their governments. More than 80 countries have enacted similar laws, with that number growing annually. In most countries, FOI or RTI is primarily used by journalists, however India has a wider user base that demand information from the government. In India, the Right to Information (RTI) Act was passed in 2005, after a nationwide campaign led by grassroots and civil society organisations. The Ministry of Information and Broadcasting considers RTI as 'the most fundamental law' as it can be used by all levels of the population beginning from the local *Panchayat (the Panchayati raj is the oldest system of local government in the Indian subcontinent, existing prominently in India, Pakistan, Bangladesh and Nepal)* to the parliament. It has emerged as a powerful tool in India's civil society to promote transparency and hold people in power accountable. In the Act's first three years of implementation, around two million RTI requests were filed in the country. There are success stories through the use of RTI in India, like the pond scam (rural Orissa); investigations into the Commonwealth Games and Adarsh society; the public distribution controversy in Assam; the appropriation of relief funds controversy; and IIM's admission criteria to name a few (these are discussed below).

The Indian legislation

The RTI has been defined by the Ministry of Law and Justice as:

> *'an Act to provide for setting out the practical regime of right to information for citizens to secure access to information under the control of public authorities, in order to promote transparency and accountability in the working of every public authority, the constitution*

of a Central Information Commission and State Information Commissions and for matters connected therewith or incidental thereto' (No 22, 15 June, 2005).

The RTI is considered to be a part of Article 19(1) (a) of the Indian Constitution, which states that 'all citizens shall have the right to freedom of speech and expression'. To enjoy freedom of speech and expression, information needs to be made available to every citizen. The Act is a fundamental right as it is absolutely essential for the healthy functioning of modern democracy. The legislation applies to the whole of India except the State of Jammu and Kashmir. When first introduced it was, and still is, considered essential to assure transparency in performance and ensure accountability amongst the workers of each public authority. It was enacted on 15 June, 2005, and it came into force on 12 October that year, making India the 48th country globally to implement such legislation. Central and state governments, and organisations funded by the government come under the purview of the Act. It compels public bodies covered by the Act to provide publicly available information, and disclose information related to their organisations on request. In that way, it is designed to act as a check against nepotism, maladministration and corruption, and protect the rights of citizens (Orissa Review, 2009).

The legislation is similar to many other such laws internationally, and includes rights to inspect work documents and records; take notes, extracts, or certified copies of documents or records; take samples of material; obtain information in the form diskettes, tapes, video cassettes or any other electronic mode or through print outs, where such information is stored in a computer or any other device. The Act provides for a right of request to Indian citizens only. Exclusions apply to a number of national security, intelligence and policing institutions, however information can be demanded from these organisations in case of corruption or human rights violations.

Before the introduction of the 2005 Act, similar legislation was in place in several states of India, namely Tamil Nadu (1997); Goa (1997); Rajasthan (2000); Karnataka (2000); Delhi (2001); Maharshtra (2002); Assam (2002); Madhya Pradesh (2003); and Jammu and Kashmir (2004). The RTI movement began in the early 1990s and was chiefly orchestrated by a number of civil society groups such as the Press Council of India (1996 by Justice P B Sawant, Chairman, PCI); and the Institute of Rural Development, Hyderabad (1997). On 2 January, 1997, a working group was established under the chairmanship of HD Shouri, and the first bill was introduced in parliament in 2000.

The RTI journey in India so far

Despite almost a decade since the legislation was first introduced, the process of accessing information is lengthy in several parts of the country, and the success or otherwise of the legislation varies considerably between states. A number of states lack enough information commissioners to process appeals – leading to severe delays – while in several other states, the hearing of appeals does not happen at all. Sunil Ahya (a RTI activist) stated that 'the Act allows maximum of 11 commissioners to be appointed and so if the pendency rates are so high then the state governments should appoint more commissioners' (Jain and Chhapia, 2014). The time taken to process requests also varies considerably – a request in Mumbai may take a couple of weeks to process whereas in places like Aurangabad, Nagpur and Pune hearing an appeal may take up to two years. States like Haryana, Punjab and Andhra Pradesh have the maximum number of information commissioners, and take around six weeks to finalise an appeal.

RTI and Political Parties
In 2011, the union cabinet approved the introduction of a Bill to amend the RTI Act, 2005 to exclude political parties from the purview of 'public authority'– meaning they would no longer be subject to requests (Agarwal, 2011). The Central Information Commission (CIC) decided on in June 2013 that political parties such as BJP, AICC/INC, CPI, CPI (M), BSP and NCP are public authorities as per Section 2(h) of the RTI Act. Section 29A (5) of the Representation of the People Act, 1951 stated that 'any small group of persons, if they so desire, can be registered as a political party by making a simple declaration' as provided in the guidelines and application format for registration of political parties). The RTI Act was enacted to provide for an effective framework for effectuating the right of information recognised under Article 19 of the Indian constitution and to ensure greater access to information by making the Freedom of Information Act, 2002 more progressive and participatory. However, the Act was vehemently opposed by the political parties as 'unacceptable'. Janardan Dwivedi, a congress party spokesman stated: 'It is unacceptable. Such a reckless approach will create a lot of harm and damage to democratic institutions as political parties are not government bodies'3. The CPI (M) opined 'to demand access to the internal deliberations of the party will constitute a serious infringement of the inner-party functioning, confidentiality of discussions and undermine the political party system itself'4 (Agarwal, 2011).

Successful RTI cases in India
In its first 10 years of operation, the RTI Act has emerged as an effective anti-corruption tool amidst all the hue and cry over corruption. In the numerous countries implementing RTI laws, journalists and media are the primary users, while India has a broader user base. In the first three years of implementation, around two million RTI requests were filed throughout the country. There were RTI cases filed to access entitlements, redress individual grievances, investigate government policies, and expose misuse of government resources and corruption. It was notable that a campaign for anti-corruption by a relatively unknown activist Anna Hazare, now considered a heroic anti-corruption crusader, incited remarkable public support. A number of right to information requests have lead to revelations of corruption by public officials; maladministration; cosy deals between politicians and businesses; and unequal access to rights by citizens. Some of these cases have been exposed by the media,

or by activists. The following are some examples of successful instances of the RTI:

The pond scam

In the pond scam of 2010, in rural Orissa, an RTI request was filed by the applicant seeking information on the number of ponds constructed in his village as per the government's national wage employment scheme. Shockingly, no pond was ever constructed though money had been spent. An experimental study by Yale University students on India's RTI Act found that RTI is 'as effective as bribery' in helping the poor access information. One of the researchers stated that: 'access to information appears to empower the poor to the point where they receive almost the same treatment as middle-class individuals at the hands of civil servants. This is something that payment of a bribe cannot do' (Shrinivasan, 2011).

Commonwealth Games

In 2010, a Delhi based NGO, the Housing and Land Rights Network, found that the Delhi government had manipulated funds from its social welfare programs for developing infrastructure in the Commonwealth Games.

Adarsh Society

A building planned to accommodate war widows and veterans, ended up being provided to bureaucrats, politicians and their relatives. A request was filed by activists Simpreet Singh and Yogacharya Anandji in 2008. The story was instrumental in bringing to light the relationship between politicians and military officials.

Public Distribution

In 2007, the online news site Krishak Mukti Sangram Samiti filed an request under the RTI Act to reveal irregularities in distributing food supposed to be for the poor. The corruption allegations were investigated and several government officials were arrested.

Appropriation of Relief Funds

A RTI request by a Punjab based NGO in 2008 showed that bureaucrats handling the local branches of the Red Cross Society used the Kargil war victim funds for their own personal benefit. The officials were subsequently charged with fraud.

The IIM's Admission Criteria

In 2007, a visually-impaired student was denied admission in the Indian Institute of Management (Bangalore), despite a remarkable score in the entrance examination. The student filed requested the institution reveal its selection process. Though she was not granted admission, the IIM was forced to make its admission criteria public. It was revealed that the entrance exam (Common Admission Test, commonly referred to as CAT) carried less weight as compared to performance in other areas.

The risks involved

Despite its extraordinary benefits, the Act has its own inherent risks. RTI activists have increasingly been threatened and attacked, with several casualties. Over the years, numerous activists were assassinated throughout the country, leading to widespread fear within civil society groups. The victims were investigating abnormalities in highly corrupt sectors like land, mining and local elections. Organisations therefore demanded the government to take measures to protect the RTI activists. While activists debate whether the RTI has reduced corruption in India, it is generally agreed that the legislation plays a crucial role in promoting transparency. RTI activist Vivek Deveshwar states:

> *'My personal advice is that if there is an issue, then only one person should not be involved in exposing it. Let hundreds of people come forward and seek the same information. This will deter the culprit in question since he cannot go around killing so many people. This issue should not just be limited to activists. Even the common man should come forward and file such applications. The government ought to take a lead in such matters and create more awareness,' (Surie, 2011).*

Despite initial difficulties, the RTI Act has continued to be popular amongst citizens and activists. RTI activist Shekhar Singh said that the main objective of India's RTI movement was to empower people, concluding that 'this law has given the people the power to challenge their government. That is no small thing' (*New York Times*, 28 June, 2010). RTI is the first step of a very long journey by public authorities to further transparency in every organisation, and can be successful with vehement public support.

References

Agarwal, Vibhuti (2011) 'A look at some RTI success stories' in *Wall Street Journal*, 14 October, available at http://blogs.wsj.com/indiarealtime/2011/10/14/a-look-at-some-rti-success-stories/ accessed 13 September, 2014

Agarwal, Vibhuti (2013) 'Political parties don't welcome RTI rule' in *Wall Street Journal*, 4 June, available at http://blogs.wsj.com/indiarealtime/2013/06/04/political-parties-dont-welcome-rti-rule, accessed: 13 September, 2014

Electoral Commission of India (2005) *Guidelines and Application format for Registration of political parties under Section 29A of the Representation of the People Act, 1951*, available at http://eci.nic.in/eci_main/ElectoralLaws/guidelinesandformat.pdf, accessed 19 September, 2014

Government of India (2005) *The Right to Information Act, 2005* [22/2005 Delhi: Government of India Department of Publication

Government of India (2013) *Amendment to the Right to Information Act 2005*. Delhi: Government of India Department of Publication

Jain, Bhavika and Chhapia, Hemali (2014) RTI Act lies buried in several states' *The Times of India* 3 February, available at http://timesofindia.indiatimes.com/india/RTI-Act-lies-buried-in-several-states/articleshow/29795652.cms, accessed 13 September, 2014

Ministry of Information and Broadcasting, National Documentation Centre on Mass Communication Research, Reference and Training Division (2000) *Right to Information*, available at www.rrtd.nic.in/right%20to%20information.html, accessed 19 September, 2014

Orissa Review (2009) 'Success story - RTI Act, 2005', pp 74-80

Polgreen, Lydia (2010) 'Right-to-know law gives India's poor a level' in *The New York Times*, 28 June, available at
http://www.nytimes.com/2010/06/29/world/asia/29india.html?emc=eta1&_r=0, accessed 16 October, 2014

Shrinivasan, R (2011) 'Don't pay a bribe, file an RTI application' in *The Times of India*, 2 May, available athttp://timesofindia.indiatimes.com/india/Dont-pay-a-bribe-file-an-RTI-application/articleshow/8137899.cms, accessed19 September, 2014

Surie, Mandakini Devasher (2011) 'Right to Information in India: an effective tool to tackle corruption' *Asia Foundation*, 28 September, available at
http://asiafoundation.org/in-asia/2011/09/28/right-to-information-in-india-an-effective-tool-to-tackle-corruption/ accessed 13 September, 2014

Note on the contributor

Sudeepta Pradhan (M.Com, LLB, Master in Business Laws) is a doctoral student at IFHE, Hyderabad, India, in the field of corporate social responsibility. Her research interest lies in the field of corporate governance, business ethics, green marketing and qualitative research. The author has research publications in numerous national and international journals including *Advertising Express; Romanian Journal of Marketing; Insights into a changing World; Journal of Transnational Management; Business: Theory and Practice; International Journal of Business Insights and Transformation*. She has also authored a number of cases in numerous journals.

FOI's emerging impact on media freedom in Malaysia and Singapore

Malaysia and Singapore are effectively one-party states with both governments retaining tight control of the media. Despite this, the shoots of democracy have begun to emerge with FOI-type laws, and social media, writes *Sankaran Ramanathan*

Introduction

Malaysia and Singapore shared the same political history until the latter separated from Malaysia in 1965. Both nations were under British rule dating from the establishment of settlements (Penang - 1786 and Singapore – 1819). Prior to the Second World War, Peninsular Malaya consisted of three political entities: 'Straits Settlements' (Singapore, Penang and Melaka); 'Federated Malay States' (Perak, Selangor, Negeri Sembilan and Pahang); and 'Unfederated Malay States' (Kelantan, Kedah, Perlis, Johor and Trengganu). The nine Malay states plus Penang and Melaka were joined together at the Federation of Malaya in 1948, and obtained independence from Britain in 1957 (Kaur and Ramanathan, 2008: 8). Media laws in independent Malaysia and Singapore were more focused on the role media could play in the nascent nations' development process. Hence there have been long-standing policies of strict media censorship. However, British colonial masters cannot be blamed for the prevailing restrictions upon media freedom. In fact, most of the *Ordinances* introduced by the British were strengthened and enacted by the Malayan Parliament in 1957, and also by the Malaysian and Singapore parliaments after the formation of Malaysia on September 16, 1963.

All media in both countries are subject to licensing for socio-political reasons, hence under the cloak of political expediency, media and the state were brought together, and still remain bonded in a symbiotic relationship. This relationship was legitimised by the proposition that media should function as tools for national unity and development and by the concept and practice of development journalism (Ramanathan and Nadason, 2012). Further restrictions upon freedom of speech and expression occurred after the 'May 13 Incident' in 1969 (the most serious racial riots in Malaya, leading to the suspension of parliamentary democracy). When it was restored in 1971, laws relating to prior restraint and post-publication controls were amended and strengthened by the Malaysian parliament. When Singapore separated from Malaysia in August 1965, both nations retained and further strengthened these repressive laws.

Government ownership strengthens stranglehold

In both countries, mainstream media are controlled by private enterprises with strong links to the ruling parties. Increasingly, there have been mergers and take-overs with media companies becoming part of large conglomerates, creating a near-monopoly in print and electronic media. This, combined with control of radio and TV stations, and by the Information Department, means that the governments and affiliated business organisations control all mainstream media. In these circumstances, media personnel tend to be cautious by downplaying the opposition and highlighting government achievements. Many journalists who present balanced reporting on contemporary issues have either been reprimanded or sidelined.

Media control and ensuing self-censorship have been cited as prime factors that enabled political parties in both countries to stay in power since independence. These governments set about modifying media laws and regulations, balancing their own need to maintain inter-racial harmony and political control with their attempts to attract domestic and foreign investors. However, they have had to implement new media regulations to deal with rapid media development. These include the need to promote a climate of liberalisation, particularly in telecommunications and broadcasting, and also the need to regulate communication in cyberspace. The bi-partisan nature of the media (especially print media, online news portals and websites) has become more evident in the last two decades. Mainstream print media and websites are divided into pro-government and opposition media, and there has been a running battle between these two groups, especially for control of cyberspace. Joining in the fray are the party organs of the opposition parties. These publications, together with online portals, constitute the core of alternate media in both countries.

Freedom of information in Malaysia

While the Malaysian constitution guarantees freedom of expression under Article 10, it permits numerous limitations to this right. The Sedition Act; Official Secrets Act (OSA); and harsh criminal defamation laws are regularly used to curb freedom of information. The ruling Barisan Nasional (BN) government has assiduously asserted that media should emphasise values that preserve the stability of the multi-ethnic nation. It highlights that Malaysia must be fully developed in terms of national unity and social cohesion; any form of initiatives that disrupt the economic system and political stability, especially those linked to freedom of expression, must be resisted. However, this view of the role of media as merely allies in the development process has come under intense scrutiny after the BN's dismal performance in the last two general elections (2008 and 2013). Studies indicate that new and alternate media were significant in influencing voters' decisions (Ramanathan, 2009; Foong Lian, 2014).

Hence, opposition parties, forming an alliance known as the Pakatan Rakyat (that now control three states and have a much stronger voice in the federal parliament) have become emboldened and more vociferous in their criticism of federal policies and practices. Furthermore, human rights activists and NGOs have become more vocal and strident, forcing the federal government to use preventive laws in order to curb the frequent demonstrations and rallies. Freedom House reports that press freedom remained restricted in Malaysia in 2012, with both positive and negative developments in the legal sphere and a number of attacks on journalists who attempted to document large protests. The BN coalition made minor improvements to two existing laws affecting the press, but it also passed an amendment to another law that expanded liability for illegal internet content.

In July 2012, Prime Minister Najib Razak kept an election campaign promise to repeal the oppressive and anachronistic Internal Security Act. However, the government replaced it with the Security Offenses (Special Measures) Act (SOSMA). The new law grants suspects the right to a fair trial, but still permits 28 days of initial police detention, after which the attorney- general must decide whether to prosecute. Since then the legislation has been used on a number of occasions to detain people, for example:

- In July, 2012, Malaysian blogger Syed Abdullah Hussein al-Attas was briefly detained after a group of people complained about his posts on the Sultan of Johor, which included documents supporting the blogger's claim that part of the fortune left by the late Sultan Iskandar was embezzled.

- In August, 2012 another blogger and opposition politician was sentenced to three months jail for contempt of court in connection with articles that were deemed to have defamed a government minister. An amendment to the Evidence Act drew particular criticism from media freedom activists, as it made those who own, host, edit, or administer websites, blogs, and online forums liable for content published through their services. Opposition to the amendment led to the designation of August 14, 2012, as 'Internet Blackout Day,' in which a host of news websites, bloggers, and civil society organisations took down their websites for the day and pledged to support the campaign against the amendment.

- In May, 2013 the Deputy Speaker of the opposition-controlled Selangor Legislative Assembly Nik Nazmi Nik Ahmad was charged under the Peaceful Assembly Act, for his involvement in an opposition rally held at a stadium. Following his conviction in the Sessions Court, he appealed to the Court of Appeal, which struck out the charge and ruled that the pertinent section was unconstitutional. However, he was charged for the second time under the same Act; the judge gave him a discharge not amounting to an acquittal, based on Article 7 (2) of the Federal Constitution (whereby an individual cannot be tried twice for the same offence). The outcome of this on-going case will have major implications for freedom of assembly in Malaysia.

- In May, 2014 an opposition MP Teresa Kok was charged in the Kuala Lumpur Sessions Court with sedition under the Sedition Act 1948 for posting a video clip entitled 'Teresa Kok "Onderful" Malaysia CNY 2014'. This 11-minute video that pokes fun at top leaders and current issues, led a group of Muslim NGOs to protest, claiming it would fan racial hatred. The charge carries a maximum fine of RM5,000 (£950) or three years imprisonment, or both. This on-going case will have an impact on freedom of information in Malaysia.

State assemblies have been quicker to promote openness and transparency. In 2011 the opposition-controlled Selangor State Assembly passed an enactment to provide for freedom of information in the state. Malaysians can access state documents including that of local councils, city halls and state government-linked companies. The federal government has questioned the legality of the law, claiming it ran contrary to the Official Secrets Act, which would take precedence. However, legal experts said Selangor could implement the law if it sidestepped matters directly pertaining to official secrecy. This government has also launched its own newspaper and a TV website. The same year, the opposition-controlled Penang Legislative Assembly also passed a bill to promote freedom of information. Chief Minister Lim Guan Eng said the law would promote media freedom and transparency. However, the federal government has questioned the legality of the law and federal government officials remain reluctant to share even innocuous information with journalists, for fear of being charged under the Official Secrets Act.

The internet remains a bright spot in the media landscape, with the government formally committed to a policy of no direct online censorship. Hence, there has been a mushrooming of news websites and blogs that offer competing points of view. Although not all these organisations are politically independent (many have suspected affiliations with politicians) they offer an array of political opinions that cannot be found in traditional media. Social networking sites such as Facebook continue to flourish, hosting vigorous debates on political issues and government policies.

In keeping with another election promise, the BN reviewed existing media licencing and censorship laws. An amendment to the 1984 Printing Presses and Publications Act (PPPA) that took effect in July 2012, repealed a provision that had required all publishers and printing firms to obtain an annual operating permit. However, the revision left all other restrictions in place, including the government's authority to grant or deny applications and revoke the required licences at any time without judicial review. The government may likewise continue to issue 'show cause' letters, which require newspapers to explain certain articles or face suspension or revocation of their permits. The Malaysian government hasn't had it all its own way, however. In 2011 a Malaysian court ruled against the government's refusal to issue a publishing licence to the news website *Malaysiakini*, in effect giving the outlet permission to publish a daily print edition. The government had argued that the licence was 'a privilege,' not a right, but the judge ruled that the decision was 'improper and irrational' and exceeded the limits of its jurisdiction. The judge also noted that the right to a permit was a freedom of expression issue and as such was a fundamental liberty enshrined in the constitution.

Physical harassment and intimidation are usually less of a danger for journalists in Malaysia than arbitrary arrest or threats of legal action. However, several instances of physical harassment and attacks on journalists were noted, especially when they covered opposition rallies. More recently, there were reports of harassment and manhandling of journalists who had come to cover the March, 2014, MH370 air disaster, however since Malaysia was the centre of international attention, government officials and the police backed down quickly.

Despite the BN's insistence that mainstream newspapers are impartial, owners' political and business interests often lead to self-censorship by journalists. Foreign print media are occasionally censored or banned, especially when they report on matters covering Islam.

Figure 5: Malaysia 2013 Scores (adapted from Freedom House Report)

Criterion	Score range	Score	Evaluation
Press Status:	N/A	N/A	Not Free
Press Freedom	(0 = best, 100 = worst)	64	Poor
Legal Environment	(0 = best, 30 = worst)	24	Quite poor
Political Environment	(0 = best, 40 = worst)	23	Average
Economic Environment	(0 = best, 30 = worst)	17	Average

(Freedom House, 2013)

Freedom of information in Singapore

Freedom of information is conspicuous by its absence in Singapore, where media remains tightly controlled and freedom of expression is a qualified right. The state's parliament has been dominated by the People's Action Party (PAP) since 1959, and ruling party members frequently use harsh civil and criminal defamation laws to silence and bankrupt political opponents and critical media outlets. The judiciary frequently returns verdicts in the government's favour and people who raise questions regarding judicial impartiality are subject to being charged with contempt of court. Although freedoms of speech and expression are guaranteed by Article 14 of the constitution, the Newspapers and Printing

Presses Act (NPPA), Defamation Act, Internal Security Act (ISA) and articles in the state's penal code constrain press freedom for various reasons. They allow the authorities to restrict circulation of news that is deemed to incite violence, arouse racial or religious sentiments, interfere in domestic politics or threaten public order, national interest or national security. The Sedition Act outlaws seditious speech, distribution of seditious materials and acts with 'seditious tendency'. The government is also empowered to prevent transmission of radio and television content and ban distribution of specific publications under the ISA and Undesirable Publications Act (Muppidi, 2012: 355-364).

Annual licencing requirements for all media outlets and internet service providers have been used to inhibit criticism of the government. Websites offering political or religious content are required to register with the Media Development Authority, and a website's owners and editors are criminally liable for any content that the government finds objectionable. Foreign media are also subject to pressures and restrictive laws such as the NPPA, and are required to post a bond and appoint a local legal representative if they wish to publish in Singapore.

Films, television programmes, music, books, and magazines are sometimes censored; all films with a political purpose are banned unless sponsored by the government. The majority of print and broadcast journalists practice self-censorship to avoid defamation charges or other legal repercussions. These practices, designated as 'Out of Bounds (OB) Markers,' have been well-documented. Hence, the vast majority of print and broadcast journalists practise self-censorship when reporting on domestic and foreign policy issues.

Nearly all print and broadcast media outlets, ISPs, and cable television services are owned or controlled by the state or companies with close ties to the PAP. Since internet use is widespread in Singapore, it carries more coverage of sensitive socioeconomic and political topics. It is believed to have played a significant role in informing voters in the 2011 parliamentary elections, in which the ruling PAP received its lowest vote share since the country's independence, and also providing space for alternative or dissenting views.

A comment made on the *Temasek Review* website led three members of Singapore's ruling Lee family (Prime Minister Lee Hsien Loong, his wife, Ho Ching, and his brother, Lee Hsien Yang) to demand an apology for allegations that they had filled top government positions with family members. In February 2012, *Temasek Review* took down the posting and apologised, but days later the Singapore parliament amended the Evidence Act allowing courts to admit deleted online posts as evidence. The amendment means computer printouts and sound and video recordings can be treated just like other evidence in Singapore courts. Months later a Facebook user was sentenced to two months imprisonment for inciting violence under Article 267C of the Penal Code for a comment posted on the Facebook wall of the *Temasek Review* blog in connection with 2010 National Day celebrations.

The Singapore media environment remained unchanged in 2012 and 2013, with few developments in the areas of freedom of the press or expression that attracted international attention. Social media sites and other internet-based sources of news continued to grow but also drew scrutiny from government authorities, with several bloggers forced to retract postings and one jailed for inciting violence. While opposition parliamentarians have repeatedly called for an FOI Act, leaders of the ruling PAP have rejected this, and ask media to be more socially responsible.

Quo Vadis FOI?

As this encapsulated account shows, ruling governments in both Malaysia and Singapore have assiduously maintained tight controls over print, electronic and new media during the past five decades or so. Their justification is that media need to support the government's socio-economic development goals and promote national unity among the multi-ethnic citizens. There are some faint rays of hope on the horizon, particularly with the mushrooming of the internet and alternate media in the last two decades. In Malaysia, two opposition states have indeed adopted FOI legislation, though no movement toward FOI type laws has taken place in Singapore. Nevertheless, the way ahead is still arduous and long, with many twists and turns.

References

Centre for Public Policy Studies (2008) 'CPPS policy factsheet: freedom of information' 21 August, available at
http://www.cpps.org.my/downloads/factsheets/Freedom%20of%20information%20factsheet.pdf, accessed 20 September, 2014

Faruqui, Shad Saleem and Ramanathan, Sankaran (1998) *Mass Media Laws and Regulations in Malaysia*. Singapore: Asian Media Information and Communication Centre (AMIC)

Foong Lian, Hah (2014) 'Social Media and the Future of Malaysian Society' Monash University Malaysia online blog, available at
http://www.monash.edu.my/research/researchers-say/social-media-and-the-future-of-malaysian-democracy, accessed 15 October, 2014

Kaur, Kiranjit and Ramanathan, Sankaran (2008) 'Wither Media Laws? Experiences of Malaysia and Singapore,' *Journal of International Communication* 14(1) pp 7-21

Malaysian Insider (2011) 'Selangor passes freedom of information enactment' 1 April, available at http://www.themalaysianinsider.com/malaysia/article/selangor-passes-freedom-of-information-enactment/#sthash.Zx71GGB8.dpuf, accessed 20 September, 2014

Muppidi, Sundeep (2012) *Asian Communication Handbook 2012*. Singapore: AMIC

Ramanathan, Sankaran (2009) 'Malaysia's 2008 Political Tsunami: Hope for Media Liberalization?' *Media Asia*, 35/4

Ramanathan, Sankaran and Marimuthu, Nadason (2012) *Media, Democracy and Civil Society*. Petaling Jaya: Consumer Research and Resource Centre

Note on the contributor

Formerly with Universiti Teknologi MARA Malaysia, and then with Asian Media Information and Communication Centre, Singapore, Dr Sankaran Ramanathan is currently Principal, Mediaplus Research Consultancy. He has authored, co-authored and edited more than 170 publications including nine books. He can be contacted at mediaplusconsultancy@hotmail.com

Freedom of information in China? The paradox of access to information in a closed regime

Chinese academic *Yongxi Chen* explores the complex and often fractious relationship between the Chinese state and its people, as evidenced through their access to information regulations

Introduction

In April 2007, the Chinese government introduced the Regulations on Open Government Information (ROGI), which implicitly grants individuals and other entities a right of access to information held by the executive branch of the government. The regulations further allow individuals to enforce the right through an external appeal channel, the court. This general and legally enforceable right marks a leap forward from the incremental transparency reforms that had been adopted inconsecutively since the introduction of marketisation reform in the 1980s. With the ROGI entering into force on 1 May, 2008, China seems to have established a regime that resembles the freedom of information (FOI) regimes installed in around 90 countries.

Yet unlike FOI regimes, which develop on the basis of, and enhance in turn, representative democracy and press freedom, the Chinese regime of open government information grows out of the context that the government is not democratically elected, and the media remains subject to institutionalised censorship by the ruling Chinese Communist Party and state apparatus under its control. The open government regime may operate in a distinctive way in the party-state, which leaves people wonder whether it would make impacts similar to those of FOI regimes, and what its implications would be for Chinese journalists.

While 'freedom of information' nowadays mainly denotes a positive access to information right that should be fulfilled by the State, the term evolved from a negative freedom from state interference with the free flow of information (Alfredsson and Eide, 1999: 401). Still in numerous countries such a 'right to know' derives from and links closely with the constitutional right to freedom of expression (Mendel, 2008: 20). In China, no statutory provisions link the access to information right to freedom of expression, though the theoretical correlation between the two is often stressed by domestic scholars. From a legal aspect, the ROGI has no direct impact on press freedom: operation of the media and content of the press is still largely controlled based on various legal rules and Communist Party directives (He, 2008; Stockmann, 2013). ROGI does not create a right for the journalist to disseminate information. Nevertheless, the professed policy goals of the ROGI share certain critical values of modern FOI laws, including enhancing government accountability, increasing public participation in decision making and curbing corruption (Cao, 2009: 4; Mendel, 2008). The open government regime thus has potential democratic significance in terms of providing an alternative access channel to information that helps citizens, in particular watchdogs on different public affairs, to monitor and check the government. Focusing on the democratic values of FOI, this chapter reviews the ROGI's performance in guaranteeing disclosure of information about government accountability, and discusses its implications for journalists.

The regulations explained

The ROGI sets a general framework for the access to information right, but leaves unresolved issues because of the ambiguity in its wording and its conflicts with other sources of Chinese law. It also imposes intensive obligations of proactive publication on government agencies. Article 9 provides as a rule that agencies should proactively disclose information that 'involves vital interests of citizens' or 'concerns issues which need to be extensively known or participated in by the public'. Articles 10 through 12 stipulate the minimum categories of information to be released by agencies at different levels, covering not only areas where people's livelihoods are directly impacted by administrative decisions - such as land appropriation or inspection of food and drug safety - but also matters which impact public interests but not necessarily relate to the material interests of individuals, such as administrative licensing standards and annual budget reports. Though proactive publication is required, agencies will not be challenged before the court for failure to do so, as has been clarified by the Supreme People's Court through judicial interpretations (SPC 2011: Art. 3).

Provisions that allow public access to information through making requests are less unequivocal. Article 13 of the ROGI creates a 'right' to request and obtain information in an implicit way:

> *'In addition to government information [provided] for in articles 9 through 12, [citizens] may also, based on the special needs of such matters as their own production, livelihood and scientific and technological research, etc., file requests [to] obtain relevant government information'*

An ambiguity is thus left as to whether the 'right' to access information is preconditioned by a test of the requester's need in obtaining the information. It can be clarified by using the contextual approach of statutory interpretation in Chinese legal doctrine. Under Article 20 of the ROGI, which stipulates the form of request, requesters are not obliged to give any reason for requesting the information. Had the legislators meant to install a 'need test', they would have imposed an obligation to give reason under this article. Hence it is more likely that the legislators mention 'special needs' to stress the *diversity* of information to be disclosed upon request as opposed to the *common features* of information to be released proactively (as indicated by Article 9). This ambiguity is nevertheless open to agency manipulations. And unfortunately indeed, the General Office of the State Council issued directives to allow agencies to reject those OGI requests 'irrelevant to requester's special needs' (GOSC 2008).

No presumption of disclosure

The absence of a presumption of disclosure is another fatal defect. The ROGI recognises a number of categories under which information can be refused, or is automatically exempt. Firstly, 'exemption clauses' allow for agencies to refuse access to information on issues including trade secrets and privacy, but these exemptions are subject to a public-interest override test. The second type of restriction is more catch-all, where disclosure shall not 'endanger social stability' (Article 8). Social stability has been widely exploited as a tool of political convenience since 2002, denoting not only the disturbance of public order but also the undertaking of petitions and protests against malfeasances of officials. Thirdly, the ROGI is subordinate to other laws, such as the Law on Guarding State Secrets that provides extremely vague and expandable standards for classification, and the Archives Law, which seals documents stored in state archives for 30 year. Lastly, Articles 7 and 14 further instruct agencies to follow 'provisions of the State' that require information release to be approved by designated authorities – potentially allowing agencies to veto disclosure through making norms with weaker legal forces than the ROGI, including documents determining the scope of state secrets and directives on news censorship. The ROGI hence fails to supersede the pre-existing regimes governing release of government information from which the journalists have suffered a lot.

Withholding information about government accountability

Despite the restrictions, the ROGI is in significant use. Figures from a number of Chinese regions show that there were around 12.4 requests per 100,000 population in 2008. The rate increased to 20.7 in 2010 and 28.5 in 2012 (Chen, 2013: 126). Compared with available data (Vleugels 2011), the request rate in these Chinese regions lags behind some countries with influential FOI laws – like the US (492 requests per 100,000 population) and the UK (72), but outperforms some other advanced democracies, such as Australia (20) and France (5). The nature of the requests corresponds generally with the hotspots of social concern such as corruption and the abuse of power that accompany China's economic reforms. Citizens most frequently requested information about rural land grabs, forced relocation of urban residents, and takeovers of state-owned enterprises that cause massive layoffs (Chen, 2013: 130). Some citizens have also taken on the role of watchdog, requesting information about the discharge of statutory duties by agencies, and documents exposing gross violations of the law by officials. These watchdogs have included lawyers, rights defence (*weiquan*) activists, NGO members, university students and journalists (Weiquanwang, 2009; ACTogether, 2014).

Interestingly, many provincial governments in China reported that around 80 per cent of the requests they received were granted between 2009 and 2012. Nevertheless, since the categorisation of subject matter and the composition of requesters are unrecorded in these reports, the accuracy of government-released statistics remains problematic, and the ostensibly high disclosure rates cannot reliably indicate how agencies have dealt with requests, especially those aiming at improving government accountability through disclosure of maladministration.

A better measure might be independent audits carried out by civil society groups, and dozens have been carried out by a range of such groups since 2008. The reported results show a positive correlation between the rate of refusal and the likelihood of disclosure arousing public criticism of the government (Chen, 2013: 134). Requests about emissions of pollutants and relevant law enforcement (matters that are subject to proactive publication under the ROGI) were generally rejected by about half of local environmental agencies. Audit requests pertaining to annual budgets were rejected by around 80 per cent of local governments. Requests for information detailing public money spent on official receptions, overseas trips and cars were denied in 90 per cent of cases. Such spending – known as the 'three public expenses' in China - have long been criticised by the public, and invariably involve overspending and self-enriching by officials. Two of these audits were conducted by newspapers (Miao and Li, 2009; Yuan and Xu, 2010), and the denial rates were as high as, if not higher, than similar requests by environmental NGOs and scholars.

Requiring the requester to represent his/her identity and purpose is a prevalent agency practice. And one of the most common reasons for non-disclosure is lack of 'special needs' in accessing information. Though in China journalists are generally considered as having the privilege to collect news (Xu 2005: 33), agencies do not readily accept ROGI requests as being relevant to journalists' 'production needs'. For instance, journalists failed to pass the need test when they requested, in the capacity of reporter, a list of organisations subject to administrative punishments for violating environmental regulations (Yuan and Xu, 2010), or when they requested, in the capacity of common citizens, details of fines imposed by law enforcement agencies on unlicensed taxies (Chan, 2010) – stories that would be routine for investigative journalists in most western democracies.

Insufficient judicial protection

When access is denied, Chinese requesters have the right to appeal to the courts. Data released by 16 provincial governments shows that judicial review cases concerning ROGI decisions have been steadily increasing between 2008 and 2012. According to a continuous study by the author of more than 170 media outlets in China (for earlier results, see Chen, 2011: 340; Chen, 2013: 39), a total of 278 ROGI cases received press coverage in the period from 1 May, 2008, to 30 April, 2014. Though the media show enthusiasm for reporting ROGI cases, very few of these cases actually concerned access to information for news-gathering purposes.

Local courts have proved to be conservative toward 'watchdog' requests, as reflected in the threshold of case admission and the endorsement of a need test not imposed by the ROGI. Some senior judges of provincial high courts have insisted that judicial protection should cover only those requests directly related to specific personal rights or property rights of the requester, and the requests based on 'general democratic supervision' should not be admitted to the court (Gao 2009: 24; Zhang 2009: 538). Following this rationale, many courts excluded from judicial review the accountability-journalism-type of FOI requests commonplace in western democracies. Though the Supreme People's Court subsequently mandated admission of all challenges towards denials of access (SPC 2011: Art. 1), that does not improve much the fate of watchdog requests, because local courts have turned to applying rigorous need tests. Most judges are inclined to find the requester lacks 'special needs' where the access is likely to expose maladministration and is not related to the requester's personal or property rights. In effect this means that, with the back-up of appeal through the courts, requests for non-personal information (especially where such information may reveal public officials' wrongdoing) are routinely refused. In the aforementioned 278 media-reported cases, 39 cases involved such non-personal requests. Among them, 22 (56 per cent) were not admitted by the courts, in addition to the 9 cases (23 per cent) that were ruled by the courts against the requesters. Most of these cases touched on large-scale corruption or controversial policies, such as an activist requesting investigation results of illegal use of land transfer payments in Beijing from the National Audit Office (Wang, 2009); a researcher requesting the income and expenses of the fund dedicated for the Three Gorges project from the Finance Ministry (Tang, 2010); a lawyer requesting documents detailing the outcome of experiments and safety evaluations on genetically engineered rice from the Agriculture Ministry (Xu and Li, 2010); a university student requesting the amount of salary of an suspected corrupt official from the Shaanxi Provincial Finance Department (Liu, 2013); and an NGO member requesting environmental impact assessment reports of a newly constructed incinerator from the Sichuan Provincial Environmental Protection Department (Jiao, 2014). In addition, local courts have been lax in examining if agencies have correctly applied public interest tests. They also tend to avoid interfering with the extensive discretion enjoyed by agencies in explaining the indefinite concept of 'endangering social stability', insulating themselves from substantive scrutiny (Chen 2013: 334, 356).

Conclusion

Because of the ROGI, Chinese journalists as well as other citizens enjoy, for the first time in history, a statutory right to access government information. While the ROGI has led to increased disclosure of non-sensitive information, it has yet to secure disclosure of information with democratic implications, i.e. enhancing government accountability and promoting civic engagement, as shown by data concerning request handling and judicial review. Under the law, journalists do not have a more privileged right of access to information than any other citizen; in practice, their rights are actually far less, as frequently a 'needs test' is applied by government agencies (news gathering has not been recognised as a valid need) in addition to other exemptions, in an effort to stymie information release, especially where such requests relate to accountability of public money; potential maladministration; or corruption. Journalists and other non-personal requests have an extremely limited right of appeal, as courts have been slow to overturn non-disclosure decisions, or even accept cases. Because of this combination of a weak legislative framework and a largely impotent judicial protection, watchdogs such as activists, NGOs and journalists find it increasingly difficult to use the ROGI to monitor and check on the workings of government, and its officials. As a result, the ROGI falls well short of a genuine FOI regime.

References

ACTogether (2014) 'Zhengfu Xinxi Gongkai Tiaoli Zhixing Qingkuang Minjian Guancha Baogao [Civic Monitoring Report of the ROGI's Implementation]' available online at http://t.cn/8s3CWZe, accessed 31 August, 2014

Alfredsson, Gudmundur and Eide, Asbjørn (1999), *The Universal Declaration of Human Rights: A Common Standard of Achievement.* The Hague: Martinus Nijhoff

Cao, Kangtai (2009) (ed) *Zhonghua Renmin Gongheguo Zhengfu Xinxi Gongkai Tiaoli Duben* [Annotations on The PRC Regulations on Open Government Information] [2nd edn.] Beijing: People's Press

Chan, Bo (2010) 'Reporter filing information request for fines imposed on unlicensed taxies', *The Beijing News*, 5 August

Chen, Yongxi (2013) *An Empty Promise of Freedom of Information? : Assessing the Legislative and Judicial Protection of the Right of Access to Government Information in China*, unpublished PhD thesis, University of Hong Kong

Chen, Yongxi (2011) 'Yu Jianduquan Wuguan de Zhiqingquan' [A Right to Know That Has Little to Know with Supervision], in Fu, Hualing and Zhu, Guobin (eds), *Constitutional Rights and Constitutionalism: Research on Constitutional Problems in Contemporary China.* Hong Kong: Hong Kong University Press, pp339-68

He, Qinglian (2008) *The Fog of Censorship: Media Control in China.* New York: Human Rights in China

Gao, Jie (2009) 'Difficult issues relating to current OGI litigation,' *Annual Conference of Administrative Law Division of China Law Society*, Changsha, 24 August

GOSC (2008) 'Opinion on Several Issues concerning the Implementation of the ROGI', 29 April

Jiao, Dongyu (2014) 'A post-80s girl who sues environmental protection agencies', *China Weekly*, 2 February

Liu, Chao (2013) 'Shaanxi department reveals why it rejected a student's request for disclosing the salary of "Director in Expensive Watch"' in *Caijing Magazine Net*, 22 March, available online at http://politics.caijing.com.cn/2013-03-22/112613476.html, accessed 1 June, 2014

Mendel, Toby (2008) *Freedom of Information: A Comparative Legal Survey* [2nd edn] Paris: UNESCO

Miao, Jing and Li, Xin (2009) 'Open government information questioned by 25 request forms', *Yanzhao Evening News*, 17 July

SPC (2011) 'Provisions on Several Issues Relating to the Trial of Administrative Cases concerning Open Government Information, 13 August

Stockmann, Daniela (2013) *Media Commercialization and Authoritarian Rule in China*. New York: Cambridge University Press

Tang, Yaoguo (2010) 'Citizen sued the Finance Ministry for not disclosing information on the Three Gorges Construction Fund; Case not admitted by the court', *Liaowang Weekly*, 12 April

Wang, Yijun (2009) 'Using state secret as a pretext to refuse disclosure of information?', *China Youth Daily*, 2 December

Weiquanwang [Rights Defence Net] (2009) 'Guanyu Zhengfu Xinxi Gongkai Tiaoli Zhixing Qingkuang de Baogao [Report on the ROGI's Implementation], available online at http://www.weiquanwang.org/archives/15131, accessed 31 August, 2014

Vleugels, Roger (2011) 'Overview of all FOIA laws' in *Right2Info.org*, online blog, 9 October, available online at http://www.right2info.org/resources/publications/laws-1/ati-laws_fringe-special_roger-vleugels_2011-oct, accessed 1 June, 2014

Xu, Chao and Li, Hujun (2010) 'Why the public fear genetically modified rice?', *New Century Weekly*, 29 March

Xu, Jiabiao (2005), *Xinwen Caifangquan de Bianjie yu Jiegou Fenxi* [Scope and Structure of the Right to Collect News]. Jinan, China: Shandong Remin Chubanshe

Yuan, Duanduan and Xu, Nan (2010) 'Why disclosure of environmental information is so difficult? The fate of 29 OGI requests', *Southern Weekly*, 24 June

Zhang, Haitang (2009) 'Studies of focal issues on OGI litigation', *Annual Conference of Administrative Law Division of China Law Society*, Changsha, 24 August

Note on the contributor

Dr Yongxi Chen is a post-doctoral fellow at the Faculty of Law of The University of Hong Kong. He participated in preparing the draft of China's first local rule of freedom of information, and has been engaged in open government initiatives since 2006. He is member of the International Media Lawyers Association. Before receiving his PhD in Law from HKU in 2013, he obtained a postgraduate diploma in *Le Droit en Europe* at Université Paris 1 Panthéon-Sorbonne and his LLM at Sun Yat-sen University, China. He has published on FOI, personal data protection and comparative administrative law.

Appraising Zimbabwe's AIPPA: Aiding information access or ambushing media freedom?

Bruce Mutsvairo examines Zimbabwe's freedom of information law – known as the Access to Information and Protection of Privacy Act – and discovers differing opinions on whether it lives up to the high expectations of a 'right' to know

Introduction
There has been widespread debate on the purpose, legitimacy and credibility of the Access to Information and Protection of Privacy Act (AIPPA), signed into law by Zimbabwean President Robert Mugabe in March 2002. Critics consider it a repressive piece of legislation, whose main objective is to stifle freedom of media and expression in the country, while those in support of the law argue that far from impeding the work of journalists, AIPPA seeks to enable citizens to easily access information held by public bodies. This chapter assesses the Act, and how it is being used by the Zimbabwean public and the media.

Background: Zimbabwe's colonial heritage
While AIPPA's credibility can always be questioned, an analysis of the history of media laws in the southern African country shows that media has always been tightly controlled and restricted going back to British colonial times. Successive white minority governments introduced draconian laws including the Law and Order Maintenance Act 1960 (LOMA, Chapter 65) to suppress press freedom while consolidating their power base. LOMA, for instance, specifically restricted natives' freedom of association, assembly, movement and expression. Other notable colonial laws, which restricted freedom of expression, include the Official Secrets Act 1970, which made reporting 'classified information' a criminal offence, further prohibiting the disclosure for any purpose information prejudicial to the safety or interests of Zimbabwe; and the Censorship and Control of Entertainment Act. Some of these laws remain intact 35 years after independence, not just in Zimbabwe, but in several other African countries that were subjected to colonialism. Charting the way forward in these countries is no

easy task. Independence may have been attained but it is no secret that African liberation heroes capitalised on the presence of these laws to strengthen their hold onto power just as their colonial masters had done. Still, at independence, President Mugabe's government notably abolished the Powers, Privileges, and Immunities of Parliament Act, which banned the media from covering debates in parliament.

AIPPA was first introduced in the Zimbabwean parliament in January 2002, before President Mugabe assented to it two months later. It is important to note that the law was enacted at a time when the government was facing unprecedented criticism from its erstwhile friends in the West, effectively triggering the imposition of 'smart' sanctions on government officials by the European Union (EU), the United States and other countries including Australia and New Zealand. The opposition Movement for Democratic Change (MDC), formed in 1999, was at that time on a high after successfully campaigning for a no vote during the 2000 referendum, which observers said had sought to substantially strengthen Mugabe's presidential powers. Although President Mugabe claimed 56.2 per cent victory in the March 2002 presidential elections, these elections were considered the closest ever, as opposition leader Morgan Tsvangirai picked 42 per cent of all votes.

In the aftermath of the 2002 elections, which the African Union (at that time still known as the Organisation of African Unity) concluded were credible, ubiquitous attacks emerged, mostly from Western governments and media outlets. In order to fight off these attacks, the Zimbabwean government saw the need to regulate media, leading to the inevitable introduction of the AIPPA, whose other aims were to help citizens gain access to records held by public bodies and protect individual privacy. In an interview as part of the research process for this article, Alexander Rusero, a media studies lecturer at one of the main training centres for journalists in the country's Harare Polytechnic College, said AIPPA was introduced to protect what he called 'ZANU-PF (Mugabe's party) hegemony'. He said:

> *The context under which AIPPA was crafted is a clear testimony on Karl Marx's view on the functions of law, that is to protect the interest of ruling class. The AIPPA was no exception. Its thrust was to sustain the perpetual hegemony of ZANU-PF, whose hold on power was loosening amid formation of the MDC. The AIPPA was clear in its mandate: report against the Mugabe regime at your own detrimental peril,'* (personal interview, August 2014).

The government had posited that openness and accessibility to information was a key component towards enhancing democracy in the country. 'When we asked the Information minister (Jonathan Moyo) why AIPPA was introduced,' said Constantine Chimakure, editor of the *Zimbabwe Mail* newspaper in an interview at his Harare office, 'he said the Americans had openly admitted that they were financing civic society organisations and the independent media in order to effect regime change. The government had to come up with mechanisations to control the media. That gave birth to AIPPA,' (personal interview, August 2014). Still, opponents of the Act said it severely restricted access to information. Section 15, for example, states that 'the head of a public body may not disclose to an applicant information relating to the President, a Cabinet Minister or a public body.'

The Act explained

Going through the cumbersome pages of this legal document, you will be forgiven for thinking there is nothing dubious about it. In fact, much of its content is largely comparable to several legislative charters guiding the work of journalists in several Western democracies. In fact, Bright Matonga, a former deputy minister of information who was partially instrumental in facilitating the introduction of the law, said 'I was living in the UK, working for the BBC. I realised there was a need to help our citizens acquire information held by public bodies then I started supplying British legal documents and books to Zimbabwe. These were then used in crafting the AIPPA,' (personal interview, August 2014). Matonga is adamant AIPPA does not seek to limit media freedom. He believes most journalists operating in Zimbabwe never read the law:

> *The problem is many journalists never read or at least made efforts to understand the law. Most decisions were emotional and as a result, they weren't successful. ZANU-PF works within the bounds of the law. When AIPPA was rolled out, several journalists attacked it because they didn't like the Minister of Information. That worked in our favour. Of course, the law can be frustrating but you always have to follow it. That is also the case in Britain or the US. Everyone focuses on the parts that specifically deal with media. No one mentions the fact that the law does allow citizens to request information from public institutions,'* (ibid).

He is right in every sense because the AIPPA has provisions governing access to information. The only problem is citizens may have other priorities or may not even know it is within their right to make such requests. It is therefore extremely difficult to obtain figures on how many requests are made annually. Further research is necessary in this regard.

While critics allege the law seeks to gag media freedom in the country, there are specific AIPPA provisions guaranteeing access to information, like the acronym suggests. Like similar laws guiding access to information in several countries, there are provisions for release of documents, within certain limits. Section 4(1) stipulates that 'all records in the custody or under the control of a public body' are subject to request, while section 5(1) guarantees access to any records controlled by a public body provided access is requested by citizens, permanent residents, holders of temporary employment permits, students or registered media agents. Section 5(3) specifically prohibits 'agents of a foreign state' from making requests. Section 17 protects disclosure of information that would be harmful to national security or law enforcement processes. Deliberations of cabinet, policy formation, and client-attorney privilege can be withheld even if it is in public interest to release records. Proactive publication is permissible in a wide range of circumstances, whether requested or not. Examples include when relating to a risk of significant harm to the health or safety of members as well as matters of national security (AIPPA, 2002).

Instrument for media control?
Despite these laudable sections in the legislation, Darch and Underwood argue that Zimbabwe should not be included on the list of counties with relevant freedom of information legislation, concluding any attempts to do so would be 'highly ironic' (2010: 212). Indeed, one of the main criticisms of AIPPA has been, according to government critics and media rights organisations, its alleged ability to control media. Opponents of the law have fiercely censured provisions imposing content restrictions. A media commission chaired by Tafataona Mahoso, a no-nonsense government apologist if his weekly columns in the government-controlled *Sunday Mail* newspaper are anything to go by, is tasked, according to AIPPA, with imposing registration requirements on all media outlets and personnel operating in the country. Mahoso's team is also tasked with hearing appeals where refusal to grant access to information has been sanctioned, further irking those opposed to the law (section 9(3)). The legislation is thus subjected to intense debate hinging on press and media rights with some journalists and civic society organisations supported by the West arguing AIPPA seeks to control and silence government critics, chiefly in the media, while others see it as instrumental in granting easy access to information.

Some find it unacceptable that in an era where anyone could potentially be a journalist thanks to the availability of digital technologies, AIPPA somehow dictates on who is allowed to carry out duties of a journalist. Sections 65 through 77, for instance, do not only clearly identify who may be a mass media owner, but they also make registration with Mahoso's commission mandatory, clearly stipulating the manner through which journalists must operate in order to retain registration with the commission. Registration may be revoked if a journalist or media organisation fails to abide by the stipulated standards (section 69). It is arguable that forcing journalists to register with a commission is the same as giving the government a veto on deciding who should practice as a journalist. Accreditation is granted on annual basis for local journalists, while, as noted in section 79(4), foreign reporters may be accredited for a maximum of 30 days.

Visas may only be granted upon arrival in Zimbabwe to journalists with prior approval from the government. Sally Sara of the Australian Broadcasting Corporation and David Blair of the British *Daily Telegraph* were denied entry in 2002 and in the case of Blair, immediately deported upon arrival (Committee to Protect Journalists, 2002). American journalist Andrew Meldrum, who had previously worked as *the Guardian*'s Zimbabwe correspondent for more than 20 years, was deported in May 2003 after 'publishing a falsehood' (Mutsvairo, 2013). Local journalist Fanuel Jongwe was arrested and charged in January 2003 for practicing journalism without Mahoso's accreditation while working for the

Daily News. However, while sympathising with the *Daily News*' legal quagmires, one wonders why the newspaper refused to register with Mahoso's commission, since other newspapers known for their ferocious rebuke of Mugabe and his ZANU PF party successfully applied and were granted a licence. On the other hand, the *Daily News* may have taken their stance based on their own conviction and in line with other democracies across the world, that it was wrong for journalists to be forced to register with Mahoso's commission. Unfortunately by taking this decision, they became victims of the "law," which with very little doubt seemed to have been designed to specifically target vocal critics like them.

Others have objected to a provision that requires media owners to be citizens of Zimbabwe (Section 65, AIPPA). Partial owners must be permanent residents of Zimbabwe further restricting potential external ownership of the local media. Under amendments to the legislation in 2008, the media landscape has since been opened up to foreign owners but foreign journalists remain barred from working permanently in Zimbabwe. Supporters of the law argue this is in line with the government's indigenisation laws, which severely restricts foreign ownership of local companies and businesses, though new newspapers and radio stations have been allowed to freely operate since then.

Regulating the media?

The Zimbabwean government argues it sees the law as critical in regulating the operations of media in the country. This seems to be one area that is highly debatable throughout the world. Who should regulate media? Is it necessary to regulate media? What restrictions, if any, should be imposed on the media? In Zimbabwe, like elsewhere in the world, the media does not always gets its facts right. In several other countries, whenever something like that happens, journalists can get away with an apology – or are subject to defamation legislation. However, in a politically polarised environment such as Zimbabwe, an apology may not be enough. There are people who feel if journalists are left to report freely they will misuse and abuse that privilege. Take stories of Mugabe's alleged health problems. Journalists in the private media have speculated and reported on Mugabe's supposed illness, yet whenever he resurfaces, no signs of fatigue or illness can be detected. Anna Miti, a senior producer at the Zimbabwe Broadcasting Corporation (ZBC) has said she believes media regulation is necessary.

> *'We need these laws. You cannot allow a situation where journalists can write and report anything they want about other people's lives. People complain about AIPPA. What they don't realise is that several other countries including in the West also have laws governing the work of journalists. Why does it become a problem when Zimbabwe passes such a law?'* (Personal interview, 2014).

What Miti's reasoning seems to miss however is the fact that journalists in the West are not subjected to threats of harassment and torture, a price that some Zimbabwean journalists, who have taken a stance against the government, have had to pay. Few journalists can get away with vocal criticism levelled against Mugabe. However, what many people don't know is that you don't simply go to jail for criticising Mugabe. Mugabe gets criticised in the independent press on a daily basis in Zimbabwe. But if you are considered a threat, it is likely you may be targeted.

Supporters of the AIPPA argue that Zimbabwe's national interest was one main reason why AIPPA was introduced. Information minister Jonathan Moyo, seen as the brains behind AIPPA, was quoted by the Media Institute of Southern Africa as saying 'these papers are trash, and they injure our national interests,' referring to independent newspapers (Media Institute of Southern Africa, 2004).

Objections to the AIPPA have also ignited a string of legal battles against the legislation. In May 2003, the Supreme Court of Zimbabwe ruled Section 80(1)(b) and (2) of the AIPPA was constitutional after a legal challenge brought by the *Daily News*, seen as the country's first independent daily. The newspaper - known for its fierce criticism of government policies - had inaccurately reported a story in which a woman was said to have been killed in front of her children by supporters of the ruling ZANU PF party. Geooff Nyarota, the editor-in-chief, and Llody Madima, the reporter who wrote the article, were summonsed before court and faced the likelihood of paying hefty fines or serving jail terms of up to two years or both under the AIPPA. Facing charges of publishing falsehoods and abusing journalistic privilege, they successfully appealed to the Supreme Court arguing Section 80(1)(b) and (2) was unconstitutional because it violated Section 20 of the Constitution, which guaranteed freedom of expression. However the Supreme Court dismissed a case brought by the same newspaper challenging the legality of the AIPPA in September 2003, arguing the newspaper was obliged to register with Mahoso's commission. This decision effectively led to the closure of the *Daily News*.

New constitution and new developments

Some critics want the AIPPA repealed on the grounds that a new constitution, introduced in 2013, specifically calls for the introduction of new legislation giving citizens access to information (Section 62(4)). Section 62(2) guarantees a citizens' rights to freely access information, stating, 'every person, including the Zimbabwean media, has the right of access to any information held by any person, including the State, in so far as the information is required for exercise or protection of a right.' In a very significant development for press freedom, the Constitution Court scrapped the criminal defamation law in July 2014 after the journalists Chimakure and Vincent Kahiya filed a challenge on alleged falsehoods published in 2009.

But with a new constitution already in place, there are suggestions the Constitution Court ruling may only be applicable in circumstances pertaining to the old constitution. According to the *Zimbabwe Mail* newspaper, media watchdog MISA's director Nhlanhla Ngwenya was the first to warn journalists against 'over-celebrating' the ruling given it was issued in the context of the old constitution (*Zimbabwe Mail, 2014*). 'The ruling that was made was based on old constitution not on act,' said Loughty Dube, the Voluntary Media Council of Zimbabwe (VMCZ)'s executive director, adding that his organisation had long campaigned against the defamation law in Zimbabwe. Dube said it was now illegal to apply some provisions of the AIPPA against journalists. 'That is positive development that has a bearing on new constitution if you look at sections, which specifically deal with freedom of media and access to information. It would transcend into the new constitution depending on how it is interpreted,' (personal interview, 2014).

Charles Laiton, a senior court reporter with Alpha Media Holdings and publishers of the independent daily *Newsday*, believes the new ruling will have little or no bearing on the AIPPA.

> *These are two different laws. AIPPA is mainly put into effect by the government in order to protect its information from being accessed or leaked to the public. The one struck by the Constitutional Court was on criminal defamation, which was being used by powerful guns in politics or business to say if you write about them, they would say they were defamed and press criminal charges against journalists. The only remedy now is to sue the journalists through civil courts and ask for damages to settle the dispute as opposed to criminalising the article. The law now says it's not criminal,'* (personal interview, August 2014).

Signs of improvement?

The new developments have been somewhat helped by Moyo's less hostile approach towards the media in his second stint as information minister. He has introduced the Information and Media Panel of Inquiry (IMPI), which he says is crucial in ending the divisions reflected in the media. IMPI's mandate is largely to assess the state of the information and media industry in the country. Ironically, and perhaps in a sign of improved relations between the government and journalists, Nyarota, the former editor of the *Daily News*, chairs the panel. Mahoso's commission has since been replaced by a more independent organisation known as the Zimbabwe Media Commission. Fights have however emerged between ZMC and IMPI with the former alleging the new organisation was taking its mandate. The new commission has overseen the licencing of new media firms including the re-launched *Daily News, Newsday* and *Zimbabwe Mail.*

In spite of the somewhat positive environment, one wonders where the future stands when it comes to AIPPA. Paidamoyo Muzulu, who is Laiton's colleague at *Newsday* and currently studying law with the University of South Africa, said despite the ruling 'AIPPA is still legally enforceable':

> *The only difference is that we have heard promises from the ministry that they want to relook at AIPPA. Nothing has materially changed except that government has made a statement of intent so the non-implementation or relaxation is at the benevolence of the minister who think the law need to be revised,'* (personal interview, 2014).

In reality the AIPPA was introduced to frustrate the work of journalists, who had operated relatively freely prior to its introduction. Depending on who you talk to, ZANU-PF, facing intensified media scrutiny, knew introducing a law to regulate and control media was one expedient way of silencing critics. Zimbabwe is uniquely difficult when it comes to access to information. This is because while perhaps only a minority of the nation's 12 million people know how to access information from public bodies, in a country where some are facing starvation and millions are jobless, this may not be a high priority. Besides, for journalists, a real predicament awaits: criticise the government and be prepared to face severe consequences or avoid politically sensitive topics but then perhaps no one will know you exist.

References

Article 19 (2003) *The Access to Information and Protection of Privacy Act: Two Years on*, available at http://www.article19.org/data/files/pdfs/publications/zimbabwe-aippa-report.pdf accessed 16 August, 2014

Government of Zimbabwe (2002) *Access to Information and Protection of Privacy Act 2002*, available at http://www.sokwanele.com/pdfs/AIPPA.pdf accessed 16 August, 2014

Committee to Protect Journalists (2002) *Attacks on the press: Zimbabwe*, available at https://www.cpj.org/2003/03/attacks-on-the-press-2002-zimbabwe.php, accessed 21 August, 2014

Zimbabwe Mail (2014) 'Be wary of defamation laws-MISA' *Zimbabwe Mail*, 28 July, available at http://www.thezimmail.co.zw/2014/07/28/be-wary-of-defamation-laws-misa, accessed 17 August, 2014

Darch, C and Underwood, PG (2010) *Freedom of Information and the Developing World: The citizen, the state and models of openness*. Oxford: Chandos Publishing

MISA-Zimbabwe (2007) *The Access to Information and Protection of Privacy Act: Five Years On*, Media Institute of Southern Africa (MISA), available at http://archive.kubatana.net/docs/media/misaz_aippa_5yrs_070629.pdf, accessed 15 August 2014

Mutsvairo, Bruce (2013) *Power and participatory politics in the digital age. Probing the use of new media technologies in railroading political changes in Zimbabwe*, unpublished PhD thesis, Leiden University

Note on the contributors

Bruce Mutsvairo is senior lecturer in Journalism at Northumbria University, Newcastle. A former Associated Press correspondent in Amsterdam, he is the current convenor of the undergraduate media law and ethics module. He covered the Zimbabwean crisis for the AP in 2008. He also reported from South Africa, Ghana and Angola on AP foreign assignments. His freelance-based articles have also appeared in the *New York Times, Washington Post, Toronto Star* and *Christian Science Monitor*. Bruce's current research explores the impact of social media in advancing political participation in Africa. He can be contacted via bruce.mutsvairo@northumbria.ac.uk

Acknowledgement

The author would like to thank *Newsday* reporter Moses Matenga for facilitating the data gathering process for this article.

Lightning Source UK Ltd.
Milton Keynes UK
UKOW07f1520280115

245291UK00001B/31/P

9 781845 496463